My Place in the Sun

My Place in the Sun

Life in the Golden Age of Hollywood and Washington

George Stevens, Jr.

UNIVERSITY PRESS OF KENTUCKY

Published by the University Press of Kentucky, scholarly publisher for the Commonwealth, serving Bellarmine University, Berea College, Centre College of Kentucky, Eastern Kentucky University, The Filson Historical Society, Georgetown College, Kentucky Historical Society, Kentucky State University, Morehead State University, Murray State University, Northern Kentucky University, Spalding University, Transylvania University, University of Kentucky, University of Louisville, and Western Kentucky University.

Editorial and Sales Offices: The University Press of Kentucky
663 South Limestone Street, Lexington, Kentucky 40508-4008
www.kentuckypress.com

Library of Congress Cataloging-in-Publication Data

Names: Stevens, George, Jr., 1932– author.
Title: My place in the sun : life in the golden age of Hollywood and
    Washington / George Stevens, Jr.
Description: Lexington : The University Press of Kentucky, [2022] | Series:
    Screen classics | Includes indexes.
Identifiers: LCCN 2021062358 | ISBN 9780813195247 (hardcover) | ISBN
    9780813195414 (pdf) | ISBN 9780813195254 (epub)
Subjects: LCSH: Stevens, George, Jr., 1932– | Stevens, George, Jr.,
    1932—Family. | Stevens, George, 1904–1975—Family. | Motion picture
    producers and directors—United States—Biography. | American Film
    Institute—History. | LCGFT: Autobiographies. | Biographies.
Classification: LCC PN1998.3.S739 A3 2022 | DDC 791.4302/330922
    [B]—dc23/eng/20220112
LC record available at https://lccn.loc.gov/2021062358

Member of the Association
of University Presses

"Let America Be America Again" by Langston Hughes excerpt courtesy
Penguin Random House LLC and Harold Ober Associates.

"The Times They Are a-Changin'" excerpt courtesy Universal Music Publishing Group,
© Bob Dylan.

For George Stevens and Michael Stevens.

Men of creativity and decency. I was blessed to have my journey nourished first by my father, then by my elder son, savoring their humor and courage.

Contents

STEVENS FAMILY TREE

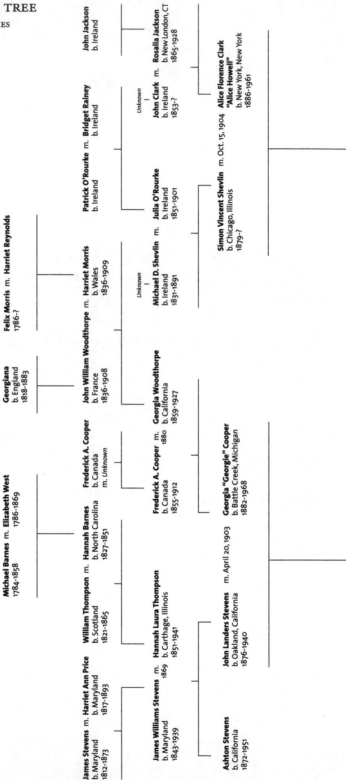

John Jackson
b. Ireland

Rosalia Jackson
b. New London, CT
1865-1928

Bridget Rainey
b. Ireland

Unknown

John Clark
b. Ireland
1853-?

Patrick O'Rourke m. **Bridget Rainey**
b. Ireland

John Clark m. **Rosalia Jackson**

**Alice Florence Clark
"Alice Howell"**
b. New York, New York
1886-1961

Felix Morris m. **Harriet Reynolds**
1786-?

Harriet Morris
b. Wales
1836-1909

Julia O'Rourke
b. Ireland
1851-1901

Unknown

Michael D. Shevlin
b. Ireland
1831-1891

Michael D. Shevlin m. **Julia O'Rourke**

Simon Vincent Shevlin m. Oct. 15, 1904 **Alice Florence Clark**
b. Chicago, Illinois
1879-?

Georgiana
b. England
1818-1883

John William Woodthorpe m. **Harriet Morris**
b. France
1836-1908

Georgia Woodthorpe
b. California
1859-1927

Michael Barnes m. **Elizabeth West**
1784-1858   1786-1869

Frederick A. Cooper
b. Canada
m. *Unknown*

Frederick A. Cooper m. **Georgia Woodthorpe**
b. Canada   1880
1855-1912

William Thompson m. **Hannah Barnes**
b. Scotland   b. North Carolina
1821-1865   1827-1851

Georgia "Georgie" Cooper
b. Battle Creek, Michigan
1882-1968

Hannah Laura Thompson
b. Carthage, Illinois
1851-1941

James Stevens m. **Harriet Ann Price**
b. Maryland   b. Maryland
1812-1873   1817-1893

James Williams Stevens m. **Hannah Laura Thompson**
b. Maryland   1869
1843-1939

John Landers Stevens m. April 20, 1903 **Georgia "Georgie" Cooper**
b. Oakland, California
1876-1940

Ashton Stevens
b. California
1872-1951

STEVENS FAMILY TREE

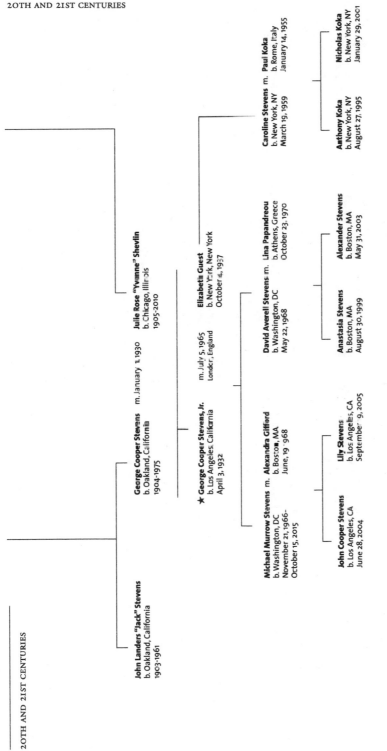

John Landers "Jack" Stevens
b. Oakland, California
1903-1961

George Cooper Stevens
b. Oakland, California
1904-1975

m. January 1, 1930

Julie Rose "Yvonne" Shevlin
b. Chicago, Illinois
1905-2010

★ George Cooper Stevens, Jr.
b. Los Angeles, California
April 3, 1932

m. July 5, 1965
London, England

Elizabeth Guest
b. New York, New York
October 4, 1937

Michael Murrow Stevens
b. Washington, DC
November 21, 1966-
October 15, 2015

m.

Alexandra Gifford
b. Boston, MA
June 19, 1968

David Averell Stevens
b. Washington, DC
May 22, 1968

m.

Lina Papandreou
b. Athens, Greece
October 23, 1970

Caroline Stevens
b. New York, NY
March 19, 1959

m.

Paul Koka
b. Rome, Italy
January 14, 1955

John Cooper Stevens
b. Los Angeles, CA
June 28, 2004

Lily Stevens
b. Los Angeles, CA
September 9, 2005

Anastasia Stevens
b. Boston, MA
August 30, 1999

Alexander Stevens
b. Boston, MA
May 31, 2003

Anthony Koka
b. New York, NY
August 27, 1995

Nicholas Koka
b. New York, NY
January 29, 2001

FAMILY

Landers Stevens' theatrical company performing *Lead, Kindly Light* in San Francisco, circa 1914. Landers, left in white hat, his wife Georgie Cooper, center. George Stevens, Sr., age ten, kneeling far left. Jack Stevens, age eleven, holding newspapers, right.

1

San Francisco

A fog-shrouded September night in 1900.

Landers Stevens was the last to leave the Dewey Theater on Twelfth Street in Oakland, the town of his birth. He secured the doors, packed the receipts in his pouch, and bid the watchman goodnight. Landers was just twenty-four but the playbill from the day lists him as "Proprietor and Manager" of the Dewey, where he directed the plays and was the company's leading man. Tall and square-jawed, always carefully dressed, he set off briskly down Broadway to catch the last ferry across the bay to San Francisco.

When he turned onto Fourteenth Street two toughs sprang from the darkness and tackled him. As the *San Francisco Call* reported the next day, "One of the robbers struck him a powerful blow on the face at the point of the jaw, staggering Landers and nearly knocking him insensible." He gathered himself, threw off one of the men, managed to draw his pistol, and "beat down the assailant with a half-dozen blows on the face with the clubbed weapon." Nursing a severely cut hand and a swollen jaw, Landers told the *Call* reporter that it was the hardest battle he ever fought. "While I was fighting the man whom I captured, the first man recovered and ran. I didn't want to take a chance of killing him so I did not fire."

John Landers Stevens was my grandfather. He was the younger son of James William and Hannah Laura Stevens. James came to San Francisco from Maryland in the 1850s with his parents and five brothers and sisters. He became a businessman and met Hannah Laura Thompson, who came west across the Sierras in a covered wagon from Liberty, Missouri, propelled by whatever dreams drove pioneers to make that grueling journey. James and Hannah Laura fell in love, were married, and fostered the Stevens family.

A few years after his encounter with the robbers, Landers sat in a darkened theater and watched an ingenue, a tall girl with fine features and a lilting

BULLETIN: SAN FRANCISCO AUGUST 7, 1898.

LANDERS STEVENS AT MOROSCO'S

Landers Stevens at age twenty-two on the stage of Morosco's
Grand Opera House in San Francisco, 1898.

soprano, perform in an operetta. He waited at the stage door and introduced himself to Georgie Cooper, undertook a courtship, and asked her to marry him—a proposal that proved pivotal to my own existence.

I knew Landers as an older man, with lines of silver showing through his black hair, living in a small house in Glendale where I would sleep on the living room sofa. He and my grandmother Georgie were then in their sixties and there were few signs of a glamorous past. But my mother, who became our family's informal archivist, left me a copy of their wedding license along with a note in her handwriting.

Landers was married to Fannie Gillette (sister of Gillette Razor) and she got a divorce so he could marry Georgie. They drove all night from San Francisco to San Jose after the show—were married at 9:05 a.m. and drove back to S.F. to do the show that night.

A yellowed clipping from a San Jose newspaper, dated April 20, 1903, supports my mother's account:

> John Landers Stevens, the actor, who was divorced in San Francisco yesterday, was remarried in this city today by City Justice Davidson to Miss Georgie Cooper, the soubrette at the Central Theater. Thomas McGoeghegan, city treasurer, was best man. The bride was attended by her maid. Eighteen year old Georgie is a second generation actress whose mother, Georgia Woodthorpe, is an audience favorite on San Francisco stages.

It was Georgia Woodthorpe, my great-grandmother, who launched five generations (and counting) of Stevens family participation in the entertainment world. She was born in San Francisco in 1859, when the Gold Rush town was becoming a cosmopolitan city. Her father loved amateur theatricals, and one afternoon J. B. McCullough, a noted impresario and one of the leading tragedians of the American stage, heard five-year-old Georgia recite an "impromptu entertainment" in the basement of the Actors Club. He persuaded her parents to let her join his company and she made her debut as young Prince Arthur in Shakespeare's *King John* at the California Theater. McCullough, a broad-shouldered man with a large head and strong features, played Falconbridge. "When he carried me—presumably dead—on to the stage," Georgia remembered, "his extended arms shook and his tears fell on my face." McCullough complimented her afterward: "The unconscious acting of childhood . . . Little Girl, you'll never know how great you were."

When she was seventeen Georgia fell in love with a schoolmate called Billy Wallace, an attraction so intense that in 1877 they ran off to Santa Clara and married. When they returned to San Francisco their incensed parents were waiting. Billy's father doubted the stability of marriage to an actress, and the Woodthorpes believed marriage would constrain Georgia's promising career, so they insisted on an immediate annulment. The tearful lovers parted and young Billy Wallace left the Bay Area to make his life in Oregon.

Georgia became a celebrated leading lady in San Francisco. She married Fred Cooper, an actor and manager, and they lived a theatrical life, touring across the United States, while finding time to have three daughters. The first, my grandmother Georgie Cooper, was born while her mother was playing in Battle Creek, Michigan. A second daughter was delivered in a Utah train station, earning her the name Edith Ogden Cooper. The third sister, Olivette, became an actress and a longtime screenwriter at Republic Pictures.

Great-grandmother Georgia shared the stage with the most commanding figures of American theater, including Lawrence Barrett, McKee Rankin and Charles Fechter. When she was only seventeen, she played Ophelia to Edwin Booth's Hamlet in San Francisco. Booth was considered America's greatest ever Hamlet, and in an era when theater was king, America's brightest star. Yet he bore the stigma of being the brother of Abraham Lincoln's assassin, actor John Wilkes Booth. Georgia, the youngest ever to play Ophelia opposite Booth, observed her Hamlet after a matinee complaining about being hungry, and ordering his dresser to run across the street and bring him food. "I stood outside his dressing room staring at the unexpected sight of the great Booth drinking beer and eating bologna." Booth noticed her and laughed, "Ah, Little Girl. Someday when you've done one big performance and are facing another, you'll know how good these are." Georgia's only comment: "I thought he would at least have champagne and truffles."

Georgia Woodthorpe enjoyed a distinguished career on the stage but in later years her life took an unusual turn, documented in a yellowed clipping I have from the August 15, 1919, *Morning Oregonian*. After the death of her husband Fred Cooper, Georgia continued performing and was touring in a play in Portland, Oregon. One night there was a knock on her dressing room door. It was Bill Wallace (no longer Billy), now an Oregon businessman, twice married and twice divorced. The two hadn't spoken or corresponded since the day of their annulment forty years earlier. Bill repeated his proposal of marriage and the two were wed. "Love's Fires Banked, Burst Forth Afresh," proclaimed the *Oregonian*. "Even willful fate cannot thwart two schoolmate lovers who insist on having things their own sweet way."

However heartwarming the story of Billy and Georgia may be, I must consider that were it not for that forced annulment in 1877, my great-grandmother Georgia would not have married Fred Cooper and given birth to Georgie Cooper, and Georgie would not have produced my father George—and the Stevens family as we know it would not exist.

My grandmother Georgie made her debut in the theater at age ten. Dr. David Burbank, a wealthy dentist, became such a fan of her mother that he built

Grandmother Georgie Cooper at the Alcazar Theater,
San Francisco, circa 1903.

the Burbank Theater in Los Angeles for Georgia Woodthorpe to star in and for her husband to manage and promote. A columnist described Fred Cooper driving a pair of zebras down Main Street to generate attention for the theater's 1893 opening in which little Georgie played the title role in *Little Lord Fauntleroy* alongside her mother. The little girl so enjoyed the glow of footlights that by the time the family returned to San Francisco the stage was her calling too.

Georgie Cooper, "Little Lord Fauntleroy."

Rose & Co., Tabor Block, Denver.

Georgie Cooper in the classic velvet Fauntleroy suit she wore in her debut
at the Burbank Theater in Los Angeles in 1893.

It was ten years later that Landers and Georgie married and started their
own stock company at Ye Liberty Playhouse in Oakland, where they performed
Shakespeare and Dickens and the new plays of the day.

Georgie gave birth to my Uncle Jack, John Landers Stevens, Jr., on November 2, 1903. The date sheds light on the hurried aspect of the wedding in San
Jose just seven months before. George Cooper Stevens, my father, was born on
December 18, 1904, which happened to be the year the nickelodeon made its
debut in New York—the device that would soon disrupt his parents' livelihood
and, in time, provide one for him.

As the twentieth century blossomed, artists came from around the world to perform in San Francisco. The legendary Enrico Caruso arrived from Italy with considerable fanfare to sing Don José in Bizet's *Carmen* at the Grand Opera House on April 17, 1906. Georgie and Landers were playing at the Ye Liberty and returned to their hotel in San Francisco after their show. My father was fourteen months old, sleeping in a bassinet on wheels, when at 5:12 a.m. the city began to shake. The Great San Francisco Earthquake sparked fires that burned twenty-nine thousand buildings to the ground and left three hundred thousand residents homeless, including the Stevens family. The great Caruso survived the quake but the Palace Hotel where he was staying did not, and the beloved tenor fled the city the next morning vowing never to return—a pledge he honored.

Half a century later Georgie Cooper Stevens described that fateful night to my mother. "The whole front of the building collapsed," she said, "and I grabbed the bassinet and just held on." When my mother heard the story for the first time in middle age, her Irish humor took over. "If you'd have let that bassinet go you would have saved me a whole lot of trouble."

In their teens Landers and his older brother Ashton followed their parents into the theater world. Ashton mastered the banjo by nineteen and was giving lessons at home for a dollar and a half, working upstairs with his customers. He paid Landers, then fourteen, five cents to ring the doorbell and inquire about lessons in such a loud voice that Ashton's students and their parents would hear. Each time he simulated a different voice and manner. "That's how I got the acting bee," Landers explained. The publisher William Randolph Hearst hired Ashton for banjo lessons, took a shine to his young instructor, and gave him a job at the *San Francisco Examiner*. Ashton gained a tryout as drama critic. "I expect excellence," Hearst told him, with a reminder that two of his predecessors, Ambrose Bierce and Bret Harte, were in the pantheon of American writers. Hearst liked Ashton's conversational style of criticism and sent him east to be drama critic at the *New York Evening Journal*.

My great-uncle Ashton believed critics should write about plays just as they would about the weather—"showing hardly any regard for the weather's feelings." He applied this principle even to his brother's performances. Landers claimed that Ashton's reputation for honesty was acquired at his expense. When readers saw Ashton's criticism of Landers' Hamlet or Sherlock Holmes, they would say, "He must be on the level, he pans his own brother."

Landers was mentored in his teens by Frederick Warde, one of the most admired actors of the day. He was invited on Warde's national tour during which he compiled critics' notices in scrapbooks with praise of his performances

My father, right, in Vancouver, British Columbia, holding the Kodak Box Brownie camera that his mother gave him on his ninth birthday that led him to begin taking pictures. His brother Jack, left. Standing above is their mother Georgie, left, and an unidentified woman.

George displays an eye for composition in this view of Vancouver Harbor taken in 1912.

underlined in red. One review in New York criticized Warde's star performance in *Runnymede* and singled out Landers for the only piece of creditable acting, perhaps straining the mentorship. Landers returned to San Francisco at twenty and was chosen to be leading man at the Alcazar. "He acts with an earnestness and finish and a degree of naturalness that are as agreeable as it is rare," wrote the *San Francisco Newsletter.* "His voice is round and musical and there is intellect in his handling of the lines."

This led to two years at Morosco's Grand Opera House after which Landers, having married Georgie Cooper, leased the Dewey Opera House in Oakland to become an actor/manager, choosing the plays and appearing in leading roles. By the time he was thirty Landers had played five hundred parts, many of them with Georgie as his leading lady.

Landers' father had a house in Boyes Hot Springs outside San Francisco, so Jack and George went to a nearby one-room schoolhouse called the Flowery School. My father remembered that his father would sometimes get "jittery" running his theater and decide to take a vacation. "He'd book himself and mother on a vaudeville tour and off we'd go to see the country—doing two or three shows a day." Dad and his brother had great fun on trains traveling the Orpheum Circuit, but three shows each day was hardly a vacation for their parents. I found photographs of the Stevens family handsomely dressed on tour in Vancouver, British Columbia, in 1912. Landers and Georgie worked hard to make ends meet, but as my mother observed, "Actors spent their money on clothes because appearances were so important."

Landers Stevens and Georgie Cooper became the toast of the Bay Area. At the Ye Liberty Landers took advantage of the world's first permanent revolving stage, which enabled him to create fast scene changes that enlivened his productions of *Camille, Trilby* and *The Prisoner of Zenda*. As director and star Landers dealt with whatever roles came his way—the Count of Monte Cristo one day, Shylock the next. He confessed that sometimes he would slip a few lines of last night's play into tonight's. Few in the audience seem to have noticed.

It was a golden era for theater. The *Oakland Tribune* sized up Landers' place in that special world: "Before the arrival of the movies and radio, the matinee idol flourished—and of all the fair-haired boys, Landers Stevens stood alone as the actor who could do no wrong."

2

The Irish Side

Alice Florence McGinnis was born in New York in 1888. Her father was a towering Irishman from County Clare who wore a long black frock coat and took the boat to Boston rather than New York because it was $7.50 cheaper. He settled in Connecticut where he became a schoolteacher. When she was eighteen Alice married Simon Vincent Shevlin, an engaging young saloonkeeper in Chicago, where she gave birth to my mother Yvonne in 1905. Alice, who loved to cook, would prepare the "free lunches" that lured drinkers into Simon's saloon, but soon discovered that her husband had an incurable case of the Irish flu and was drinking away the pub's profits.

Alice left Simon and returned to New York to raise Yvonne, earning a living as a vaudeville chorus dancer. She met Dick Smith at a New York saloon where Irving Berlin was a singing waiter. Dick got his start in show business singing in a quartet on Broadway with his friend Mack Sennett, who soon decamped to Hollywood to start a movie company. Alice and Dick married and created an act, performing three a day on the Orpheum Circuit, where she practiced her comic moves and timing. They were booked on short notice to replace a comedy-dance team in Pittsburgh and arrived at the theater to find a skinflint manager. "Kids, you've got the job," he grumbled, "but I can't afford a new billboard. For this run your act is called Howell and Howell." From that day on my grandmother's stage name was Alice Howell.

In 1913 Dick was diagnosed with tuberculosis, and Alice, just twenty-five, decided they should head west in search of warmer climes. Anxious to escape the fickle life of vaudeville, she hoped the new business of movies might provide a more dependable living. Perhaps Mack Sennett could help. Hollywood was a continent away and the movies were a gamble, so she asked her good friends Jack and Millie Kennedy to care for eight-year-old Yvonne. Alice had met

My maternal grandmother,
Alice Howell, in Hollywood
after arriving from New York,
circa 1914.

Millie, a dancer from an English ballet company, when they worked in the chorus for the actor-impresario DeWolfe Hopper. Jack was the drummer at the
New York's Keith Orpheum, and he took little Yvonne with him on Friday
nights and let her sit in the front row while he played for Eddie Cantor, Jack
Benny and other headliners. Yvonne adored those Friday nights and learned to
love comedy and music.

In Hollywood, Sennett hired Alice for crowd scenes and extra work. She
rented a small farm house on Allesandro Street so Dick would have a place to
convalesce and she could walk the half mile to Sennett's Keystone Studio. "It
wasn't easy to be funny on six dollars a week with an invalid at home," she told
a reporter, "but I had to make a living." Alice had been a swimmer and a basketball player, and was physically graceful. She recalled filming a police raid scene
with half a dozen women and plunging into the thick of the fray as others drew
back. "We all had on evening gowns and the girls didn't want to spoil them, but
I had no scruples. I fell downstairs and literally wiped up the floor with my
gown." Sennett was impressed and began giving Alice small parts.

Earlier that year Sennett sent a telegram to the Fred Karno British pantomime
troupe that was touring in Philadelphia asking, "Is there a man named 'Chiffin' in
your company or something like that?" A few weeks later twenty-three-year-old
Charlie Chaplin arrived at the Sennett studio, and after a few stints in front of the

camera he was ready to make his debut as a director. He recognized Alice's comedic skill and cast her in his first six two-reelers. *Laughing Gas*, the first, was released in 1914. Charlie plays the careless assistant to a dentist, Dr. Pain. Alice plays the fashionably dressed Mrs. Pain, whom Chaplin accosts, pulling off her skirt and exposing her bloomers as she desperately tries to evade his pursuit. Alice was in tune with Chaplin's comic pacing, which was slower and more graceful than Sennett's.

Sennett cast Alice in *Tillie's Punctured Romance*, with Marie Dressler, Mabel Normand and Chaplin, the first feature-length comedy ever made. Then he put her in two-reelers that the pun-loving Sennett promoted as "Every One a Howell!" But Sennett was in love with Normand, who got the prize roles, so Alice moved to L-KO Pictures on Gower Street. Having watched Chaplin create his tramp persona, she conceived her own eccentric wardrobe of ill-fitting clothes, her hair piled high. With large eyes, bee-stung lips and a Rubenesque shape, Alice blended roughhouse comedy with feminine delicacy in more than a hundred films, perfecting a stiff-backed, penguin walk that became her signature.

"Funny make up without a funny personality inside is only pitiful to me," Alice observed in a 1916 interview. "You must know how just one comic touch in the middle of a serious situation will upset everybody's gravity." She was billed as "The Funniest Girl on the Screen," and in *Cinderella Cinders* engaged in a rollicking chase in which she wore roller skates pulled by a bulldog. She also did a spoof of ballroom dancing with her husband Dick Smith (who it turned out didn't have tuberculosis after all) that dated back to their vaudeville act.

Alice was inclined to be modest about her career, but in September 1917 a reporter for the *Los Angeles Herald Examiner* provoked a response that revealed the extent to which she had to stand up for herself in a man's world. "To get Alice to show some temperament there are three good ways. Call her the female Charlie Chaplin or the lady Douglas Fairbanks or the skirted Max Linder." She countered with: "I don't want any borrowed glory, I am just as much a star in my own way as the famous male comedians."

Anthony Slide, in his book *She Could Be Chaplin! The Comedic Brilliance of Alice Howell*, explains that Alice, a star in her own right, with her "unique and original style," was the centerpiece of her films, as opposed to being a leading lady present merely to support the male comedian.

When Stan Laurel was asked to name the ten greatest comediennes of all time, Alice was on his list. Movie historians say her career is unfairly neglected because so few of her films survived, the majority lost because of the instability of nitrate film stock. Alice, by her own account, went into movies to support herself and family, not for a place in history, never forgetting what it was like to

Alice taking matters into her own hands in *Her Barebacked Career* (1917), from Century Comedies. Eva McKenzie, left, and unidentified actor.

stand in line for extra work. And her Irish heritage gave her a belief in the value of land. "They're not making any more of it," she often reminded my mother, spending her savings on corner lots on Santa Monica Boulevard and managing the properties when she retired in 1927.

When I was in my teens Alice lived nearby. She was a delightful woman with red hair and a hint of the distinctive penguin walk that had served her so well on the screen. We never talked about her career, so I had no idea of the tenacity this easygoing woman exercised to make her way to the top. Still, the humor that made Alice a gifted comedienne also made her great company. She once told me of having to take some hats to be blocked the same day she had an appointment at her bank on Hollywood Boulevard. Leaving her house she couldn't carry everything so she put the four hats on her head, drove in her open car to the bank, and did her business without anyone telling her she was overdressed.

3

A Man of the Theater

A movie theater was built right across the street from our theater," my father, then playing boy parts in the family troupe, recalled. "Americans were flocking to the movies. There was just not enough money coming in, and Mother and Dad had to move to the Wigwam Theater in the Mission District that didn't have the stature of the Dewey or Ye Liberty."

Growing up my father and his brother spent time at the theater because their parents couldn't afford help, and Landers used the boys in children's roles. Dad made his debut at age five in *Sappho*, playing the illegitimate son of Nance O'Neil, an actress critics hailed as the American Sara Bernhardt. O'Neil was six feet tall and known for her beauty and passion, so it must have been an intense experience for a youngster.

My father and his brother were big as teenagers and Landers had them play kids' parts that they were too old for. The July 1919 issue of the *Wigwam Weekly* describes a production of *Sherlock Holmes* starring Landers and Georgie, with the role of Billy played by Master George Stevens. By then my father was nearly fifteen, doing one of those children's roles that he felt self-conscious about. People later wondered why this handsome man worked behind the camera rather than in front of it. He would say, simply, "I guess I got the acting out of my system."

Yet those days and nights in the theater made a lasting impression. I discovered a recorded interview in which my father described doing his homework under the stage while his parents performed. His favorite moment was when his father played Sydney Carton in *A Tale of Two Cities*. Sitting in the dark he would wait for the last act and the sound of his father's footsteps climbing the guillotine. I sensed a tremor in his voice as he recited his father's lines: "It is a far, far better thing that I do than I have ever done; it is a far, far better rest that I go to than I have ever known." He would hear the crack of the guillotine blade

My father, performing in his father's company in 1914 with an
unidentified actor, shows an air of mischief onstage.

landing, feel "the breathless silence of the audience," then listen to the applause
build to an ovation as the footlights came up for curtain calls.

My father's gift for storytelling was spawned as he sat in the darkness under
the stage at the Dewey.

Many of Landers' San Francisco colleagues made the move to Hollywood,
but Landers postponed the inevitable. "D. W. Griffith, known as Larry then,
worked with Landers in San Francisco," my father recalled, "and many who
became stars in Hollywood were good friends—fine actors like Bert Lytell,
Hobart Bosworth and Alia Nazimova. But my father stayed with the theater
business until it finally went right out from under him."

In 1921 Landers surrendered his pride and took his family south to look for
work in the movies. He and Georgie and the boys moved into a $35 a month
house in Glendale. My father was sixteen and looking forward to going to Glendale High School, but Landers, infected with a healthy measure of actor's vanity,
had other ideas. He was, at forty-five, unwilling to learn to drive, so he insisted
that young George drop out of high school and drive him to casting calls—a

cruel disappointment to a sensitive young man fired with curiosity. Later, when asked where he went to school, my father would say with quiet authority, "H. K." If that didn't end the conversation, he would add, "School of Hard Knocks."

His formal education was over but he set up his own ambitious program of reading and study, borrowing books from the Glendale Public Library and discovering the plays of Eugene O'Neill, who, like him, had a headstrong matinee idol for a father. He filled notebooks with observations: "Read *Notre Dame* by Victor Hugo . . . a fine story but less convincing than some of his others." He loved *Liliom* by Molnar and John Drinkwater's play *Abraham Lincoln.* Drawn toward a life of imagination he began to write, and regularly hike two miles from his parents' house to see movies in Glendale, and then walk all the way home "dreaming that damn film out as if it were happening to me." After seeing Abel Gance's *J'accuse,* he noted, "It was splendid and required much thought—the best foreign picture I have seen."

Landers and Georgie started working in movies. Captain of his ship in the theater, Landers found himself on unfamiliar sound stages surrounded by technicians. It was confining when directors instructed him to hit marks chalked on the floor to accommodate the camera, but he still managed to appear in eighty films, among them *Public Enemy, Little Caesar, Mr. Smith Goes to Washington* and, under the direction of his son, *Swing Time,* where he plays the dignified father of the bride (Betty Furness) who Fred Astaire stands up early in the film. Most of Landers' roles were small, as were most of Georgie's forty-five screen appearances, which included *Theodora Goes Wild, Hollywood Hotel* and *Mr. Deeds Goes to Town.*

Landers' brother Ashton had moved from New York to Hearst's *Chicago Herald American,* where his success earned him the sobriquet "dean of American critics." His next-door neighbor was guardian to a precocious boy with a theatrical appetite, Orson Welles. Ashton was one of the first to recognize his talent. He saw Orson in *Richard III* at age fifteen and wrote in his column, "I am going to put a clipping of this paragraph in my betting book. If Orson is not a leading man by the time it has yellowed, I will never make another prophecy."

Welles modeled Jedediah Leland, the Joseph Cotten character in *Citizen Kane,* on Ashton. "Jed was based on a close childhood friend of mine, George Stevens' uncle Ashton," Welles told a biographer. "He was one of the great ones . . . a gentleman very much like Jed." When Welles came to Hollywood in 1940, he brought Landers, then sixty-three, to RKO for a small role in *Citizen Kane.* It was his last performance. Less than a year later he died of a heart attack. I was eight years old. My grandfather's funeral at Forest Lawn was my first.

My father started a business in Glendale when he was sixteen, taking pictures for tradesmen posing at their shop doors or at store openings, but when he

George Stevens, Sr., at age twenty-one as assistant cameraman on *Black Cyclone* (1925), on the Crow Indian Reservation near the Little Big Horn River in Wyoming.

drove his father to auditions he roamed studio lots calculating how he might get a job. One day he came home full of excitement and told his father that he had been hired as a second assistant cameraman on *Kismet* (1920) at MGM. Landers, nursing his first Scotch of the evening, exclaimed, "No son of mine is going to be a stagehand!"

So Dad didn't take the job, but made up his mind that he would find another opportunity. "There were no unions, so if a cameraman didn't have an assistant he didn't know where to find one," he remembered. "If you happened to be around when they were starting a picture, you could become an assistant." His persistence led to a job at the Roach studio. Fred Jackman, a respected cameraman-director, hired the twenty-year-old for a series of films he was making starring Rex the Wonder Horse on the Crow Indian reservation in Wyoming. The city boy learned to ride and rope and live in the outdoors, making friends with the cowhands and the Indians who set up camp and rode before the cameras. Jackman let his young assistant experiment with film stock and filters and make his own shots. "When I first came out I was just working for a

Oliver Hardy and Stan Laurel in *Leave 'Em Laughing* (1928), photographed by George Stevens.

place on the team," he wrote in a letter to his mother. "Four weeks later I belonged."

He honed his skills in the high country with Jackman and on movie lots until one day he learned that studio boss Hal Roach had a problem. He wanted to cast an English music hall comedian in a new series of two-reelers. "But," lamented Roach, "his pale blue eyes won't register on black-and-white film." The young camera assistant explained that the orthochromatic film in common use was "blue blind." "Jackman and I have been experimenting in Wyoming with highly sensitive panchromatic film," he told Roach. "I can get some and shoot a test." He screened the test for Roach and the actor's eyes stood out. The problem was solved. As a reward, in 1927, George Stevens, at age twenty-three, became the cameraman for Roach's new comedy team: Stan Laurel—he of the pale eyes—and Oliver Hardy.

Nobody knew that Laurel and Hardy would become stars, and my father came to the assignment with a dim view of the comedy work he had seen at Roach, which he described as "the comedian falling into stuff and getting back up." But the opportunity to be the cameraman and work as a gag writer on more than thirty Laurel and Hardy films, including classics like *Putting Pants on Philip, Battle of the Century* and *Two Tars,* enabled him to observe Stan Laurel's genius. It changed the course of his life.

Stan Laurel and his young cameraman exchange looks, observed by Oliver Hardy
on the set of *Angora Love* (1929), the final silent film in the Laurel and Hardy
series. The goat who costarred stands at Laurel's side.

Stan was the story man, Babe was the golfer, and Babe liked it that
way. One day I walked into the projection room at Roach and Stan
was the only one there. He was watching some Laurel and Hardy
rushes, howling with laughter. I recall his feet were in the air—he was
bicycling them furiously in a reaction of utter merriment. He laughed
at Babe, not only because Babe was such a superb comedian, but
because Stan had the chance that creative people get so rarely—to see
his own ideas not only brought to life, but brought to life more
magnificently than he dared to dream.

My father watched and learned from the two comedians as they stoically faced
the indignities that befell them. "Until I met Laurel and Hardy, I didn't know
that comedy could be graceful and human," he said. "By some artistic instinct
they had this quality of being in touch with the human condition." With Stan as
his mentor, the young cameraman set his eyes on becoming a director. "As time
went on," he remembered, "I left comedy, but Laurel and Hardy never left me."

4

Yonnie

When it came time for Yvonne—who throughout her life was known as Yonnie—to join her mother in Hollywood, she took the train west all by herself. As an adult she stood four feet, eleven inches and wore size three shoes, so she must have been a tiny eleven-year-old when she made that six-day journey. Alice arranged for Pullman conductors to look after her. The charm and openness that became my mother's defining qualities must have eased her way on her cross-country adventure.

She stepped off the train at Union Station in 1916 to find a quiet and modestly populated town that was on its way to becoming the movie capital of the world. One day she rode her bike below the graceful pepper trees on Sunset Boulevard past the Triangle Studio, where she noticed actors rehearsing on a stage with an open-air roof that let in the bright sunlight required by cameras. She stopped. I remember her telling me that she was standing there—not causing any trouble—when she saw a tall man wearing a cowboy hat and puttees giving instructions to the leading man Richard Barthelmess.

The tall man looked over and said, "Well now, whose little girl are you?"

The inquiry was from the foremost of the movie pioneers, David Wark Griffith. "Well, everybody says I look like my mother," she replied. She remembers Griffith slapping his puttees and laughing, then inviting her to stay and watch them work.

My mother attended the Gardner Street school and would bike with her friends to Hollywood Boulevard and watch workmen building Grauman's Chinese Theater. An interviewer once showed her mother's passport indicating that Alice was born in 1888. "Oh no," Yonnie responded. "My mother was born in 1886 but she always took two years off—I was ten for about three years." She graduated from Hollywood High in the same class as a tall athlete named Joel McCrea who did stunt work on Westerns. One of her teachers told her she had talent for advertising and would regret not going to college. "I never regretted it because it was so much fun working in the movies," she said. "Gee whiz. $7.50 a day!" She and her friends would stand outside the Lasky Studio on Sunset and Vine for cattle calls. "They wanted flappers and you'd walk by, and they'd say, 'Hey you!' Little people like Gloria Swanson and Mary Pickford were in style so I got a lot of good chances."

One of those "Hey you's" led to Yonnie becoming a Mack Sennett Bathing Beauty, working under the name Yvonne Howell, with her good friend Carole Lombard. In September 1924 the *Universal Weekly* reported:

> The newest addition to the famous group of youthful beauties known as the Century Follies Girls, is already claiming distinction. She is Yvonne Howell, daughter of the famous comedienne Alice Howell, and claims to be the youngest and most beautiful member of the famous Century Comedies group of beauties. Modesty prevents the young lady from admitting it.

After she was cast in the FBO Pictures series *Grimm's Progress, Exhibitors Herald* had encouraging words. "We have just finished chapter 5 and it is the best one to date. Yvonne Howell is a comer, or I miss my guess. Good luck to you, Miss Howell." Later she took a serious role as Mimi in *Fashions for Women* (1927), working for the pioneering female director Dorothy Arzner, followed by an adventurous experience in *Somewhere in Sonora,* a Western with cowboy star Ken Maynard. My mother and another girl were driving a buckboard when the horses became frightened and sped off, turning a planned make-believe runaway into a real one as the buckboard headed down a narrow canyon path alongside a chasm several thousand feet deep. It was reported that Maynard, a gifted stuntman, leapt on his horse Tarzan, caught up to the speeding wagon, grabbed the reins and brought it under control. "Fifty members of the company testify to its happening," the account concluded.

No wonder my mother found movies more exciting than advertising.

Oliver Hardy had been a vaudeville singer in Georgia. When he came to Hollywood he worked in silent films with Alice Howell before teaming up with Stan Laurel. Yonnie remembered evenings at the Hardy house above the Cahuenga Pass that links Hollywood with the San Fernando Valley. Oliver, known to his friends as "Babe," had a rich tenor voice and after dinner he sang, with his actress wife, Myrtle Reeves, at the piano and Alice's husband, Dick Smith, playing the guitar. "Babe was like an uncle to me," my mother recalled.

My mother at the Sennett studio in 1924.

Alice took the train east in 1928 when her mother died suddenly to deal with funeral arrangements. Yonnie had just broken up with a fellow and recalls sitting around "moping" when her stepfather, Dick, said that Babe wanted them to come for dinner. They drove up to the Hardy house where dinner was delayed because Babe was shooting late at the Roach Studio in Culver City. Word finally came that he was on his way home and bringing along his cameraman. My mother thought, "Oh lord, some old coot." The front door opened and Babe, light on his feet for a three-hundred-pound man, glided in followed by his lean, dark haired and handsome twenty-four-year-old cameraman. "I thought he must be the *son* of the cameraman," Yonnie remembered. "I had what they called a Kewpie Doll haircut, and George always talked about seeing me sitting there in a big wing chair with my feet underneath me doing a crossword puzzle. He thought I was fourteen years old."

She remembers Babe and others making jokes at dinner, and time after time George would top them. "I'd been raised around comedians all my life, and I thought, 'Well, he heard that someplace, he couldn't have thought it up.' But he had this quiet way of knowing what was funny—the best sense of humor of anyone I ever met. And it turned out I wasn't fourteen—so one thing led to another . . . and you can take it from there."

5

Just Married

George and Yonnie were married by a justice of the peace in Glendale, California, on New Year's Day 1930. It was the depth of the Depression. My mother sold her car to pay for wedding clothes.

Newlyweds. January 1, 1930.

Matthew Beard, George Stevens, Jr., and Spanky McFarland
in *Wild Poses* (1933).

My mother's next movie was her last. "I had a tight fitting grey costume that Edith Head designed, and to my surprise I discovered I was pregnant," she remembered. "I was really worried when the leading man got sick and shooting was delayed—but it all worked out. Babe and Myrtle Hardy gave the baby shower."

I was born at the Hollywood Hospital on April 3, 1932, a respectable twenty-seven months after the wedding. My mother put aside her acting career to become a full-time mother. She must have wondered from time to time, like many women of her generation, what she might have achieved had she continued her career. One thing she did was become a dedicated saver of mementos, preserving countless pieces of family history. I was surprised to find a Certificate of Identification and Permit to Be Employed in Motion Pictures, dated August 8, 1933. It records my age as 16 months and my height as 32 inches, and enabled my acting debut at the Roach Studio, alongside George "Spanky" McFarland, in *Wild Poses,* one of the *Our Gang* series—a performance of which I have no memory that marked the beginning and end of my acting career.

Dad loved his steady job photographing Laurel and Hardy comedies, but one night confided a deeper yearning to my mother. "Pictures are gone in a week. I wish I could write a novel. I want to do something that will *last.*"

When Roach started a second series, *The Boy Friends,* with the *Our Gang* kids grown to teenagers, he gave the young cameraman his first opportunity to direct and my parents rented an apartment on Arnaz Avenue not far from the Roach Studio. My mother recalled my father's routine at day's end.

> He'd work from seven at night until one or two in the morning. Our apartment had a long hallway and he'd walk up and down that hall. He wanted to think. He did that until the day he died. He would just walk and walk and walk. I felt neglected because I'd always had a lot of attention, but I understood he had responsibility for the picture—the director can't blame the result on anybody else.

He directed seven pictures in the *Boy Friends* series, reworking the scripts during those late nights, until the day Roach gave him a script that was too weak to fix. Roach ordered him to shoot it anyway. Dad told his boss that *he* should direct it. "Roach wanted me to direct gag comedies," he explained, "but I liked humor that came from believable characters. It became a contest as to whether I would make pictures his way or make them my own way." That night during the depth of the Depression the company manager informed my father that his contract was canceled. The conflict revealed a trait that would define my father's career—his belief that a filmmaker must be in control of his work. He spent the next six months job hunting during his wife's pregnancy, a time my mother remembered well.

> It was just before Christmas during the Depression—that's always the way. We were going to meet and go to his mother's house for Christmas dinner. I thought he said in front of Grauman's Chinese, but it turned out he said Grauman's Egyptian. It was a cold night and George was half an hour late. I was furious because it was Christmas and my condition. Then I saw him ambling up the street—Hollywood Boulevard was nothing then—and I said, "Who are those people you were talking to?" And he said, "They were bums and wanted some money." So I asked, "What did you say." And he said, "I told them to get out of the way, I'm working this side of the street."

Dad began to wonder if he would ever get another directing job before Universal hired him to do some comedy shorts and his first feature, *The Cohens and Kellys in Trouble.* Then RKO signed him to do two feature comedies—*The Nitwits* and *Kentucky Kernels,* starring vaudevillians Bert Wheeler and Bob Woolsey, which allowed him to display his sense of timing and dexterity with actors. This led to the opportunity to direct his first drama, *Laddie,* from a Gene Stratton-Porter novel. Luckily for him an important star took notice.

Katharine Hepburn's career had taken a bad turn by 1935, leading critics to label her "box office poison." She was set to play the lead at RKO in *Alice Adams,* the Booth Tarkington story of a young woman from a poor midwestern family trying to find her way. William Wyler, already a top director, was in line to direct. "I was very desirable to work with at the time," Hepburn told me with an air of self-mockery in 1983. "I was considered absolutely fascinating. But I was suffering from the usual classiness of new stars, and I talked to one nice director after another and decided they didn't have the right *artistic attitude.*" After an assistant director told Hepburn she should take a look at George Stevens, they met and she was intrigued. When RKO chief Pandro Berman found out that Hepburn was torn between Wyler and Stevens, he suggested they flip a coin. Hepburn agreed and Berman tossed the coin. It came up Wyler. After a long moment of silence, Hepburn said, "Let's flip it again." It came up Stevens. "Pandro was obviously delighted," Hepburn concluded. "I think George was getting ten cents an hour and everyone else wanted about a hundred and fifty thousand dollars."

Alice Adams was my father's first chance at an important film with top stars. Fred McMurray played a young man from a wealthy family and the extraordinary Hattie McDaniel was the disgruntled maid hired for the evening when McMurray comes calling to the modest house of Alice's parents. The young director guided McDaniel through the memorable dinner table scene that combined pathos and hilarity, as she glumly serves a hot dinner on a humid night with her servant's hat sliding down her perspiring brow.

Alice was a girl of modest means. My father, sensing Hepburn's desire to show her skills as an actress, sought understatement. At one point Alice comes home after a dance where she was ignored, greets her mother pleasantly, then goes to her room. Hepburn fell on the bed sobbing. My father thought it would be more interesting if she walked to the window—with her back to the camera, rain spattering on the pane. "I don't know whether she cries or not, but I know she's heartbroken." And that's the way he shot it.

These two strong individuals came to respect one another. "I think his knowledge of comedy is unique," Hepburn told me. "When we filmed the dinner table scene I thought it was as funny as a baby's open grave, but it was one of the most brilliant comedy scenes ever played. That was totally George. He timed the angle of that headpiece she was wearing. I thought, that's too much, it's not going to be funny. But he knew—too much, too little—just great."

My mother went with Dad to the sneak preview of *Alice Adams.* Studios used to book an entire theater and the public would show up not knowing what they were going to see. The executives sat in the back, assessing the audience

George Stevens and Katharine Hepburn on the set of *Alice Adams* in 1935.

response. "On those nights your life was on the line," my mother remembered. "Sometimes you'd bring along an uncle who knew how to laugh." The lights went down and before long the audience was laughing and crying. The executives left the theater lighting their cigars, exchanging wide smiles. Mom and Dad went for coffee, and then, rather than going home, drove around until dawn when they could pick up the *Hollywood Reporter* at the paper's offices on Vine Street. "You've never read such a rave in your life," my mother enthused. "*Alice Adams* was a smash."

The picture was nominated for the Academy Award for Best Motion Picture and Hepburn for Best Actress, but the raves came from beyond Hollywood. The esteemed young critic James Agee wrote, "The direction of George Stevens, who at 30 is the youngest important director in Hollywood, is almost flawless."

6

Toluca Lake

Not long after Dad finished *Alice Adams* we moved from our apartment in Hollywood to a two-bedroom house with a sloping English roof that my parents built in Toluca Lake, a quiet village that surrounds a five-acre lake in the San Fernando Valley. The Lakeside Golf Club was built on undulating land between the lake and the Los Angeles River. Warner Bros. is half a mile to the east and Universal Studios is across the river to the west. Our corner house with wood beamed ceilings, designed by Robert Byrd, a rising new architect enlisted by my mother, cost $3,000 to build during the Depression. We were on Forman Avenue, which was connected by Navajo Street to the Valley Spring Lane entrance to Lakeside. During the day neighborhood children harvested polliwogs in the pond across the street, and at night we listened to coyotes howl.

Amelia Earhart, the intrepid aviatrix who would disappear over the Pacific in 1937, was the first to build on Valley Spring Lane, followed by stunt flyer Paul Mantz, and Bert Wheeler of the Wheeler and Woolsey comedies. Al Jolson and his wife Ruby Keeler lived on Navaho, and on the next corner was Bing Crosby, his wife Dixie and their five sons. But most of the houses were modest and the majority of our neighbors were ordinary people. My friend Jackie Faul's dad was a dentist, Mary Ann Kerans' father taught at LA City College, and Bobby Brewster's was an accountant at Universal.

All the moms, except for Ricky Arlen's actress mother, Jobyna Ralston, were what today we call homemakers. In later years my mother would repeat her conviction that the kids turned out well because their mothers were at home raising them. My closest pal Alfred Werker lived across the street. His father, like mine, was a movie director. We played baseball in the street and when movie tour buses invaded our space we shouted "Rubbernecks!" at the faces staring through the windows. I have a slightly off-color front tooth from a collision with

Framing my first shot in 1935.

a manhole cover when I dove past Peter McHugh while stretching a two-base hit into a triple. Peter's dad, Frank McHugh, was the ruddy character actor who appeared in 150 films including Leo McCarey's Oscar-winner *Going My Way.* Along with Pat O'Brien and Jimmy Cagney, he was a pillar of Hollywood's Irish mafia. The neighbors, even the ones whose fame attracted the buses, behaved like regular people. Everyone felt safe growing up in Toluca Lake.

Raised by comedians, my mother was a marvelous audience for a husband for whom comedy was a way of life. When he touched her funny bone she would rub her hands together, throw her head back, and laugh. And Dad loved to make Mom laugh. One morning Alfred, Mary Ann, Bobby and Jackie came over to play. Jackie brought along his brindle and white bulldog Vicki. While my parents were eating breakfast, Dad said to Jackie, "Vicki looks like a smart dog." Jackie nodded. Dad turned to the dog. "Vicki . . . how old is Jackie?" Vicki stared at my father with bulging eyes, then went—"Woof, Woof, Woof, Woof, Woof, Woof." Dad watched her. "Jackie, are you six?" Proud of his pet, Jackie smiled and the kids leaned in closer. Dad had more questions, and the acquiescent bulldog correctly indicated how many boys were in the Crosby family (five), how many cars the Werkers had (two), and how many toes my mother had on her right foot (yes, five). It had escaped our notice that Dad would slip Vicki a piece of bacon under the table when her "woofs" totaled the desired number. Every Saturday the kids would come over and Vicki would perform like a Quiz

George, Jr., and his dad at home
in Toluca Lake, 1937.

Kid. The children were enthralled, my mother adored it, and Vicki's prowess
became the talk of Toluca Lake.

One morning we assembled in the dining room and Vicki, enjoying her
new role, arrived with Jackie and stared expectantly at Dad. She knocked off
a few questions with characteristic precision, savoring her clandestine treats. At
that point my father looked at my mother, assumed an innocent Stan Laurel
expression, then turned slowly to the dog. "Vicki," he said. "What is Jackie's
mother's name?" The kids leaned in. Vicki stared at my father blankly. The room
was silent. Dad turned to my mother who was stifling laughter. In the tradition
of climaxing a sequence of gags, he'd provided the unexpected topper, wanting
to amuse her—even, it seems, at the risk of confusing the children. Vicki ran off
with us to play in the eternal California sunshine, and soon our minds were on
to other matters.

On other mornings Dad would finish breakfast, put on his linen jacket
(directors had not yet discovered blue jeans and baseball caps), shoulder his
leather bag of scripts, and walk out the front door toward his tan Lincoln Continental Cabriolet convertible parked by the curb, pointed in the direction of
RKO Radio Pictures. "Goodbye, Da," I would call out, and he would smile and
wave. My mother and I held hands as he went down the path with an exaggerated Charlie Chaplin flat-footed walk. Then I noticed he wasn't wearing shoes.

"Da! . . . your shoes!" He didn't seem to hear me. The walk became more pronounced. "Da! Your *SHOES!* You forgot your *SHOES!*"

He would stop, turn around with a puzzled look, and stare down at his stocking feet. And then at me—yes, with that Stan Laurel expression. Then he would hurry back to the house for his shoes and thank me for my watchfulness, making me feel important. This became a ritual in which I played my role—until the day when, no matter how loud I yelled, he seemed unable to hear me and drove off to RKO in his stocking feet. My mother paid a price for being such a good audience. She spent the morning convincing me that Dad must have shoes at the studio. Happily I developed no neuroses from these experiences, only a tendency to play practical jokes.

The neighborhood kids learned to swim at Lakeside. A large rectangular pool with a diving board was situated on a grassy expanse not far from the lake, just a short walk from the clubhouse. We waited anxiously through spring for the summer ritual when one of our mothers would take us each day for swimming and club sandwiches. During our first summer of swimming we five-year-olds made good progress. On the first day of the next summer we walked down to Lakeside with my mother. I ran with elation toward the pool and leapt into the deep end, then splashed a few times and went under. I had forgotten what I learned a year before. I bobbed and went under again, feeling at once helpless, embarrassed and terrified. There was a volcanic splash and I felt an enormous hand grab my trunks and cradle my bottom, lifting me to the surface and plopping me, sputtering, on the warm tiles at the side of the pool. When my eyes cleared, I was looking into the black eyes of a massive stranger with wavy black hair and white teeth. His name was Johnny Weissmuller—the five-time gold medalist at the 1932 Olympics—who was a member at Lakeside. I was too young to have seen him in Tarzan movies, but I knew I was in good hands.

I must have been six when I swam my first race at Lakeside. The contest was simply to swim one width of the pool. I remember getting to the other side, then treading water and hearing the poolside instructors yelling, "Touch, touch!" while I watched everyone else finish. I had neglected to touch the other side and lost the race. I think it may have been a reaction to my father and the way he made things look so easy and nonchalant, never seeming to expend much effort.

Around this time I made a discovery in our dark-paneled Forman Avenue den. A scientist's boy might have a chemistry set, but I discovered my father's 16mm Bell and Howell projector. Once he taught me how to thread the film, I screened prints of his Wheeler and Woolsey comedies, giggling at the gag humor. His print collection grew and in 1939 my favorite arrived. I delighted in setting up the screen on its tripod legs, turning on the projector, seeing the lamp pierce the darkness, hearing the "beeps" of the RKO Radio Pictures logo, and absorbing myself in the captivating adventure and comedy of Dad's *Gunga Din,* starring Cary Grant, Victor McLaglen and Douglas Fairbanks, Jr. I steeled myself for the dread of the snake pit in the underground prison where the three British sergeants were captive, into which Eduardo Ciannelli, playing the erudite but crazed Thuggee cult leader, leapt to his death. (I was even more intrigued when I found out that the actor was the father of my schoolmate Eddie Ciannelli.) But I was drawn most to Gunga Din himself, Rudyard Kipling's regimental bhisti, played by Sam Jaffe. Din is the water boy who aspires to be a soldier and sacrifices himself to save the regiment. For the first time I had deep feelings watching a film, touched by the dignity of the outsider, a theme at the heart of so many of my father's movies. During Din's funeral, I waited for the gruff commandant's declaration to the lilt of bagpipes. "You're a better man than I am, Gunga Din." My father's humane and beautifully crafted films were, unbeknownst to me, shaping my taste and sensibility.

George Stevens on location in Lone Pine, California, in 1938, directing *Gunga Din.*

7

My Dad

When I was in kindergarten at Rio Vista School, a couple of miles from our house, each child was asked to tell the class what their fathers did. I was a shy boy, a disorder that seemed to recede as years passed, so I muttered softly, "He's a director." The teacher tried to draw me out. "Georgie, why don't you tell the class what a director does." I was at a loss. My mother told me Dad was a director but we didn't discuss what it meant. I learned soon enough that his way of making a living was out of the ordinary.

Rio Vista had a small amphitheater called the Bowl at which the children did an annual performance for parents. I was to enter wearing a delivery hat and carrying a small flowerpot, then cross in front of the audience and call out, "Flowers for Mrs. Brown." I repeated this entrance three times after intervals, on each occasion with a larger pot and a taller flower. The laughter increased with each appearance. It was a modest but well-remembered early exposure to the satisfaction of pleasing an audience.

Dad loved sports, and he told me stories that brought that world to life, setting me on the path to becoming a sportswriter. He told me about working out as a teenager in Boyes Springs during spring training with famed Boston Red Sox left fielder Duffy Lewis who, with Tris Speaker and Harry Hooper, formed what many consider the greatest outfield ever. He told me about seeing "the long count" in the Dempsey–Tunney fight, and stories about the Notre Dame backfield, under Coach Knute Rockne, reading aloud Grantland Rice's account of the Fighting Irish victory over Army in 1924. "Outlined against a blue-grey October sky," Dad would recite in his mellow and stirring voice: "The Four Horsemen rode again. In dramatic lore their names are Death, Destruction, Pestilence and Famine, but those are aliases. The real names are: Stuhldreher, Crowley, Miller and Layden." None of the four was six feet tall and none weighed more than 175 pounds, but they are the most famous backfield in football history and my father made them come alive. I loved sitting at night playing checkers with him, or passing the *Sporting News Baseball Guide* back and forth, picking our all-time favorite players.

The Philadelphia Athletics came to southern California for spring training in 1940. A pal of my father's, Al Horwits, was the baseball writer for the *Philadelphia Ledger* and later became a top Hollywood publicist. We went to watch the Athletics practice and Al introduced me to Connie Mack, who managed the team for fifty years, winning more games than any manager in history. (He also lost more games than any manager.) Mr. Mack, whose given name was Cornelius McGillicuddy, was a slender, seventy-eight-year-old man with white hair who stood over six feet. He wore a starched white shirt, blue suit and tie, even when managing in the dugout. He shook my hand and said, "How old are you, Georgie?" I told him I was seven. He asked whether I batted right or left-handed. According to my Dad, I looked the Hall of Fame manager in the eye and said with assurance, "Switch, Mr. Mack." Dad said he knew at that moment I was going to turn out all right.

I would visit my father's parents at their little house in Glendale. Boss and Granga (Landers and Georgie) were simply my grandparents, and I'm not sure I even knew they were actors. Landers' mother, Hannah Laura—Nana to me—had her own bedroom, and I slept on the old-fashioned sofa in the living room listening to the whistles of the passenger trains heading east in the night. Sometimes Uncle Jack would visit. He was a year older than my father but had the spirit of a big kid and was a good athlete. He would crouch with a catcher's glove and receive my pitches, giving me signs for curveballs and changeups. Jack was mischievous and I was fond of him, but I overheard conversations that hinted at problems. He was an accomplished camera operator, but drink was his demon and good studio jobs were often lost, regained, then lost again. In 1941, shortly after Landers died, my grandmother called Dad at the studio. She said Jack was outside her house and she was frightened, so Dad walked off the set of *Penny Serenade,* leaving cast and crew idle, and drove to Glendale. When he arrived at the house the door was ajar. As Dad walked in, Jack caught him across the face with a chair, breaking his nose. The brothers grappled until Jack was subdued. His demons were painful baggage in the Stevens family.

Dad and I played football in the street and pitcher and catcher in our backyard. He aligned my tiny fingers with the seams in my efforts to master the curveball, and the screwball that breaks in toward the right-handed batter, showing me how to snap my wrist at the end of the throw. He worked with Al Werker, Peter

McHugh, Bobby Brewster and me on the Notre Dame shift in our backyard, instructing us to swing our arms right to left. Then we would shift and hand the ball off in the deceptive patterns designed by Knute Rockne for the Four Horsemen, where all the backs were in motion when the ball was snapped—a system so successful it was outlawed. Dad was patient and always made it fun. He was the favorite father in the neighborhood.

He employed a man named Roy Fisher as a right-hand man, and sometimes the three of us would go to Palm Springs for the weekend. I was bundled into the backseat of the tan Lincoln Continental convertible, enjoying the smell of the brown leather seats as I fell asleep. Dad would drive and Roy would sit in the passenger seat. We stayed at a rustic resort and I tried hard to stay awake after dinner listening to cowboys singing "My Little Buckaroo." In the morning Dad and I rode for an hour on horseback to a chuckwagon, where cowhands were cooking breakfast. Then I would watch Roy and Dad play tennis. Roy was a fine athlete and would play football with the kids in Toluca Lake on a grassy area by the second fairway at Lakeside. He was special because he could fire long spirals that arrived flush in our stomachs, which he called our "breadbaskets." Roy was the only Black man I spent much time with as a child, and the easy relationship he had with my father made an impression.

Dad told a story about Roy. Katharine Hepburn was coming over with a script she wanted him to direct. Roy's training in domestic work was, let's say, informal. He came in with a tray and set it carefully on a side table, placing a cup and saucer in front of Miss Hepburn, then pouring her tea. She thanked him and, fanning herself said, "It's so warm isn't it? If it's not too much trouble, I'd prefer *iced* tea." Roy glanced at my father, the kind of "take" seen in his comedies. Then he hurried to the kitchen and returned with a bowl of ice and tongs. "One lump or two?" he asked. This delighted Dad, who liked keeping things down to earth. And Kate, too. She was her own variation of a man's man.

Dad would take me to the Los Angeles Coliseum with a hundred thousand other fans to watch the USC Trojans face the crosstown rival UCLA Bruins. All the USC players were white at that time, but UCLA was a state university and had two young African American stars, Kenny Washington and Jackie Robinson. One Saturday we watched USC punt to the UCLA three-yard line and the Trojan defense sprint down and huddle around the ball waiting for it to come to rest. Suddenly Robinson reached in, snatched the ball, and took off around the USC men for a ninety-seven-yard touchdown, demonstrating the audacity that would one day make him an American legend.

Washington and Robinson were not welcome in the National Football League because of their race, so Washington signed with the Hollywood Bears in the Pacific Coast pro league, and Robinson with the Los Angeles Bulldogs, before he turned his hand to baseball. Jackie claimed Kenny was the greatest football player he had ever seen and believed he carried "a deep hurt" because he never had a chance to become a national figure in professional sports.

One Sunday December afternoon Dad and I went to Gilmore Stadium to watch Kenny Washington play for the Bears. I was happy in the sunshine, clutching my Zeiss binoculars on the fifty-yard line beside the father I loved. The spell was broken when the public address announcer interrupted the game with a report. Japanese aircraft had bombed American ships in a sneak attack on our base at Pearl Harbor. I remember riding home in the front seat of the Lincoln beside my Dad, aware that something of consequence had occurred that I didn't fully understand.

PART TWO

WAR

Major George Stevens, Yvonne Stevens and George, Jr., at the Empire State
Building, March 1943.

8

Changing Times

The next day the children at Rio Vista assembled outdoors in the Bowl and listened to President Roosevelt describe December 7, 1941, as a date which will live in infamy, and then declare war on Japan. We had no way of knowing how lives might change. Rio Vista was a two-mile ride from our house and before long I was doing my part for gas rationing by walking to school in formation with my friends, singing, "We are the army of the Flying Feet." The fourth graders staged a patriotic show in which I played George Washington and my friend Roy Murakami was Benjamin Franklin. My mother was enchanted by Roy, a husky nine-year-old of Japanese descent, wearing wire-rimmed glasses and a white wig, gamely portraying a founding father. Roy and his younger brother George were sons of the owner of a popular plant nursery.

Californians became apprehensive when J. Edgar Hoover, the imperious head of the FBI, warned of an espionage network of spies. There were reports of unidentified aircraft over our city, where airplane factories were located, and of hostile submarines off the coast. Volunteer air raid wardens in tin hats patrolled Toluca Lake, the Rose Bowl game was moved to North Carolina out of the range of Japanese bombers, and President Roosevelt created the War Relocation Authority to manage the removal from designated areas of persons who might compromise national security. Then one day I learned that Roy and George Murakami had left Rio Vista. The Murakami home and nursery had been confiscated and the family sent to the Manzanar Relocation Center in the Owens Valley. We had no opportunity to say goodbye.

Our little village had lost its innocence.

My father turned thirty-seven two weeks after Pearl Harbor. He was well beyond draft age and with a dependent child there was no prospect of him being called up. His career had soared at RKO after *Alice Adams*. He made eight pictures in five years, starting with *Annie Oakley* starring Barbara Stanwyck as the beguiling sharpshooter, followed by *Swing Time,* with Fred and Ginger, of which dance historian Arlene Croce wrote, "There was never a more star-struck movie or a greater dance musical." Then *Quality Street,* a period piece with Katharine Hepburn and Franchot Tone; *A Damsel in Distress,* with Astaire, Joan Fontaine, George Burns and Gracie Allen with music by George Gershwin; *Vivacious Lady,* a romantic comedy with Jimmy Stewart and Ginger Rogers; *Vigil in the Night,* a drama of wartime in London with Carole Lombard; and finally *Gunga Din,* which became a huge hit for RKO.

The first title on the screen for the last three films was "A George Stevens Production," a credit that signaled *he* was the person telling the story.

Gunga Din was his first outdoor picture and the script was being rewritten at night and filmed the next day. They shot six days a week in 100-degree heat in Lone Pine, California, with hundreds of extras, a process Dad called "cavalry scale improvisation." One night he wrote to my mother about family concerns. He had helped his troubled brother Jack get a job as a cameraman in Italy, but after three weeks Jack went on a bender and was fired, leaving him stranded with debts in Rome.

I thought your idea of the steamship company handling the details of bringing Jack back here was very good. I didn't know just what to do. This is just a lusty example of Jack's attitude of doing nothing for himself. Mother wrote me not to send her check this month, feeling that the big loafer could deprive her for his own greedy indolence.

I hope my little boy is being a good little man, and is sweet to his Mama. So he thinks his Dad is the only one who is good to him? Isn't that always the way, the one who's away and doesn't have to drill them is the sugar coated one? He is a fine boy and his Dad sure does love him, although it probably doesn't look much like it. Give him a big hug from his Da. I've got to get some sleep now. Lots of love to two dear little people.

My father was at the top of his game at RKO, but the studio resisted his desire to address more serious themes. He brought them *Paths of Glory,* Humphrey Cobb's World War I novel about three soldiers in France who are court-martialed for turning their backs on a hopeless battle. He saw drama in the questions of patriotism and power, but RKO wanted no part of it. (Stanley Kubrick made *Paths of Glory* in 1957. I once asked Dad if he'd seen the film. "No," he said. "Not out of carelessness, I just didn't want to attend another man's wedding.")

George Stevens and Fred Astaire at work on the classic *Swing Time* at RKO in 1935.

He became determined to gain greater control over his work. Harry Cohn, the famously abrasive head of Columbia Pictures, urged him to move up Gower Street to his studio. Aware of Cohn's intrusive, sometimes abusive, reputation, Dad told him he needed full control of his pictures. Cohn signed him by promising, "You'll have final cut and I'll never come on your set." As evidence of his growing stature, the Screen Directors Guild, founded in 1935 with King Vidor as its first president, and Frank Capra as its second, elected him to succeed Capra.

My earliest memory of being on a movie set is as an eight-year-old standing next to a passenger train at RKO as artificial snow tumbled down on Irene Dunne and Cary Grant. In *Penny Serenade* my father wove together romance, heartbreak and humor, helping Cary to the first of his two Oscar nominations. Next he mixed drama and comedy, casting Cary in *The Talk of the Town,* as a fugitive who hides out in a house occupied by Jean Arthur and a law professor, played by Ronald Colman. The film brought Columbia seven Academy Award nominations, including one for Best Picture.

Then Katharine Hepburn sent him a script. She was under contract at MGM, a studio at which Dad had vowed never to work because directors had to answer to Louis B. Mayer. Mayer was known for liking directors with big mortgages. Recalling that she chose him to direct *Alice Adams,* Hepburn said, "George paid an old debt. I needed him and he said, 'Okay, here I am.'" He went to MGM and made history bringing Hepburn and Spencer Tracy together in *Woman of the Year.* Hepburn played a sophisticated world affairs columnist and Tracy a baseball writer. Hepburn loved her *Alice Adams* director's way of keeping comedy real, and counted on his steady hand with her new leading man.

In 1942 he was back at Columbia with Joel McCrea and Jean Arthur shooting *The More the Merrier,* the blithely witty and erotic comedy set in wartime Washington, DC. Jean Arthur was enchanting and shy, and her rawboned leading man and her handsome director enjoyed flattering her by seeming to be at war for her affections.

Dad and Joel were men of the West and enjoyed one another's laid-back humor. The unassuming McCrea was known for saying that he had never received a script that didn't have Gary Cooper's fingerprints on it. He had already made two pictures the year he received *The More the Merrier* screenplay, and only reluctantly agreed to meet with George Stevens. "I was kind of lazy and had a ranch to run and didn't feel like going to work right away," Joel told me in 1983. "George didn't do any of the things an ordinary director would do to try to get an actor to do a part. He brought out all the stills with Rex the King of Wild Horses, and said he carried the camera and he helped build the pole corrals up in Utah. And I saw what a regular guy he was, so I said, 'I want to do the picture.' George said, 'You've *got* to do the picture.' So we did and we had the greatest time." Joel added that if someone were to tell George he could make *The More the Merrier* over and have Clark Gable, George would say, "No, for this I want McCrea." Then he made a self-effacing observation I can't imagine coming from any other movie star. "You see, George had that kind of confidence in himself, so even if it were somebody better, like Gable or Cary Grant, he'd say, 'No for this I want McCrea.'"

One night in a Columbia projection room my father watched *Triumph of the Will,* the propaganda masterpiece by Leni Riefenstahl documenting the Nazi Party Congress in Nuremberg that juxtaposes chilling rants by Adolf Hitler and sweeping shots of goose-stepping troops cheered by civilian throngs. The young director was struck by the cinematic power Riefenstahl achieved in glorifying Hitler and the invincibility of the German army. "It affected me more than any

"He was kind of like the best cup of coffee you ever had," said Jean
Arthur of the director for whom she starred in three films. Above with
Joel McCrea in *The More the Merrier* (1943). Also, *The Talk of the
Town* (1941) and *Shane* (1953).

film I would ever see," he said later. He concluded that when good and evil were
at odds in the world, he couldn't sit on the sidelines. Within days he was commissioned a major in the US Army Signal Corps with the assurance he would
serve overseas. He advised colleagues at the Directors Guild that he was resign-
ing as president, and received orders to fly to North Africa with a combat camera
unit that he would lead.

"George Stevens is leaving at the end of the week to enter the Service of his
Country," wrote Harry Cohn in a memo to studio management, adding with
some optimism: "Anyone to whom you assign his office must take it with the
understanding that he will vacate it when Mr. Stevens returns." Cohn notified
the payroll office that Stevens' $3,000 a week salary would cease at the end of the
week.

I keep in my desk the officer's pay data card my father was given in 1943.
Major George C. Stevens, 0-921,866, would receive a base pay of $250 monthly,
a rental allowance of $105 and subsistence of $63, for a total of $418 a month.

On a clear January morning Dad put the top down on the Lincoln Continental
and we drove on Ventura Boulevard to Joel McCrea's Santa Rosa Valley ranch.
This was our last father–son outing before Dad went to war. McCrea's spread

was 2,700 acres where he ran 150 head of cattle. (Joel once listed his profession as rancher and his hobby as actor.) He and his nine-year-old son Jody were waiting with saddled horses by the old bunkhouse that Joel used for an office when Dad and I got out of the car wearing our western hats and boots. We spent the day roaming the hills and valleys of the McCrea ranch, and even herded some cattle in the afternoon sun. Joel and Dad were models of strong warm-hearted men. I remember riding home in the car beside my father wondering how long he would be away.

My bedroom was down a short hallway from my parents on the second floor. That night lights stayed on and the phone rang. My father had agonizing stomach pain but was unwilling to let my mother take him to the hospital. He suspected it was an ulcer, and if the army found out he wouldn't be allowed to go overseas. At five in the morning my mother finally prevailed and an ambulance took Dad to the Hollywood Hospital, where he underwent emergency surgery. The doctors said his appendix was removed just in time to avoid a fatal rupture. I recall the disturbing sight of a jar beside his bed containing the swollen organ.

Fred Guiol, Dad's director pal going back to the Roach days, came to visit, bringing word that the air transport carrying the men he was assigned to travel with had crashed off the coast of Brazil on the way to North Africa. All aboard were lost. That long day on horseback had inflamed the appendix and diverted my father from a tragic fate.

Two weeks later Dad, in uniform with a major's golden oak leaves on his shoulders, was hurriedly signing documents at the direction of his lawyer, including a power of attorney for my mother. It was the only time I remember feeling tension in our house. We went to the Burbank airport where he boarded a DC-3 bound for New York to undergo orientation. My mother and I followed by train and joined him in a small suite at the Waldorf Astoria, at the military rate of five dollars a night. He went to the Army Pictorial Center on Long Island each day where he discovered an army bureaucracy that rivaled the studios. He reported to a career Signal Corps colonel, Melvin Gillette, who was blocking his efforts to recruit professional cameramen. I heard tense phone conversations and began referring to Colonel Gillette as "Old Blue Blades," which delighted my parents. One day I telephoned from the bedroom to the living room and, deepening my voice, impersonated Old Blue Blades. My father bought into it for a few moments, or at least he and Mom let me think they did, indulging their rascal son.

Dad took me to Ebbets Field to see the Brooklyn Dodgers, my first major league ball game. Then he came down with pneumonia and was sent to the army hospital at Fort Jay on Governor's Island. He was bedridden for three weeks, and my mother brought him fresh sheets and pajamas every day, providing this ten-year-old a measure of freedom that included choosing dishes in New York's coin-operated automats and seeing *Yankee Doodle Dandy* five times. I was captivated by James Cagney's singing and dancing and I loved the patriotic songs—*Yankee Doodle Boy* and *Over There*—with lyrics that were close to home: "Send the word, send the word over there, That the Yanks are coming, The Yanks are coming."

When Dad recovered we took the train to Washington and stayed in the new Statler Hotel a block from the White House. I loved looking through the window and seeing the lights of Griffith Stadium where the Washington Senators played, and visiting Ford's Theater where Lincoln was shot. We were joined by Irwin Shaw, the young novelist who worked with Dad on *The Talk of the Town* and had signed up for his unit. We were in the dining room on a Saturday night waiting for Irwin to join us when there was a ruckus at the headwaiter's station. We looked over and saw Irwin, a private first class, close to blows with the maître d'. Dad, wearing his officer's uniform, rushed over. Irwin had assumed that the man refused to seat him because he was Jewish, whereas in fact the hotel policy excluded enlisted men from the dining room. My father patiently persuaded the agitated maître d' that there must be a place for one of America's most respected authors. Irwin joined us and the two men nursed a bottle of Scotch on their last night on American soil.

Mom, Dad and I had breakfast early on Easter Sunday and took a taxi to Washington's new National Airport where I watched my father stride with his B-4 bag to a twin-engine military C-47. We watched it take off to the south and disappear toward Rio de Janeiro where it would refuel, head east to the Azores and on to North Africa, where British and American forces were fighting General Erwin Rommel and his Afrika Corps. I found a note in Dad's diary that he must have written in flight.

> I had a hard time to keep my eyes dry when I kissed my dear little boy and my dear little wife good-by. I'm so happy when I'm with those two. They are both so fine. I will be very happy when I can come back to them.

My mother took me to Lafayette Park across from the White House and we rested on the grass in the afternoon sunshine, two little people who, for the foreseeable future, would be living alone together on Forman Avenue. I wrote to my father that evening. It was my first use of V-mail—letters written on a special form that could be checked by censors, thumbnail photographed, shipped overseas, then blown up for delivery at their destination, saving thousands of tons of transport space for war matériel.

Easter Sunday, April 25

Dear Dad,
I thought I would write you a letter so you would receive it when you got there. I don't have much to say because you just left this morning. Do not go out of your way to write me but when you write mother or

me tell me if you need a calendar. If there is any special information you want me to write to you or any equipment you want me to send you. We watched the plane fly out of sight today.

> Best of luck and love.
> Your son George.

It was my father's nature to save things. He kept all the letters he received from us overseas, and my mother saved his. Among his papers I found the letter my mother wrote that night.

Dear Da,

You sure left two sad little people behind today. Your little man held out until he got back to the hotel and then he threw himself on his bed and just sobbed. I was so surprised. It just broke my heart. He's been so sweet to me. He went out scouring the town (it's Sunday, you know) to get this V mail stationery so we could write right away. Lots of love from us and we sure do miss you tonight.

> Mama and Georgie

9

A Time of War

A tan parcel secured with twine arrived at our house addressed to me. I unwrapped it to find *The Human Comedy,* a novel by William Saroyan. The author was in the motion picture unit my father was assembling in London to cover the invasion of Europe. He was, along with Irwin Shaw and intrepid war photographer Robert Capa, a poker buddy of Dad's in pre-D-Day London. The book was inscribed in the author's hand.

> Dear George,
> All I can say is that getting to know your father has been one of the
> greatest bits of good luck I have ever had. He is the best friend in
> the world, because besides understanding things so well, he is full
> of fun, and whenever I am with him I am in a better happier world—
> *his* world.
> I'll be seeing you someday.
>
> Your friend, Bill Saroyan
> June 2, 1944
> England

Saroyan's feelings, written just four days before D-Day, mirrored my own about my faraway father, and I was flattered by the grown-up gift from a fine writer. Before it was a novel, *The Human Comedy* was a movie starring Mickey Rooney as Homer Macauley, a messenger boy in a small California town who is assigned to deliver telegrams from President Roosevelt informing families that a loved one has been killed in action. I don't believe a day would pass when the prospect of the Western Union man coming to our house bearing a yellow envelope didn't cross my mind. *The Human Comedy* stayed at my bedside.

Mom and I placed a small flag with a blue star in our dining room window, signaling that a member of the household was serving. A father at war became the subtext of my otherwise normal childhood. My mother was raising a son by herself while her high-earning husband was now drawing army pay. The only mother in the neighborhood without a man in the house, she volunteered three days a week as a nurse's aide in the burn ward at the Birmingham Hospital in Van Nuys.

Mom learned from teachers' reports that I was the "spitball king" at Rio Vista, so she decided I needed a more demanding environment. Her generous interpretation was that I completed my schoolwork with such ease that too much time remained for mischief. Before Dad left they interviewed with the English-born headmaster of Harvard School, the Suffragan Bishop of Los Angeles, Robert B. Gooden. Apparently they passed muster because I was accepted as a sixth grader at Harvard, which had a Junior ROTC program.

Mom and I went to Desmond's for fitting of three uniforms—khaki shirt and trousers worn with a web belt, tie and garrison cap; olive drab trousers and a blouse; and dress blues for Thursdays.

I entered the sixth grade as the second shortest boy at Harvard, standing in formation on the parade ground with my carbine rifle in the Third Platoon of D. Company, next to the shortest, my new friend Buck Zuckerman, whose impish humor made close-order drill tolerable. Another pal was the best looking among us, Robert "R. J." Wagner, who would leave early to pursue an acting career but remained a friend for life. Our company commander was a senior, H. R. "Bob" Haldeman, the scion of steadfast Republican parents. Haldeman wore a flat-top haircut that was unchanged a quarter century later when he arrived at the White House as chief of staff to President Nixon. At a party at Joan Collins' house in Beverly Hills in the sixties I was introduced to Buck Henry, the rising young screenwriter who created Get Smart with Mel Brooks and was Oscar-nominated for The Graduate. I recognized Buck Zuckerman—my mischievous comrade from the Third Platoon of D. Company.

Harvard had recently moved to the twenty-two-acre site of the bankrupt Hollywood Country Club on Coldwater Canyon Road, where one fairway was turned into a football field that doubled as a parade ground. Bishop Gooden was slight and benign without a hair on his head, earning the whispered moniker Old Cue Ball. Kinter B. Hamilton was our erratic headmaster, known for taking five thousand words to say, "No." Master Sergeant August J. Kunkel was a retired regular army man with ramrod posture, gravelly voice, and a bulbous nose protruding from a leathery face. He would greet us after the bugle sounded for early morning formation. One day I arrived without my uniform cap. Sergeant

In my senior year at Harvard School with Coach Hanson, 1949.

Kunkel barked at me to the stifled delight of my fellow cadets: "Stevens, you'd lose your balls if they weren't in a sack!"

Dr. Baron von Jacobs was our gymnasium instructor. He was fit and muscular in his tight trousers, tee shirt and pointed gym shoes. And how should I put it? *Germanic.* The performance he demanded on the high bar often exceeded the capacities of us under-muscled twelve-year-olds. When a boy would struggle and plummet to the mat and moan, Dr. Jacobs would stand over the crumpled specimen and exclaim, "Achh . . . der iss no pain!" He raged when an unidentified boy hurled a baseball that cracked one of the gym's dusty elevated windows.

We rebelliously traced in the dust, "Achh . . . der iss no pane."

Most fondly I remember Wilbur Hanson, my Mr. Chips. He drove our Toluca Lake group to school in his station wagon, taught English and coached basketball. He was tall and rangy, a fine athlete with a dazzling smile. His brother Jack played third base for the Los Angeles Angels of the Pacific Coast League. There were occasions when a motorcycle cop would pull us over because of Mr. Hanson's heavy foot. We would fall silent and watch him flash his killer grin at the officer, then be sent on his way with just a warning. He encouraged me on the basketball court and he liked to win, but there was no Bobby Knight in him. He was there to teach teamwork and sportsmanship, to build our confidence and let us discover the joy of competition. It was Mr. Hanson in his English class who put me on the path of being a writer. I discovered that I enjoyed writing, which later led to me serving as sports editor for the school paper, then as editor, and in our senior year as editor of the yearbook.

My father had arrived in North Africa in the waning days of the Allied campaign. He was filming in Tunis when the Germans surrendered. From there he went to London where in late 1943 General Eisenhower gave him the most important assignment of his life. He was put in charge of organizing motion picture coverage for the invasion of Europe. He set up the Special Coverage Unit (SPECOU), attached to the Supreme Headquarters Allied Expeditionary Force (SHAEF), and recruited top professionals, among them Joe Biroc, his camera operator from *Swing Time* at RKO, Bill Hamilton, his sound man at Columbia, and William Mellor, a camera mainstay at Paramount. The unit, composed initially of forty-five men, became known as the Stevens Irregulars.

I wrote to Dad at least once a week, but my mother wrote almost every day. He, preoccupied by fatherly concerns, responded to her from London:

> I have thought much about what sort of job George should try and
> get for the summer. It will be his first job. . . . He will have to learn
> to get along with his boss and do things that are not designed for his
> pleasure. He will get the satisfaction of personal accomplishment, the
> realization that he as a person can do something himself, independent
> of the parental organization which has made all things possible so far.
> He will earn some money, a portion of which should be designated for
> the community welfare. By that I mean his home should benefit from
> this new found earning power. This I hope does not have to be told
> to him, but I will pass a guarded hint. I say guarded hint because
> important things like that are much better if they come from him as
> part of his character development. You are the Supreme Court to him;
> your decisions should be based on judgment and wisdom so that he
> will respect those decisions, because from that pattern he will develop
> his own code of conduct. A boy must learn to decide things that affect
> other people in a code of fair play. I don't think you need advice on
> how to do what you're doing but I just want you to know I am
> interested too and feel very far away.

No job materialized for this twelve-year-old that summer, though I did find in my mother's papers a polite rejection letter from the Security National Bank. She knew I was interested in writing so we enrolled together in a typing school on Hollywood Boulevard. Mom and I would go to class, searching the keys as the instructor intoned, "Semi . . . L . . . K . . . J . . ." Then we would cross the street for flannel cakes at the Musso and Frank Grill, a favored hangout of picture people where she and Dad and I had enjoyed dinners sitting in red leather booths, tended to by waiters in red jackets. Afterward we would cross the boulevard again to the NewsView, a theater that showed one-hour programs of newsreels. I loved the sports stories, but my mother and I were drawn to reports on the war, always hoping that one of those helmeted Americans we saw would be Dad.

I was delighted that we had a surfeit of vehicles—a black 1941 Ford convertible, as well as Mom's white Chrysler coupe, with its state-of-the-art automatic transmission, and Dad's 1939 Lincoln Cabriolet. Mom would sit in the passenger seat and let me drive her Chrysler, even though I was too young for a learner's permit. When she went to Hollywood for the afternoon, I would become adventurous and back the Ford out of the garage and drive around the block.

An enterprising developer, Paul Trousdale, had built thousands of houses in Beverly Hills by age twenty-nine, and one day came to our door unannounced and asked to speak with my mother. He had seen the tan Lincoln Continental with the spare tire mounted on the back in front of our house. "I want to buy that Lincoln Continental," he said. "I'll pay top dollar." My mother, a warm and open person, found him brazen, and explained that the owner was also fond of the car and, despite being well beyond draft age, was overseas fighting to keep America free. He was, she added, looking forward to driving his Continental when he returned home. I was proud of my mother.

The New York Film Critics Circle honored my father with the 1944 best director award for *The More the Merrier,* and soon after the Motion Picture Academy nominated it for best picture and best director. I could recite the batting averages of the entire Hollywood Stars lineup and was looking forward to a doubleheader between the Hollywood Stars and the San Francisco Seals when my mother informed me we were going instead to Grauman's Chinese. If my father won, I would accept the Oscar for him. I got dressed up in what I remember as an itchy suit and set off with my mother and grandmother Georgie. Jack Benny was host. We were seated down front near the nominees for best actress—Jean Arthur (*The More the Merrier*), Greer Garson (*Madame Curie*), Joan Fontaine (*The Constant Nymph*), Ingrid Bergman (*For Whom the Bell Tolls*) and Jennifer Jones (*The Song of Bernadette*). When one of the ladies' films would win for costume design or art direction, her competitors would smile gracefully and applaud their colleague.

The Special Coverage Unit, London 1944, Major George Stevens back row, center. First row, left to right: Tom Henry, Norton McMillan, David Mott, Jack Muth, William Hamilton, Hal Lee, Forrest Weller, Ken Marthey, John Hines; second row: Gordon Bush, Russell Day, Curtis Albertson, Pinkney Ridgell, Sandy Brooke, Andrew McCarthy, Phil Drell, Dick Kent; third and fourth rows: Irwin Shaw, Ivan Moffat, Leicester Hemingway, Henry Moritz, Lt. Branham, Captain Reis, Captain Starling, Colonel Jervy, Lt. Morse, Major Stevens, Captain Mellor, Lt. Biroc, Lt. Montague, Lt. Herman, Lt. Johnson.

Dad's comrade in arms, Bill Saroyan, was nominated for best original story for *The Human Comedy*, opposite *The More the Merrier*. Saroyan's name was called and, as the proud owner of an inscribed Saroyan book, I enjoyed seeing the gold statue go to him in absentia. Toward the end of the evening Mark Sandrich, my father's successor as president of the Directors Guild, read the names of the director nominees, opened the envelope, and called out, "Michael Curtiz, *Casablanca*!" My mother recalls that I had a deep and resonant voice for a twelve-year-old, and—untutored in the decorum of the gracious ladies surrounding me—exclaimed in the silence before the applause, "We was robbed!" My mother dined out on that moment. "You never heard such *laughter*," she would say.

My father was busy organizing for D-Day when he received my mother's letter reporting on the Academy Awards. He responded promptly.

I feel like a big loafer letting you down like that. We didn't hear anything where I was at the time and I certainly didn't know my darlings were going. I would have felt very blue thinking about their disappointed little faces as they walked out of the theater. The Academy Awards hooey seems so far away and unimportant, then I realize my dear family was there and it made me wish terribly that I had won. I felt bad about disappointing George. Then along came his 'we wuz robbed' letter and I didn't worry any more about my boy. I remembered that the black cloud on his face when [Hollywood Stars first baseman] Babe Herman struck out only lasted an hour or two and then the sun would come out and light up those freckles of his like neon.

Dad wrote separately to me.

Dear Son,
You are all a lot of big shots going to high-powered affairs like that. I bet we darn near won it. And I must agree with you that as long as we didn't win it we must have been robbed. Dem bums. We'll moider em!

Love from your Dad

10

The Fifty Yard Line

At dawn on the sixth of June 1944 the Royal Navy cruiser HMS *Belfast* approached the coast of Normandy near Saint-Aubin-sur-Mer. My father, huddled against the wind in his helmet and flak jacket, standing with the crew assembled on the deck, may have thought of his Shakespearean father as the captain recited the Saint Crispin's Day speech at the battle of Agincourt from *Henry V*:

> And Crispin Crispian shall ne'er go by,
> From this day to the ending of the world,
> But we in it shall be remembered—
> We few, we happy few, we band of brothers;
> For he today that sheds his blood with me
> Shall be my brother.

Belfast was the flagship assigned to initiate the bombardment that would launch the largest amphibious landing in history. She commenced firing at German shore batteries and bunkers at 05:30—preparing the beach code-named Juno for the landing of Allied forces.

In North Hollywood I was getting ready for school when my mother and I heard on the radio that the invasion was under way. The report said that British, Canadians and Americans had made their way ashore and were battling Germans entrenched on the bluffs above the beaches. We drove to St. David's Episcopal Church and joined a crowded prayer service. The churchgoers were somber. I never prayed harder than I did that day.

Mom and I sat together that evening listening to the CBS report that opened with Edward R. Murrow's distinctive baritone: "This . . . is London." He played

Lt. Col. George Stevens on deck of HMS *Belfast* on D-Day, 1944.

General Eisenhower's message to the troops: "You are about to embark upon the Great Crusade toward which we have striven these many months. The eyes of the world are upon you. The hope and prayers of liberty-loving people everywhere march with you."

Reports confirmed that ten thousand Americans shed blood on D-Day alone. Days passed before we received word that Dad was alive and his unit was part of the American beachhead in Normandy. He was required to censor letters written by his men, as well as his own, so we learned little about his whereabouts, other than he was at the heart of the action. "It was like having a seat on the fifty yard line," he wrote in his diary, "and seeing men at their best and their worst." Jack Muth was a cameraman on *Belfast* who filmed the first bombardment. He recalled that Stevens had to persuade the admiral to give permission for them to disembark: "We climbed down the side of the ship with Eyemo hand-held cameras into a 'Duck' that carried us ashore to cover the beachhead."

The Stevens Irregulars dug out a camp and set up tents in a pasture near Carentan, next to a landing strip for fighter planes within artillery range of the Germans. From there they fanned out in jeeps through the hedgerows and villages, covering the savage fighting with 35mm black-and-white film that they shipped to the United States to be screened as newsreels in movie theaters. My father's instruction to his men was simple: "Shoot what you see." He wanted them to capture in vivid detail for history how American soldiers confronted a fierce German army. He crossed Western Europe in the front seat of a jeep, a .45 strapped to his hip, a carbine at his side. The Indian word "Toluca" was stenciled in white letters on the windscreen. Behind him, a rifle between his knees, rode twenty-six-year-old Ivan Moffat, a British-educated PFC who spoke French and German. Ivan's father was American and his mother was the whimsical English poet and actress Iris Tree. Ivan would become my father's lifelong friend and creative associate, and, in time, best man at my wedding.

By mid-August, after sixty days of merciless combat, the Germans were retreating and the Allied armies were nearing Paris, each one hoping to liberate the city. My father learned that Eisenhower had assured General de Gaulle that the French would have the honor, so he took several jeeps and weapons carriers and caught up with the 2nd French Armored Division (*Deuxiéme Division Blindé*). Dad had with him the 16mm Bell and Howell Cine Special that he used on *Gunga Din,* so in addition to the official 35mm black-and-white coverage, he and his men shot a personal diary on Kodachrome, a cache of footage that when discovered decades later would provide a unique record of the war in Europe in color. In that footage we see my father in combat gear, a pipe clenched in his teeth, cross a fog-shrouded pasture outside of Paris and, with Moffat as interpreter, persuade a French general to allow SPECOU vehicles to join the assault on the German-occupied capital. Then we see three American jeeps making their way through cheering crowds of flower-throwing French women that disperse when firing rings out. Dad's letter to my mother describes August 25, 1944.

> Dearest:
> There is so very much to tell you that I don't know where to begin.
> First, from the time I last wrote until two days after the fall of Paris,
> I did not at any time have my clothes off. The days and nights all ran
> over themselves and became pretty much one thing, the struggle to get
> to Paris. We had a small party in jeeps with the armored column, with
> the responsibility of getting in first and photographing the activity.
> That we did, but the doing and the two weeks before were the most
> exciting, most unbelievable time of my life. Including some of the
> great moments with you my little angel.
>
> The morning we came into Paris was the wildest thing I have ever seen.
> The civilians lined the streets and went mad as the tanks and armored

cars came in. They stood and cheered as the shooting went on all around them. Our jeeps brought in the first cameras and I believe the first American flag, which we got from a Frenchman just outside the city. We were only eight or ten miles out when we halted about two a.m. and waited for daylight and the artillery fire to cease. Then at the break of day we were off and three hours later after a ride that [the famed Hollywood stuntman] Yakima Canutt would have wanted $500 to do, we stood under the Eiffel Tower. But not for long. The Jerries were up in it and French resistance was fighting them from the ground below, and it was too hot for some lonesome jeeps. We holed up in a railroad station, stood off the last attack the Nazis made before they surrendered. The Jerry general was brought to the station for the surrender.

The "Jerry general" was Dietrich von Choltitz, commander of the German garrison of greater Paris, and the railroad station was the Gare Montparnasse. In the black-and-white newsreel coverage we see von Choltitz led from his armored car through a door into the dingy station building. Then we see General De Gaulle arrive and enter. Inside the darkened station the German signed documents surrendering the city. In the color footage we see the same arrival scenes, but also shots of Lt. Colonel Stevens who, in his combat helmet, wearing a sidearm, goes inside the station and comes out leading von Choltitz, in his gray uniform with red epaulets and gold braid. He stands the general on the platform in the bright sunlight in front of the cameras, then steps out of the way so history can be recorded. Irwin Shaw, viewing this scene after the war said, "Of course. The man is a film director."

Dad ended his letter with what was for him a rare expression of pride:

There is so much I could tell you and will in further letters but I do hope you and Georgie have seen the newsreels that carried our film. We have heard that the films of the Liberation of Paris were the best ever taken of anything like that. We are completely exhausted and hoping to get a chance for a few days rest.

Ivan Moffat wrote in his diary that Paris on that day had the atmosphere of a bullfight: "This roaring welcome and this extraordinary sense of not liberating Paris, but our being liberated by Paris. Our spirits opened like balloons shooting up in the sky. And this marvelous embrace, this genuine love affair which took place between the people of Paris and the Allied soldiers . . . and you knew it was a love affair that couldn't possibly last, but whilst it did it had this incredible intensity."

Stevens and General Dietrich von Choltitz as he surrenders the city of Paris at
Gare Montparnasse, August 25, 1944.

The next day Irwin Shaw stood next to my father as SPECOU cameramen
photographed the 28th US Infantry Division marching down the Champs-
Élysées with the Arc de Triomphe in the background, receiving salutes from
Generals Eisenhower and de Gaulle. As they watched the 28th move through the
city toward the Rhine, Irwin bet my father the war would be over by October.

The men who served in the Special Coverage unit were experienced professionals.
Two cameramen would earn Oscars after the war—Bill Mellor for *A Place in the
Sun* and *The Diary of Anne Frank,* and Joe Biroc for *The Towering Inferno* (after
missing out for *It's a Wonderful Life*). They took pride in their service, believing
they were providing more effective coverage and a better record of history than less
experienced GIs would have. I spoke with them to gain impressions of my father
at war. When they worked together in Hollywood Irwin Shaw was just twenty-
three and received a modest fee for writing *The Talk of the Town.* He recalled sitting with my father in a muddy foxhole in Normandy, having just received their
first mail after D-Day. "George passes a paper to me from his accountant showing

his share of profits from the movie we did together," Irwin explained with a crooked grin. "He was teasing me and I was furious." He went on:

> George was taciturn, very courageous, stubborn. He ran our outfit
> his own way . . . not really "GI," and he got better results that way.
> I don't know whether it's true or not—but the way he behaved it
> might be—that he's part Indian. Taciturn, always grave looking, even
> when he was cracking jokes. He was patriotic in a very quiet way, an
> honorable man. He was a brave man, but he didn't want the guys to
> get hurt doing anything reckless.

Ivan Moffat's fluent French made him a useful interpreter. Irwin said my father would become impatient if Ivan dallied when seeking directions from attractive French women along the roads in Normandy. On one occasion after Ivan returned to the jeep, my vexed father said, "Moffat, from now on I forbid you to even *think* in French."

William Saroyan, a keen observer of the human condition, wrote of poker games in London before D-Day.

> Of course during a game I was the loudest, while George Stevens
> quietly sat and sipped whiskey, and then suddenly from nowhere took
> the biggest pot of the night with something unbelievably magnificent
> or astonishingly paltry, but not so paltry that it didn't beat the other
> gambler's hand. . . . Whenever George Stevens noticed that members
> of his outfit were losers in a game, he would pick up their I.O.U.'s and
> pay them off out of his winnings. And then while their backs were
> turned, he would tear up their I.O.U's.

Saroyan went to him later insisting, "I always pay my gambling debts, I'd sooner not pay the grocer," and handed over his check for $800. "Stevens carefully folded the check and put it in his wallet, but the check was never cashed."

Packages arrived from Europe from time to time. I don't know how Dad pulled it off but these boxes contained items he had, in his preferred term, "liberated," including a German helmet, wrapped in a red Nazi flag emblazoned with a black swastika, with a deep indentation from a bullet. Dad explained that he saw the helmet beside a dead Wehrmacht soldier and had fired a round to insure it wasn't booby-trapped, suggesting, "You can make a flower pot of it for the shelf by the front door." These souvenirs brought the war up close for kids in the

The Irregulars poker game in London, 1944. Left to right: William
Saroyan, Irwin Shaw, George Stevens, Robert Capa.

neighborhood. There were street signs from liberated towns, German military
flashlights, mess kits, and perhaps most intriguing, an officer's black leather
swagger stick. If the owner extended the stick and another person grabbed it, a
sheath would slide off in his hand uncovering a twelve-inch metal spike capable
of eviscerating the enemy. Thankfully, the lads of Toluca Lake managed not to
impale one another. Toward the end of the war Dad and his men went to the
Eagle's Nest, Hitler's mountaintop chalet in Berchtesgaden. He sent home ma-
sonry bricks from the fireplace, along with a Bible with an "A.H." bookplate, a
leatherbound score of Wagner's *Der Meistersinger von Nürnberg* inscribed by
Heinrich Himmler to "Der Fuhrer" for his birthday, and porcelain dinnerware
decorated with small swastikas. After the war Dad reconsidered his liberation
policy and the Hitler items were dispatched to a museum.

The year 1944 was an election year and Franklin Roosevelt waited until the
Democratic Convention to confirm that he would run for an unprecedented
fourth term. Four years earlier my parents had been for the Republican Wendell
Willkie. I never asked why they made that choice, but it may have been because
my father, having grown up without money, was a big earner in 1940 and his tax
rate under Roosevelt was 81 percent. In 1944 my mother and I had a picture of
the Republican governor of New York Tom Dewey in our window. I remember
our surprise when we received a letter from Dad telling us that he had voted for
Franklin Roosevelt, saying simply, "He is my Commander in Chief." From that
election forward my mother, my father and I were Democrats.

11

Winter

Six days before his fortieth birthday in December of 1944, having joined General Omar Bradley's First Army as it pushed the Germans toward the Rhine, Dad wrote to his mother, Georgie.

> As for coming home, I have a hunch that might not be too far in the future. I have a suspicion that the Great Wehrmacht is getting close to fighting its last battle. Anyway, just clip this paragraph and paste it in your bonnet. I would like to be able to say I told you so.

Four days later Hitler launched a blitzkrieg counteroffensive with a quarter of a million men, surprising the Allies in the snows of the Ardennes Forest and triggering the Battle of the Bulge. The Sixth SS Panzer Army attacked Malmedy in Belgium, forcing Allied units to retreat, and the next day nearly ninety American prisoners of war were massacred nearby by the SS.

My father wrote in his diary by candlelight in Malmedy.

> 18 December 1944 — Happy Birthday to Da.
> Last night it was finally announced that there was a major German counter offensive. We had heard shells landing around us in Malmedy during the night. We were bombed first around five-thirty when I was writing a letter to Yonnie. I heard aircraft about 1:30 a.m. Some more bombs and the Germans dropped parachutists. [They] have been raising hell all over the place. . . . I loaded an extra box of ammo for the Forty-five and a box for the Carbine in my canteen bag. I sent Hamilton down the road to find our jeep. I know now how the Jerries felt all through France—I was reluctant to leave anything, even a piece

of K-ration for them to gloat over. The "Welcome Liberator" signs are down from the windows and the Allied flags disappeared. We pull out. No cheers.

While Dad was in the thick of it in the Ardennes Forest, I was in Toluca Lake fending off dark thoughts about him not coming home. Memories of his affection became precious, his graceful hand tousling my head or the hug when he came home at night from RKO. Dad rarely called me George. It was "Son" or "Red Dog," his allusion to the hair color of my youth. My mother and I went shopping for small presents which we wrapped and mailed, hoping they would reach him by Christmas.

One week after pulling back from Malmedy, my father and his men shot color film on Christmas Day. We see the Toluca parked near piles of rubble with Dad standing beside it, wearing a bulky greatcoat, a cigarette between his lips. On the hood are his rifle and helmet and a wrapped package from which he removes a leather shaving kit filled with colored candy. We see a small card that reads "To Dad." He looks to the camera, flashes a smile and thumps his chest, then looks suddenly to the sky. The camera tilts upward and we see a descending Messerschmitt fighter. The men scramble into the jeep and speed off.

> I opened my Christmas present on the road on Christmas Day. We
> took some pictures that I have to show you. The party was broken
> up by some Jerry 109s strafing. Three of them were shot down, a
> Jerry pilot bailed out. We picked him up, he had his leg shot off.
> We took some pictures and carried him to battalion aid station.
> He died there.

The Allies battled in the snow for forty days, eventually forcing the German retreat, but at the cost of eighty-one thousand American casualties. The Stevens Irregulars continued with Bradley's army on the advance into Germany and were among the first to cross the Rhine. On April 15 at Nordhausen, a small town in the Harz Mountains, they found a secret factory with forty miles of tunnels, where fifty thousand slave laborers built the V-2 ballistic missiles that terrorized England. The workers lived in a concentration camp. Dad's report to Washington that accompanied film his unit shot at Nordhausen depicted a scene of mass murder: "So completely without a record of their past lives had these creatures been left, that out of two thousand men and women and children it was possible to identify but four men by a name and nationality." His eyewitness account of Nazi atrocities was among the first received by the War

Battle of the Bulge, Belgium, on Christmas Day, 1944.

Department. It ended: "Nordhausen is as stark an example as could be found anywhere of the utter German indifference to human life, side by side with a supreme example of technical perfection in the science of mass destruction."

The Stevens Irregulars received orders to push east to the old fortress town of Torgau on the Elbe River. My father and eighteen men took an improvised ferry to the east side of the river for the historic linkup of American and Russian forces—an exuberant meeting of allies, the Russians dancing on their haunches with American GIs clapping, then showing off their Eyemo cameras to smiling Red Army soldiers with gold teeth. My father expected to go north to Berlin to photograph the final collapse of the Third Reich, but an urgent order from divisional headquarters directed him south to Bavaria. "We just loaded up our jeeps with weapons," Dad noted in his diary. "We had a 50 caliber and one Tommy Gun in each jeep . . . and we took off down country." They drove three hundred miles without escort, skirting active German units.

There were patches of snow on the ground on the last day of April when the Special Coverage Unit drove their jeeps through the brooding iron gates of the

Dachau Concentration Camp, marked by words wrought in black metal: *Arbeit Macht Frei* (Work Sets You Free). Before them were stacks of corpses in the central compound, thirty thousand emaciated prisoners infected with cholera and typhus, and snow-covered bodies in cattle cars at the railroad siding. It was at Dachau, my father said, that he learned about life.

He knew that the atrocities must be documented, lest they later be denied, so he became a gatherer of evidence, lugging his camera through snow and ice into railroad cars to photograph half-frozen corpses. Mark Harris, in his book *Five Came Back,* about five directors who left Hollywood to go to war, described his process. "He didn't stop or sleep for days. . . . His eye was unwavering and unsentimental. He was not in search any more of small, personalizing details but of images that would capture both the vastness and the specific sadism against humanity."

My father, who in his life and films took the side of the outsider, was now witness to humiliation on a scale he could never have envisioned. He was unnerved when, wearing the uniform of liberator, he approached prisoners and saw fear in their eyes.

> Everything evil will be exposed in a day in a concentration camp.
> It's deplorable because it undercuts one terribly. I would examine
> it on the basis of what would happen if I was in the other army, the
> German army. I hated the bastards—what they stood for was the
> worst, the worst possible thing that happened in centuries. And yet,
> when a poor man hungered and unseeing because his eyesight is
> failing grabs me and starts begging, I feel the Nazi in any human
> being. I don't care whether I'm a Jew or a Gentile. I feel a Nazi
> because I abhor him and I want him to keep his hands off me. And
> the reason I abhor him is because I see myself being capable of
> arrogance and brutality to keep him off me . . . that's a fierce thing
> to discover within yourself—that which you despise the most.

Rabbi David Max Eichhorn, a military chaplain, arrived at Dachau and worked to comfort Jewish prisoners and restore morale. In 1994 Eichhorn's grandson sent me the rabbi's report from Dachau in which he writes about being approached by a Signal Corps lieutenant colonel who said his name was George Stevens and that he wanted to film a Jewish service. Eichhorn told him there would be a camp-wide Sabbath service the following morning in the main square, with the platform decorated with the flags of all twenty-eight nations represented in the camp.

Gathering evidence. Railroad siding at Dachau Concentration Camp, April 30, 1945.

When Eichhorn arrived he saw no decorations. The non-Jewish Polish inmates had threatened to break up the service, so it had been canceled. The rabbi moved his group to the cramped camp laundry which held eighty people. During the service Colonel Stevens made his way to the front, telling the rabbi that his camera crews were set up in the main square. The rabbi explained what had happened. As he recalled it, "Stevens flushed in anger, said he gave up his job in Hollywood to fight fascism, and he sure as hell wasn't going to tolerate it here." He took the rabbi to the American commandant of the camp, an Irishman who was a former police commissioner of Boston. The commandant assured the rabbi that the service would take place the next day and he would provide an American "guard of honor." Rabbi Eichhorn recalled how the meeting ended.

> Colonel Stevens requested that I teach some of the girls in the
> women's barracks to sing "God Bless America." I spent two hours
> teaching fifteen Hungarian Jewish girls to sing the Irving Berlin
> composition even though they knew not a word of English. Thanks to

the decent instincts of an American movie director, the service was
held in the main square, attended by every Jewish male and female
whose health permitted. And ringing the outer rim with faces turned
away from the platform was the American "guard of honor" with
loaded rifles and fixed bayonets. The forty-five minute service was
filmed with sound by Colonel Stevens and his crew.

Hitler committed suicide in his bunker in Berlin on the day the Stevens Irregulars arrived at Dachau. A week later, on May 8, 1945, my father and his men listened together on their small radio to the announcement of the unconditional surrender of German forces in Reims, France. The Third Reich, after twelve years, was finished. The war in Europe was over.

Ivan Moffat told me of the day they left Dachau. He was riding in the back of the Toluca when they passed the camp post office. My father instructed the driver to stop, entered the building by himself, and returned a few minutes later. They drove off in silence and made camp along the roadside that evening. Ivan asked my father why he had gone into the post office. Dad rustled his musette bag and withdrew a circular metal stamp with a four-inch wooden handle. It was the stamp used to mark the letters the prisoners sent and received from Dachau. The rotating metal numbers were frozen at 4-28-45, the date the camp was liberated. It was my father's totem marking the end of the Nazi assault on humanity. He passed the stamp to me, which to this day I keep in the top drawer of my desk.

When we heard news of V-E Day, my mother put the top down on our Ford convertible and the neighborhood kids piled in with little American flags for the drive over the Cahuenga Pass to Hollywood Boulevard, where confetti rained and horns blared in jammed traffic, with strangers hugging in the street. I had just turned thirteen and now knew my father would be coming home.

News of the harrowing discoveries at Dachau had not reached us, so we could not imagine how different the setting was where Dad learned that his war was over. We did not hear from him until a letter arrived dated May 30 written by the Elbe River at Magdeburg, Prussia.

Dear Yonnie and Dear George:
I have been going nuts for a month trying to get a cable off to you.
This frightful anti-climax is driving us mad, everyone is so anxious to
get home. . . . When I sit down to write to you in the east of
Germany, and realize I am going to be beside the same river for the

next few days, I find it impossible to continue to write. I get so homesick and anxious. Anyway, I am sure I will be back in touch soon. I do so want to be home during the summer.

Tons of love from your anxious and devoted Dad.

He added a paragraph of frustration that was unusual for a man known for his composure and self-control.

We are living out of a jeep trailer and camping beside the roads at nite and we still have the same dirty clothes that we had on when the war was on. We are FED UP and want to get back and clean up and stop itching and COME HOME.

The US Army had other priorities. My father would not see summer in Toluca Lake. He was directed to Berlin to photograph the aftermath of surrender, including poignant scenes of German women clearing the rubble of that once grand city, then to Potsdam, where he served as a delegate at the conference where America's new president Harry Truman joined Stalin and Churchill to negotiate the reconstruction of postwar Europe.

Dad and his men drove north in the Toluca. One day they set up camp in a meadow where they bathed in a stream and washed their clothes. Warmed by the spring sunshine, Dad saw a fair-haired German boy about my age in short leather pants playing downstream. He realized how long it had been since he spoke to a child, so he ambled down to say hello. "I wanted to talk to the boy because I had a boy at home," he wrote. "Suddenly the boy's mother appeared from the woods and angrily herded him away. She was terrified of me, an officer in the enemy army."

The Nuremberg War Crimes Trials were soon to take place in Germany where Herman Göring, Martin Bormann, Rudolf Hess, Albert Speer and other architects of the Final Solution would be judged. My father was assigned to make two documentaries with writer Budd Schulberg, culling footage that he and others had shot, to provide proof of Nazi atrocities. On November 29 the Palace of Justice was darkened and *Nazi Concentration Camps* was shown before the judges, defendants, prosecutors and reporters. The image at the beginning is an affidavit of authenticity signed by Lt. Colonel George C. Stevens, US Army. Then, as one reporter at the trial wrote, "On the screen there is no end to the bodies, tumbling bodies, and bodies being shoved over cliffs into common graves and bodies pushed like dirt by giant bulldozers, and bodies that are not bodies at all but charred bits of bone and flesh lying upon a crematory grave." There were scenes of gas chambers and ovens, lampshades made of human skin, a tableau of abandoned eyeglasses and a harvest of gold teeth. The light on the defendants' box remained on as they were confronted with the evidence. One defense counsel remarked that he found it intolerable to sit in the same room with his clients. "Stevens' films had done what weeks of testimony had not," wrote Mark Harris. "It had made their crimes irrefutable, and their fates inevitable."

My father's work was done. In November he arrived home, thirty-three months after leaving Toluca Lake. My mother drove to Burbank Airport to meet him. Dad in his uniform, carrying his khaki B-4 bag, walked with her from the plane to the car.

"It was the tan Lincoln Continental with the tire on the back—there were only three of them in town," my mother recalled. "George got in and sat at the wheel, and he just started shaking." After a pause she added, "Well, it was a long time away."

12

Together Again

I was overjoyed to have my father home. He was drawn to the simple things he described in his letters—to be with his beloved Vonnie Girl and his Red Dog. A week after he returned he took my mother, his mother and me to Chasen's on Beverly Boulevard, a chili parlor transformed by a former comedian from the Ukraine into the flagship of Hollywood restaurants. Dad, not yet discharged, was in uniform and an eager Friday night crowd was waiting for tables. I remember him telling me later of a greeting by a studio executive, "George, what are you doing in that monkey suit?" After a few moments a short man with a wistful smile eased through the crowd and saw my father. They embraced, not having seen one another for three years.

This was Dave Chasen. He escorted us past those waiting into the main room to a half-circle red leather booth, seated my mother and grandmother with Old World courtliness, and gestured for a bottle of champagne. I remember people looking over to see who was receiving this attention.

Just then George Burns and Gracie Allen, the former vaudevillians who starred with Fred Astaire in Dad's *Damsel in Distress,* passed by. Gracie, a tiny comedienne who became a television favorite on *The Burns and Allen Show,* noticed my father and stopped to say hello. Then she saw his mother and went silent. Gracie grasped the older woman's hands and said with emotion, "I used to wait outside the stage door in San Francisco to see Georgie Cooper!" My grandmother, who had long been out of the limelight, bowed her head. She seemed, at that moment, so refined and elegant beside her son the director.

I noticed no outward change in my father. His affection and good humor were constant, but speculation would emerge about how the war changed him. When he joined the army he thought he might be retiring from the movie business, that by the time he came home new people would have filled his place. Yet now studios were keen to sign him and independent producers like Sam Goldwyn and David Selznick were calling—and he was listening. But he was in no hurry.

He rented a house on Lido Isle in Newport Beach for July. We were sitting on the sand one morning when he said, "Shall we swim to the other side?" It was half a mile to the shore across the bay. We plunged in. We were both good swimmers and stroked side by side. If I speeded up he would draw alongside, and it was soon evident that we were racing. I swam hard and scrambled ashore, touched a log to signal the finish, and collapsed on the hot sand. Dad came ashore, walked up to the log and touched it. Then, without a word, he splashed back into the water. I leapt up and followed, matching him stroke for stroke. My chest became heavy and my arms weary, but again I hit the shore a few strokes ahead of him. This time we both lay flat on the beach catching our breath. I was beside my father, newly home from war, warmed by the sun. I felt a surge of pride for my win, but wondered whether he let up a little to give his son a victory.

When my pals Al Werker and Peter McHugh came to stay we devised a game of water football and realized it would be more fun with four players so we recruited my father. A big part of the game was the player in the backfield diving underwater with a tennis ball and swimming some distance, then popping up to throw a pass to his teammate, or advancing the ball by swimming downfield. Dad had a special capacity for holding his breath and fooling the opposition, so he became a valued teammate. Moreover, in the fashion of the day we teenagers wore bright neon swimming trunks, while Dad found a pair of olive drab army trunks that made him hard to locate underwater. He was competitive and patient and would play with us until the sun went down.

Wilbur Hanson, my mentor at Harvard School, was a Quaker and had standing as a conscientious objector, which excused him from military service. A faction of parents led by Darryl Zanuck moved to have him fired. Zanuck entered the army for a brief but widely publicized tour of duty while retaining his job as head of Twentieth Century Fox, where he expected to be called "Colonel Zanuck." My father appreciated the influence Wilbur Hanson had on me while he was overseas and respected the teacher's right to his religious views. There was a contentious hearing process in which the two colonels took sides, and when the dust settled my schoolmates and I were delighted that Mr. Hanson retained his job.

I had a lunch meeting in Hollywood in the nineties to discuss a project with the talented screenwriter and director of *LA Confidential* and *Wonder Boys*. I was happy to tell Curtis Hanson that his father was one of the important influences in my life.

My father and I and Buddy Friese at the Stork Club, New York, 1948.

One summer morning Dad slid into the driver's seat of the Lincoln Continental, my friend Buddy Friese climbed into the back, and I rode shotgun. With pillows and a blanket in the back and navigator's maps in front, Dad gunned the twelve-cylinder engine, heading east on Route 66 with two baseball fans brought up on Pacific Coast League games. We were driving two thousand miles to the 1948 Major League All Star game in St. Louis, where Buddy and I prowled the lobby of the Chase Hotel and succeeded in getting autographs from Joe DiMaggio, Ted Williams and Bob Feller. Dad snapped pictures with his Leica at Sportsman's Park as we watched the American League win 5 to 2, with Stan "The Man" Musial's two-run homer the only score for the Nationals. The next morning we took the train to Philadelphia to see a doubleheader under the lights at Shibe Park between Connie Mack's Athletics and the visiting Cleveland Indians. Pitcher Bob Feller was leading the Indians to a World Series championship, so Buddy and I saw major league baseball at its best. In the dugout I had a second opportunity to say hello to Connie Mack in his blue suit and starched white collar. This time he didn't ask me how I batted, but if he had, the answer would have been the same. "Switch, Mr. Mack."

Dad's wartime letters are filled with admiration and love for my mother, and appreciation for her burden as the parent who had to impose discipline while he was away. As a director making several films a year before the war his time at home was limited, but now we were going to ball games, to the races at Santa Anita, and having dinners together at Lakeside and Musso's. I adored my mother and father and during our years together I never heard a cross word between them. During the war she wanted to build a unit of seven two-story town houses on Riverside Drive, about a mile from our Forman Avenue house. It was an ambitious project and she told me with satisfaction that when she proposed it, Dad was immediately supportive. She had his confidence and trust.

But all was not as it seemed.

I remember in 1940 when I was eight going with my mother to live and attend school for six months in Palm Springs. I was too young to see it as a sign of trouble in the marriage, but in 1947, she told me unexpectedly that I was going to be a boarder at Harvard School for a semester. My father's work through the years involved six-day weeks and long hours. The intimacy and emotional nature of life on movie sets was known to lead to marital challenges, and unbeknownst to me, this had affected my parents, causing strains that led my mother to ask for a divorce. By the end of my semester as a boarder details had been worked out, and my mother and I moved into one of her newly completed two-bedroom town houses. It was confusing to see this split between two people who had such respect and affection for one another, though I now realize how considerate they were of me. What might have been an upheaval was managed in a way that allowed me to feel that my life was stable.

Only late in her life did my mother and I discuss the divorce. She told me that once negotiations among lawyers led to an agreement, she and my father met in the attorneys' office to sign documents. As papers were passed out Dad excused himself. When he returned a half hour later he instructed the lawyers to change the agreement to further favor her. Of the man she found it necessary to divorce, my mother said, "George was the most honest and fair person I ever met."

She would reflect on my father when we had dinner at the Hamburger Hamlet, often with her tart Irish humor lubricated by a late-in-life practice of a nightly cocktail—gin with a splash of tonic, lemon on the side. One night she mused on the difficulty of being married to an attractive director. She recalled going on the set of *Swing Time* one night to watch Dad shooting the famously romantic "Never Gonna Dance" number with Fred and Ginger. She sized up the implications. "Young people working together fifteen hours a day dedicated to the same goal," she said. "Forget it!"

Mom lived to be 104 and retained her humor even as she became forgetful. One day we were sitting in her apartment when she asked, two decades after my father's death, "Where's George?" I was caught off guard. After a moment I simply pointed to the sky. Glancing upward, she gave me a knowing look. "Oh, I bet he's got them straightened out."

The Forman Avenue house went to my mother in the divorce, and like all situations in the Stevens family humor wasn't far away. She told me that Dad had no plans so he lingered in the house, even as the furniture was removed. The writer Gene Solow, his genial war correspondent-screenwriter pal, joined him and they slept on cots and cooked with army Sterno kits. My mother, though somewhat amused by this eccentricity, was keen to sell the house and during Dad and Solow's stay real estate prices dipped, muting her amusement. She managed to get him out of the Forman Avenue house by allowing him to rent the town house on Riverside Drive two doors from ours. My father's proximity may have limited my mother's ability to move on with her life, but she condoned it because she believed it was best for me. For years to come we would go together to premieres, ball games, and my friends' weddings, like a normal family. I don't think I bear the scars that so many children in these situations do.

I made my way through Harvard School with a circle of close friends. We were preoccupied by girls, cars, sports and girls. By our senior year we smoked cigarettes now and then, but hadn't discovered the pleasures of drink, and the girls at Marlborough and the Westlake School were strictly raised and kept us a step removed from complications of a sexual nature. A glance at the senior yearbook shows that my moniker was "leader of the incorrigibles," a nonconformist label I must have considered flattering since I was the editor and could have chosen something more aspirational. During our senior year Don Weber, Mike Bagnall, Freddie Martin (his father was the popular bandleader) and I got in trouble. It seems a donkey was discovered on a Monday morning after spending the night in the small classroom of our history teacher, Aaron "Bulldog" Burr. I was identified as one of the conspirators. Our transgression was deemed sufficient for the four of us to be reduced to the rank of private and placed on probation. I neglected to mention this to my parents, and my father heard about it at a school event. It was the only time I recall him being angry with me, more for the failure to inform him than for the misplaced donkey.

My friends and I muddled through our senior year. As graduation day approached, I realized that those boys who worked harder and kept out of trouble would be receiving prizes. Seeking redemption, I auditioned to be the reader of scripture in the graduation chapel service. The school chaplain couldn't conceal his surprise when I turned up, yet to my astonishment I was chosen. My parents were proud to see me in St. Savior's Chapel, decked out in my dress blue uniform, albeit with insignia of rank removed, in the presence of the bishop of Los Angeles, reading from the Book of Wisdom. I suspect my father sat there imagining how to shoot the scene.

Much later my mother told me they had gone to see Bishop Gooden during this period. She recalled the bishop looking out the window and saying, "I can't think of a boy who's done more for the school than George." I have no idea what led His Eminence to that conclusion, or whether his words were a simple act of Christian charity. It would have saved me some heartache if my mother had not waited fifty years to tell me.

In 2001, Harvard, now coeducational and known as Harvard-Westlake, published a history of the school. I was surprised to find a chapter titled, inexactly, "The Horse in a Classroom." It addressed our deed with the donkey in a more benign light than had been done in 1949.

PART THREE

MOVIES

George Stevens, Jr., Elizabeth Taylor, James Dean, George Stevens,
filming *Giant,* Marfa, Texas, 1955.

13

Seventeen

I chose Occidental College, a small liberal arts school thirty minutes from home, where I was joined by a handful of Harvard School classmates. The tuition was $500 a year. I was starting at seventeen, which allowed for four years of sorely needed maturation. I enjoyed camaraderie on the freshman basketball and baseball teams, and was glad to have a chance to work on the *Occidental,* where in my junior year I became sports editor. I majored in English and speech and gained some experience on stage in the Oxy drama program. These were four enjoyable and stimulating years, but looking back, the experiences that most influenced my thinking and guided my career took place away from college.

My father joined forces with fellow colonels Frank Capra and William Wyler to start Liberty Films, the first company run by directors. Their objective was to have control over their films. The launch coincided with the explosion of television in American homes which shook the movie business, and Liberty completed just one film before the colonels felt the financial squeeze. Each had anted up $150,000 to pay operating expenses, but because they owned the company's stock, the Internal Revenue Service required them to pay themselves $3,000 a week, equal to what they would earn elsewhere, and pay 80 percent tax on that income. Capra and Wyler, who lived more elaborately in Beverly Hills than we did in Toluca Lake, became so pressed that they voted with Liberty's business partner Sam Briskin, three to one over my father, to make a deal with Paramount in which the partners received Paramount stock in return for each director making five pictures.

Liberty's only completed film was *It's a Wonderful Life,* a box-office flop in 1947 that in time became an American treasure. Capra, in his memoir *The Name Above the Title,* recalled my father warning his partners that they were selling their freedom. Capra concluded that his own soul "stopped leaping upward after

I forced my partners to sell Liberty Films. . . . I traded the élan of courage for the safety of money."

Paramount provided the directors with "final cut" but retained approval of stories. My father, after a year during which Paramount refused to green-light the projects he proposed, engaged Vincent Hallinan, a brilliant criminal attorney from San Francisco. Hallinan was in no way beholden to movie studios and sued Paramount for obstructing my father's right to make a living by rejecting his proposal to film Theodore Dreiser's *An American Tragedy.* My father laid it on the line in a letter to Paramount: "I will stake my professional reputation, which I have been called upon to do many times, on my judgment of this property." The gulf between filmmaker and management was evident in Paramount chief Henry Ginsburg's response.

> We refuse to admit that your judgment is better than that of our
> entire production organization, our sales department and our New
> York home office executives combined. . . . We had expected that you
> would be most appreciative of the time and effort expended not only
> by me but by everyone including [Paramount president] Mr. Balaban
> in studying the advisability of proceeding with this story, and
> therefore you can well imagine our surprise and chagrin when instead
> of being grateful you seem resentful because we rejected this story.

So strong was my father's resolve that Paramount finally consented to making *An American Tragedy,* which would receive a new title: *A Place in the Sun.* Audiences would have an opportunity to make their own judgment.

During the summer before I entered Occidental my father put me to work on two tasks. One was to take Dreiser's *An American Tragedy* and list every character and event in the novel. The other was to read and comment on scripts and books sent to him by Paramount. Most were saccharine romance novels and formulaic screenplays, tedious reading for a seventeen-year-old, but one day I picked a small novel from the pile and finished it before sundown. That night I went to my father's apartment two doors down the courtyard from my mother's. I found him reading in bed. "Dad, this is really a good story," I said, handing him the book. "I think you should read it." He put down his magazine and said, "Why don't you tell me the story?"

So I started pacing, telling him the story of *Shane,* as I remembered it from my afternoon with Jack Schaefer's novel. I was grappling for the first time with the challenge of storytelling, trying to remember details and order them in a way that would hold my father's attention. I now realize his request was—as was the

George Stevens in 1949 directing Montgomery Clift and Elizabeth Taylor
in *A Place in the Sun*.

entire summer assignment—his way of helping me discover if I had an appetite
and aptitude for his creative world.

While I navigated my freshman year at Occidental, Dad prepared the Dreiser story and cast Montgomery Clift and Elizabeth Taylor in the leading roles.
One Saturday he invited me to the studio to watch him work. Clift was a sensitive thirty-year-old who drove a banged-up black convertible with a tattered top,
a statement to the world about his indifference to material things. He had studied at the Actors Studio and had a reputation of being insecure.

When Monty and Elizabeth arrived on the sound stage, Dad asked the crew
to stand back, giving the actors privacy to explore a challenging new scene.
"Why don't you just go in there and find your way?" he said gently. "Monty,
you find a place at the pool table, and Liz you just find a spot where you're comfortable." The actors worked through the scene with the script clerk cueing lines.
My father watched from the shadows. When they finished he said, "Good. Why
don't we try it again?" They did the scene once more. And then one more time,
after which Monty came over to my father and whispered a question. Elizabeth

moved closer to listen. I stood for the next hour watching a director and two actors build a scene that was intriguing and believable. Only then did my father, who had at times been holding a small viewfinder to his eye, choose the first setup and the cinematographer, his wartime comrade Bill Mellor, went to work.

Later, I asked Dad why he had Monty and Elizabeth do the scene three times before he offered any direction. "Sometimes," he said, "it's useful to allow actors time to discover that they may need some help."

During a break he took me to a dressing room trailer and introduced me to Elizabeth. She was nearing eighteen, a month older than I, vivacious and light-hearted, much more a girl than a star. Yet her exquisite face, accented by her violet eyes with double lashes, took my breath away. I was certain I had met the most beautiful woman in the world.

When the company broke for lunch Elizabeth asked if I would like to join her. I tried to make my acceptance suitably casual, but my heart rate was in overdrive. We walked together along the studio street to the commissary. She breezed inside with me in her wake, the hostess making an appropriate fuss and showing us to a corner table, while the eyes of other diners followed. To this college freshman she seemed sophisticated, yet she proposed that we have hamburgers and chocolate milkshakes. The next three-quarters of an hour passed quickly, an occasion so beyond my expectations that I recall little of what we talked about. It did occur to me that my report of the event would be eagerly received that night at the Phi Gamma Delta house.

I spent most of the next four years at college, but was discovering that the movie studio was an intriguing place. And how could I know that an enduring friendship had begun over those milkshakes?

14

Higher Learning

I was home from Occidental one Saturday morning in 1950 when my father suggested we drive into Hollywood. He had finished shooting *A Place in the Sun* and begun his lengthy editing process. We settled into his Lincoln with the top down and drove to Crossroads of the World, a modest office complex on Sunset Boulevard, where the Screen Directors Guild was housed in a two-story bungalow. He parked on the street and ambled to the entrance, tried the front door without success, then peered in a side window before returning to the car. As we drove away, he told me he had received a four-page telegram that morning, signed by fifteen directors, including Cecil B. DeMille and Frank Capra, urging members to vote to dismiss the Guild's president. He had telephoned the Guild office which was normally open on Saturday, got no answer, and concluded there was mischief afoot. The actions of this quiet weekend sparked a conflict that to this day resonates in Hollywood history, and provided a son with a fuller understanding of his father.

The Screen Directors Guild was founded in 1934 to secure rights for directors and assistant directors who worked for the powerful studios. The board was led by the industry's most respected directors, but during the war a number of them, including my father, left for military service and a faction led by DeMille gained control. DeMille, who directed Hollywood's first feature film *The Squaw Man* in 1914, was a self-dramatizing figure who often wore puttees and carried a swagger stick. He hosted the *Lux Radio Theater*, which broadcast versions of Hollywood films to forty million listeners, making him the most famous of directors. Nearing seventy and fearing the industry was being infiltrated by Communists, he established the DeMille Foundation for Political Freedom that compiled dossiers on "subversives" and fed names to the House Un-American Activities Committee.

The studios started using a blacklist in the late forties to prevent suspect individuals from working in movies or television. Congress raised the ante when they ordered ten screenwriters and directors to testify in Washington. Membership in the Communist Party was not against the law but the wrong answer to the question "Are you now or have you ever been a member of the Communist Party" could torpedo a career. Witnesses who declined to testify became known as the Unfriendly Ten and were sent to prison for contempt of Congress.

Anticommunism was a launching pad for politicians, including two Californians who would later be American presidents. A young congressman from Whittier, Richard Nixon, hitched his star to the cause in his campaign for the United States Senate, and Ronald Reagan, president of the Screen Actors Guild, became an advocate for Hollywood "housecleaning."

In 1950 DeMille endorsed Joseph L. Mankiewicz for Guild president. A forty-one-year-old director-writer from New York, Mankiewicz had won two Oscars for *A Letter to Three Wives* and would soon receive two more for *All About Eve*. He was a Republican and with DeMille's support was elected. The Taft-Hartley Act of 1947 required union officers to sign loyalty oaths and Mankiewicz did so, swearing that he "was not now nor ever had been a member of the Communist Party." At the next meeting DeMille proposed that the Guild require *all* members to sign the oath. Mankiewicz rebuffed the idea, and then sailed to Europe on a planned vacation.

DeMille called an emergency board meeting, warning Frank Capra beforehand that the communist-hunting Senator Joseph McCarthy planned to investigate the Guild. They persuaded the board to pass a bylaw requiring that all members sign the noncommunist oath to demonstrate the Guild's patriotism. It required ratification by members. The ballots were numbered so they could be monitored, and anyone who failed to vote in favor was reported to the studios. The bylaw passed by 547 to 14, with 57 ballots not returned.

When Mankiewicz arrived back in New York he was met at the dock by a throng of reporters asking about the new bylaw of which he had no knowledge. When he got to Hollywood he found letters and telegrams from directors complaining that the bylaw had been invoked without discussion. Mankiewicz called a board meeting and argued that the failure to provide a secret ballot was a violation of members' rights, and that those who voted "no" were now subject to a "blacklist." DeMille took umbrage at the term and excoriated Mankiewicz, who knew then that he had to call a meeting of the membership.

DeMille and his allies gathered secretly at his office at Paramount to engineer a "recall" of Mankiewicz before he could call a meeting. DeMille had an ally in Vernon Keays, the Guild's executive secretary, who for many years had been his assistant director. On Thursday morning October 12, Keays instructed the Guild staff to mimeograph ballots: "I hereby vote that Joseph Mankiewicz be recalled as President of the Directors Guild of America." There was a blank line for signature. The DeMille group prepared a mailing list, crossing off the names of fifty-five directors thought to be close to Mankiewicz. On Friday Keays instructed the staff to close the office early and not to report for work on Saturday, then took the ballots and envelopes to DeMille's office. That night, in a scene worthy of a Hollywood film noir, they dispatched couriers on motorcycles to deliver recall ballots to the chosen members, with orders to wait for signatures and return the ballots to DeMille's Paramount office.

Directors sympathetic to Mankiewicz, including John Huston, William Wyler, Billy Wilder, Elia Kazan, Richard Brooks and Fred Zinnemann, got wind of the DeMille plan and met after work at Chasen's. They made calls through the night to obtain signatures from twenty-five senior members, which would oblige the Guild to call a meeting. When they called the Guild offices on Saturday morning to file the petition, the phone didn't answer.

Realizing their secret was out, the DeMille faction sent a seven-hundred-word telegram to members for Saturday morning delivery. It cited Mankiewicz's opposition to the mandatory loyalty oath and his referring to a blacklist at the board meeting, arguing that he had "pitted himself against the Board of Directors. . . . We must disavow Mr. Mankiewicz's right to use the office as president in such a dictatorial manner [and] recommend that he be recalled according to the democratic method provided."

The Huston group's petition for a meeting of the membership was accepted. The next day gossip columnist Hedda Hopper demanded in the *Los Angeles Times* that all industry workers sign a loyalty oath, adding, "Those who aren't loyal should be put in concentration camps before it's too late."

My father, a two-time president of the Guild, wanted facts, so he went to the Guild offices with an attorney, Martin Gang, to question the staff. My mother used to tell me, "George should have been a lawyer. I've never seen anyone win an argument with him." I found minutes of that meeting among my father's papers. They show Gang stating that the purpose of the meeting was "to seek statements and facts as to certain occurrences with reference to the operation of the Screen Directors Guild." Gang led five secretaries through an account of their activities. They testified that they were provided a list of

Board meeting of the Directors Guild of America, 1948. At desk, George Stevens,
president. Seated on sofa, left to right, William Wyler, Frank Capra, Cecil B. DeMille.
On chair with pipe, John Ford. Seated elbows on knees, Irving Pichel.
Far left near desk, Tay Garnett. Others unidentified.

members by Vernon Keays on which fifty-five names had been scratched out,
and instructed to prepare ballots and envelopes that Keays took to DeMille's
office on Friday afternoon, after instructing the staff not to report for work on
Saturday.

Gang tried to pin down who had possession of the list. Adele Salem testified
that she put two copies of the list with the fifty-five names crossed out in the
safe on Friday, and that Keays called her at home on Saturday to ask where
the lists were. She told him she had locked them in the vault and given the
key to Jane Woerner. Woerner testified that Keays came to her house on Saturday and she handed him the key to the safe, "directly from my wallet to his
hand."

Genevieve Steck then testified that Keays called late Sunday night and instructed her to meet him in the Guild parking lot at six on Monday morning,
where he handed her the key with the instruction, "You had this in your purse
all weekend."

Gang asked Ms. Steck if she knew who had the missing list with the fifty-five names crossed out. She replied that Keays had the list. The transcript continues:

> Mr. Stevens left the room.
>
> Mr. Stevens returned to the room and said, "Mr. Keays says he has no list on which any names were crossed off."
>
> Mr. Stevens and Miss Salem left the room to confront Mr. Keays with Miss Salem's statement that she gave the list to him.
>
> Mr. Stevens and Miss Salem returned to the room.

At that point my father informed the others, "Mr. Keays told us that on the advice of Guild counsel and his own personal counsel he does not wish to answer." He ended the meeting saying, "I have a responsibility as a board member. My interest is finding out if another board member is attempting to run this Guild and the people employed by this Guild in a manner he shouldn't."

Two nights later, on Sunday, October 22, five hundred members, including many of the world's most celebrated directors, filed into the ornate Crystal Room at the Beverly Hills Hotel.

Mankiewicz took his place on the dais with the other board members. He described the scene to me when I interviewed him in 1983: "The assistant directors at the time had no vote and they were relegated to the balconies, like the rabble, and below them sat the majesty of the senior directors. And without exception they were there. I have never witnessed a more emotional meeting." He noticed that my father had taken a seat at a small table and placed a notebook in front of him. Dad later explained that he picked "a beautiful red binder out of my library and let it sit there during the meeting, and every now and then one of these guys would take a look at it. They didn't like it."

Mankiewicz spoke for an hour refuting the accusations against him, admitting that he could not report on the recall process with even a hint of objectivity because of the "politburo quality" of its execution. He then gave the floor to DeMille.

"I first want to compliment the president on his splendid presentation," the older man said in his rich theatrical timbre. "I have come before you neither to praise Caesar or bury him . . . my race is nearing its end so I have nothing to gain but the welfare of this body." DeMille recited the text of the loyalty oath with fervor: "I am not a member of the Communist Party or affiliated with such party, and I do not believe in and I am not a member, nor do I support any organization that believes in or teaches the overthrow of the United States government by force." He declared that the oath would assure the industry that the men who direct American movies are "not ashamed to declare their loyalty to the United States."

He then spoke of directors who were at what he called the "Friday the thirteenth dinner at Chasen's," asking, "Who are some of these gentlemen?" DeMille proceeded to name organizations he considered subversive that the directors belonged to. "One of them was Chairman of a testimonial dinner for the Hollywood Ten; five were on the Committee for the First Amendment; one was on the board of the Actors Lab; two were on the Committee of Arts, Sciences and Professions . . ." He surveyed the room before adding, "Troubled waters attract strange specimens." His implication that twenty-five fellow members were Communist dupes led to a chorus of boos.

Among the twenty-five were several who had put aside lucrative careers to serve overseas and returned from combat to find that DeMille, who along with Ronald Reagan and John Wayne had remained in Hollywood throughout the war, was now posing as a patriot anxious to serve as judge and jury. When John Huston, tall and angular with the Legion of Merit for wartime service in his lapel, managed to get recognized, he was trembling with anger. He challenged DeMille: "In your tabulation of the twenty-five men, C.B., how many were in uniform when you were wrapping yourself in the flag?" And Wyler, who lost most of his hearing flying B17 missions over Germany, stood and exclaimed, "I'm sick and tired of having people question my loyalty to my country. . . . The next time I hear somebody do it, I'm going to kick hell out of him. I don't care how old he is or how big." When DeMille challenged my father by asking where he had been when DeMille was fighting a labor union he believed was obstructing his radio show, Dad stared at him, then said quietly, "I was up to my ass in mud at Bastogne, C.B., while you were at home fighting the battle of capital gains."

But it was tall and courtly Rouben Mamoulian, the Russian-born director of Gershwin's *Porgy and Bess,* who struck home. He said sorrowfully that he knew he spoke with an accent, and that for the first time he feared having one. "I feel," he declared, "I have more reason to stand on my being a good American because I *chose* it. I wanted to become an American."

Mankiewicz recalled giving the stage to my father, "George just raised his hand. It was his sense of timing. He resigned from the board saying, 'I want no part of this as an American, as a director, or as a human being, because this is a conspiracy.'" He then declared that the recall was rigged, and had there not been a slipup, Mankiewicz would have been forced out overnight. He recommended that "every man on this Board who is responsible for this—by omission, as I am, or by being a party to this conspiracy—resign."

Then—in what Mankiewicz described as a performance worthy of Clarence Darrow—my father opened his red binder and recited facts, detailing the sworn testimony of the Guild secretaries. The members heard for the first time what had been done in their names by the self-appointed recall committee. He charged that the board had lost sight of its responsibility by allowing itself to become preoccupied with the fight against Communism instead of fighting for increased wages and improved conditions for workers:

> The only other time I resigned an office in this Guild was in 1942 because the United States was at war. I believe in defending my country. I didn't believe you can win wars of the United States speaking at the board table. I think you have to do something about it over there.

Mankiewicz recalled that my father's presentation was decisive and that he received an ovation, and soon after, "John Ford got up and said, 'My name is Ford. I direct Westerns.' And then he looked over at DeMille and said, 'Cecil, we've been together since 1916, or was it '15? . . . I respect you, Cecil.'" Mankiewicz feared that Ford was going to wipe out what my father had accomplished, but then he quotes Ford saying, "You make movies the world wants to see and nobody in this room can touch you . . . but I don't like you, Cecil, and I don't like a God damned thing you stand for." Mankiewicz added that Ford, clutching a pipe, introduced a motion echoing my father's call for the entire board to resign.

Mankiewicz's heroic story about John Ford has been repeated through the decades, but new research and writing tells a different story. Ford's comments were, in fact, more evenhanded toward DeMille, and he wrote to him the next day saying he was "a great gentleman." But Ford made a film called *The Man Who Shot Liberty Valance* with the newspaper editor's famous line, "When the legend becomes fact, print the legend." So I'm printing the legend, with this alert to the reader.

The meeting ended with DeMille isolated. The entire board, including DeMille, resigned and a committee composed of Mankiewicz and five past presidents was put in charge of creating a new board of directors.

It was twenty past two on Monday morning when Mankiewicz banged the gavel and the members, most of whom were due on sound stages in just a few hours, filed out. My father remembered walking out of the Beverly Hills Hotel and getting into his car.

"That was during the height of the McCarthy time. I drove fifty miles up the road to Ventura and back. I was so exhilarated seeing that victory won."

This was the first time I was aware of my father facing a crisis. At the age of eighteen I discovered the depth of his conviction, his sense of justice and his willingness to put his reputation on the line. Moreover, I admired the men at his side who earned a rare victory over Hollywood's reactionary forces. In time Willy Wyler, John Huston and John Ford would become friends of mine, as would Zinnemann, Mamoulian and Mankiewicz. They were men of integrity and creative vitality who I looked up to, whose values and independent thinking were markers for my professional life.

They don't teach you that in college.

A postscript: I remember my father telling me about a meeting of the Academy of Motion Picture Arts and Sciences the following spring. The board of governors was voting on the prestigious Irving Thalberg Award for "sustained production achievement," judged by a candidate's number of Oscar nominations. Studio heads who received credit on several pictures a year regularly received the award. DeMille was proposed because he had a high total of nominations as a director-producer. Some board members objected because he was a director, not a studio head, and others because of his recent behavior at the Directors Guild. My father surprised me when he told me he weighed in on behalf of DeMille and he was chosen. I suspect he thought there was a lesson for me.

This letter arrived days later.

PARAMOUNT PICTURES CORPORATION
WEST COAST STUDIOS

5451 MARATHON STREET   HOLLYWOOD 38, CALIF.
      TELEPHONE   CABLE ADDRESS
   HOLLYWOOD 9-2411   "FAMFILM"

26 March 1953

Mr. George Stevens
10506 Riverside Drive
North Hollywood, California.

Dear George:

          The best-kept secrets do leak out.
I have heard from several sources something which
warmed my heart and added to the respect I have
always had for you.   When a man goes to bat for
someone with whom he has strongly differed on
occasion, he shows that he is a man indeed.

                    Sincerely,

                    Cecil B. deMille

CBdM-C

15

Company Clerk

Our chartered DC-3 descended through the clouds, revealing the snow-capped peaks of Wyoming's Grand Tetons and the sprawling valley below.

My father was leading an advance party to Jackson Hole in June of 1951 to scout locations and create a visual framework for *Shane*. The grandeur of the Tetons would provide a cathedral effect under which, as he put it, the mortals in the valley could work out their little play. We bounced along in Jeeps and hiked until he found an idyllic but isolated spot by a stream to build the hewn-log homestead for the Starrett family, two miles from the spare 1880s town consisting only of Grafton's Saloon, an attached company store and a livery stable, constructed on a one-sided street at the foot of the mountain. On a hill a half mile from the town Dad marked a spot for three aspen trees to be planted, a distinctive portal past which all visitors would ride.

This was the summer of my sophomore year and my first job on a movie. I was hired as company clerk at, for me, a robust $125 a week, and was expected to record each shot and camera angle on a clipboard. My duties kept me near the camera, offering an unforgettable seven-week window into filmmaking of the highest order.

But the first important lesson had come earlier. Paramount was initially enthusiastic about making *Shane*. Montgomery Clift had expressed interest in the title role and William Holden in the part of Joe Starrett, but the success of Hopalong Cassidy and Wild Bill Hickok cowboy shows on free television led the Paramount front office to worry that the era of big screen Westerns was over. Then Monty Clift, who was volatile, dropped out without explanation and Holden decided he had been working too hard and needed a break. Y. Frank Freeman, a white-haired former theater manager from Georgia who was head of production at Paramount, called my father to say that *Shane* would be indefinitely postponed. "Without Clift and Holden," he explained in his slack southern drawl, "you just don't have a picture, George."

My father was back where he had been when the studio resisted making *A Place in the Sun* two years earlier. He held his fire for a week before walking into Freeman's office, catching the old gentleman off guard. Freeman started rambling about the projected cost of *Shane,* about audiences not going to see Westerns anymore, and how the loss of the two stars made a postponement necessary. Dad listened with what Katharine Hepburn called his "Indian impassivity," a silent look that unsettled people and fostered the rumor he was part Comanche. Finally Freeman ran out of gas and Dad let the silence linger.

"Frank, let's take a look at that list of actor commitments in your left-hand drawer."

Freeman pulled a single sheet from his desk. Dad studied it.

"Well, Frank, it looks like Alan Ladd owes you two pictures. He can play Shane. And Van Heflin—I saw him in *Tomahawk,* that Jim Bridger picture. He'd be good as Joe Starrett. And Jean Arthur has never let me down. She can play the woman."

We will never know if Freeman feared another lawsuit or whether the director's imposing self-confidence got to him, but after a long silence he nodded.

"All right, George, we'll go ahead."

Shane had been recast in ten minutes.

We began shooting in Jackson Hole on July 25, 1951. The one-hundred-person production unit was billeted in motels, houses were rented for Ladd, Arthur and Heflin, and the creative team and supporting cast were put up at the Wort Hotel, which also served as location headquarters. The hotel's Silver Dollar Bar, boasting 2,032 silver dollars embedded in the bar top, was headquarters for drinking, poker and courtship, and a spot where the occasional fight broke out. Two rawboned Wort brothers, who owned the hotel, had a yen for violence that harkened to an earlier time. I was startled (and sobered) one night to see the two Worts casually bloody a boozy customer and dump him outside on the wooden sidewalk.

Tourists coming into the Silver Dollar did double takes at the familiar faces of character players like Elisha Cook, Jr., whom they had seen in *The Maltese Falcon,* Ellen Corby from *I Remember Mama,* Edgar Buchanan from *Penny Serenade,* John Dierkes, the tall soldier in John Huston's *The Red Badge of Courage,* and a menacing looking newcomer, Jack Palance, whose distinctive face was partly the result of corrective surgery following a wartime flying accident. Brandon De Wilde, nine years old with blond hair and glittering blue eyes, arrived from two years on Broadway in *Member of the Wedding* to play Joey, the Starrett's son.

In the spring my father had enlisted A. B. "Bud" Guthrie, Jr., a Pulitzer Prize winner for his novel *The Big Sky,* to write the screenplay. He valued the authenticity of Guthrie's ear for western dialogue. When Guthrie arrived at Paramount on a Friday afternoon he announced that he had actually never seen a screenplay before. Dad gave him his *A Place in the Sun* script. Guthrie returned to his hotel and on Monday handed over the work he had completed.

"If the Writers Guild ever finds out you showed up with twenty pages on the first day," said Dad, "they'll ban you for life."

Fred Guiol and Ivan Moffat, my father's close collaborators, could not have been more different. Fred was a large man of Mexican descent, handsome and taciturn. He and my father became pals in the twenties on the Hal Roach lot where Fred was a successful director before he ran into a bottle problem that stalled his career. Dad used to talk of the days when Freddy would single-handedly clean out a saloon. Ivan, Oxford-educated and a brilliant conversationalist, was thirty-three. He came to Hollywood after wartime service in the Stevens Irregulars. Dad valued the story sense of both men who worked with him revising the script at night.

At six each morning Fred, Ivan, my father and I climbed into the back seat of a black Cadillac for the forty-minute trek to the location. Our driver Harry was a teamster with a weathered face and a frog-like voice who would stand by until sunset waiting for us to return to the car where, once settled in from a long day's work, Dad's only words were, "Kick it in the ass, Harry"—and we would speed off leaving a funnel of dust.

Having just turned nineteen it was my first experience with expert professionals. My father was effortlessly in charge, rarely raising his voice, patiently answering questions, calmly making a hundred decisions a day—setting a tone for the company. On occasion he defused tense situations with humor, at other times letting tension build as the crew strained to meet his expectations. Looking back on my early life I realize that Dad never seemed to instruct me, or to offer bromides or paternal pearls of wisdom. It was his example that formed me. And now, in the same way, I was learning about leadership in the workplace.

We filmed *Shane* in the Technicolor process that involved three strands of film running synchronously through a massive and unwieldy camera, "blimped" to mute the motor sound. Technicolor assigned a special consultant, or watchdog, to insure that shooting conformed to company standards. Unfortunately the Technicolor standard in America, as distinct from work being done in England or Italy, was what Dad referred to as the "Oh, What a Beautiful Morning" look, conspicuous for bright colors which were at odds with the realism he sought. He made certain nothing got in front of the Technicolor lens that wasn't authentic. He told wardrobe he wanted the actors to wear only what would have

George, Jr., in Jackson Hole with the Grand Tetons in background, 1951.

been available to them in the Old West: "These people didn't have the Western Costume Company to make them look conspicuous." He showed paintings of western masters Frederic Remington and Charles M. Russell to the designers, and worked with cinematographer Loyal Griggs to place actors in shadow and render scenes with muted tones.

Strangers drinking coffee from steaming metal pots at the chuck wagon on the first day soon became friends, and I relished the stimulating companionship. My one perk was a gray horse with a yellow slicker cinched behind the saddle that enabled me to go exploring at lunchtime. We worked twelve-hour days, six days a week. The cast and crew realized that their director was determined to perfect each scene. His exacting standards and a spate of mountain storms soon put us days behind schedule, causing budget concerns at Paramount. My father, maintaining his calm demeanor, internalized the stress, which provoked a chronic stomach ulcer. There was no dependable treatment in those days, so I would see him loosening his belt and munching crackers to ward off the pain. It was distressing to see him shouldering responsibility in such discomfort.

We watched dailies each night at the hotel in a jerry-built screening room. The footage was splendid. My father's understanding of the camera, nurtured as a young man in neighboring Montana photographing Rex the King of Wild Horses, was pivotal on *Shane*. I was discovering how his choice of lenses affected

Lunch with my mother and father on the set of *Shane*.

the story. He employed long focal length lenses that gave height and structure to the snow-covered peaks and brought them close, looming over the action—images that let us feel the isolation of a human being in that landscape.

The preparation and shooting of one scene awakened me to the way film-making technique can communicate a story's central theme, how attention to detail and a touch of serendipity could achieve classic cinema. Dad told me of a basic idea he wanted to convey. He had come home from war having watched only one movie in three years, and went to see a John Wayne Western in which, as he put it, they were using six-guns like guitars—shooting, falling down, getting up and shooting some more. In combat he had seen what a round from a .45 could do to the human body. In *Shane* he wanted to undermine the glamor of gunplay by dramatizing the significance of a single bullet. "A gunshot, for our purposes," he said, "is a holocaust."

The scene centers on two characters. Stonewall Torrey, portrayed by Elisha Cook, is a brash little southern homesteader, and Jack Wilson, played by Jack Palance, is a gunslinger imported by head cattleman Rufe Ryker to bait Torrey to draw on him. Palance, the son of a coal miner from Pennsylvania and former boxer who had appeared in just one film, Kazan's *Panic in the Streets,* spent weeks on location in his menacing black garb, mounting and dismounting the small bay horse that my father had selected to make him appear even taller and more menacing than his six-foot, four-inch frame. He worked with a fast-draw cowboy to perfect a move with his pistol—tugging a black glove over his fingers before a lightning-fast pull from the holster—to become a poetically evil gunslinger. My father had water trucked in from the Snake River to make the street in front of Grafton's Saloon muddy and slushy. He was blessed on the day with ominous storm clouds lying low over the Tetons, as Torrey rides into town for supplies with another homesteader, Swede Shipstead. They tie up their horses at the livery stable, and Wilson, standing on the raised wooden sidewalk in front of Grafton's, calls out to Torrey. Shipstead cautions him, but the proud little southerner makes his way toward the saloon, slipping and sliding on the mud, as the gunslinger baits him onward.

The camera, trained on Shipstead, captures the Swede's growing concern. Serendipity came at that moment—the sun disappeared behind the clouds, casting a dark shadow over the scene. It was Hollywood practice for the cameraman to tell the director they had lost the light, then cut the camera. "Keep rolling," Dad whispered to Loyal Griggs as the cloud passed over Shipstead. A dark rumble of thunder—added later to the soundtrack—foreshadows the violence to come.

A mattress had been buried in the muddy street and a harness was built for Elisha Cook to wear under his shirt. It was attached to a line with three burly wranglers at the other end. When Torrey reaches the front of the saloon Wilson looks down at him, taunting, tugging on his black glove.

"I'm saying that Stonewall Jackson was trash himself—him, Lee, and all them Rebs . . . and you, too."

Torrey responds, "You're a low down lyin' Yankee."

Wilson half smiles, then purrs, "*Prove* it."

Torrey draws. Wilson draws faster, and after a chilling hesitation, fires. The three wranglers violently yanked Torrey back, splaying him in the mud, avoiding the cliché of the victim clutching his stomach and falling forward. To magnify the moment, my father recorded an eight-inch Howitzer firing in a canyon and combined it with a high-pitched rifle shot. Two decades later Sam Peckinpah, himself a director of Westerns, would say, "Killing used to be fun and games in Apacheland. You fired a shot and three Indians went down. You always expected them to get up again. But after Jack Palance shot Elisha Cook, Jr. things started to change."

Elisha Cook, Jr., and Jack Palance in front of Grafton's Saloon.
"A gunshot for our purposes is a holocaust."

The burial of Stonewall Torrey was shot at the raw hillside cemetery over-looking the town in the distance. It was a complex scene that would conclude the location work and enable the company to return to Los Angeles—to the great relief of Mr. Y. Frank Freeman. All of the homesteaders were in the scene, in addition to assorted livestock and extras. Rudd Weatherwax, from the re-nowned Weatherwax family of animal trainers, was in charge of the several dogs in *Shane,* including the scraggly cur that belonged to Torrey.

The funeral is a linchpin scene that occurs after two of the frightened settler families decide to pack up and leave. Shane and Joe Starrett are trying to hold the community together. Ryker and his men watch from the distant porch of Grafton's saloon, and at the end of the burial torch one of the homesteads. Par-adoxically, the sight of the black smoke rising in the sky unites the homesteaders and they decide to soldier on.

Dad carefully choreographed the animals, women, children and Ladd and Heflin, who stand beside the grave holding ropes that will lower the coffin. A special effects crew stood ready in the distance to fill the sky with smoke. One of the homesteaders plays a mournful "Dixie" on his harmonica as his comrade is lowered, and Torrey's dog whimpers at the graveside as the pine coffin descends. The players were intently engaged, feeling the lonely desolation of this ritual. Except for Torrey's dog. Weatherwax was feverishly offering inducements, begging for obedience, finally taping a hunk of sirloin to the coffin—but in take after take everything went as planned except for the dog, who showed no interest in his master's misfortune. It was magic hour and the sun was about to set behind the mountain. Camera assistants reloaded the massive Technicolor camera and I watched my father in his western hat and sunglasses.

He spoke softly in the strained silence. "Mr. Weatherwax?"

The director silently points to the grave. The frazzled trainer gets the message, and warily climbs down into the grave avoiding contact with the hovering coffin. The attention of the dog is now directed, promisingly, toward the grave. Dad looks through the camera and sees the noticeable disparity in height between Heflin and five-foot, six-inch Ladd. "Slide an apple box under Mr. Ladd," he whispers to the head grip. Nerves are at the breaking point. The grip, eager to please, and please quickly, shouts to an accomplice, using the argot of their trade, "Sam, bring me a man maker!"

Mr. Ladd flinches, then turns and walks in the direction of his trailer. The sun disappears below the horizon and the company is dismissed.

As happens in the movie world, on the next day in the same place with the same people, the same dog, and Alan Ladd in fine form, everything went perfectly and we recorded a scene that would earn a place in film history.

My most valuable learning experience was still ahead of me, during borrowed time when I was back at college. I was able to explore the most mysterious facet of moviemaking in a small projection room at Paramount. Joe Mankiewicz worked with my father when he was at MGM directing *Woman of the Year*. "George shot voluminous amounts of film," Mankiewicz told me much later, "and then, after the actors and technicians were gone, there was nothing left but George Stevens and his film. It seemed to me that's when George made his films. I don't know any other director who worked that way."

Films were normally edited on a Moviola, a four-foot-high machine in use since 1924 that could run separate 35mm picture and soundtracks synchronously and display an image on an attached five-inch-square screen. My father concluded that the tiny picture could never give him a true impression of how scenes would play for audiences in movie theaters, so he constructed a screening room where he spent a year editing *A Place in the Sun*. There was a booth in the rear with two 35mm projectors and an operator to load reels. My father had devices on either side of his chair in the front row of the auditorium with which he could start, stop and reverse the projectors. The machine on the right would show an assembled version of the scene he was working on, the one on the left would contain alternate takes. He was able to watch the scene on the large screen, then refine it by using the second projector to review different versions of an actor's performance or search for a preferred camera angle or different image size. On *A Place in the Sun* he sensed subtle emotional distinctions in the performances of Montgomery Clift and Elizabeth Taylor on the large screen that weren't evident on the Moviola. He would comb through close-ups, looking for the exact moment that was most convincing.

Dad shot 362,102 feet of film on *Shane*—sixty hours of screen time—that would be distilled into a two-hour motion picture. It was a trove of thousands of individual takes. I came to realize that each shot has no essential meaning until the director makes a choice to splice it to another. It's the linking of shots that makes a scene and the linking of scenes that makes a story. "Cinema, at its most effective," my father explained, "is one scene effectively superseded by the next."

Shane's editors, Bill Hornbeck and Tom McAdoo, organized large looseleaf albums that contained the first and last frame of each take, carefully labeled, so they could locate the exact piece of film needed at any moment. The studio felt the amount of exposed film was excessive, but my father saw it as an investment that gave him the means to tell the story most effectively. William Wyler was known for making take after take—sometimes as many as eighty. He drove some actors crazy but they loved what they saw in the finished film. The Stevens method was to cover scenes from many different angles with fewer takes. He could protect the actors, either by showing the most convincing reading of a line or cutting away to emphasize another performer's reaction. Or he might simply omit the line. "Morning noon and night, Saturdays, sometimes Sundays," remembered Ivan Moffat, "George was running and re-running the film, squeezing different meanings, different nuances into a scene, sometimes changing the whole concept of a scene."

There is a sterling illustration in *Shane* of how a scene can be created in the editing room. I sat in the dark beside my father and watched him craft it. Shane is shamed in the eyes of the homesteaders when he goes into Grafton's Saloon to buy a bottle of soda pop for Joey and fails to retaliate when mocked by Chris Calloway, a strapping Ryker gang cowhand played by Ben Johnson. Now he enters Grafton's to return the empty bottle. Calloway approaches him at the bar.

"Set 'em up bartender," says Shane, and the bartender fills two shot glasses.

"You ain't gonna drink that in here," Calloway says.

"You guessed it," Shane responds.

He empties one shot glass on Calloway's chest, the second in his face, then sends him sailing with a right cross. The two men fight and when Shane gets the upper hand, the other Ryker men come to the rescue. Brandon De Wilde as Joey, watching near the door, warns, "Shane . . . there's too many!" He runs to tell his father. Joe Starrett enters the saloon and joins Shane in a titanic battle to overcome the Ryker gang. The scene runs nine minutes and contains 202 separate cuts, each filmed with the hard-to-maneuver three-strip Technicolor camera in the days before portable cameras. Many consider it cinema's greatest fight scene.

It was fascinating to observe the detail involved in choosing establishing shots and reaction shots, close-ups and inserts—paring it down to a coherent whole—then orchestrating a soundtrack to enhance the drama. There are twenty-three cuts of Brandon De Wilde—first, watching under the swinging door, later biting off a piece of his candy cane at a climactic moment. My father was telling the story through the eyes of the boy, a device that enhanced the believability of the outsized fistfight.

There was a widely accepted studio mantra that the intelligence level of the audience was that of a twelve-year-old, condescension that encouraged producers to aim at the lowest common denominator. What I learned from my father was the opposite—*respect for the audience.* "I often watch the audience at work and I'm profoundly impressed by their intelligence," he said. "Get five thousand people and seat them in the Music Hall in New York, and calculate the energy of those minds surpassing themselves."

We took *Shane* at two hours and twenty minutes—to San Francisco for a sneak preview. The audience was captivated but there were moments of restlessness, so we were back in the editing room the next morning going through the reels. We pared away twenty-two minutes, every change and refinement made with the audience in mind. The director had control and was making the most of it.

One night in March, as finishing touches were being put on *Shane,* I went with my father, mother and grandmother to the 1952 Academy Awards at the Pantages Theater. It was my first Oscar outing since *The More the Merrier* and the first time Dad had attended. I was beside him when his friend Joe Mankiewicz read the nominees for best director: John Huston for *The African Queen,* Elia Kazan for *A Streetcar Named Desire,* Vincent Minnelli for *An American in Paris,* William Wyler for *Detective Story,* and George Stevens for *A Place in the Sun.* Mankiewicz opened the envelope and called out, "George Stevens!" Dad gave me a quick squeeze and I watched him go to the stage and receive his first Oscar, one of six that went to *A Place in the Sun* that night.

Later, when he was driving us home, with the Oscar resting between us on the front seat, I was still excited. Perhaps too excited in his eyes, because he turned to me with these words.

"We'll have a better idea what kind of a picture this is in about twenty-five years."

There were no cinematheques or retrospectives then, or videotape or DVDs or streaming. Films came and went. I was moved by what he said, and though I didn't realize it then, he had with a single sentence instilled in me an idea that would define a large part of my professional life. He was talking about the test of time.

Alan Pakula, who would become a first-rate director and a good friend, was a twenty-two-year-old assistant in the Paramount front office when we were editing *Shane*. He told me later that the studio lost confidence in the picture and that Y. Frank Freeman was negotiating to sell *Shane* to Howard Hughes at RKO for its negative cost (no wonder Dad referred to him as Why Frank Freeman?). The studio ledgers told Freeman that no Alan Ladd picture had ever grossed more than $2,600,000. There was jubilation in the executive hallways when Hughes offered Paramount $3,000,000 to take *Shane* off its hands. The deal fell through but it was a learning experience for Pakula: "What Mr. Freeman didn't realize was that *Shane* wasn't an Alan Ladd picture, it was a George Stevens film. And Paramount was stuck with one of the biggest hits in its history."

The *Shane* opening at Grauman's Chinese was the first time I sat at a premiere and watched a film that I had worked on. It was stirring to see a large audience respond moment to moment to the thousands of calculations made during the preceding two years. Although I was little more than an observer of the creative process, it gave me a taste of the gratification that comes when an audience is fully transported. Archer Winston in the *New York Post* seemed to foresee the film's place in history. "*Shane*," he wrote, "is 'only a Western' in the same sense that *Romeo and Juliet* is only a love story."

Years later, when I described to an accomplished older friend my experience sitting by my father's side in that editing room at Paramount, he said, "You know, don't you—that's your inheritance."

16

The Wild Blue Yonder

I graduated from Occidental in June 1953. Surprisingly, considering there was substantial achievement in our family, it was our first degree since my great-great-grandfather William Thompson, father of my covered wagon great-grandmother Hanna Laura, earned his a century before from William Jewell College in Liberty, Missouri. (He became president of the college in 1857.) That is, unless you count my father's phantom degree from "hard knocks."

The Air Force ROTC had come to Occidental in 1951 as the Korean War was heating up. My military experience at Harvard School, slender as it was, meant that I could complete the four-year program in two. I received a commission as a second lieutenant on graduation day along with orders to report for active duty at Lackland Air Force Base in Texas, but the armistice ending the Korean War reduced the need for young lieutenants, so my service was postponed for a year.

Suddenly I was adrift, but by chance my father had just chosen his next project. Edna Ferber, the best-selling author of *Show Boat, So Big* and *Cimarron*, had published her saga of a Texas family, *Giant*. Her previous books had become successful films but studios balked at her lofty asking price for *Giant*, so Dad and one of his former antagonists at Paramount, Henry Ginsberg, crafted a partnership with Ferber, and negotiated a production deal with Jack Warner. My father was willing to work without salary, as were his partners, in exchange for owning 50 percent of the film and a "final cut" guarantee for him. Dad invited me to join him as he worked on the screenplay—filling my dance card until Uncle Sam beckoned.

For the next ten months I showed up at nine-thirty each morning at my father's apartment. I had a fifty-yard commute. Our family now occupied four of my mother's seven town houses, she and I on one corner, my grandmother

Alice Howell across the way, and Dad occupying two units in the center. Alice, contentedly retired from starring in silent comedies, made tasty dishes for my now bachelor father. I would see her—red hair and Charlie Chaplin walk—carrying casseroles to his door.

Fred Guiol and Ivan Moffat joined my father and me in his living room. I sat on one end of the sofa, Fred on the other, with Ivan and Dad in easy chairs. We started at fade-in and organized a detailed step outline which became the foundation for *Giant*. It was a masterclass in screenwriting, observing three experienced storytellers examine a four-hundred-fifty-page novel, explore character and plot, pare away nonessentials, devise new scenes, and end up with a sturdy cinematic structure for the complex story of three generations.

The Magnavox television in the corner provided occasional distraction, notably the mesmerizing Army–McCarthy hearings—my first exposure to a political villain, Senator Joseph McCarthy, and a political hero, Joseph Welch (who asked the senator, "At long last, have you left no sense of decency, sir?"). We were heartened when Edward R. Murrow, whose broadcasts from London I listened to during the war, set the course for McCarthy's downfall with his episode of *See It Now,* in which he dissected the senator with his own words. All that and the Yankees trouncing the Brooklyn Dodgers in the World Series, and lunch breaks at the Lakeside Golf Club followed by putting contests on the practice green. Despite our penchant for diversion the storytelling progressed, and by the time orders came in 1954 for me to report to my new assignment in Florida, we had completed a carefully crafted first draft screenplay.

After a steamy July drive across the American Southwest in my 1950 Mercury Sedan, with a portable metal cooling system attached to the window, I pulled through the gates of Orlando Air Force Base, the headquarters of the Air Photographic and Charting Service. APCS was responsible for providing aerial charts for pilots and producing training films and newsreels. Orlando was a sleepy, sticky southern town that offered no hint that it would one day become a jewel in the Walt Disney crown.

I was one of a dozen motion picture officers in the 1365th Photo Squadron who were dispatched to bases around the country to direct training films, a provident assignment for a young officer leaning toward a movie career. The claim to fame of our motion picture unit was John Frankenheimer, who had cut his filmmaking teeth in the unit and was now directing *Playhouse 90* in New York. I inherited John's cameraman, Sergeant Kazumplik, a crusty New York cab driver, and together our training films ranged from *Meat Cutting by the Rail Method* for butchers to *How to Navigate Icy Roads* for military drivers. Officer's pay was $100 a week but we did most of our filming away from Orlando on temporary duty orders, which triggered a per diem allowance that provided comfortable living for a bachelor. Our movie unit had its own flavor of Joseph Heller's *Catch-22*. Fraught relationships with senior career officers provided a touch of the absurd that kept us laughing.

This was my first experience living in a southern town and coming face to face with the routine exclusion of people of color in restaurants. There were separate restrooms and "whites only" drinking fountains in public places. I remember a captain who I would see at the Officers' Club, an African American named Eugene Rock. He was dark-skinned and handsome, a few years older than me, and usually by himself. I wondered what his life was like off-base in Orlando. I've never forgotten him, nor, to my regret, my failure to make an effort to get to know him. My time in the South reinforced my awareness of the outsider, a perspective gained from my father. I was distressed by the injustice but today I must rank myself as having been only a passive observer.

On assignment to Maxwell Air Force Base in Montgomery, Alabama, in December 1955, I witnessed the bus boycott initiated by the activist seamstress Rosa Parks, who refused to yield her seat to a white passenger. The nearby house of a young activist preacher, Dr. Martin Luther King, Jr., was bombed in retaliation. The bravery and determination of Parks and her allies was inspiring. A year later I would read in the *Orlando Sentinel* about the Supreme Court decision that outlawed segregated buses in Alabama and ignited the Civil Rights Movement.

Jeff Meisser, a classmate in the theater program at Occidental, and Billy Hale from Rome, Georgia, were fellow officers. Billy was my first southern friend, a sardonic Phi Beta Kappa graduate from the University of Southern California film school. Jeff and I were assigned a ten-week mission at Tyndall Air Force Base on the Florida gulf. We each headed a four-man camera team making training films for fighter pilots, shooting in the searing heat on the flight line. Our actors were swaggering jet jockeys who sported mirrored sunglasses, blue nylon flight suits with silver wings on their chests, and parachutes on their backs. We non-flyers hung out at the Officers' Club with these intrepid fellows, feeling a bit wimpish. Jeff and I were driving on a country road one afternoon and spotted a red hangar beside a grass landing strip. Whitewashed on its side was "RIDES." A slender man wearing a leather jacket and a jaunty red cap ambled toward us, flashing a smile. "My name is Jack," he said. "I'll teach you to fly for a hundred bucks." He showed us a bright red Aeronca Champion, a ninety horsepower "tail dragger," promising that we would be ready to "solo" after ten hour-long lessons.

I was directing a film called *The Walk Around Inspection of the F-86D* to explain the preflight routine for pilots of the new all-weather interceptor, shooting cockpit shots of gauges being checked and switches being toggled. After work Jack taught me the walk-around inspection of the Aeronca Champion. During my first flight he sat in the rear seat, issuing precise instructions over the intercom. I experimented with the throttle, the control stick between my knees, and the rudder controlled by foot pedals, adjusting to the sensation of this heavier than air machine gliding above the clouds. Then, to teach me how to extract myself from an unintended tailspin, Jack pulled the nose upward, stalled the plane, and threw us into a stomach-turning downward spiral. After a few moments of spinning toward the earth he told me to jam the left pedal and shove the throttle, miraculously righting us onto a forward path.

I became proficient at touch-and-go landings—flying downwind at five hundred feet parallel to the runway, turning on the carburetor heat, making two left turns into a final approach, then lowering the wing flaps to assist the descent. When we touched down Jack would shout, "Accelerate!" I would shove the throttle forward and we would rise again without stopping. I showed up for my seventh lesson realizing that only three hours of instruction remained. We came in for a landing and Jack directed me to taxi our little craft to the end of the runway and come to a full stop. With the engine still running Jack opened the door and climbed out. He leaned in close in his red cap.

"You're ready, George. Take her up, climb to five hundred feet, make left turns, put her down nice and soft, and taxi back to this spot."

SLAM! The door closed and I was alone. I checked the instruments and shoved the throttle forward, pulling the control stick back as I gained speed—the Aeronca Champion was ascending. Soon I was at five hundred feet, surveying the gorgeous blue waters of the Gulf of Mexico. "I'm flying! Goddamn it, I'm flying!"—it was the most exhilarating feeling, doing something thrilling that had first occurred to me just three weeks earlier.

And then, just as suddenly, the thrill dissolved and my mind was racing. How do I get this sonofabitch down?

I wouldn't be writing this if my first solo landing had been unsuccessful. Jack watched a smooth landing and greeted me proudly as I taxied up to him. I shouted over the engine, "You said I'd solo in *ten* hours. This is my *seventh*!" He climbed into the rear seat. "You looked like you were ready. Take us around again."

When Jeff and I returned to Orlando we bought a Cessna 140—a handsome cream-colored single-engine tail dragger with green trim for $3,500—which we parked at a small field on the other side of town. We were restless twenty-three-year-olds and our free time was occupied by logging the thirty hours required by the FAA for certification as pilots. Abandoned World War II

Flight planning with Jeff Meisser and Cessna 9496 Alpha,
Orlando Airport, 1956.

navy airfields in central Florida were ideal for afternoon hops to develop our
takeoff and landing skills, but Jeff and I soon tired of this routine.

"Let's try something more adventurous," I said one night at dinner.

"Like what?" Jeff asked.

"How about Cuba!"

We unleashed our Cessna from its mooring on Friday morning, stuffed
what we called our "survival kit" behind the seats—a box containing fried chick-
en, Scotch whiskey, Band-Aids, sunscreen and a flashlight—and prepared for
takeoff. (We did prevail upon an air force friend for two life jackets.) Three
hours later we parked on the apron at Key West Airport and strolled into the
flight center. "We want to file a flight plan to Havana." The operations man gave
us a wary look, but within twenty minutes we were airborne for the ninety-
minute overwater flight. When the island with its white sand beaches came into
view we called Air Traffic Control at Jose Marti International Airport: "Cessna
9496 Alpha requesting permission to land." The accented voice responded in
English, guiding us into the landing pattern behind a Pan American flight
packed with tourists. We touched down, grinning with satisfaction.

Except for forays along the Mexico–California border, neither of us had ever been abroad. We were now in the Cuba of dictator Fulgencio Batista, who maintained power with support from the United States. Havana, with its casinos, beaches and brothels, was a playground for American tourists. Little attention was being paid to the Castro brothers in the hills, Fidel and Raoul. Jeff and I checked into a small hotel, and were soon joined by our Florida roommate Billy Hale. He had flown down on a commercial flight and we became Three Amigos in Havana. Outside our hotel a Cuban in a flowered shirt, who bore a striking resemblance to an American singer, approached. "My name is Frankie Sinatra," he chirped. "Twenty dollars a day and I show you Havana."

Frankie took us to a cigar factory, on a tour of Morro Castle, to the Bacardi Rum Distillery and on nighttime visits to the Tropicana Casino and the Copacabana. The topper was on our final day at four in the afternoon when we strolled into the famous Floridita Bar, found a table, ordered three Papa Dobles—the double Daiquiri favored by Ernest Hemingway. We gazed across the dimly lit room. Seated in his preferred corner wearing a tan bush jacket, getting the drinking part of his day started, was Papa himself. We ordered another round. Our mission to Havana was complete.

Back in Orlando I was diagnosed with infectious hepatitis and quarantined on complete bed rest in the base hospital, where I followed the 1956 presidential election on the radio. Four years earlier my father had taken me to an event in Beverly Hills where we had a picture taken with the Democratic candidate, former Illinois governor Adlai Stevenson. He was the first political figure I'd met. His wisdom and wit appealed to me and I was crushed when he lost to Dwight Eisenhower. Now, during my confinement, I read an eloquent speech by Stevenson and typed a letter of support to him. A few weeks later I received a letter from Governor Stevenson thanking me for my encouragement, as he put it, "at a time when it was sorely needed." I was surprised and happy that he responded, and look back on this exchange as fostering my growing interest in politics. It also inspired my lifelong practice of replying to people who write to me.

My service time was near an end when I was released from the hospital. I took my savings and ordered a $2,500 gunmetal gray Mercedes Benz 190SL convertible with red leather seats, to be picked up at the factory in Stuttgart. We had access to air force transport flights to Europe, so a friend and I flew to Frankfurt. I shall never forget the husky German mechanic at the Stuttgart factory who checked me out on the new vehicle. He concluded by bumping his fist on the hood and declaring, "Simple but *puff-fect!*" It proved to be a guarantee for the best car I ever owned.

When Jeff and I let it be known we intended to fly our Cessna to California, our commanding officer questioned our transcontinental expertise (and our sanity), insisting we show our charts and flight plan to two experienced air force pilots. They vetted our plan and we flew at ninety miles an hour cruising speed for three days, with overnight stops, before touching down safely in Burbank. I asked my mother to meet us, not having troubled her with the news that we were piloting our own plane. We embraced in the terminal, then I led her across the tarmac to our ninety-horsepower Cessna. As she studied the plane, it slowly dawned on her that this tiny aircraft had carried her only child across the United States. She pointed to its nose, and said, "That poor little propeller."

Reunion with my mother, Burbank Airport, July 1956.

17

The Eyes of Texas

G*iant* was never far from my radar screen during my two years in the air force. Dad spent an arduous three and a half years on the film—from our first work on the screenplay in the spring of 1953 to its premiere in October of 1956.

Strong independent producers were challenging studio power at the time my father struck a deal with Jack L. Warner for his studio to finance and distribute *Giant*. Dad retained authority over all creative decisions and was assured final cut. He and his partners, Edna Ferber and Henry Ginsberg, gambled that *Giant* would succeed at the box office and their ownership share would reward them.

Jack Warner made his way to the top of the movie industry with a fifth-grade education and an abundance of grit and toughness. He relished taking stars and directors to the window of his Warner Bros. office and asking, "Whose name do you see on that water tower?" He could be jovial and was known for telling lame jokes, but he wielded the hammer at Warner Bros. He and my father believed that *Giant* could be an enormously successful movie, but after reading the script Warner betrayed uneasiness in a memo: "Is there some way in your rewriting and polishing that you can maintain the same dramatization and still aim for a two hour show rather than the length I am sure you're going to wind up with—two hours and twenty-five or thirty minutes?"

When they sat in Warner's office to discuss the final screenplay Dad noticed that Warner's copy was heavily marked in red pencil. Warner spoke in generalities before referencing a couple of marked items, then he laughed and tossed the script aside. "Hell, George, you know what you're doing, I don't have to go through all this."

The cost of the picture was originally pegged at $1,850,000, but a budget based on the final 178-page script grew to $2,700,000, with seventy-two shooting days. Time would tell if the thinking of these two strong-willed men would remain aligned.

Dad took my mother and me to dinner at Musso's in March of 1955 on one of my visits home from Orlando, after which we went across the street to the Egyptian to see Elia Kazan's *East of Eden*. At dinner he told of his secretary complaining about a scruffy twenty-four-year-old actor in dirty jeans who loitered around their office bungalow. He and Fred Guiol found the young man to be intuitive and smart. I will never forget the feeling that night at the Egyptian when James Dean appeared on the screen. He was arresting and mysterious with hooded eyes, moving across the CinemaScope frame with a catlike grace.

Dean was physically slight compared to Ferber's burly ranch hand Jett Rink, and my father had been talking to bigger men like Robert Mitchum and Richard Burton. The role called for Dean to age into an oil tycoon in his fifties, and his response to the script was direct. "That guy is me. I could do that."

The other leads were Texas rancher Bick Benedict and Leslie Lynnton, the young Virginia woman who Bick courts and marries. Audrey Hepburn and Grace Kelly were considered for Leslie but Audrey declined and when MGM refused to release Kelly, my father turned to Elizabeth Taylor. Clark Gable, Burt Lancaster and Gregory Peck were proposed for Bick Benedict, but Dad borrowed a young contract actor from Universal, Rock Hudson. He was, with Rock at twenty-eight and Elizabeth at twenty-three, reversing the convention of casting older stars who would play younger in the early scenes, believing that audiences were more likely to believe a romance between young actors. He was confident Rock and Elizabeth could be convincing as grandparents. The rising new actress Carroll Baker, making her screen debut as Elizabeth's younger daughter Luz, was a year older than Taylor.

I had lunch one day in the exclusive Green Room at Warner Bros. with Jimmy and his friend Dennis Stock, the Magnum photographer whose pictures of Dean are now celebrated. He was mercurial and enjoyed being a rebel on the studio lot. I noticed him studying the large framed portraits of Warner stars on the dining room walls. As we got up to leave, Jimmy nudged Dennis, and as other diners watched he posed between portraits of Bogart and Cagney, scrunching his shoulders to fit in the narrow space while Dennis snapped a picture. It was evident that Jimmy intended to create his own history in front of the camera.

In New York Carroll Baker took me for a visit to the Actors Studio, a converted church where Dean had studied. Descending the brick steps into its dim interior required an adjustment of the eyes. I observed two hours of scene work guided by the Studio's director Lee Strasberg and witnessed the intensity of the actors performing before their peers. There was a reverence for Strasberg, perhaps also a strain of fear. Afterward Carroll took me to the side of the room to meet him. She introduced me graciously, explaining that I was in the air force and describing my Hollywood background. I looked to Strasberg, ready to shake hands. He studied me with a sober glance and turned away. As Carroll and I walked toward the door she whispered, "Lee doesn't say anything unless he really feels it." Some of the most extraordinary actors of a generation came out of the Studio, more than a few of whom developed behavioral traits that complicated their lives.

In May I took leave from the air force and flew from Orlando to Washington National Airport (where twelve years earlier my mother and I had watched my father fly off to North Africa) and observed a white TWA Super Constellation with red stripes taxi to the terminal. When the door opened Elizabeth Taylor, cradling a Lhasa Apso puppy, Rock Hudson and my father stepped out and paused for photographs, followed by the cast and crew of *Giant.* I joined them on the night train south to Keswick in the heart of Virginia's hunt country where the first scenes of the picture would be shot. Rock, as Bick Benedict, comes from his Texas ranch to buy the black stallion War Winds and falls in love with the owner's raven-haired daughter Leslie.

Dad was working again with cinematographer Bill Mellor. The first scene showed Bick watching from the window of an old train as it winds through lush green hills to the tiny Keswick station, juxtaposed with Leslie riding to the hounds on War Winds. I hadn't seen Elizabeth—now married to Michael Wilding and the mother of two infant boys—since *A Place in the Sun.* She was more beautiful than ever and her horsemanship superb. For an air force second lieutenant, a few days lolling on the grass taking pictures of Elizabeth and her silky Lhasa Apso gave added dimension to serving one's country.

Descending on a Trans-Texas flight into tiny Marfa, population 3,600, six weeks later, I spotted the set of Bick Benedict's Victorian ranch house isolated on bleached prairie grass, providing stark contrast to Leslie's emerald green Virginia. This sixty-foot-high structure, shipped to Marfa on six railroad cars, as well as the interior built on a Warner Bros. sound stage, would change in appearance as the Benedict family evolved, with the addition of a modern interior, a tennis court and swimming pool. Hundreds of head of cattle were imported at substantial cost, different breeds for different stages of the film, and the herd was enlarged by wooden cutouts of cows placed among the real animals.

The townspeople of Marfa were engaged to work on and appear in the film, providing a financial windfall for the tiny town. My father made it an "open set,"

With Rock Hudson and Elizabeth Taylor on *Giant* location in Keswick, Virginia. At left,
Judith Evelyn, who played Elizabeth's mother. At right, Carolyn Craig, who played
her sister. May 1955.

allowing as many as five hundred visitors a day to watch the filming. They became goodwill messengers for the picture.

When a director is also the producer it means that the principal artist in
charge of working with actors and shaping the story is also, in the case of *Giant*,
responsible for a complex logistical enterprise involving hundreds of performers,
technicians and livestock. My father also managed the relationship with the
studio which became strained when *Giant* fell seven days behind schedule. The
primary causes were Elizabeth's absences because of sickness, Dean developing a
habit of being late to the set, and my father's comprehensive coverage of scenes.
Dad received a brusque telegram from Jack Warner complaining about what he
called the repetitious shooting of scene after scene. My father was strong-willed
but never arrogant, the tone of his reply respectful. "Deeply aware of the urgency expressed in your wire and most appreciate its humane tone. Doing utmost
repeat utmost to pick up time."

In the late summer I visited the *Giant* set on the Warner lot. Dad arranged for
me to view two hours of inspiring footage. Elizabeth and Rock were compelling

Stevens, Sr., and James Dean in Marfa, Texas. The iconic Benedict family ranch house is in the background.

and Jimmy Dean was fascinating as the truculent ranch hand Jett. Mercedes McCambridge also stood out as Bick's brusque older sister. (It might have reduced tension if Jack Warner had known then that Rock, Jimmy and Mercedes would all be nominated for Oscars.)

There were many striking images but one in particular took my breath away. After seeing Sal Mineo's smiling face in uniform in a newspaper proclaiming "Angel Obregon Comes Home Today," we see a train pull away to reveal a coffin covered by an American flag on a baggage cart, with a silent group of black-clad mourners silhouetted against an evening sky. Angel's funeral in a segregated cemetery combined themes of sacrifice and racial divide. The power of what I saw convinced me the film would score with audiences.

The 72-day schedule expanded to 114 days. As the picture progressed Elizabeth called in sick more frequently and lost days added up, and during the last fortnight of shooting she reported abdominal pains that stopped work for nine days. My father had first sensed these tendencies six years earlier on *A Place in the Sun*, when she was just seventeen. Child actors were tutored at MGM, and he concluded that like many youngsters her inclination when she didn't want to

Elizabeth Taylor showing her director who's boss. Left to right: Mercedes McCambridge, Taylor, Rock Hudson and James Dean.

go to school was to say she was sick. It became a habit, intensified in her later years by serious illnesses.

In the midst of this tension Dad got a call one Sunday night with word that Mercedes McCambridge had fallen at home, sustaining serious cuts and loss of blood. She was due at eight a.m. on the process stage to film a scene with Dean. Dad called her in the emergency room and proposed she take a day to recover. "George, I'm a professional," Mercedes responded. "I've seen too much bad behavior on this picture. I'll be made up and in my place in the morning."

Early Monday Dad went to the process stage and found McCambridge in costume sitting in the passenger seat of Jett Rink's truck. The crew was tinkering with lights—but there was no sign of Dean. At nine-thirty he ambled in, climbed into the driver's seat, peered through his sunglasses at McCambridge, and muttered with a chuckle, "I thought you were dead." My father looked to the woman who had covered her stitches with makeup and arrived on time. Furious, he moved to Dean's side of the car, telling me later, "I was thirty years older than he was and I figured I may have to find out how long I could go with him." Looking directly at the actor he said, "Miss McCambridge has been waiting for an hour and deserves an apology." There was a long silence as crew members watched from the shadows. Then Dean took off his hat and glasses and told the actress he hoped she was feeling better.

Jimmy's last scene was the banquet at the opening of Jett Rink's new hotel. Jett, now middle-aged, passes out drunk at the head table without delivering his speech, then later wakes up and stumbles through his remarks, drifting into his feelings for Leslie Benedict, a scene my father described as a man's rendezvous with despair. Dean had difficulty during rehearsal. "I could do this damn scene better if we do some work on it," he said to my father. "Can you come back at night?" So the two men rehearsed together alone for two nights on the cavernous sound stage, doing the scene over and over. When they finally shot it, Dean was utterly convincing as the troubled oil baron.

Jimmy had finished shooting but happened to be visiting the set the last time I was there. A racing enthusiast, he assured my father that he wouldn't race cars during the production. Jimmy was true to his word, but now he had bought a Porsche Spyder 500 that he named Little Bastard. We were watching a rehearsal when he said, "She's outside." Then squinting through his tinted lenses, "Wanna ride?" A studio lot with towering sound stages and narrow streets is a far cry from a grand prix racetrack, but as soon as we settled into the cockpit of the low-slung silver roadster, Jimmy gunned it. We sped around the studio with engine roar reverberating off the sound stage walls, fortunate not to cross paths with a prop truck or studio police. Minutes later we were back at the *Giant* stage. "Not bad, eh?" Jimmy grinned. I grinned back.

He decided to enter a race in Salinas. He told my father he was going to truck the racing car to the track in northern California, but at the last minute decided he wanted the experience of driving the car on the highway, so on the morning of September 30, 1955, he and his mechanic set out for Salinas in the Spyder. It was after six on that Friday at Warner Bros. when my father and the editors met to view dailies. Rock, Elizabeth and Carroll Baker were there. The telephone was off-limits in the projection room but it rang that evening. My father picked it up. "You just saw all the blood drain out of him," remembered Carroll. "I thought, George Junior, knowing he was in the air force. George turned to us and said, 'Jimmy's dead.' I remember we sat there for the longest time. There was no crying or talking, there was just silence."

I heard the news in Florida. It was my first experience with the death of a contemporary. Jimmy had been so alive and filled with such promise—it was a confounding loss. There was a long-held belief in Hollywood that the death of a star actor doomed a movie at the box office, adding to Jack Warner's worries.

My father worked with three film editors to shape 875,000 feet of film into a finished motion picture. I joined him in July when I got out of the service. No feature film had run longer than three hours since *Gone with the Wind* in 1939 and the first time I saw *Giant* it ran nearly four hours. The challenge was to sharpen the story by trimming the film to its proper length. Race and feminism—themes rarely addressed in Hollywood films of the era—were at the heart of *Giant*. Elizabeth Taylor, as Leslie, is a maternal figure who challenges assumed masculine superiority and brings about change, including in her husband, who moves beyond his prejudices when he steps up to fight the beefy owner of a roadside diner who insults his Hispanic grandson.

The moment of truth was our first preview at the California Theater in San Diego. Jack Warner, who had hoped for a two-hour movie costing $2,500,000, settled in on the back row with the studio brass from New York, bracing themselves for a three-and-a-half-hour film that cost $5,445,667. I sat next to my father halfway to the front where he could get a better sense of the audience. Scenes that I had seen dozens of times suddenly came alive as I watched them through the eyes of viewers around me. The packed house was engaged from start to finish as confirmed by preview cards: 307 rated *Giant* excellent, 64 good, 9 fair, and 3 poor.

We went upstairs where Jack Warner and his aides were huddled along with Ben Kalmenson, who ran advertising and distribution from New York. Kalmenson, stocky with a gray complexion and a blunt manner, had complained to one of our editors downstairs that the film was full of communist ideas. He opened the meeting by declaiming, "This picture is at least an hour too long." Then, referring to a scene that occurs half an hour before the finish: "Your picture is over when James Dean passes out at the banquet." Warner defused the explosive moment and mustered some laughter by saying, "George, why don't you and I have a drink and toss around some ideas."

Kalmenson's bucket of ice water dimmed the euphoria for only a few minutes. Warner wrote to my father the next day: "Believe me, in my estimation it is a better picture than *Gone with the Wind*, and I'm glad the preview patrons agree with me."

Warner called a meeting to review the ads displayed on easels. My father studied them, then asked quietly, "Is there a reason that none of the people in these ads are wearing western hats?" The situation was reversed—Kalmenson's work was now being evaluated. "You see, George, we commissioned a Sindlinger

& Co. study," Kalmenson replied, referring to the research organization, "and they found audiences don't want to see movies with people wearing western hats."

Dad took another long look at the ads and turned to Kalmenson. "Ben, I think that's a survey you should have taken before we spent five million dollars shooting a picture where everybody wears western hats."

"Jack," he said, turning to Warner. "We agree that we've got a fine picture. Our advertising must tell the public—in a dramatic way—the truth about what kind of a picture they're going to see." Warner ordered a new ad campaign to capture the spirit of *Giant*.

One day Jack Warner walked over to my father's bungalow. He came to discuss the scene in which Bick Benedict, Senator Bale Clinch and their cronies are sitting beside the new swimming pool at Reata discussing the 27½ percent depletion allowance on oil revenue. The controversial tax law, engineered by Senate Majority Leader Lyndon Johnson, was (and is today) a financial windfall for oil companies. Leslie walks by from the tennis court and hears the men talking. "How about an exemption," she says, "for depreciation of first-class brains, Senator?"

"Whose, yours?" asks Bick.

"My father's for instance—he spent his life saving other people's lives. How about some tax exemption there?" Leslie hoists a tennis ball and whacks it over the fence.

Warner had earlier asked my father to remove the scene because the biggest theater owner in Texas was threatening not to show *Giant*. Now, he explained, Serge Semenenko, head of the First National Bank of Boston, was going to cancel the studio's line of credit unless the scene was removed. Warner was desperate, arguing that it was just two minutes in a three-hour movie and that no one would miss it. Dad said he was sorry that Warner was in a difficult situation, but he couldn't compromise the film to mollify one banker's discontent. "Just tell him the truth, Jack. You can't cut it. Tell him to talk to me." My father had worked for three years without salary as a means of gaining control. The public was going to see his version of *Giant*.

Dad and I flew to New York for the October premiere. It was a heady time and we shared a two-bedroom suite at the St. Regis. Scoop Conlon, a pixyish, silver-headed publicist in his sixties, a former reporter with rapid fire patter out of *The Front Page,* hurried in and said, "You're coming with me." He led me downstairs and into the backseat of a waiting limousine. "Yankee Stadium," he instructed the driver. "Don't spare the horses."

I listened as Scoop, his voice rising above the din of midday Manhattan traffic, recited baseball tales and movie lore. His patter reminded me of the day when another publicist, Alan Delynn, was with my father in our Toluca Lake living room. The phone rang and Dad picked it up. "Hello, Scoop. How are things?" Delynn said my father listened for what seemed like five minutes, then put the receiver on the coffee table and beckoned. The two men went outside, got into Dad's car and drove two blocks to the Conlon house on Valley Spring Lane. Climbing the front steps Dad gestured to Delynn to ring the doorbell. After a few moments Scoop breathlessly opened the front door, saw Delynn, and said, "Come on in, Alan, I'm on the phone with George Stevens."

Scoop and I walked into Yankee Stadium, decorated with World Series bunting, and found our seats on the third base line. It was game five between the Yankees and Dodgers, and we watched Yankee pitcher Don Larsen methodically shut out the Dodgers for eight innings. In the top of the ninth the young Dodger announcer Vin Scully spoke carefully, avoiding the no-hitter jinx, saying, "Let's take a deep breath as we go to the most dramatic ninth inning in the history of baseball." It was just a few minutes after three o'clock, when Dodger pinch hitter Dale Mitchell stood looking at a high fastball for a third strike, and catcher Yogi Berra sprinted to the mound and leapt into Don Larsen's arms.

Larsen had completed the only perfect game in World Series history, a record that still stands. It teed me up for another sort of history the following evening.

Dad and I arrived together for the black-tie premiere of *Giant* at the Roxy Theatre. Elizabeth, having hastily divorced Michael Wilding, arrived with her new beau Mike Todd. The audience cheered and the *New York Times* called it "the best film of the year—every scene and every moment is a pleasure." *Time* said it was "an act of singular artistic courage." Enthusiastic reviews and solid word of mouth led to box office joy for Jack Warner, and come Academy Awards time I would be at my father's side when he collected his second Oscar for directing.

Jack Warner continued to receive calls from the American Petroleum Institute complaining about the depletion allowance scene, but Serge Semenenko agreed to buy out brothers Harry Warner and Albert Warner, giving Jack sole control of the studio. Henry Ginsberg got his windfall by selling his share of *Giant* to investors for $900,000. Edna Ferber would sell her interest to Warner Bros. and collect $1,500,000, the greatest literary payoff in movie history. My father, after gambling on *Giant* for three years, believed in the film's long-term value and held on to his share—to be rewarded over the years by his belief in the test of time.

That Oscar night is now more than sixty years in the past and *Giant* has more than met the rigors of the passing decades. Friends often say that when *Giant* appears on television at home they become absorbed once again for the entire three hours and twenty minutes. Historians and critics now write of the way the film's penetrating insights into race, gender and class relate to America today. The closing scene is set in the Reata library. Leslie and Bick are reflecting on their lives, babysitting their grandchildren, a blond girl and a dark-haired boy in a playpen. The film, known for its grand scale, ends on an extreme close-up of the boy's brown eyes, as Bick, the patriarch, accepts that the future of the proud Benedict family name will be carried forward by his Hispanic American grandson.

The British historian Neil Sinyard wrote in 2019, "For an epic, *Giant* might seem deceptively modest. What is gigantic in the film is not the scale of its setting and action but the breadth of its humanity."

Rock Hudson, his wife, Phyllis, and the Stevenses at the Hollywood premiere of *Giant* at Grauman's Chinese Theater, 1953.

18

On the Town

I had been mustered out of the air force several months before the *Giant* premiere. My military paycheck had sustained me nicely for two years and I was now home in North Hollywood helping my father edit *Giant,* looking for work and spending idle time at Lakeside tuning up my golf game. When I last saw Elizabeth Taylor she suggested I call when I got back in town and come to her and Michael Wilding's house for dinner. One day, after a long bout of shyness, I rang the number she had given me. A housekeeper answered and soon after I heard Elizabeth's voice. She seemed happy to hear from me, inviting me to come to the house at seven the next evening.

My father was out of town so I borrowed his gray gullwing Mercedes 300SL, arguably the hottest car on the road in those days. I guess it gave me a feeling of security. I drove up Benedict Canyon, turned onto the curling road up the hill, and pulled into the porte cochere of 1275 Beverly Estates Drive, wondering who else might be invited for dinner. I sprung the 300SL door upward, lifted my rear to the doorsill, and swirled my feet to the pavement. The housekeeper showed me in as two small children, Elizabeth's sons with Michael, scampered by. Then Elizabeth entered in a short dark blue dress looking breathtaking. After a warm greeting she said, "Well, where are we going?"

I blinked. Then, rapidly processing the startling news that Elizabeth was planning to go *out* for dinner, I began calculating. I was not a man about town with a phone book of maître d's, so I punted. "What would you like, Elizabeth?" She said, airily, "Trader Vic's is always fun." I went to a phone and dialed information for Trader Vic's, then the number. The maître d' answered and I said, simply, "I wonder if you can have a table for two in fifteen minutes. The name is Stevens." He responded, matter-of-factly, "Certainly, come right over." I worried about having a table up to the expectations of my companion, but pride prevented me from dropping her name.

As we walked outside Elizabeth's violet eyes widened on seeing the gray jewel in her driveway. The process of advising her to sit on the doorsill and swing her legs over to get in was agreeable, as was sealing her in with the overhead door. Then, nestled in the cockpit, we roared down the winding road to Beverly Hills. It seems Michael Wilding was making a film in London, and I was now taking it in that I was driving the most beautiful woman in the world to dinner. The parkers at Trader Vic's were duly impressed by the car and its cargo as I pulled up and popped the gullwing doors. "You don't need a ticket," the lead man assured me. Elizabeth and I entered and walked the carpet toward the maître d' stand. I watched the captain assess us. He looked carefully at Miss Taylor, then, turning to me as we drew close, said with authority, "Mr. Stevens, your table is ready." It was my good fortune that this man knew enough about movies to connect the Stevens name with Elizabeth. He showed us to what I later would come to know as the much-preferred second room, and seated us at a corner table for two in large fan-like wicker chairs.

We ordered two Navy Grogs, a signature drink at Trader Vic's, and reminisced about good times in Marfa on *Giant*. Several people came over to say hello to Elizabeth, some of whom were friends of mine, including William Wyler and his wife Talli, and my old Harvard School chum Robert Wagner, who stopped by with Natalie Wood. After a delightful dinner we pulled out of Trader Vic's onto Wilshire Boulevard. "Why don't we go see Rock and surprise Phyllis," Elizabeth said, referring to Hudson's new bride, Phyllis Gates. So we drove east, turning up Doheny Drive to Rock's small hillside house above the Sunset Strip. We rang the bell, and the surprised Hudsons invited us for a nightcap. We told stories until Phyllis reminded Rock that he was due for makeup at 6:30 at Universal.

Elizabeth and I rumbled along Sunset Boulevard and ascended Beverly Estates Drive, and I wheeled the 300SL into the Wilding porte cochere. As I raised the passenger door for my companion to exit, I discovered she had become expert at swinging her legs around and landing gracefully. I had wondered just what our goodnight might be like, but when we reached the door she put her key in the lock and entered without looking back, saying over her shoulder, "I'll open some champagne." I followed her, feeling much like Montgomery Clift in a corresponding circumstance in *A Place in the Sun,* the outsider bemused by his good fortune. I helped with the Dom Perignon and soon we were sitting on the sofa, my blazer tossed casually on the adjoining chair. Conversation flowed freely in this unanticipated opportunity of sitting with a flute of champagne and the most attractive woman on the planet.

There was a light in the bedroom through the open door behind us, and at some point the phone rang. It was close to midnight. Elizabeth sighed, and with an annoyed roll of her eyes made her way to the bedroom. Music was playing in the living room, but fragments of the phone conversation could not be missed.

"Oh, Michael, it must be breakfast time in London." Then some indistinct conversation with Elizabeth sounding cross. Then I heard her say impatiently, "No, Michael . . . not *Douglas Fairbanks, Junior*."

This sentence was sobering. I realized that Elizabeth must have announced my midnight presence, her husband had misheard my name and she was correcting him. In any case, my cover was blown. By the time Elizabeth returned to the living room I'd placed my glass on the bar and put on my blazer. After what must have been a disagreeable transatlantic conversation, she cheerfully accepted my departure, and was full of thanks and a warm embrace for what she assured me was a wonderful evening.

In no time I was back in the sealed cockpit of the 300SL making my way over Coldwater Canyon to my mother's town house in the Valley where I was staying. Yes, I was going home to mama.

19

A Young Girl's Diary

Television was thriving in Hollywood in 1956 when I was looking for work. One of the most popular shows was *Dragnet,* the series centered on Sergeant Joe Friday of the Los Angeles Police Department. Friday's signature phrase—"Just the facts, ma'am"—was spoken by Jack Webb, the laconic former radio actor who produced, starred in and directed the series. I'd met Webb with my father, and he sent a cheerful letter of encouragement when I was hospitalized at Orlando Air Force Base, with an "if I can ever be helpful" closing. I went to see him at the old Republic lot in Studio City. He was about to make a feature film, *The D.I.,* based on a television drama by James Lee Barrett about a Marine Corps drill instructor at Parris Island. After an hour's conversation he invited me to come work with him. Jim Barrett and I were both young and feisty and ready with opinions, which Jack liked—up to a point. I came to relish those occasions when his patience ran out and in his irritation he would stand in his Marine sergeant pose and intone, in the voice loved by millions, "Stevens, you miserable shit!"

There was much to learn from the efficient and stylish way Webb ran his company. He was among the first to have IBM typewriters with a carefully chosen font. He had a nimble way of using teleprompters, shooting at a pace far different from my father, wherein we prepped, shot, edited and released *The D.I.* in six months. One of the most difficult challenges in Hollywood is to get your first directing job, and Jack took a chance letting me, at age twenty-five, direct a television pilot, *People,* that starred Ben Alexander, his sidekick from *Dragnet.* He then assigned me episodes of another series, *The D.A.'s Man,* enabling me to become a member of the Directors Guild. I was responding to opportunities that put me on the path of following my father's footsteps without ever making a calculated decision to do so. Having observed my father's wisdom and artistry

Stevens pére et fils, 1958.

firsthand, I had some internal doubt as to whether my skills would measure up. Yet the work was exciting and I was having a good time.

One day Dad invited me to lunch at the Polo Lounge at the Beverly Hills Hotel. There was mellow good feeling and affection whenever we met. He came with important news. His next film would be *The Diary of Anne Frank,* based on the Broadway play that dramatized the diary of a young Jewish girl hiding from the Nazis in Amsterdam during World War II. He had been looking for a story that could address his wartime experience, and in an odd way this one, even though confined to an attic, was to become his war film. "What would you think about coming over to Twentieth Century Fox and we make this film together?" he asked. Before the waiter brought the check we had agreed. I would join him as his associate producer and continue to direct television shows and pursue my own projects as time allowed.

In May 1957 Dad and I flew to the South of France where he served on the jury at the Cannes Festival, and I was provided a delightful plunge into the international film scene. We stayed at the belle epoque Carlton Hotel on the Croisette overlooking the Mediterranean, saw new jewels of European cinema, including Fellini's *Nights of Cabiria* and Bergman's *The Seventh Seal,* enjoyed gourmet dinners with filmmakers from around the world, and impromptu gatherings at the Carlton Terrace Bar. One evening I joined Greek director Michael Cacoyannis, actress Irene Pappas, matador Luis Miguel Dominguin, a young Israeli writer with a captivating smile, Yael Dayan, tanned and fit from her service in the Israeli military, and humor columnist for the *International Herald Tribune* Art Buchwald, who would become my lifelong pal. Yael, the daughter of heroic General Moshe Dayan, brightened my days and nights at the festival.

Dad and I rented a car and drove from Cannes to Munich, where we checked into the Bayerische Hof Hotel. He spent his first night in Germany since the winter of 1945 enjoying a luxurious suite instead of sleeping on cold ground in army gear. We rose early and on a gray morning drove to a nearby Bavarian town where we approached the Dachau concentration camp with its forbidding *Arbeit Macht Frei* black metal gate. I had seen the harrowing footage my father shot and edited for the Nuremberg Trials, and our walk through the site of such horrors was solemn. He was a man of extraordinary composure who revealed little of what was going on inside, but I sensed the intensity of his memories when he entered the crematorium. I discreetly took my Leica and snapped a picture of him standing stolidly in a tan raincoat with the stenciled word *"Brausbad,"* meaning shower bath, visible on the wall above him. His face told the story of another time.

We went next to France and parked on the coastal road at Saint-Aubin-sur-Mer on the Normandy shore, where we walked onto the sands of the beach code-named Juno where he came ashore on D-Day. As we looked out at the now tranquil seaside, he described that June morning in 1944 when HMS *Belfast*, positioned offshore, initiated the Allies' shelling at dawn. He told me of receiving permission from the admiral to go ashore with one cameraman and join the turmoil on the beach. We then drove inland through hedgerow country and found the area near Carentan where the Stevens Irregulars dug in during early fighting. As we drove through Caen I noted how many modern buildings there were in this old city. Dad mused in a tone of contrition, "We touched up this town pretty good," referring to the Allied barrage that hammered SS Panzer divisions occupying the city. As we drove through Normandy we could have been father and son tourists, but I was at the side of a master storyteller with his memories both haunting and humorous.

On the bluff at Colleville-sur-Mer overlooking Omaha Beach we were moved by the sea of white marble crosses marking the final resting places of ten thousand Americans. The story we were about to film made us conscious of the graves that were capped with Stars of David. That night Dad and I were huddled over our map and noticed the proximity of Amsterdam. He calculated that when he was in Malmedy during the Battle of the Bulge he had been less than a hundred and thirty kilometers from Anne Frank.

We were driving along a back road when we saw a German graves detail recovering the remains of soldiers buried in a meadow. We got out of the car for

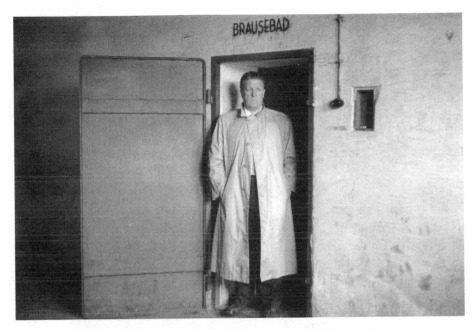

George Stevens returns to Dachau, a photograph taken by his son. May 1957.

a closer look. A stocky man in a black leather jacket stepped in our path, shouting, "*Raus! . . . Raus!*" and signaling us to leave. My father bristled and stared at the man before we walked to the car, where he mused with a smile about his transition from an officer in the conquering army to being bossed around by one of the vanquished.

The next morning in Amsterdam we pressed the buzzer at a modest building in the business district. An erect man with receding silver hair wearing a suit and tie opened the door. This was Otto Frank. He led us to a small office where coffee awaited on a wooden table, and introduced us to his wife, Fritzi, a woman in her fifties, who, like him, was a survivor of Auschwitz. Otto's first wife Edith had died there and their two daughters at Bergen-Belsen. Mr. Frank listened intently as we spoke over coffee about the film. This was his first look at the director to whom he had entrusted his daughter's story. Then, without comment, he went to a filing cabinet and pulled open a drawer. He removed an object and placed it on the table in front of us, carefully parting the cloth wrapping to reveal a small album with a red, white and beige plaid cover. We sat in silence. The pages before us bore Anne's distinctive penmanship and photos she had pasted in of her family and her favorite movie stars. This child had captured the world's imagination and in that moment we felt the weight and responsibility of telling her story.

George Stevens, Jr., holds Anne Frank's diary in Amsterdam, 1957.

Otto Frank's family had lived in Frankfurt for generations. He studied eco-nomics at Heidelberg and had been an officer in the German army in World War I, but in 1933, when Nazi persecution made life perilous for Jews, he moved his family to Amsterdam, where he started a small but thriving spice business in a four-story building at 263 Prinsengracht. When the Germans oc-cupied Amsterdam they ordered Jews to wear yellow Stars of David, and soon many were being arrested and shipped away. So in August 1942 Otto Frank took his family into hiding on the top floor of the spice factory.

Mr. Frank guided us to a taxi boat that took us along the canals to a build-ing standing in the middle of a tree-lined block. The spice business was long gone so it was a vacant building that Otto Frank, my father and I entered. We climbed four flights of darkened stairs to reach what Anne called the Secret An-nex, space behind a false bookcase where the Franks and another family hid for two years. The room was bare with no furnishings, only faded spots on the walls where pictures once hung.

Mr. Frank showed emotion for the first time as he led us to the spot where the Green Police snatched his briefcase and shook the contents to the floor. He said his captors gathered up money, jewelry and silverware before herding the

Otto Frank and my father explore the Frank family hiding place at 263 Prinsengracht.

two families down the stairs. In a hurry and interested only in items of obvious value, the men left on the floor the diary that would one day bear witness to the outrages of Hitler's persecution and find more than thirty million readers.

The Diary of Anne Frank was the first American film centered on the experience we know as the Holocaust, although the word was not yet used in that context. Frances Goodrich and Albert Hackett wrote the screenplay based on their adaptation of Anne's diary for the Broadway stage. We discussed the possibility of "taking the story outside," movie parlance for expanding the scope of a play by creating new scenes that took the characters to different locales, but my father decided that the story's power came from the confinement of the family in hiding. This led to the construction on Twentieth Century Fox's Stage 14 of an ambitious set with a profile that enabled us to photograph four levels—the top floor hiding place and its attic skylight above three floors of spice factory offices and machines. The top floor was duplicated for convenience at ground level, where most of the filming took place.

We shot for 112 days on Stage 14 between March and August 1958 with the primary cast of nine actors working every day. Joseph Schildkraut as Otto Frank and Gusti Huber as his wife Edith reprised their Broadway roles. Susan Strasberg, who portrayed Anne on the stage, was deemed too old, so casting director

The three-story multipurpose set designed by George Davis shows the spice factory on the ground floor—and the family in the hiding place, upper left. The camera was able to crane upward and reveal the entire building. The duplicate hiding place on the ground level was built on springs that shook the structure during bombing scenes.

Owen MacLean and I managed a worldwide search to find a girl to play Anne, which led us to Millie Perkins, who Dad decided captured Anne's spirit. Diane Baker, Shelley Winters, Gusti Huber, Lou Jacobi, Richard Beymer and Ed Wynn rounded out the cast. Wynn was chosen for Dr. Dussel, the elderly bachelor dentist. My father knew that Ed, in his seventies and a veteran of vaudeville, could bring humanity and humor to the role.

Fox's new CinemaScope widescreen projection process was suited for outdoor epics, but its wide horizontal frame posed challenges in the confined hiding place. My father proposed that the process not be used, but Fox chairman Spyros Skouras believed CinemaScope was central to his company's future, so Dad had to find ways to work with it. With his cameraman's eye he recognized that the anamorphic lenses were faulty, distorting faces in close-ups. We met with Robert Gottschalk, head of a company called Panavision, whose new anamorphic lenses had no distortion, and conducted a covert experiment, smuggling a

Panavision lens on the lot and shooting a close-up test of Millie Perkins, first with the Fox lenses and then with Panavision lenses. We intercut the two tests and ran the reel for Sol Halperin, head of the Fox camera department, in the studio theater. It became a comic opera. Millie's face would go in alternating shots from a beautifully drawn classical face to one with swollen cheeks. Halperin, knowing the depth of Skouras' commitment to CinemaScope, soberly insisted he saw no difference. Realizing we were at a dead end, we shot *Anne Frank* with Fox's lenses, but for important close-ups of Millie Perkins used a normal spherical lens, then blew up the shots to fill the CinemaScope screen, which gave true renderings of Millie's face. Eventually Panavision became the industry standard and Skouras was forced to abandon Fox's lenses.

The Diary of Anne Frank required considerable ensemble rehearsal. My father liked to watch the scenes unfold and give actors an opportunity to introduce their ideas. He would circle the set with his viewfinder looking for camera angles, making adjustments to the placement of actors.

Joseph Schildkraut was born in Vienna and his mannerisms from the Old World were helpful, but he had a tendency to upstage other performers. In one rehearsal, after my father settled in on one side of the set with his viewfinder, Schildkraut shifted his movements so as to be facing the director, leading Millie Perkins to end up with her back to the viewfinder. My father instructed the crew to put marks on the floor to set each actor's position. Then he told the grips to take out the back wall and put the camera on the opposite side, thereby leaving Schildkraut in the least conspicuous place, facing a wall, not the camera. Schildkraut would eventually be covered with close-ups but Dad's unpredictable approach encouraged the cast to concentrate on the scene and forget about the camera.

A hallmark of a Stevens set was silence. He wanted the actors emotionally tuned, on the right wavelength. On many sets after a scene is rehearsed the assistant director shouts, "Quiet!" Assistants echo the call and a loud bell rings. After setting an emotional tone in rehearsal, Dad didn't want noise to alter the mood, so he arranged for red lights to go on without any shouting. He would gesture for the camera to roll, then say quietly to the actors, "All right—action."

He liked to have music available, and on *Anne Frank* he took this to a new level. The prop department built a six-by-three-foot gray box that stood four feet high on wheels. On top were three reel-to-reel tape decks. He had a control panel next to his chair and a library of tapes from which he would select three he wanted for a particular scene. This sound system was dubbed the Lease Breaker. On one deck my father might place an emotional piece of music, like Franz Waxman's love theme from *A Place in the Sun*, that would serve like a pitch pipe, getting actors who had been in the midst of pounding hammers into a pensive mood. For the scene when Amsterdam is bombed at night he used Hitler's thundering speeches and the crowd responding, "*Sieg heil, sieg heil!*" plus bombs, airplanes and antiaircraft fire. After a scene was completed and the crew had to tear down a wall and revamp the set, he would get them moving with the University of Southern California fight song.

Casting director Owen MacLean arrived with six candidates for the roles of two German soldiers. The men were beefy and hard looking, what we used to call Otto Preminger Germans, after the portly actor-director who specialized in playing Nazis during the war. My father excused the men, then said to MacLean, "Bring me the boy next door." When the casting veteran looked perplexed, he added, "Bring me a boy from that Annette Funicello picture shooting on Stage 12." He didn't want to allow audiences the comfort of distancing themselves from the German soldiers because of their appearance. Instead they would see someone who could be their own son.

We fell behind schedule and at first, because the rushes were superb, the studio was patient. But with August approaching they proposed that location filming in Amsterdam should be delegated to a "second unit," something Dad normally avoided. On Friday morning he came by my office. "Considering where we stand, it makes sense that the work in Amsterdam be separated," he said. "I'd like you to head the location unit and direct the shooting over there." My first impulse was to question whether I could rise to his standards, especially on this film that meant so much to us both. "For me," he said, "it's a matter of taste and sensibility." "All right," I replied, "but I'll need an excellent cameraman," adding, half joking, "someone like Jack Cardiff." It turned out to be no joke. The master British cinematographer of *Black Narcissus* and *The Red Shoes* was between pictures and agreed to do it.

Three weeks later I arrived in Amsterdam and had drinks at the Krasnapolsky Hotel with one of the most charming and fun-loving men I would ever know. Cardiff came over from London with his wife Julie and a friend of hers, Lydia Stevens, who was separated from the actor Warren Stevens. Jack and I discussed ways to make the black-and-white images capture the look and mood of wartime Amsterdam, and Jack, who deferred to me as director despite the difference in age and experience, loved the challenge. He was also a bon vivant and proposed a fine dinner for good luck. He took Julie, Lydia and me to an elegant restaurant. By the second bottle of vintage Margaux I was feeling fine about the job that would begin at dawn with this gifted cinematographer at my side. At that point Jack raised his glass. "Let's drink to the good work ahead of us," he said. Then, with a devilish twinkle, "George, I think you should know one thing. I've never shot a frame in black-and-white." Jack had come up through the ranks at

Cinematographer Jack Cardiff, in raincoat and hat. George Stevens, Jr., seated, directing a scene at Anne Frank's hiding place, Amsterdam, 1958.

Technicolor and never had reason to shoot in black-and-white. I watched him revel at my momentary discomfort

The dinner was delightful, especially so since Lydia and I had discovered one another. She was tall with fine features and dark hair. Her father was a Russian-born vaudevillian who had a popular night club in Paris. She had inherited a sly sense of humor. In those days hotels were vigilant about checking the marital status of couples and the dual Stevens passports were a convenience. I not only had a congenial and brilliant collaborator in Cardiff, but a sympathetic and beguiling companion in Lydia.

Outside the building on the Prinsengracht that we had explored with Otto Frank a year earlier there was now barbed wire and wartime rubble on the sidewalks. Onlookers, fascinated by the first sight of German uniforms in more than a decade, watched on a rainy night as we shot a scene of German soldiers firing at a fleeing resistance suspect. Cardiff was bold and didn't want the scene flooded with light.

We shipped the first night's negative to Hollywood for processing. It was two days before we had a report. Cardiff came to me holding a terse cable from

Fox camera department head Sol Halperin, who had been frosty toward our choice of a British cinematographer: "Cardiff's footage printing on light one." This was notice that in Halperin's opinion the film was underexposed. When we returned to the hotel a second cable awaited us. This one from George Stevens, a rare breed: a gifted cameraman who became a great director.

> GEORGE STEVENS JR
>
> KRASNAPOLSKY HOTEL AMSTERDAM
>
> JUST LOOKED AT THE FIRST DAYS WORK. NIGHT SHOTS WITH THE
> MILITARY POLICE AND WATCHMAN. THE FILM IS ABSOLUTELY
> MAGNIFICENT. VERY BOLD AND EXCITING. BEST REGARDS TO MR
> CARDIFF THE OTHER GENTLEMEN AND YOURSELF.
>
> STEVENS

We completed our work in Amsterdam and I returned to join the editing process. Once more my father had gathered a vast amount of film and was in the projection room with controls next to his chair. Albums identifying every take were prepared by the chief film editor, David Bretherton, and his bearded young assistant with hair to his shoulders and a mellow smile, Hal Ashby, who would one day find fame as a director.

Dad and I spent a good part of every day in projection room 7A. The challenge was to keep the story moving forward within the confines of the hiding place. Watching him seamlessly integrate the scenes I shot in Amsterdam with his own work was deeply satisfying. However, after the invigorating challenge of directing the location shooting I was beginning to feel that time was standing still. "Dad, this film looks awfully good," I said, one afternoon. "Why don't you just lock it up?" I shall never forget his reply. "Just think how many hours people will spend watching this film over the years. Don't you think it's worth us spending a little more of our time working to make it a better experience for them?"

While we were editing Spyros Skouras proposed that my father make *The Greatest Story Ever Told.* Twentieth Century Fox had acquired Fulton Oursler's popular telling of the life of Jesus, a project close to Skouras' heart. Charlie Feldman, who had been my father's agent before the war, led elaborate negotiations and ensured that my father retained the control he needed. Moreover Skouras was prepared to provide co-ownership of the film and a one million dollar fee, quadruple the going rate for premier directors. We began preparation of *The Greatest Story.*

The Diary of Anne Frank opened in March 1959 to critical acclaim and received eight Academy Award nominations. We went to Cannes for a red carpet "out of competition" closing night premiere. It was Millie Perkins' first film festival. Renowned poet, painter and filmmaker Jean Cocteau was chairman of the jury, and as the lights came up in Festival Hall he strode over to Millie in his cape, doffing his hat and bowing to kiss her hand. Millie, a cultivated but shy person at her first premiere, not keen on the spotlight, was entranced.

Years later Dr. Michael Berenbaum, director of the Shoah Foundation, described *The Diary of Anne Frank* as "the earliest attempt to take the Holocaust from the private domain of a bereaved community and to bring it out to humanity as a whole—that is its power." At the Academy Awards Dad was nominated for best director and best picture. We watched his dear friend and former partner Willy Wyler win both for *Ben-Hur*. Shelley Winters took one home for best supporting actress in *Anne Frank*, as did George Davis for production design and William Mellor for cinematography. And, perhaps best of all, the former Texaco Fire Chief and pioneer vaudevillian Ed Wynn gained enormous satisfaction at age seventy-two from his nomination for best supporting actor.

The *Diary of Anne Frank* had consumed close to two years, a long hire for a fellow in his twenties, but it was one of my richest life experiences.

20

The Unexpected

In 1960 I was working with my father on *The Greatest Story Ever Told* while exploring projects of my own. I loved working with him, nourished by his companionship and humor. I enjoyed the reflected prestige, always pleased when identified as "George's son" or "George's boy," while conscious that the recognition was simply for being the son of a prominent father. The magnitude of my father's talent and experience left me with buried questions about my own capability. I joked that I might devote my entire life to becoming the second best film director in my family. But it was an invigorating life with a bachelor's pad in the Hollywood Hills, a new Mercedes 220SL convertible, a passport into the movie world social scene, and blossoming creative challenges.

I was blessed with opportunities to direct prestigious television shows like *Peter Gunn* and *Alfred Hitchcock Presents*—a job that included a stimulating acquaintance with the Master of Suspense himself and working with excellent actors. I was comfortable being on sets with people many years my senior and taking charge. I dealt with actors in the manner of my father—leaving latitude for them to find their way, taking them aside for private conversations when necessary.

Hollywood was changing. Spyros Skouras sold half of the Twentieth Century Fox studio to a developer to build Century City, and the MCA talent agency bought Universal Pictures to produce television. A new generation of cutting-edge comics and satirists like Mort Sahl, Jonathan Winters and Don Rickles were making us feel smart at Hollywood clubs, as were Lenny Bruce, Mike Nichols and Elaine May in the East.

I wanted to make a film of Hawthorne's *The Scarlet Letter*. The procedure with public domain material was to register the title with the Motion Picture

Producers Association, but the request from the newly formed Stevens Company came back in third place behind Selznick Productions and Selznick International Ltd. One morning my secretary Pat Woodward buzzed. I picked up and heard the gravelly voice of the producer of *Gone with the Wind.* "George, it's David Selznick. I hope you'll come up and have lunch with me." I felt I had won the lottery. Selznick, a bearish, spectacled man with easy charm, greeted me at the door of the Tower Road house he shared with his actress wife Jennifer Jones. We had a delightful lunch discussing how to produce Nathaniel Hawthorne's story of Hester Prynne. I felt my fortunes soaring until David said, almost parenthetically, "We will surround Jennifer with other fine actors." I was taken aback. David's plan was to cast his forty-year-old wife in the part of the young adulteress. That was our last conversation about *The Scarlet Letter,* but my disappointment was compensated a thousand times over by David and Jennifer's friendship—David for the few years he had left, and Jennifer for decades.

In *The Greatest Story Ever Told* my father wanted to tell the story of Jesus in a way that would engage Christians and nonbelievers alike. He was also determined to "take the mischief out of the story" by ridding it of the anti-Semitism that too often infects the narrative. Expansive research into the four gospels and other religions covered the walls of our conference room at Fox. Dad, who found young people stimulating, enlisted colleagues of mine: James Lee Barrett as a collaborator on the screenplay, and as story and production assistants Antonio Vellani, an aspiring producer from Italy, and Billy Hale, my fellow director of training films from our days at Orlando Air Force Base.

We went to Europe and the Middle East for more research, stopping in Rome for a private audience with Pope John XXIII. He was a breathtaking presence and warmly expressed his belief in the importance of the film. The next afternoon offered a sharp contrast when Federico Fellini arranged a private screening of his new film *La Dolce Vita,* which opens with a farcical scene of a helicopter flying over Rome toward St. Peter's with a statue of Jesus suspended beneath it—a second coming of Christ. The film was condemned by the Vatican, but its brilliance took Fellini beyond the art house circuit to the forefront of world cinema. In Istanbul we met the bearded six-foot, four-inch Athenagoras I, charismatic patriarch of the Greek Orthodox church, who had a passionate belief in ecumenical unity and believed our approach to the story would enhance his cause. We looked at holy sites in Lebanon, Syria, Jordan and Israel, reinforcing my father's conviction that the landscapes of the Middle East had

Stevens, Sr., and Carl Sandburg, foreground, in a *Greatest Story Ever Told* script conference with, left to right, Toni Vellani, James Lee Barrett, Stevens, Jr., and Billy Hale. 20th Century Fox Studio, 1961.

eroded over centuries and that dramatic vistas of the American West would more effectively represent the Holy Land.

Toni Vellani and I stopped in Paris and came upon my father's pal William Saroyan in the Hotel Georges V lobby. I introduced myself and over a drink told him how much I treasured the copy of *The Human Comedy* he sent me before D-Day. Saroyan explained that he was at the George V because he had run up a gambling debt at the famed Aviation Club on the Champs-Élysées, and Darryl Zanuck, the head of Twentieth Century Fox, who was having a public romance with French singer Juliette Greco, offered him $50,000 to write a screenplay for Greco to star in. Zanuck provided Saroyan a room at the hotel where he agreed to stay until the script was finished. The next morning I found the screenplay at my door with a note from Bill. It was a whimsical "Saroyanesque" story that I was certain would never be filmed. Greco's character was a woman living in the George V with a talking dog. Zanuck did nothing with the script and Saroyan took his fifty grand to the Aviation Club with predictable results. But he got back on his feet and later wrote of his proclivity: "I certainly didn't gamble away every penny. I drank some of it away, and I bought a raincoat."

Twentieth Century Fox chairman Spyros Skouras was passionate about *The Greatest Story Ever Told* and believed my father would make an extraordinary film. He was having problems in Rome with *Cleopatra,* where his star Elizabeth Taylor had left Eddie Fisher for her British costar Richard Burton. Their frolic filled the tabloids as delays exploded the budget. We met with Skouras at the Fox Studio to discuss the *Greatest Story.* He was the canny immigrant son of a Greek sheepherder who spoke with a heavy accent ("Spyros has been here for thirty years but it still sounds like he's arriving next week," quipped Bob Hope). We explained that the script included brief cameo roles in which we intended to cast prominent actors. Spyros was devoted to the Greek Orthodox religion and keen about the role of Mary Magdalene. He asked my father who he was considering.

Musing, Dad—referring to the star of the two films for which he won Oscars—said, "Elizabeth might want to do that part for us." He noticed Skouras blanch and added quickly, "It's a small part, Spyros . . . a vignette. It will only take a couple of days. We can work around any delays she might cause."

"George," Spyros pleaded, clutching his yellow worry beads, "that woman is a nightmare. Even if it's only a *vinaigrette* . . . I don't want her in this picture."

Diversity was one of our goals. My father was aware that the Holy Land in the time of Jesus was a crossroad of cultures and ethnic groups, so people of color would be seen throughout the film, including the Inbal Dancers brought from Israel, who added authenticity. Simon of Cyrene, the man who helps Jesus carry his cross on the path to crucifixion, was usually played by a white man, but Dad hoped we could enlist Sidney Poitier. To illustrate the concept an artist did an arresting drawing of Poitier as Simon of Cyrene for a press announcement should he agree to play it.

I knew Sidney only slightly but flew to New York to see him. We sat across from one another at the new and short-lived restaurant Sardi's East. At six foot three he was an imposing presence, extremely courteous yet reserved. He had accepted the meeting without asking the topic. I told him of our goals for the

Greatest Story and my father's intention to enlist prominent actors for pivotal smaller roles, then described the sequence with Simon of Cyrene and Jesus. Lifting the drawing from beside my seat, I said, "My father would be honored if you would agree to play this role." Sidney's eyes widened as he looked at the image. I expected him to ask for time to talk with his agent or to simply say his schedule was crowded. After a moment he spoke in what I like to call his "princely" manner, choosing each word with care.

"Please tell your father I will consider it a privilege to work with him."

I had made my first offer to a star and it was accepted. I was proud to have delivered for my Dad.

He was troubled that every one of the assistant directors hired to run the *Greatest Story* set on location in Utah was white, so he asked the Directors Guild about Black members and was told there was just one—a television stage manager at NBC. Wendell Franklin remembered the day he was assigning spaces in the NBC parking lot when he was told he had a call for an interview at George Stevens Productions. "I was paralyzed," he recalled in his memoir. "I couldn't believe I was sitting in the office of this man—a great director and a past president of the Guild. All he said was, 'Well, are you ready to go to work?'" Franklin described the hostility he faced when he arrived on location, and how the lead assistant director insisted he sign a paper promising he would return to television at the end of the picture. "Everyone in the production office was trying to get rid of me," he said, "but Stevens was not going to have it." Franklin wrote that there was never a biblical picture that cast so many people of color: "I honor the Stevens picture because people of my race were used throughout, in every essence, even down to soldiers."

Carl Sandburg, who earned Pulitzer Prizes for his poetry and his six-volume biography of Abraham Lincoln, and my father admired one another's work. Carl, at age eighty-two, agreed to work on the screenplay of the *Greatest Story*. We arranged for him to have Marilyn Monroe's spacious dressing room that my father had used as his office during *Anne Frank*. He would arrive mid-morning from the Bel Air Hotel with his shock of white hair parted at the center framing his chiseled features, his sturdy right hand clutching a black briefcase harboring copies of his books. Carl would look at me, in the green corduroy jacket I often wore, and intone, "*Hello, corr . . . durroy . . . boy.*"

Monroe heard that Sandburg was in her old dressing room and came to visit. I had the prime assignment of greeting Marilyn and introducing her to Carl. Her blond hair cut short and pushed back with a bandana, she blended reverence for the eminent writer with breathtaking allure. Carl became ceremonial and flirtatious, reaching into his case and pulling out books to inscribe in his bold black script, spinning a story in his soothing voice for each one. He then looked closely at his visitor and purred, "*You're* not the trouble with the world." It was a phrase Carl reserved for special people and it came with a twinkle. Marilyn was in awe.

Carl was a discerning observer of the world around him. One day during the 1960 campaign President Eisenhower was being interviewed on television, and in support of Nixon made a strong assertion about private enterprise being the bedrock of the American way. Carl growled, "Ike has been on the public payroll ever since the day he left the creamery in Abilene."

At a press conference announcing his association with the *Greatest Story,* he was asked by a *Variety* reporter if this would be his first screenplay. He responded that in 1930 D. W. Griffith asked him to write the script for *Abraham Lincoln.* "I asked for $10,000 and Griffith wouldn't pay it. So I said, 'Nuthin' doing.'" There was a silence and the reporter followed up. "So what happened, Mr. Sandburg?" Referring to his fellow Civil War historian Stephen Vincent Benet, Carl muttered, "Stevie Benet did it for five."

On another occasion we were watching television and a young director of modest reputation was being interviewed. He began a response with the words, "Well, as an artist I . . ." Carl turned to me and declared, "Artist is a *praise* word. You don't call *yourself* an artist."

It occurred to me that I never heard my father or his fellow masters refer to themselves as artists, preferring to let their work speak for itself.

A nervous Twentieth Century Fox board feared that *Cleopatra* might bring down the studio and Skouras was struggling to retain his job. We had a visit from two Wall Street bankers, members of the Fox board. One began, "I always become terribly anxious when I set foot in this movie studio atmosphere." My father nodded, recognizing the implication that frivolous people were at large. "Do you remember 1930?" he asked. Then, referring to his days as a cameraman for Laurel and Hardy during the Depression, he said, "Everything I had was in the First National Bank in Culver City—it closed with all my savings. So I get a little nervous around bankers."

Not long after that Skouras notified us that Fox had decided not to proceed with *The Greatest Story Ever Told.* We were soon on a plane to New York accompanied by the audacious agent Charlie Feldman. He demanded a meeting for Dad with the entire Fox board to which they reluctantly acceded. My father summoned his Clarence Darrow skills and made a compelling case about the violation of his contract and the damages that would result, leading the board to make a beneficial settlement that enabled us to take the picture elsewhere.

Arthur Krim and Bob Benjamin, the widely admired leaders of United Artists, picked up the project and our work continued.

This was the summer of the Democratic Convention in Los Angeles. I favored Adlai Stevenson but was swept away by John Kennedy's thrilling speech outdoors at the Los Angeles Coliseum, where he first said, "We stand today on the edge of a New Frontier," and by his inspiring challenge at his inaugural, "Ask not what your country can do for you, ask what you can do for your country."

Among my friends on the Fox lot was a writer, Leslie Stevens. One day we read a report in the morning paper that Jacqueline Kennedy was planning a goodwill trip to Pakistan. We decided it would be a good subject—in the "ask not" spirit—for a documentary we could produce to demonstrate America's concern for other countries.

One of Kennedy's most noteworthy appointments was of America's most respected newsman, Edward R. Murrow, to head the United States Information Agency. Leslie and I wrote to Murrow proposing that we make a film, pro bono, about Mrs. Kennedy's trip that could be shown overseas. "The key, as we see it," we wrote, "is that she comes to learn from Pakistan: who its people are, what they hope for, their wants and needs, their culture and accomplishments." We added that we felt Mrs. Kennedy's warm personality and intense curiosity made her ideal for such a film.

A few weeks later *Variety* reported that Murrow was coming to Hollywood to speak to senior figures in the motion picture industry at a Sunday night dinner at Chasen's. Leslie and I hadn't received a reply to our letter, so we sent a request to Murrow's office urging that he allow time to meet with some younger people when in Hollywood. To our delight he agreed and we set up a meeting at the Directors Guild on the Friday afternoon he arrived for his Sunday speech. Paul Newman, three young producers, George Englund, Alan Pakula and Richard Zanuck, and writers Gore Vidal, Stewart Stern and Ivan Moffat were there.

Murrow stepped out of a black limousine at three p.m., wearing dark-rimmed glasses and a dark blue chalk stripe Savile Row suit. His keen intelligence and reporter's curiosity blended with his wry humor, and he seemed to enjoy discussing the ways in which film could enhance America's image overseas. There was talk of a nonprofit film foundation for making documentaries and providing opportunities to young filmmakers who wanted to tell America's story.

The next day I was reading on the balcony of my small bachelor pad in the Hollywood Hills when Samuel Goldwyn, Jr., called. "George," he said, "Ed Murrow is staying at my father's house and he wonders if you could come by and meet with him on Sunday." Surprised and intrigued, I asked if he knew why

Murrow wanted to see me. "Ed's looking for someone to run motion picture operations at USIA." I responded quickly, "Sam, I'm now my father's partner. We're preparing *The Greatest Story Ever Told* and I'm fully committed. I wouldn't want to waste Mr. Murrow's time." Sam understood and we signed off. Twenty minutes later he called back. "Come to my father's house at one o'clock tomorrow. Ed says you won't be wasting his time."

I drove up the curved hillside driveway above the Beverly Hills Hotel and parked in Samuel Goldwyn's shaded courtyard, noticing the famous Sunday croquet game under way on the lawn, a contest that involved heavy wagers and skilled players like Louis Jourdan, Tyrone Power, Darryl Zanuck and Mike Romanoff. Murrow and I sat in the Goldwyn living room. He lit a Camel and I a Chesterfield. He spoke about his work at USIA and I asked what it was like working with President Kennedy. Murrow described the president's steadiness during the recent Berlin crisis, before adding, "He's a very impressive young man." Hearing our president referred to as a young man amused me, at age twenty-nine. Murrow asked me about the Jacqueline Kennedy idea. Earlier he had mentioned that people who helped USIA's work might be invited to dinner at the White House. I was describing our film proposal when I caught myself and said, "I'm not looking for a dinner invitation." Raising one dark eyebrow, Murrow fixed me with a steady look.

"You wouldn't want to come to Washington?" And after a pause, "I believe you could make a difference."

It sent a shiver through me. This exceptional man, whose broadcasts from London I listened to during the war and whose reporting led to the downfall of Senator Joseph McCarthy, had sized me up and was now offering me a job. I gathered myself, explained the obligation to my father, and how it wouldn't be right for me to leave him. We parted with Ed saying he would welcome a visit in Washington "so you can see what we're doing."

Three days later my father and I were walking to lunch on the Fox lot and Murrow's name came up. I hadn't told him of our meeting so I described the offer to go to Washington. He stopped walking and turned to me. "You just may have to do it." There was no elaboration. It was a father sensing this was an opportunity for his son to find a place of his own. Or, perhaps, a place in the sun. The burden to him was secondary. It didn't occur to me at the time, but he was teaching me how to be a father.

I flew to Washington and met with Murrow at his Pennsylvania Avenue office. We talked about USIA. He explained that the agency produced three hundred documentaries a year to help the world better understand our country. "I believe the quality of USIA films can be elevated—that they can be more persuasive," he said. Sensing my apprehension that I might disappear in his twelve-thousand-person bureaucracy, he offered knowing assurance, a phrase from his North Carolina roots: "We won't hide your light under a bushel."

I promised he would have an answer in the morning, then set out on a wintry walk toward Washington's historic National Mall weighing pros and cons, including trading an $80,000 a year salary for the top foreign service rate of $18,000, and putting aside an ascending career in Hollywood. Soon I found myself at the Washington Monument. I went inside and decided that by the time I reached the top, I would make my decision. Eight hundred ninety-eight steps later I looked out over the majestic vista of the memorials to Jefferson and Lincoln and the Potomac River beyond. And I decided.

I was the boy throwing his cap over the wall—I would give myself a new opportunity. I would find out what was on the other side.

PART FOUR

A NEW FRONTIER

Edward R. Murrow, director of the United States Information Agency, Lionel Mosely, personnel director, and George Stevens, Jr., February 1, 1962, Washington, DC.

21

Telling America's Story

I had a nice surprise on a frigid first day of February 1962, when I walked past the motto "Telling America's Story to the World" and reported for duty at the United States Information Agency. I discovered that my third-floor corner office in the twelve-story building at 1776 Pennsylvania Avenue was just one flight of stairs below that of Edward R. Murrow. I was eight weeks shy of my thirtieth birthday and had seen my share of men of accomplishment, but I looked upon Murrow as a beacon of integrity and was proud to be working for him. Like many, I was inspired by his 1958 speech at the Radio-Television News Directors Association Convention, where he declared that television "can teach, it can illuminate, and it can even inspire. But it can do so only to the extent that humans are determined to use it to those ends. Otherwise it is merely wires and lights in a box."

At USIA he would marshal that idea in service to his country.

Ed's right-hand man sat in a small office across from his. Reed Harris, gray-haired, soft-spoken, in his fifties, showed me into Ed's office where I was welcomed with a handshake and a smile, and the news that Murrow would swear me in at his director's meeting in the afternoon. I learned that in 1953 Harris had been forced out of the State Department as a security risk by Senator Joseph McCarthy and was later interviewed on Murrow's CBS exposé of the Wisconsin senator. Harris was the first person Murrow hired at USIA, introducing him at a senior staff meeting in his understated fashion: "Gentlemen, I want to welcome back Reed Harris after an absence of eight years." A foreign service officer recalled, "These men around the table were old hands. They remembered. The tears started running down their faces—the McCarthy Era was over." This was the nature of the man I had signed up with, and USIA veterans told me that career officers were punching above their weight in response to Murrow's leadership.

The agency's mission was to tell America's story around the world through the Voice of America radio, an International Press Service, the Motion Picture Service that I was to lead, and by public affairs specialists stationed at more than two hundred United States Information Service posts abroad. The law that established USIA restricted its programming to overseas distribution—a congressional caveat to assure that agency funds not be used to influence American public opinion for political purposes.

Murrow made just one request when he discussed the USIA job with Kennedy. He asked for and received a seat on the National Security Council so he would have a voice in framing the foreign policy that USIA would be called upon to defend. As the veteran newsman put it to the young president, "I want to be in on the take-offs as well as the crash landings." He established "themes of emphasis" to assure that USIA media services were speaking with one voice: the Alliance for Progress, civil rights, our quest in outer space and the pursuit of peace. It was the height of the Cold War and we were trying to persuade the world that our democratic system was better than the communist way. Murrow described our job as "trying to make United States policy everywhere intelligible and wherever possible palatable."

I was surprised to see a newsreel crew on hand at my swearing in. I was caught up in the sound of Murrow's famous voice reciting the oath of office for me to repeat, and only later understood that this Fox Movietone crew was one of the units the Motion Picture Service hired regularly, and that their presence had to do more with currying favor than breaking news. As we left the room Ed handed me a small booklet. "Have you read the Federalist Papers?" he asked. "It's worth your time." Murrow must have felt his young Hollywood recruit would benefit from the ideas of Alexander Hamilton and James Madison on the nature of the government he would be serving.

The Motion Picture Service had a substantial staff in Washington and men and women on the ground at USIA posts overseas. We were expected to produce three hundred documentaries a year and distribute them in as many as eighty languages in more than a hundred countries—in theaters, on television, in schools, at libraries and on mobile units in the developing world. When President Eisenhower established USIA in 1953 its first director made a contract with Cecil B. DeMille to advise on motion pictures and put Turner Shelton, a conservative bureaucrat, in charge. Historian Nicholas Cull, in his book *The Cold War and the United States Information Agency,* describes USIA films made during the Eisenhower years as "stiff and ideologically charged." Murrow wasn't getting the kind of films he wanted from Shelton and took a risk replacing him with a person with limited executive experience.

I was in a new city and in charge of a complex operation with worldwide reach—yet somehow didn't feel out of my depth. I was stepping into a new flowing stream and it seemed navigable. Anthony Guarco, my deputy, was a veteran civil servant nearly twice my age. Down-to-earth and a straight shooter, Tony knew that Murrow hired me because he wanted more compelling films, so he used his bureaucratic know-how to achieve our objectives, occasionally talking me down from ideas that were a bridge too far. I arrived with an outsider's skeptical view of the civil service, but soon came to respect Tony and others working around me. Turner Shelton stopped by and introduced me to his right-hand woman in a small office adjoining mine, assuring me that her expertise was indispensable. I sensed otherwise and Guarco did me the great service of arranging for Patricia Woodward, my assistant at Twentieth Century Fox, to be hired, providing me with a bright, energetic and loyal right hand.

The work was intense and exhilarating. No longer did *Daily Variety* and the *Hollywood Reporter* sit atop my inbox. Each morning stacks of classified cables arrived from embassies in Addis Ababa, Moscow and New Delhi, assessing political issues and providing reaction to agency films. These were my primers on international affairs. I never dreamed of participating in government at a high level and loved the challenges and responsibility. Colleagues told me that this was the most exciting time ever to be in Washington. It certainly felt like it to me.

As a new bachelor in town, invitations arrived from Washington hostesses seeking an "extra man," including one from Mr. and Mrs. R. Sargent Shriver to a black-tie dinner on February 13, 1962. It was a celebration of the recent marriage of our new ambassador to Denmark William McCormick Blair and his enchanting and accomplished wife Deeda. Eunice Shriver was the eldest surviving sister of President Kennedy and Sarge was the charismatic director of the new Peace Corps. Snow was falling as I guided my tiny rental car on slushy streets to the Shriver house on River Road. An orchestra was playing when I arrived and Senator Hubert Humphrey was holding court in a group that included Ethel Kennedy, the wife of the attorney general. Robert McNamara and McGeorge Bundy stood at the bar with the British ambassador, David Ormsby-Gore.

At dinner I was seated at a rectangular table for ten, directly across from Newton N. Minow, the thirty-eight-year-old chairman of the Federal Communications Commission who the previous year had made his maiden speech to the National Association of Broadcasters, famously declaring that American television was "a vast wasteland." I was delighted to get to know Minow and we talked across the table for much of the dinner. On my left was an attractive woman whose place card read, "Mrs. Smith." I would have spent less time talking with Minow had I been worldly enough to know that Mrs. Smith was the president's sister, Jean Kennedy Smith. Before leaving Los Angeles I had been taken by my producer friend George Englund to lunch at Romanoff's with Patricia Lawford, also a Kennedy sister, and Pat must have passed the word, hence my invitation to the Shrivers and my favored seating. Jean and I later became friends but Kennedys have long memories and my innocent gaffe was not quickly forgotten.

There was dancing after dinner. I was savoring a Scotch and water toward the rear of the Shriver's circular entrance hall, enjoying my good fortune, when the front door burst open with a wintry gust. Through the door, hatless with no coat, glided John Fitzgerald Kennedy in a tuxedo, followed by Lyndon Johnson, arriving from a stag dinner for King Saud of Saudi Arabia. When the guests saw him they gradually backed up to form a circle, and he worked his way around the group. This was the first time I had set eyes on a president. It was still the era of black-and-white television, and seeing John Kennedy in color was breathtaking—he was radiant with a tanned face, somewhat fuller than I expected, flecks of gray dotting his brown hair. I was in a second row of onlookers and when he passed our eyes did not meet, but it was stirring to see him from just a few feet away. He moved easily, laughing with the guests, occasionally brushing back his hair. I had been in Washington less than two weeks and had already encountered our president.

Later I was talking again with Newton Minow when he interrupted to ask me if I had met President Kennedy. I said that I hadn't and continued with whatever I was saying, until I sensed Minow was no longer listening. I looked to my right—and there he stood. "Mr. President," said Minow, "this is George Stevens. He's come from Hollywood to work with Ed Murrow," whereupon the president interrupted, shaking my hand. "I know about George. We're happy you're here." Then adding, "I have something I want to talk to you about." I was astonished. It never occurred to me that President Kennedy knew of my existence. And before I could wonder what he wanted to talk about, he turned back to Minow. "Newt, CBS made ninety-one million dollars last year. Couldn't they afford to broadcast Jackie's tour of the White House in *color*?" He was referring to the program to be shown the following night that would draw fifty-six million viewers in which the First Lady showed correspondent Charles Collingwood the restorations she had overseen. The remark squared with what one heard about Kennedy—his appetite for high standards and how, sparked by chance encounters, he pursued matters that interested him.

As he moved away he nodded to me, "We'll be in touch."

Driving home in the snow I reflected with some astonishment on the new world I was now a part of.

On Monday morning White House press secretary Pierre Salinger's assistant called to arrange a meeting. I walked the block down Pennsylvania Avenue from my office to the Northwest Gate of the White House and showed my driver's license at the modest guard enclosure. One is unlikely to forget his first visit to the White House. The simplicity of the building expresses the concept of a great country with an elected leader directed by the will of the people, and in 1962 America was fascinated with the glamorous young family living there. As I made my way along the tree-sheltered driveway, I heard the iron gates open behind me and saw a black limousine circle toward the residence. I was curious but vowed not to behave like a tourist. Still, as the car passed I stole a glance. Perched on the backseat was a white rocking horse on its way to the North Portico. This surprise for four-year-old Caroline sealed the memory of my first time at the White House.

Salinger sat in his cluttered office, a portly figure with teeming energy in shirtsleeves and a PT-109 clasp clinging to his necktie. At thirty-four he had established himself as a candid and witty spokesman, earning the honorific Plucky Pierre. The president had initiated a physical fitness campaign, based on a Marine Corps tradition of fifty-mile hikes—long before jogging became a popular hobby—and Robert Kennedy pressed New Frontier colleagues to join him on a fifty-mile hike. Salinger was asked at a White House briefing if he would be joining the attorney general. Pierre didn't hesitate, declaring, "I may be plucky, but I'm not stupid."

As I sat down beside his desk he offered a hurried but winning smile before telling me that Warner Bros. was preparing a film based on Robert Donovan's book, *PT 109*, the story of JFK as a young navy lieutenant rescuing his shipmates when their boat is sunk by a Japanese destroyer. It would be the first movie about a sitting president and I had already discussed it with Murrow, suggesting that a bad commercial film could undercut our efforts. Joseph Kennedy, the president's father, made a deal with Jack Warner in which the family retained approval of the actor to play JFK. Salinger said they were considering Peter Fonda, Roger Smith and Warren Beatty. I suggested what was self-evident to me, that the principal factor in determining the quality of a movie is the director. Pierre explained that Bryan "Brynie" Foy was producing and Raoul Walsh directing.

Eddie Foy, Sr. was a vaudeville entertainer with seven children and became the subject of a Bob Hope comedy, *The Seven Little Foys*. Brynie Foy, the eldest of the seven, became a producer of second-tier pictures at Warner Bros. where he was known as "the Keeper of the B's." He specialized in women's prison pictures because, they used to say, it meant he could give jobs to at least fifty girls. Walsh had been a top director who began as an actor in 1915 playing John Wilkes Booth in D. W. Griffith's *The Birth of a Nation.* He directed many fine films including *White Heat* and *What Price Glory?* but his recent films were less distinguished, including his most recent, *Marines Let's Go,* which I had seen shortly before coming to Washington. Salinger, ready to discuss actors, was thrown off when I spoke about directors. "How do you know if the director is the right person?" he asked. "You look at his work," I replied. Walsh had been great, I explained, but *Marines Let's Go,* for which he wrote the story, showed a sensibility that might be off the mark for a film about President Kennedy. It centers on four boisterous marines on leave in postwar Japan. I remembered a scene in the picture of two Americans sliding a hapless Japanese back and forth on a saloon bar top with much forced hilarity. "Thank you," said Salinger. "I'll talk to the president."

Later, to sharpen my recollection, I retrieved the 1961 review in *Variety* that described *Marines Let's Go,* calling it "as dated, corny, juvenile and predictable an entry in the war film genre as has come along in years." Pierre called a week later: "Warner Bros. sent a print of *Marines Let's Go* and the president's screening it at three. Come to my office at 2:45." Raised by a director father, it was against my nature to criticize directors, but my job now was to advise the president of the United States. I had a cordial relationship with Jack Warner from my time on *Giant,* but he was a tough customer and would likely see my fingerprints on any change of course.

I was shown into Salinger's bustling office where he juggled two phones as assistants walked in and out with wire copy. The energy in the West Wing came from the top. "John Kennedy loved being president, and at times he could hardly remember that he had ever been anything else," wrote presidential aide Arthur Schlesinger, Jr. "He never complained about 'the terrible loneliness' of the office or its 'awesome burdens.'" McGeorge Bundy, the national security advisor, likened the young staff to "the Harlem Globetrotters—passing forward, backward, sideways and underneath." After a couple of brisk phone conversations Pierre muttered, "Let's go." As we entered the colonnade that connects the West Wing to the residence I had my first glimpse of bright tulips and dogwood blossoming in Jackie's newly restored Rose Garden, all while Pierre was breaking the news that the president was dealing with a communiqué from Soviet premier Nikita Khrushchev and wouldn't have time to watch the film. As we walked the red-carpeted main hall toward the White House screening room Pierre grinned, saying he hadn't seen a movie in six months.

The small theater had four upholstered armchairs in the front row and a single rocking chair at the center. Pierre sank into the chair on the left side and I sat next to him. He gestured to the projectionist while lighting a cigar. The lights went down and the opening credits of *Marines Let's Go* filled the screen. It was as I remembered it—a bawdy account of the four marines living high in Japan that was conspicuously insensitive to the Japanese, who were from time to time called "Japs." Soon Pierre was chuckling and I realized he was having a good time. Sitting in the dark at the White House it was dawning on me that I had engineered a mess. I had created distress at Warner Bros. by inciting doubts over their choice of director, and now the arbiter was Pierre, a man starved for moviegoing pleasure. The door to the theater was in front of us and to our left near the screen. About twenty minutes into the film it opened and a butler held it as a figure entered in silhouette, walked through the beam of light, and sat in the rocking chair beside me. We couldn't see in the dark but there was just one person who would take that seat. At that moment a somewhat respectable dialogue scene played, as I sat very still. Then came a scene of more hijinks by the marines. It seemed like an eternity but after what must have been less than fifteen minutes the president said, "Turn it off, Pierre." Salinger scrambled to his feet, waved his arms at the projectionist, then sat again looking to the president. John Fitzgerald Kennedy leaned across me and said to Salinger, "Tell Jack Warner to go fuck himself."

The president got it. He had in only a few minutes sized up the storytelling sensibility and made a decision. There were a few words about how to find the right director, then a word of acknowledgment to me, and the president was gone, back to Nikita Khrushchev and the Cold War. As a consequence Pierre arranged for Jack Warner and Brynie Foy to fly to Washington for lunch. We met at Le Bistro, a tavern on M Street, where the gourmand Salinger could enjoy a fine French meal at Jack Warner's expense. Warner was armed with tired jokes that he sold with his gruff charm. Foy was disgruntled from the start. Pierre explained we were there to discuss prospective directors and that he had asked me to bring suggestions. Foy's blood pressure was rising. I said that I had two thoughts—Fred Zinnemann and John Huston, both Oscar winners with good taste. That's when the Keeper of the B's turned to me, in front of the press secretary to the president of the United States, and growled, "Kid, you're not going to tell *me* how to make an *exploitation* picture." It went downhill from there.

Pierre called the next day to let me know that Jack Warner was "batshit," but resigned to getting another director. It turned out that Zinnemann and Huston weren't available. Lewis Milestone, who won directing Oscars for *Two*

Arabian Knights in 1928 and *All Quiet on the Western Front* in 1930, was eventually picked. "Millie" was a gentleman and had good taste, but he was near the end of his career. Cliff Robertson was cast as JFK and filming began in Florida. Brynie Foy quickly became irritated with Milestone and Milestone with him, and after a few weeks Milestone quit to be replaced by Les Martinson, a television director.

The film was completed, and while not embarrassing neither was it distinguished. The *New York Times* described the story as "synthetic and without the feel of truth." Robertson did a respectable job but the *Times,* unfairly I thought, called his performance "pious, pompous and self-righteously smug." Jackie and the president screened *PT 109* at the White House and were said to be pleased with it. In the end there was no need to worry about his reputation. He was, after all, the man who when asked how he became a naval hero replied, "It was involuntary. They sank my boat."

22

Jackie's Journey

Jacqueline Kennedy's trip to Pakistan that Murrow and I discussed when we met in Los Angeles took place six weeks after my arrival at USIA and became my first filmmaking challenge. Mrs. Kennedy was also going to India, and the agency's area director for Asia advised me that due to the enmity between India and Pakistan a single film wouldn't work. So we decided to make three films: *Invitation to India* and *Invitation to Pakistan* for showing in the host countries, and a combined film, *Jacqueline Kennedy's Asian Journey,* for the rest of the world. I then faced the core question: who is going to make these films? The practice at USIA was to put projects out for bids from the three American newsreel producers and other documentary companies, and accept the lowest. I wasn't familiar with the people who made documentaries in the United States. Unlike World War II we couldn't ask top Hollywood directors to put aside their careers, so we had to find new or lesser-known people who could bring style and substance to USIA's work.

I was schooled by my father's independent approach—a strong person at the helm with a point of view who would not be buffeted by dictates from studio executives. I began screening documentaries, including two by a New Yorker named Leo Seltzer. I asked him to come to Washington with his screenwriting collaborator, his wife Doris Ransohoff. I concluded that they had a sensibility that could communicate respect for Indian and Pakistani cultures and make the story of Jackie's trip compelling. Guarco arranged for Seltzer to bid for the job of covering the trip in 35mm color and delivering completed films. To my dismay Seltzer's bid came in at $79,800. Hearst Metrotone News was lowest at $44,300, with Fox Movietone News next at $45,800. Newsreel companies featured "Voice of God" narrators and by-the-numbers storytelling, and I told Guarco we couldn't achieve the result Murrow expected if we hired Hearst, the newsreel subsidiary of MGM. He went to work and the next day told me he had talked with Hearst and they were prepared to hire Seltzer as director and Ransohoff as writer. Hearst had estimated only $600 for a writer, so Guarco engineered an amendment to the contract to increase the fee.

Guarco told me that Paul McNichol, a former FBI agent who headed the security office of USIA, was coming to see me, explaining that the government required an FBI clearance for anyone working on contract. Prior to Kennedy taking office the FBI decided whether someone could be hired, but Kennedy changed the procedure. Now, as the person proposing Seltzer, I would have a voice in the decision. McNichol was a fit man in his fifties with close-cropped gray hair and rimless glasses. He sat on my government-issue brown leather sofa and placed a three-inch-high file on the coffee table. I leafed through the pages, reading observations from unnamed people described as "reliable informants" who cited Seltzer's association in the 1930s and '40s with left-wing organizations, along with press clippings reporting activities the FBI deemed subversive, including Seltzer's participation in Franklin Roosevelt's Federal Arts Project. To my eye Seltzer's activities were not compromising, simply the actions of someone involved in progressive causes. Having watched my father fight DeMille and the guilt-by-association crowd at the Directors Guild, I now found myself in a parallel circumstance. McNichol was courteous but firm. He insisted that Seltzer—who I pointed out had been a first lieutenant in the Signal Corps during World War II—had subversive connections that could compromise USIA in the eyes of Congress and the press. "What happens if Mr. McNichol and I don't agree?" I asked Guarco. They looked at one another. "In that case," McNichol said, "we go to Mr. Murrow and he decides." I said, "Respectfully, sir, I believe Leo Seltzer is highly qualified and it seems unreasonable to deny our agency his services when he hasn't been accused of doing anything unlawful." McNichol nodded and said, "I'll arrange a meeting with the Director." Here I was, the new kid on the block, and already complicating Ed Murrow's life. What happens if he doesn't agree with me?

McNichol and I were shown into Murrow's office the next morning at eight. Ed was reading the morning papers at an upright stainless steel drafting table next to his desk. The only memorabilia on display were the large microphone he used in London during the war and a bust of Franklin Roosevelt. He gestured to the brown leather sofa beside a long coffee table, with two chairs opposite. Ed never sat behind his desk with visitors, a practice shared by my father. The Leo Seltzer file was on the table and McNichol stated his concerns. I lit a cigarette and made my case. Ed listened attentively before saying soberly, "Gentlemen, let me look at this file and ponder overnight." As I left, Ed took me aside, confiding, "Paul is a good cop. I think you'll like working with him." I went down the stairs to my office, puzzled and concerned. The next morning at 8:30 the phone rang. "Mr. Stevens," said McNichol, "we're going to be able to work out the Leo Seltzer situation. You can proceed." I was learning about leadership. Ed made the decision but allowed his good cop to give me the news.

Seltzer and his team flew to India and in the coming weeks the striking color footage of the First Lady's trip that we viewed confirmed that Seltzer had a good eye. There was stunning coverage of thousands cheering Jackie in New Delhi on the road from the airport. There were magnificent vistas of the Taj Mahal and Jaipur, a scene of Jackie and her sister, Lee Radziwill, riding an elephant, touching moments with schoolchildren, and a moving scene of a crowd in the sacred city of Benares waving as Jackie's boat sailed past on the Ganges. I was feeling confident when I got off a plane in Los Angeles on March 21 until I saw a wire service story on the front page of the *Los Angeles Herald Examiner.*

HOLLYWOOD DIRECTOR FILMS JACKIE TRIP

A Michigan Republican reported today that a Hollywood director and cameraman—one paid $1000 and the other $1500 a week— are making a movie of Mrs. Jacqueline Kennedy's Journey through Pakistan and India. Rep. Elford A. Cederberg said Edward R. Murrow, director of the United States Information Agency, advised him the film is being made under a $45,807.50 contract and that the government also will pay certain expenses.

Cederberg, the ranking Republican on the House Appropriations Subcommittee that ruled on USIA's budget, had turned my low-key New York documentarian into a "Hollywood director," a sure way to get a headline. He claimed there was adequate newsreel coverage available without spending taxpayer's money. Follow-up stories charged that USIA had become politicized by making a film publicizing the president's wife.

I had dealt with the press in Hollywood, but the provocative tone of the stories shook me—I was now working on a much bigger stage and felt I had embarrassed the president and his wife, Ed Murrow and the USIA. I flew back to Washington on the red-eye and remember sitting by myself in the little park at Dupont Circle, demoralized, wondering if I should submit my resignation. I went to see Murrow. He greeted me with a raised eyebrow and asked a few questions. "The press will find other fish to fry," he said. "Soon we'll be out of the spotlight." He walked me to the door with the words, "You make a good film and we'll make that the story."

We intensified our efforts and I worked with Leo Seltzer in room 308, the thirty-seat screening room down the hall from my office. This was our "situation room" where we would review, shape and fine-tune films to insure they were true to USIA policy objectives and that the storytelling was sharp and engaging. When we were satisfied we would schedule a screening for Murrow and the area directors, senior advisors who represented the policy views of each geographical region. The India and Pakistan films were visually splendid and each was scored using indigenous music. We enlisted Raymond Massey, the Shakespearean-trained actor who was now a television star, to voice the script that gracefully communicated respect for the histories of the two countries. The films captured the vitality and glamour of America's thirty-one-year-old First Lady, who rode a camel in Pakistan as a complement to her Indian elephant ride. Her respect for her hosts and their national traditions was evident.

I had confidence in what we had done but was tense on the morning Murrow and the area directors came to room 308 to see the result. As the lights came up at the end, everyone turned to Murrow. He allowed a twinkle of his eye to pierce his furrowed brow, before saying, "We'll be all right."

The India and Pakistan films were distributed in their respective lands, and *Jacqueline Kennedy's Asian Journey* was sent to seventy-eight countries with soundtracks in twenty-nine languages. "The monuments, the people, the colours have all been captured before," wrote the *New Delhi Statesman*, "but seldom with such exquisite taste, such lovely lighting, and, above all such obvious grace. . . . Obviously deep research and a natural sympathy for all things Indian have gone into the writing."

One morning Don Wilson, a thirty-six-year-old former *Life* magazine correspondent who was Murrow's deputy, called to say that I should send a 35mm print of *Invitation to India* to the White House right away. A few days later I received an engraved invitation from the President and Mrs. Kennedy to attend a screening on June 13 at the White House. I had started going out with Pamela Turnure, Jackie's intelligent and attractive press secretary, and I asked her if she thought it would be possible to bring my mother as a guest, and if they might invite Leo Seltzer and Doris Ransohoff. The response was affirmative and my mother flew in from California.

The Kennedys invited Ed and Janet Murrow and the Indian ambassador to dinner before the showing. My mother and I arrived at the East Wing reception area and were led along marble floors to the screening room, which had a more relaxed and inviting aura than on my previous visit. Several senators and their

Jackie Kennedy on Lake Pichola in the state of Rajasthan in northwest India during the filming of *Invitation to India,* March 17, 1962.

wives were talking with other guests outside the entrance when the president and Jackie approached with the Murrows. They greeted us, and my mother for the first time shook a president's hand. She was thrilled to meet Ed Murrow as the lights went down and we took our seats. The president sat in his rocking chair next to Jackie in the front row. From sitting through sneak previews of my father's films I was all too familiar with the tension that invariably hangs over a filmmaker who sits watching his work with an audience. The anxiety is offset by the exhilaration one feels if the film succeeds in enthralling its audience, and on this night the onlookers in the White House theater seemed transported. The First Lady was a captivating ambassador for her country, and the audience seemed especially moved when, toward the end of the film, she says to Prime Minister Nehru, "I hope that with my husband I will be able to return again soon." When the film was over the president, winningly proud of his wife, stood beside her for a few moments talking with their guests. After they went upstairs, Ed walked over, looked me in the eye and said, "It was worth all the trouble."

It was a fine night for USIA—and my mother. The frosting on the cake was that Leo Seltzer, who had been blacklisted by his government, watched his film in the White House with the president of the United States. As Murrow had predicted the controversy died away, but not before the *New York Daily News* ran an editorial cartoon showing the Kennedy family watching a home movie called "My Trip Abroad," with Caroline asking her father, "Daddy, when does Cleopatra come on?"

Murrow and I hosted VIP screenings in Washington and the word of mouth created such an appetite to see the film that Congress passed a resolution making an exception so Americans could see *Jacqueline Kennedy's Asian Journey.* United Artists paired it in theaters at Christmas with Yul Brynner in *Taras Bulba.* I was becoming steeled to bad publicity, so when Raymond Massey complained in the press about the domestic showings, and contributed his three hundred dollar narration fee to the Republican National Committee, I turned the other cheek.

23

Cannes and Venice

I discovered to my surprise that my office was responsible for our country's participation in international film festivals and was expected to designate an official American entry to the festivals at Cannes, Venice, Berlin and Moscow. My predecessor's practice had been to send the least controversial films, which meant that America was often represented by mediocre work that earned little respect among the world's film community. With Murrow's blessing we set up a committee of filmmakers to oversee a selection process that favored excellence. Fred Zinnemann of the Directors Guild chaired the Film Festival Selection Committee, joined by Gene Kelly from the Screen Actors Guild, Ernest Lehman from the Writers Guild, and John Houseman of the Producers Guild.

In 1962 the committee chose Sidney Lumet's *Long Day's Journey into Night* to represent the United States at Cannes, where the jury awarded an unusual major prize to the group ensemble of actors—Jason Robards, Katharine Hepburn, Dean Stockwell and Bradford Dillman—which gave our committee a respectable start. I seized the opportunity to appoint myself as the official American delegate to Cannes, a ridiculously pleasant assignment that involved waking up at the Carlton Hotel to a view of the Bay of Cannes, enjoying fresh croissants at the hotel's terrace cafe, watching the newest in world cinema, and seeking to represent the Kennedy administration to good effect at events and evening soirées.

I was having coffee one May morning on the terrace when a large, rumpled, bespectacled Frenchman approached and announced in heavily accented English that he must speak with me. This was Henri Langlois, director of the Cinémathèque Française, a pioneer in the preservation of classic French and American films. I ordered coffee for him and he embarked on a feverish account of the deteriorating state of America's film heritage. He insisted that John Ford's first feature, *Straight Shooting,* was lost, that nothing remained of Greta Garbo in MGM's *The Divine Woman,* and that all but two of Theda Bara's fifty films had been incinerated in a Twentieth Century Fox library fire. He claimed that less than one-tenth of the two hundred thousand films produced in the United States since 1894 were preserved in film archives. Langlois was addressing me as the American delegate, but he was also conscious of my Hollywood lineage. He declared the American government was derelict in allowing nitrate-based film negatives to deteriorate in vaults while studios ignored the problem. This crisis of film preservation was news to me. The irrepressible Monsieur Langlois would be on my trail at future festivals.

My most exciting discovery at Cannes was a beautifully told story of one family's involvement in the Algerian war by a young American, James Blue, who had studied at the Institut des hautes études cinématographiques (IDHEC) in Paris. *The Olive Trees of Justice* received the Critics Prize in the new filmmakers section, and when I met Jim Blue I knew immediately he was the kind of filmmaker we needed at USIA. I urged him to come see me when he got back to the United States.

On my return to Washington I found an engraved invitation to come in black tie to the White House for "dancing at ten," followed by word from Bill Walton to come for dinner at his house in Georgetown beforehand. Bill, a writer and painter close to the president and Jackie, had been a war correspondent and a pal of my father's in France after D-Day. JFK named him chairman of the US Commission of Fine Arts and Bill worked so effectively with Jackie to save Lafayette Square and other Washington architectural treasures that President Kennedy chided him, "You can't spend *all* of my political capital on Jackie's projects."

The Kennedys invited seventy people to dinner at the White House and arranged supper for another seventy at the houses of friends, all of whom would appear later for dancing. The White House group included the Lyndon Johnsons, Attorney General Robert Kennedy, the Averell Harrimans, the Douglas Dillons, the Robert McNamaras, the Hubert Humphreys, Adlai Stevenson, Joan Fontaine, George Plimpton and Jackie's sister Princess Radziwill. Walton's dinner was composed of a dozen friends. My dinner partner was the vivacious painter Mary Pinchot Meyer, who was divorced from Cord Meyer, a ranking CIA operator. In a 1964 tragedy that remains a mystery, Mary was found murdered near the Georgetown canal. In her diary it was revealed she had an affair with President Kennedy when he was in the White House.

We then headed to the White House where other after-dinner guests were arriving, including the Ted Kennedys, the Arthur Schlesingers, Ben Bradlee of *Newsweek* and his alluring wife Tony, who was Mary Meyer's sister. It was an era before enhanced security, so I drove my Thunderbird through the Southwest Gate with the top down and parked on the South Lawn circle.

Walking through the Diplomatic Reception Room I heard the violins of the Lester Lanin Orchestra, and as I neared the top of the stairs I saw the president in a tuxedo with a glass of champagne in hand, having a relaxed conversation. He looked over and saw me. I could see his mind sorting me from the scores of others he had seen that day. He shook my hand. "What do you think is happening with Marlon Brando, George?" he asked with no preliminaries. "Did you see *The Ugly American?*" The movie, set in Vietnam, had just opened and he must have screened it at the White House. Fortunately I had seen the picture, directed by my friend George Englund. The president pressed for my views on Brando, until interrupted by other arriving guests. In those few moments JFK demonstrated his distinctive capacity to fasten on an area of interest and engage in conversation with whomever came his way.

The next film festival I would attend was Venice, the world's oldest, founded in 1932. Our Hollywood committee met to review prospects and chose *Birdman of Alcatraz,* John Frankenheimer's film starring Burt Lancaster as Robert Stroud, a convicted murderer who kept birds in his Leavenworth prison cell and became an ornithologist.

I was invited to dinner at a friend's Georgetown house where I met Robert Kennedy for the first time. We were getting our coats after dinner preparing to leave when the thirty-seven-year-old attorney general appeared before me. I was conscious of his penetrating blue eyes when he inquired, "Why are we sending *Birdman of Alcatraz* to the Venice Film Festival?" Astonished that he was even aware the festival was happening, let alone what picture had been chosen, I somewhat defensively described the committee we had established and our effort to elevate the quality of American films at international festivals. When I finished he said, "I don't see how that elevates anything." Then, referring to the Birdman, "He's not a very admirable figure." I was taken aback. I had been getting a good deal of favorable attention and now my judgment was being questioned by the second most powerful figure in Washington.

The next morning I went directly to Don Wilson's office and described the conversation. I told him I was here to try to help USIA, but if I'm on the wrong side of the president's brother I didn't see how I could be effective. Don was a friend of Bobby's and advised me to settle down. He explained that the *Birdman* premiere in California led to a stream of letters to the attorney general asking him to free Robert Stroud, whose criminal record is soft-pedaled in the film.

It was decades before I would discover the source of my problem. A friend gave me a 1962 letter she found at the Kennedy Library from Bobby's sister Jean, to the attorney general, saying, "George Stevens, Jr. is sending *The Birdman of Alcatraz* to the Venice Film Festival and you should be concerned." Jean's letter was written shortly after my inattentiveness at the Shrivers' dinner, and it was widely known that Bobby was dutiful in responding to his sisters.

Burt Lancaster was shooting a film in Rome and arranged a day off to attend the festival. He was to appear at a major press conference and beforehand told me he was going to make a plea for the release of Robert Stroud from prison. I told him of my run-in with the attorney general, so Burt shifted gears and spoke instead about the importance of free expression, even though I had just constrained his. As the American delegate I went with him to the gala showing of *Birdman* on the Venice Lido, and before he returned to Rome he told me that should he win a prize he would like me to accept it. The jury awarded Burt the Volpi Cup for Best Actor and I decided to memorize a few sentences in Italian for the televised ceremony. The next morning a telegram arrived at the Excelsior Hotel: "George. Thanks for accepting my award. I must say it reminded me of an Italian beer commercial. Regards, Burt." Going forward I curtailed my linguistic experimentation.

The festival presented a magnificent fifty-film retrospective dedicated to the birth of the talking picture in the United States. It was focused on directors like King Vidor, Ernst Lubitsch, Lewis Milestone, Rouben Mamoulian and Howard Hawks, and played to full houses every morning. It was praised as the finest of its kind ever assembled, though the Italian organizers told me they had struggled to obtain American films. In my obligatory chairman's report to Secretary of State Dean Rusk I made a plea:

> The United States desperately needs a coordinated archive arrangement. The Italian effort to assemble films for this retrospective was monumental. The organizers were shocked that many of the films could not be traced, and certain American films had to be borrowed from Moscow. . . . Film students and historians from around the world remark on their concern that the United States is allowing these motion picture treasures to be destroyed.

My persuasive friend Henri Langlois would have been pleased.

Attending these festivals was changing my outlook. Venice showed outstanding work by new filmmakers from state-sponsored film academies in Czechoslovakia, Argentina, Sweden and Brazil. I concluded my report to the secretary by saying that the United States should be attentive to the development of young filmmakers.

The day I left Venice an Italian friend invited me to a Frank Sinatra charity concert in Rome, and since I had my black tie I stopped overnight. It was a glittery affair at the Teatro Eliseo. At intermission I heard a familiar voice call out, and there was Elizabeth Taylor seated across the aisle—*Cleopatra* was still shooting in Rome. I slid over as the lights went down and was greeted with a hurried hug. After Frank closed with *"Arrivederci Roma,"* bringing the crowd to its feet, Elizabeth, looking ravishing and Cleopatra-like with a spray of tiny flowers in her hair, took my arm and whispered, "I'm alone—do you want to ride with me?" It was a question needing no reply. Elizabeth and I had not seen one another for a few years so we exchanged information in bursts, speeding along winding roads with the paparazzi following on Vespas—pulling alongside Fellini-style—removing their hands from the handlebars to flash pictures.

Eventually we passed through formal gates and parked in front of an imposing villa. We went inside and she directed me to a high-ceilinged living room, reappearing in seconds with a bottle of Dom Perignon and two glasses. She had made no mention of her current circumstances and while delighted to be there, uncertain of my status. She signaled me to pour the champagne and, loosening my tie and tossing my jacket on a chair, I did as instructed. We resumed our conversation with Elizabeth inquiring about my new career and life in Washington. As I paused to refresh my glass I noticed a tall figure in a bathrobe descending the staircase.

"Oh, Richard," Elizabeth said. "I thought you were asleep. I don't think you've met George Stevens, Jr."

Richard Burton and I shook hands. Seeming not to take exception to my presence, he settled in a high-backed chair and added his smoky baritone to our conversation, displaying relaxed charm considering the hour. In due course Elizabeth offered her car to take me to the Excelsior. On the way home I noticed that I was unencumbered by paparazzi.

24

The Best in the Country

The work at USIA was intense and exhilarating. Producing films for the Motion Picture Service was like running a small studio, and included deliberations with Murrow and his foreign policy staff on how best to influence opinion in the Cold War. My immediate challenge was to find filmmakers—I was looking for individuals, not production companies, who had the imagination to tell stories and the discipline to produce films on our limited budgets. The USIA policy of awarding production contracts to the lowest bidder discouraged participation by the most creative filmmakers, until Tony Guarco worked his bureaucratic magic to obtain authority from the General Accounting Office to select producers and negotiate contracts. His success opened the agency's doors to a new breed.

We began receiving documentaries that applicants believed best represented their talents. Many who came for interviews were inspired by President Kennedy's "ask not" appeal. I made the ground rules clear: we choose filmmakers for their imagination and creativity, but their job is to communicate an agreed-upon point of view—not to satisfy their artistic yearning. This balance worked because they received considerable independence in crafting USIA films.

Based on his success with Jacqueline Kennedy I asked Leo Seltzer to film President Kennedy's trip to Mexico. He gave it a sense of spectacle that raised the bar for these state visit films—a confetti-laced parade through the avenues of Mexico City was surprisingly stirring. We had a blip when I asked the distinguished Cuban-born American actor José Ferrer to be the narrator, and was presented with his FBI file in which "a reliable source" accused Ferrer of plotting to take over MGM and make it a tool of Soviet propaganda. This time, after McNichol and I made our presentations, Murrow stood and declared, "There's no reason for this agency not to have the advantage of Mr. Ferrer's talents."

George Stevens, Jr., and James Blue are presented the Venice Film Festival's Lion of St. Mark at the Italian Embassy, Washington, DC. 1963.

We got the desired outcome but the breadth of government blacklisting was insidious. The victims were unlikely to ever know their loyalty had been questioned, or have the opportunity to question their accusers.

Jim Blue accepted my invitation at Cannes and paid a visit. We proposed that he go to Colombia and make three films about the villagers who were improving their lives with assistance from Kennedy's Alliance for Progress initiative. In three moving ten-minute documentaries Jim showed his skill at layering in the message with a light touch. One was filmed in a town called Rincon Santo that had no school until the townspeople built one with materials provided by the Alliance. In the last scene—as their children take their seats for the first day of school—we see the proud faces of their parents peering through the window.

The School at Rincon Santo was shown in theaters throughout Latin America, and later in the year Jim and I received the Silver Lion for best documentary from the Venice Film Festival.

One morning a member of my staff reported that a filmmaker from St. Louis had met with Murrow's deputy for policy, Tom Sorensen (brother of

JFK speechwriter Ted Sorensen), and told him that the previous year he had seen USIA films on a trip to Brazil that "made him ashamed to be an American." These being films from the previous regime, I decided to find this fellow from St. Louis. He turned out to be Charles Guggenheim, a wiry forty-year-old who was an intellectually curious craftsman, and would in time become a dear friend.

We hired Guggenheim to direct a documentary on President Kennedy's trip to Central America that would depict the benefits of the Alliance for Progress for people aspiring to better lives. He captured vivid color scenes of the president engaging with a spirited crowd of campesinos in Costa Rica with verve and humor. The film was called *United in Progress.* Less reverently, alluding to the most imperialist of American companies in Latin America, we dubbed it "United Fruit in Progress."

Terry Sanders, a UCLA graduate whose *A Time Out of War* had won an Oscar, directed a documentary on the state visit of Leopold Senghor, the poet who served as the first president of Senegal. USIA regularly made films about foreign leaders coming to Washington, but the creativity of our new directors— and the grace with which the charismatic couple at the White House welcomed visitors—made these color documentaries crowd-pleasers with audiences in the home country.

Billy Hale, my motion picture officer friend in the air force, signed on to make *Grand Central Market,* designed to show entrepreneurial spirit among diverse nationalities in downtown Los Angeles, and asked an up-and-coming young cameraman named Haskell Wexler to photograph it. William Greaves, a New Yorker who was one of the few Black filmmakers of the era, came to see us with samples of his work, and we engaged him to document *The First World Festival of Negro Art.* Bill's film was well received and he next wrote and directed *Wealth of a Nation,* an ode to creativity and free expression.

We launched a student filmmaker program through which Carroll Ballard made *Beyond This Winter's Wheat,* the story of a farm boy's decision to join the Peace Corps. It was so effective that we assigned *Harvest* to Ballard. The film became a virtuoso color portrait of American farming that was nominated for an Academy Award. Ed Emshwiller, an avant-garde artist and experimental film-maker, created a pictorially brilliant documentary, *Art Scene USA,* that showed the vitality and range of American artists. It brightened my days to see iconoclastic Ed, sporting his long beard and ponytail, winning over my foreign service colleagues with his impressive work.

Tensions developed when the time came for reviewing and approving films. I enjoyed considerable authority over the filmmaking process but the area directors who managed the different regions were charged with reading proposed scripts, viewing rough cuts, and appraising the effectiveness of the films. They were highly educated and articulate but often brought conflicting opinions. It could be true at USIA—just as at television networks and Hollywood studios—that seeking consensus among differing opinions watered down the resulting film. My job, as I saw it, was to protect the films.

I was fond of the story about Frank Capra going to Washington during World War II for a meeting at the Pentagon about his *Why We Fight* series. He walked into a room to find ten generals waiting. Capra, short in stature in his major's uniform but a three-time Oscar winner, shook the hand of each general, then moved to the long conference table. "Fellas, are we going to talk about motion pictures?" After nods from the generals, he said, "Then I sit at the head of the table." I wasn't Frank Capra, but knew that success depended on controlling the shape and content of our films.

When we screened films for Murrow and the area directors in room 308, my task was to listen respectfully but to guard against a film being diluted. My starting point was a phrase that was becoming my lodestar—*respect for the audience.* This meant not talking down to the viewers but leaving room for them to bring something of themselves to the experience. We developed a simple rule: nothing is communicated if it isn't *felt.* I had been inspired by Carl Sandburg's stories about his years as a movie critic for the *Chicago Daily News.* "Anything that brings you to tears by way of drama," he explained, "does something to the deepest roots of your personality."

We aspired to this with USIA films. Ambassadors and foreign service officers reported that viewers were being emotionally affected by the films. Yet some area directors measured films by how much "freight" they carried—the overtly stated policy message—unaware that when films are propagandistic, audiences are turned off and lose interest. Agreeing on the right balance was a challenge. Working in my favor was Murrow's experience at CBS, where he had defended his documentaries from the opinions of executives and advertisers. Ed listened to comments and criticisms, and would sometimes say, "George, you fellows should give that some thought." But when the chips were down he supported our films.

One Sunday, as I neared my first anniversary at USIA, I read an inspiring *New York Times Magazine* article, "Little Rock Revisited." It was the story of nine Black children who entered an all-white high school in Arkansas at the start of the Civil Rights Movement. It occurred to me that *Nine from Little Rock* would be a compelling title. Research showed that racial intolerance was a prime source of overseas criticism of the United States, so I called Charles Guggenheim in St. Louis and proposed a film that would begin with the disturbing confrontation the children faced when they entered Little Rock High with National

Guard protection. We tracked down the students and told the largely affirmative stories of their lives after graduation.

Months later when we screened the film for the area directors they proposed deleting the scene of the angry crowd jeering the children. We made the case that showing this crowd was necessary to set the stage for the positive story of racial progress. Yes, for a moment viewers would see ugly behavior that had already been widely publicized overseas, but they would discover that the United States government was on the side of the students and that these young men and women went on to lead productive lives. You give a little, you get more back.

The discussion became heated but Murrow quietly guided it and the film was approved. Afterward I walked Ed to the elevator. As the doors opened he paused before entering. "If you stay around here long enough, you may learn how to make motion pictures from those boys." A wry smile and he disappeared.

Murrow was required to testify on Capitol Hill for USIA's funding, often dealing with powerful figures who were skeptical about the value of USIA. Ed brought senior aides as witnesses, and each time I was reminded that Ed Murrow was the most famous man in government after the president. His bearing and eloquence set the hearings apart. Legislators listened when Murrow reported that six hundred million people in more than a hundred countries had viewed USIA films. On my first appearance before crusty John Rooney, the powerful chairman of the Appropriations Committee, I was treated with less deference than Murrow. I began by politely asking permission to make a few preliminary remarks. Rooney, referring to the amount of our requested budget increase, put me in my place: "You'd better make $7,163,400 worth of remarks."

One morning Ed Murrow came on the phone with the words, "Shall we go to lunch?" We climbed into his black government sedan and were driven to the Washington Hotel, where he showed me to the rooftop restaurant. Ed asked for Cutty Sark "neat," a preference cultivated in World War II London, and I joined him. He had no agenda, just some quiet assurance: "The work you're doing is important." I was green, a quarter century younger than Ed, but he had made time to take me to lunch. It led me to think about accidents of life. What a gift it was to be exposed to Ed Murrow's clarity of thought and purpose, his patient leadership and integrity.

The morale of the Motion Picture Service staff and our dedicated young filmmakers soared weeks later when Murrow, addressing the Advertising Federation of America, declared, "This agency has spearheaded the intelligent use of the motion picture in the national interest to a degree unprecedented in the United States, with the possible exception of World War II."

25

Grace and Beauty

Jackie Kennedy believed the White House should be a place for excellence in artistic performance and in 1961 she invited the celebrated cellist Pablo Casals to play at a dinner that included two dozen other eminent musicians. She had a temporary stage constructed in the East Room, and in months to come welcomed Jerome Robbins and his ballet troupe, the American Shakespeare Festival, and singers from the Metropolitan Opera. In 1962 she hosted an elegant dinner for forty-one Nobel Prize winners, where the president famously remarked, "I think this is the most extraordinary collection of talent, of human knowledge, that has ever been gathered together at the White House, with the possible exception of when Thomas Jefferson dined alone."

My interest in the arts had been centered on motion pictures, but I found that the Kennedy initiatives were broadening my perspective. President Kennedy understood the importance of culture to a great nation, yet some questioned his depth. Jackie, not above teasing him, used to say his favorite song was "Hail to the Chief." He assumed leadership of the stalled Eisenhower initiative to build a National Cultural Center in Washington, DC, which had neither an opera house nor a concert hall. He wrote to Vice President Johnson and Speaker of the House Sam Rayburn on March 10, 1961, asking for legislation to set aside land for a cultural center that would establish "new horizons for the performing arts."

The president enlisted New York real estate investor and Broadway producer Roger L. Stevens (no relation) to chair the effort, named an advisory committee, and met with them the morning after the Casals concert. "I am hopeful that it will not be necessary always to have a special stage put in the White House for hearing a distinguished musician," he said, "but that in Washington we can have a great cultural center which expresses the interest of the people of this country in this most basic desire of mankind."

The United States was unique among major countries in not providing government funding for the arts. The president discovered that he didn't have the votes to move arts legislation through Congress, so in June of 1963 he created the Advisory Council on the Arts, which would one day become the guiding force for the National Endowment for the Arts. The attitude toward motion pictures in the 1960s was a far cry from today. Film was considered popular entertainment and not taken seriously as an art form. This was demonstrated when legislation was eventually introduced to create the National Endowment for the Arts, and motion pictures were omitted.

I had become acquainted with Senator Hubert Humphrey of Minnesota, a sponsor of the bill, so I placed a call to the ebullient and approachable senator. He listened to my plea that film was an indigenous American art form and must be included. In the next draft motion pictures joined theater, opera, music, dance and painting among the American arts.

Ed Murrow and I were discussing ways to elevate our efforts to use motion pictures to greater effect, even revisiting the discussion we had when we first met in Los Angeles about a nonprofit film foundation. We decided to ask President Kennedy to host a luncheon for the motion picture community that would encourage support from creative leaders and studios. I drafted a letter for Murrow and he decided we should discuss it with Arthur Krim, the progressive head of United Artists who was a leading fundraiser and close to the president. Arthur agreed, and he wrote to Kennedy, explaining, "There is much that private enterprise should be doing in cooperation with our government and in furtherance of its objectives, over and above the single objective of private profit."

President Kennedy spoke about the arts more eloquently than any of his predecessors, notably in an address honoring Robert Frost at Amherst College. "I look forward to an America which will not be afraid of grace and beauty," he said. "And I look forward to an America which commands respect throughout the world not only for its strength but for its civilization as well."

Historian Arthur Schlesinger, Jr., special assistant to the president, had a hand in crafting his statements on the arts and I was delighted when a friend arranged for me to meet Schlesinger in his office in the East Wing. He was concerned with Latin America policy, but his intellectual curiosity led him to see and admire some of our USIA films. He wore a dotted bow tie and dark-rimmed glasses and I found him surprisingly lighthearted and accessible. He told me that as a boy he began writing in his journal about every film he saw, and now, while serving in the White House, he was moonlighting as the movie critic for *Show* magazine.

Arthur became a sounding board and ally. He and another Kennedy aide, Richard Goodwin, an erudite contemporary of mine who graduated first in his class at Harvard Law School, were leading an effort to rescue Abu Simbel, the thirteenth-century BC Egyptian temples that were about to be destroyed by construction of the Aswan Dam. Arthur surprised me with an invitation to join a Saturday meeting at the White House. Science advisor Jerome Wiesner led discussion of a strategic plan to save this far-off cultural treasure—an example of the energy and breadth of the Kennedy team. Jackie helped persuade Congress to provide funds to dismantle the temples and move them safely to higher ground.

I came to Washington with a primary mission of making films, but I now had a passport into a range of activities that I never imagined. I clipped and kept a quotation of President Kennedy's on my desk. "The ancient Greek definition of happiness is the full use of your powers along lines of excellence."

It spoke to the opportunity I had been given.

26

Moscow

The Cold War and the contest of ideas with the Soviet Union were high on USIA's agenda as I made plans to lead the American delegation to the 1963 Moscow Film Festival. "I've agreed to serve on the jury in Moscow," producer-director Stanley Kramer informed me in a phone call from Hollywood. Stanley was a friend who was known for making successful films with social content. I suggested that this was an opportunity to screen American films behind the Iron Curtain. Stanley was keen on the idea, so working with a young foreign service officer in the American embassy, Terry Catherman, I put together a list of Kramer films to determine if the Russians would be receptive. With surprising speed they indicated a willingness to host showings of *Judgment at Nuremberg, Inherit the Wind* and *The Defiant Ones* at the Moscow Filmmakers' Union, and invite Kramer to speak. I knew Stanley would effectively represent an American point of view.

Word came that the State Department had concluded that the proposed films were "not appropriate." They thought *The Defiant Ones,* with Sidney Poitier and Tony Curtis as clashing chain gang prisoners, would confirm the Soviet line that the United States was a racist country, and *Judgment at Nuremberg* would undercut our ally West Germany by reminding viewers of Nazi atrocities. Bureaucratic tussles escalate quickly and views harden, so I reached out to a new acquaintance, Averell Harriman, a senior figure in Kennedy's State Department. Averell had served as governor of New York and was our ambassador in Moscow during the war, attending the Yalta Conference with Roosevelt, Churchill and Stalin. Now in his seventies, he understood the levers of power. His mental agility and tough-mindedness led colleagues to call him "the Crocodile." ("He just lies up there on the riverbank, his eyes half closed, looking sleepy. Then, *whap,* he bites.") I made my case about Kramer and the kind of films we wanted to screen, and was heartened that he shared my view.

Harriman called me at home at seven the next morning. (I later quizzed him about these early calls. "I like to get people thinking about my issues before they get busy thinking about their own.") "Your problem is Tommy Thompson," he said. "I'll arrange for you to see him."

Llewellyn E. Thompson, twice American ambassador in Moscow, was now Kennedy's ambassador-at-large serving on the National Security Council, advising the president on Soviet affairs. I felt like a Hollywood rookie when I got off the elevator on the seventh floor, where power resided at the State Department. Ambassador Thompson was cool but courteous, and seemed prepared for a serious discussion. He listened while I explained my view that Soviet filmmakers whose creativity was constrained by the state would respect these films and envy the freedom of Americans to address controversial issues. The ambassador surprised me by reversing himself and approving the showings, with the caveat that Kramer's films be shown only to the film community, not the general public.

In June of 1963 Kennedy spoke at American University about what he called the most important topic on earth: world peace. He called for a nuclear weapons treaty and committed the United States to halt atmospheric testing, a position Ed Murrow had strongly advocated within the National Security Council. He announced that Averell Harriman would travel to Moscow in July, during the time I would be there, to negotiate a test ban treaty with the Russians.

Kennedy planned a European trip in June to include Berlin, the embattled city divided by a wall erected by the Soviets in August of 1961. I met with Bruce Herschensohn, a thirty-year-old from Los Angeles who cut his filmmaking teeth at NASA, who I had enlisted to make an Alliance for Progress documentary, *Bridges to the Barrios*. Bruce not only wrote and directed his films but was the editor and composed the music, offering efficiency as well as creativity. We engaged him to make a film about Kennedy's trip to Europe.

I flew to the Berlin Film Festival on the way to Moscow. One of the perquisites of my job was a coveted black diplomatic passport that enabled me to be waved through customs, and I admit to relishing the status it conferred. I was processed quickly upon my dawn arrival at Tempelhof, the airport serving the western sector of the divided city. My itinerary showed that a car from the festival would meet me at the baggage area. I was greeted not by a driver but by a representative of the festival, unexpected at this hour. Moreover, the representative was a striking dark-haired woman in her twenties named Christine who led me to a black Mercedes. I was looking forward to dozing on the way to the hotel but Christine climbed in the back, facing me from a jump seat. It was clear there would be conversation. She inquired in lightly accented English where I lived. "Washington, DC," I replied, "originally, from Hollywood." When she asked, "Did you live on a street called Forman Avenue?" I felt like a player in *The Third Man,* Carol Reed's classic of postwar intrigue, but her manner was congenial, so I responded directly. "I lived on Forman Avenue for the first sixteen years of my life." "Do you recall your mother sending packages to a family in Germany?" she asked. I remembered after the war my mother wrapping canned goods, soap and clothing on our dining room table, and nodded affirmatively. The young woman's dark eyes filled with tears. "My mother and my brother and I depended on those packages," she whispered. "Blankets and clothing and food . . . at the end of the war." I pictured my mother, having obtained the family's name from a relief organization, wrapping parcels and explaining the importance of helping families in need, even if they were our recent enemy.

Soon we were at the hotel and I checked into a cheerful suite provided by the festival and began my duties, stirred by the unexpected emotional encounter. As the official American delegate one of my duties was to spend time with a demanding but captivating Joan Crawford, who had just completed *What Ever Happened to Baby Jane?,* costarring her rival, Bette Davis. I accompanied Miss Crawford to a screening and, after the lights went down, noticed her remove from her handbag what appeared to be a silver container of perfume. I saw her put the container to her lips. A moment later she passed it to me, her round eyes shining in the darkness. I accepted her consideration and downed a long sip of cold vodka. Subsequent sips made the Polish film about factory workers tolerable, and this interlude with Miss Crawford stood out as the highlight of my official duties.

Christine became my companion for three days and nights, my mother's good deeds and the romantic atmosphere of divided Berlin bonding two young people who had been on opposing sides of a great war. She invited me to visit her mother at her apartment and I was moved when shown blankets I recognized from our house. We had an emotional parting when I flew off to Moscow and made plans to meet again, a vow thwarted by distance and the pressures of my work in Washington. Twice in later years she called when visiting the United States and we discussed our lives, but we never met again.

Terry Catherman met me at Sheremetyevo Airport on a gray July day and took me to the Hotel Moskva. He was working on preparations for Harriman's test ban negotiations but was excited by his concurrent duties with our delegation. Moscow was drab and grim and inhospitable to tourists, even in midsummer. We would soon be referring to the Moskva—a massive gray neo-Stalinist building near the Kremlin with a lobby that resembled a train station—as the Comrade Hilton.

There were delegations from sixty-four countries, including Soviet client states North Vietnam, Cuba and East Germany, which gave the festival a political aspect not seen at Cannes or Venice. Minister of Culture Yekaterina Furtseva, who worked her way up from being a weaver in a textile factory to the first woman to sit on the powerful Presidium, was on hand. There was a saying: "Whatever Khrushchev thinks, Furtseva says." She dressed with more style than was customary for Soviet women and was especially hospitable to the glamorous, left-leaning Simone Signoret and her husband Yves Montand, and to Federico Fellini, who arrived with his wife Giulietta Masina and his new film, *8½*. But when it was time to negotiate, Furtseva displayed the steel of a party apparatchik. Her deputy, Vladimir Baskakov, a towering man with a static eye that gave him a menacing look, controlled the festival. A Russian friend warned that Baskakov was a nasty piece of work.

The opening ceremony was in the newly constructed Palace of Congresses inside the Kremlin, the six-thousand-seat auditorium with marble columns where major political events took place. Senior officials and astronauts were seated on the stage decorated with flags of participating nations. To our surprise Stanley Kramer received an ovation when the jurors were introduced. Later when his films were screened the audience chanted, "Krah-mer, Krah-mer."

Our delegation also included Danny Kaye, Geraldine Page, Shelley Winters, composer Elmer Bernstein, screenwriter Abby Mann, and Ilya Lopert, a Lithuanian-born American who was head of United Artists in Europe. Ilya, clever and tough and able to swear in seven languages, became my counselor and good friend.

"Hollywood—A Hit in Moscow!" was the banner headline in *Variety*. "Hollywood," wrote correspondent Harold Meyers, "has accomplished a major breakthrough at the Moscow Film Festival in striking contrast to its participation in previous years."

So far, so good.

Minister Baskakov saw the response to the Kramer films and surprised us by announcing—contrary to my agreement with Ambassador Thompson—a Sunday evening public showing of *The Defiant Ones* in the Palace of Congresses. I went to see Baskakov and took Ilya Lopert with me. "Vladimir," I said, "our agreement is that the Kramer films are to be shown only at the Filmmakers Union." Baskakov was obdurate. He had the film and he was going to show it on Sunday, demonstrating that in the Soviet Union possession is 100 percent of the law.

Ilya and I retreated to my suite. I was distressed about violating my understanding with Ambassador Thompson, but it occurred to me that if we could get Sidney Poitier to come to Moscow, his charismatic presence would cast a positive light on the public screening. Ilya and I grappled with the maddening Soviet phone system, and three hours later connected with Sidney, who was filming in London. I told him about the screening in the Kremlin Palace of Congresses.

"Sidney, your presence would make it a great night for America in Moscow. Ilya can arrange with United Artists for you to get Saturday off. Will you come?"

"I'll be there," Sidney said after a pause. "I'll get my own ticket."

On Saturday afternoon Ilya, Terry Catherman and I were about to go meet Sidney's flight at Sheremetyevo when the phone rang in my suite. It was Baskakov. "Mr. Stevens. Kremlin Palace no longer is available. *The Defiant Ones* now is at Palace of Sport on Sunday morning." Shell-shocked, I looked up from the phone. Ilya grabbed it and began cursing Baskakov in several languages. We now faced telling Sidney that the prestigious Kremlin Palace screening was now taking place outside of town on Sunday morning. Sidney, gentleman that he is, accepted the news gracefully and Stanley Kramer joined us for dinner at Aragvi, a Georgian restaurant favored by the cultural elite (we called it Sardi's Very East). We had a vodka-laced dinner, joked about Soviet duplicity, and returned to the Moskva for an early morning pickup.

The American delegation had a major asset in our assigned interpreter Vladimir Posner. In his mid-twenties, Vlad had gone to Stuyvesant High School in New York until his father, a Russian-born film executive, was charged as a spy and returned to Moscow. Vladimir's English had a New York patina, and his fluent Russian made our translated remarks accessible and our events enjoyable. (Two decades later he would become a prominent Soviet affairs commentator on ABC's *Nightline*.) Vlad joined Sidney, Stanley, Ilya and Susan Strasberg, who was on our delegation, in a van for the Sunday morning ride to the sports arena. We turned off the highway, circled the parking area, and approached a vast wooden building—at which point we saw a serpentine line of eight thousand Russians standing in the morning chill. They were waiting to see the American film.

We took the stage and I spoke of the freedom we enjoyed in the United States. "I'm glad so many of you can see *The Defiant Ones,* a film that explores tensions in our society." Vlad translated my words, then Kramer's. "This film deals with some of our faults and it reaches out to you for your understanding," he said to applause. "We hope one day you will be able to explore issues in your own country that concern you." Sidney, dignified and magnetic, said, "I live my life as an actor and relish the opportunity to play challenging roles." The lights went down and *The Defiant Ones* unspooled.

Sidney Poitier expresses appreciation to interpreter Vladimir Posner on return from screening of
The Defiant Ones at the Sports Palace in Moscow, July 1963. Left to right: John Strasberg,
Susan Strasberg, Stanley Kramer and Stevens, Jr.

Tony Curtis, a surly chain gang prisoner shackled to fellow inmate Poitier
as they try to escape, says, "You know the trouble with us? We spend all of our
life not saying a word—we wait until we die before we shout." This evoked a
spontaneous ovation. At the climax, their chains broken, the two men run to
leap on a moving train. Sidney hoists himself up. He extends his hand and Curtis clasps it. Poitier struggles to pull him aboard. The audience began applaud-
ing, only to see both tumble from the speeding train and be recaptured.

Henry Tanner's report in the *New York Times* described the Russian spectators jumping to their feet. "In an extraordinary display of emotion almost the
entire audience began streaming toward the corner of the huge hall where Sidney
Poitier, the Negro star of *The Defiant Ones,* was standing. There were mostly
young persons. Many wiped tears from their eyes as others cheered and clapped."
I saw Sidney look down and observe how moved Susan Strasberg was, and
watched as he drew her to her feet, her sunglasses falling, revealing tears as she
wept openly. Sidney embraced her and the roar of the crowd strengthened. Tanner observed in the *Times,* "The young Soviet artists and intellectuals who are

struggling for greater freedom of expression have reason to be gratified by what happened here during the Moscow's Third International Film Festival."

Federico Fellini's bold and surrealistic *8½* became the most talked-about film, but the Eastern bloc majority on the jury refused to vote for it because it was inconsistent with "socialist realism" and recommended that no Grand Prize be given. After a day of debate the final vote was nine to six against giving a grand prize. Stanley Kramer challenged the jury, "If we cannot award the prize to the gem of the festival, I must withdraw." Satyajit Ray, the revered Indian director, then rose and excused himself, followed by the French, Japanese and Italian jurors. The Italian, a communist, shouted at the Russian jury chairman, "What your country needs is a good Communist Party!"

Hours later the jury was ordered to reconvene. Madame Furtseva and Baskakov had made a decision. The jury now awarded the Grand Prize to *8½* by unanimous vote.

The next day the chairman of the USSR State Committee of Cinematography was in damage control mode, declaring, "We reject any attempts to interpret the judgment of the international jury as a concession of Soviet artists in the ideological struggle." According to the *Times,* "Soviet cinematographers, some almost tearfully, told their foreign colleagues, 'You don't know what this means for us.'"

Ambassador Thompson and his colleagues at State saw the *Times* article, which contained this straightforward paragraph: "The American delegation to the festival had reason to be pleased. It came to Moscow with a new approach. It took a calculated risk and its members, State Department officials, as well as moviemakers, feel it has won the gamble."

Any reproach I might have earned because of the rogue public screening of *The Defiant Ones* was blunted.

As I departed Moscow, my distinguished ally in getting Kramer's films approved for the festival, Averell Harriman, remained there at the center of world attention, successfully concluding negotiations for the historic Nuclear Test Ban Treaty with the USSR and the British. I was back to Washington in time to join a candlelight vigil in Georgetown outside the Harriman residence celebrating the American statesman's return.

27

Five Cities

The USIA film that was initiated by President Kennedy's trip to Europe took new shape. Bruce Herschensohn, inspired by Sergei Eisenstein's documentary classic about the Russian revolution, *October: Ten Days That Shook the World,* proposed that rather than simply film Kennedy's trip we make a 30-minute documentary *The Five Cities of June.* It told five stories, the pageantry of the coronation of Pope Paul VI in Rome, Kennedy sending the National Guard to Tuscaloosa to enforce the admission of Black students to the University of Alabama, the launching of a female cosmonaut into space at a secret site in the Soviet Union (using their grainy black-and-white film in contrast to the open photography of US launchings), and American advisors assisting South Vietnamese soldiers in a hamlet in Vietnam.

The climax was vivid 35mm color film that Bruce and his team shot of Kennedy's stirring challenge to the Soviets before 250,000 cheering Germans in a huge square near the Berlin Wall. "All free men, wherever they may live are citizens of Berlin," he declared to a thundering roar. "And, therefore, as a free man, I take pride in the words 'Ich bin ein Berliner.'" The color footage was magnitudes more dramatic than black-and-white newsreel coverage.

The Five Cities of June was edited and scored, and 35mm prints were shipped throughout the world within thirty days.

Then came exciting news that President Kennedy had agreed to host a luncheon for motion picture leaders at the White House on December 10. The guest list went beyond heads of major studios to include a broad representation of directors, writers and producers from the creative community. I wrote to Fred Zinnemann, who headed our film festival committee. "This will be the first time that the White House has come forth and recognized the motion picture as a major art, an important economic factor, and a primary psychological force in American life. The president will say as much to those present."

President Kennedy addresses 250,000 West German citizens in Rudolph Wilde Platz not far
from the Berlin Wall, June 26, 1963, as seen in *The Five Cities of June.*

Ed Murrow held weekly staff meetings where area directors and heads of the
media divisions reported on progress and discussed plans. I was at his meeting
one afternoon when my deputy Tony Guarco entered unexpectedly, came to my
chair, and handed me a folded note. I looked at it, exchanged a look with Murrow, and left the room. The note from Pat Woodward said that Evelyn Lincoln,
President Kennedy's secretary, had just called saying he wanted to speak with
me. Pat started to dial as I went into my office and closed the door. She buzzed
and I heard the voice of Mrs. Lincoln.

"Mr. Stevens . . . I'll put the president on." Then the unmistakable Boston
accent.

"George. I saw your film, *The Five Cities of June*. It's one of the best documentaries I've seen."

"Thank you, sir."

"Where is it being shown?"

"In over a hundred countries. I can get the exact figure. In some places in movie theaters, others on television. In Africa it goes out on mobile units."

"That sequence in the Vatican was terrific. The Russian piece. All of it. Has John Rooney seen it?"

"We have a hard time getting Chairman Rooney to watch films."

"Maybe I can do something about that. Get a detailed report on the showings over to us."

And he was gone.

I sat still for a moment. I had never anticipated getting a call from an American president. This one had an appetite for firsthand knowledge and was known to bypass cabinet officers and heads of agencies to call whomever he thought would have the information he wanted. Moments later the White House called back asking for *Five Cities* to be sent over for another showing that night.

When I returned to the meeting, Murrow, with a flicker of a smile, said, "Do you want to tell us about your phone conversation?" I did so, enjoying the intense expressions of my career foreign service colleagues, reflecting their pride in the personal vote of confidence from the president.

Three weeks later I was in Los Angeles, asleep at the Sunset Tower, where my father lived, after what would aptly be described as a late night, when the phone rang at 6:30 a.m. It was Pat Woodward in Washington with a heads-up. "Mrs. Lincoln just rang. I gave her your number."

I jumped out of bed and headed toward the bathroom for a splash of cold water, but the ringing phone stopped me halfway.

"George, I think you should enter *The Five Cities of June* in the Academy Awards."

"Thank you, Mr. President. We submitted an entry."

"Oh, good. Keep up the good work."

I was left with that distinctive voice echoing in my head, wondering who was in the Oval Office with him and what matter of state this man would turn to next.

I had become friends with the Chilean ambassador, Sergio Gutierrez Olivos, and a few weeks later went to his residence for a luncheon. It was a bright and clear fall day, and when I arrived several guests were gathered in the entryway. I ended up beside Ralph Dungan, a senior White House aide, who was telling Senator

Hubert Humphrey that the president expected Barry Goldwater to be his 1964 opponent and how he was looking forward to running against the Republican senator. We were shown into the dining room and seated at a long table. John Brademas, the ambitious young Rhodes Scholar congressman from Indiana, who would one day become Democratic majority whip, was seated on my right, and Lady Margaret Walker, the white-haired wife of the director of the National Gallery, was on my left. The columnist Drew Pearson was two seats away.

During the first course I noticed the ambassador leave the table, which seemed unusual. He returned and whispered to Humphrey, then led him and Dungan into an adjoining room. We continued talking but fell silent when Humphrey returned and stood opposite us at the center of the table. He collected himself.

"President Kennedy has been shot in Dallas."

After a moment he added with some difficulty, "We're trying to get more information. He's young and strong. We should be hopeful."

The senator left and we sat in a sepulchral silence, food going cold on our plates. Mrs. Walker took my hand and held it tightly. A few minutes passed before Humphrey returned. His voice cracked as he choked out the words, "He's gone." And the tears came.

Returning to my office by taxi I was struck by the beauty of the city in its fall colors and how John Kennedy had galvanized it. I was absorbing the unimaginable. At USIA I gathered a few stunned colleagues in my office. I explained it was our responsibility to organize camera crews overseas to photograph the world's reaction to the president's death.

My friend Pamela Turnure was with the Kennedys in the motorcade in Dallas and I was concerned for her. I watched the grim nighttime arrival of Air Force One at Andrews Air Force Base on black-and-white television, and the lowering of the flag-draped casket from a cargo door as Jackie looked on holding Robert Kennedy's hand. I called Pamela's house until she answered at close to midnight, then went to see her. This lovely young woman, devoted to the Kennedys, had endured hours of trauma and seemed numb. She had flown home on Air Force One at the side of her employer who was still wearing her bloodstained Chanel suit. Pam knew self-control was necessary because as press secretary to the First Lady she would be on duty for the next four days, coordinating delegations of world leaders arriving to pay respects to our fallen president.

By coincidence my father was making his first visit to Washington since I had been there, for an East Coast meeting of the Directors Guild. He heard the news at the Los Angeles airport and decided to come anyway. We had breakfast the next morning. He carried his own grief but I could sense his heartbreak that his son's bright new world had been turned upside down. Overnight I had been restlessly contemplating what USIA's role should be in the wake of the assassination, and discussed with him an idea for a film, then went to my office.

Ed Murrow had been hospitalized for lung surgery in October and I hadn't seen him for several weeks. I heard that he had come to the office and I asked to see him. He was wearing dark trousers and a green cardigan sweater, no tie, no Savile Row suit. We shook hands in silence and he sat on the sofa as I settled in a chair across from him. For the first time he didn't light a cigarette, and neither did I. Ed looked gaunt, his handsome face gray, his voice raspy. I heard that on an earlier visit to the office he'd cracked, "Whoever said talk was cheap had two lungs."

He picked up a letter from the coffee table and passed it to me. The legend at the top: The White House, Washington, and the date, October 21, 1963. It was addressed to Murrow at the Washington Hospital Center.

Holding this letter I was overcome knowing that it had so recently been in the hands of the president. I was moved to know that his lively mind, so heinously extinguished, had just days before been engaged with our film. I passed the letter back to Ed. He lifted his hand, rejecting it.

"You made the film. You keep the letter."

This magnanimous gesture came at a raw moment from a great man who had seen so much and was fighting for his own life. It spoke to the nature of Edward R. Murrow.

"I have a proposal," I said. Ed nodded and sat back. "I believe this is the time to make USIA's first feature-length film." I explained that we had cameramen in a dozen countries gathering reactions to the president's death. It was an opportunity to tell the story of the Kennedy presidency and address USIA's major themes, set in the frame of the four days of his funeral. I said it would cost $250,000, a big number for USIA in 1963 dollars. Ed asked a few questions, leading me to say that I had spoken to Bruce Herschensohn and we were going to meet to flesh out the story. Then he went silent, before getting to his feet and speaking one sentence.

"First, make a ten-minute film about Lyndon Johnson." He walked me to the door, with me cradling the Kennedy letter. "Then," he said, "you can make your Kennedy film."

Youthful enthusiasm had encountered age and experience. Ed understood immediately what I was slow to grasp. He knew that the world must see Lyndon Johnson serving as our leader after a swift and orderly transfer of power, and that USIA would be vulnerable in Johnson's eyes if we were preoccupied only with Kennedy. Ed understood our mission and the politics.

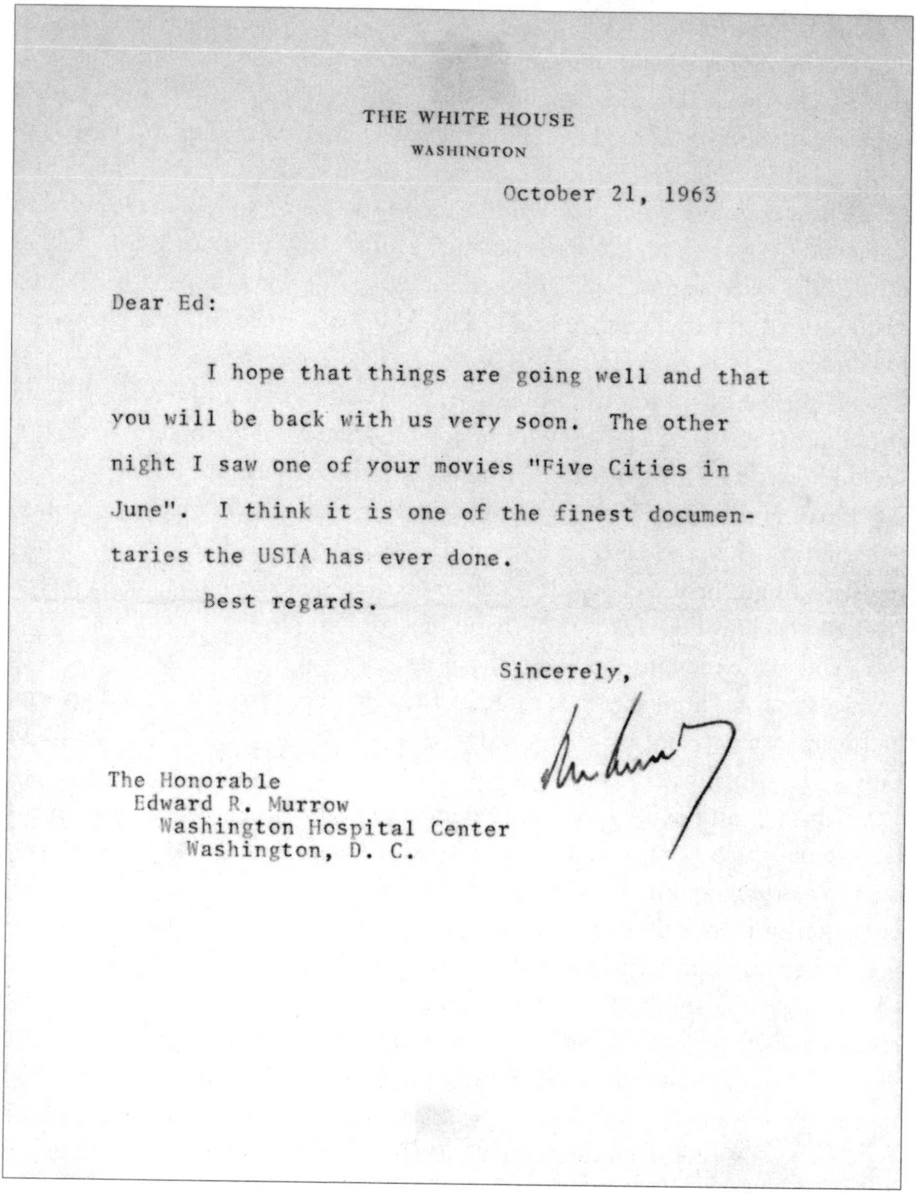

THE WHITE HOUSE
WASHINGTON

October 21, 1963

Dear Ed:

I hope that things are going well and that
you will be back with us very soon. The other
night I saw one of your movies "Five Cities in
June". I think it is one of the finest documentaries the USIA has ever done.

Best regards.

Sincerely,

The Honorable
Edward R. Murrow
Washington Hospital Center
Washington, D. C.

I called half a dozen staff members into my office and told them we had
Murrow's approval for two films related to the tragedy and both had to be organized on the fly. These were senior figures in our unit who were shaken by this
decapitation of the government they served, but they were pleased to be in action and set out to recruit the best cameramen and secure prime positions to
cover the four ceremonial days of laying our president to rest. I met with Herschensohn and asked him to take on both the Kennedy and Johnson films, and

spoke with Gregory Peck, who agreed to narrate both. We wanted the Johnson film in theaters around the world within four weeks.

There was comfort in having my father in town, and on the afternoon of Kennedy's burial at Arlington he dropped me at my apartment building on his way to the airport. As I settled dolefully into my black leather Eames chair to watch television replays, I took a cigarette from a pack and lit it, taking a deep drag. I had become a two pack a day man. I looked at the curling smoke, then stubbed it in the ashtray. I'd tried quitting before, but this proved to be my last cigarette, ending a ten-year habit.

A month later I was in Los Angeles having dinner at La Scala with my father. In those days ashtrays with matches adorned restaurant tables and we would have a cigarette with cocktails and one with coffee. My father took notice that I wasn't smoking and I told him the story. He had a story to tell me. When he rode away in the taxi that afternoon in Washington, he "lit up, took a few puffs and threw it out the window, and that was it."

Dad and I had never discussed smoking. We both decided within minutes of one another on the day Kennedy was buried to abandon cigarettes.

I pulled down the curtain on 1963, looking with uncertainty at a world that had lost its brightest light.

28

Transition

I sent a handwritten letter of consolation to Robert Kennedy saying how powerfully his brother's vision and idealism had affected me, also offering to help with the planned presidential library. Two days later he called. "I have your letter," he said softly. "I hope you'll work with us on the library." It was my first phone call from Robert Kennedy, and it was the first but not the last time I would experience the predisposition of Kennedys to comfort others in their own time of grief.

Buried in the aftermath of the assassination was a *New York Times* report that Kennedy's December 10 luncheon at the White House had been canceled. It said that forty-five individuals had received invitations in the mail on November 22. The *Times* description of the occasion—"the first White House event ever for the motion picture community, one that would be a backdrop for Kennedy acknowledging the status of films as an art"—spoke to the change he was prepared to initiate and how sorely he would be missed.

We called the Murrow-inspired ten-minute film about Lyndon Johnson *The President,* and received a Sunday night appointment in early December to film in the Oval Office. It was ghostly quiet in the West Wing as Bruce Herschensohn worked on lighting and I exchanged gallows humor with Pierre Salinger, who remained in place as press secretary. We placed a small table lamp with a glass shade on the president's desk to provide more textured lighting than would come from the ceiling. Pierre protested, saying he had never seen a lamp on the desk. Bruce and I pushed back saying we had seen a lamp of that sort in White House photos and needed dramatic lighting for this portrait of the new president alone in the Oval Office.

Pierre relented. It seemed that some of the swagger had gone out of Plucky Pierre.

An hour later the door to the Rose Garden opened and Lyndon Johnson walked in followed by Pierre and two secret service agents. I had last seen him two months before at a crowded charity premiere of *Charade,* starring Cary Grant and Audrey Hepburn, at Loew's Palace that Jackie had organized with Ethel. Cary joined Bobby and Ethel and New Frontier friends at a spirited pre-show reception in the lobby. I remember noticing Vice President Johnson standing to the side in a full cut dark suit seeming disconnected from the young crowd.

He was now president of the United States.

Pierre introduced Bruce and me and we explained our purpose. Johnson and Pierre had been in the White House swimming pool and it seemed they'd had a drink or two. As we filmed the president at his desk I noticed he had signed a response to a letter of resignation from Arthur Schlesinger, before writing intently on a yellow pad as the cameras rolled. Once we had the footage we needed, he rose, nodded a goodnight, and left for the family quarters. As for the lamp with the green shade, it was effective in creating an expressive shot that introduced the new president, preceded by an exterior night shot of the White House with music and the magisterial voice of Gregory Peck: "The light in the White House window flickered, but it did not go out."

Bruce and I remained confident of our assertion that we had seen a similar lamp in a White House photo but neither of us could remember where. Several years later I was watching *Yankee Doodle Dandy* and saw James Cagney, playing George M. Cohan, walk into the Oval Office to meet President Roosevelt. There on the desk was the lamp with the glass shade. Not quite the authenticity we professed, but no one ever complained.

Three weeks later we had a completed film that evoked continuity of government and Johnson's determination to lead. Pierre invited me to the White House for an afternoon preview for the president, Lady Bird and some of their friends. Herschensohn flew in from Los Angeles. As the Johnsons took seats in the first row with Senate Majority Leader Mike Mansfield and his wife, I noticed the rocking chair was gone.

Pierre explained to the Johnsons that a thousand prints of *The President,* translated into thirty-nine languages, were on the way to theaters overseas, and that United Artists and MGM would be pairing it with major feature films. There was applause at the end and LBJ, looming above us, shook my hand with both of his fists and thanked me. As we hurried back to the West Wing, Pierre summoned his plucky spirit to offer a sardonic observation. "Well, it looks like you just conned another president."

Ed Murrow was seriously ill and tried to resign, but Johnson—eager to demonstrate continuity by retaining Kennedy people—ignored the request. Ed being a

Filming *The President* in the Oval Office, December 1963. George Stevens, Jr., and
Lyndon Johnson with the disputed lamp on the left.

good citizen went along with it, but in late January notified the White House
that he absolutely had to leave, a loss that was deeply dispiriting. I had once
complimented Ed on his stainless steel drafting table where he stood to read
newspapers. The day he departed the table was delivered to my office with a note
encouraging me to press on.

Arthur Schlesinger resigned to write *A Thousand Days* and Ted Sorensen left
to write *Kennedy,* two firsthand accounts of the New Frontier. My contemporary Dick Goodwin stayed on, taking a job in the White House.

A host of Texans were soon in prominent positions. During my three
years with *Giant* I became familiar with the Texas accents that now supplanted

the Boston inflection. The spare elegance of JFK's oratory was replaced by more flowery language, except on occasions when the holdover Goodwin wielded the pen. It was a "the king is dead, long live the king" upheaval. Jack Valenti, a personable advertising man from Houston, became one of Johnson's closest aides. Jack was captivated by *The President* and became an enthusiastic supporter of my work. He also saw himself as a peacemaker and took on the unenviable task of trying to bridge the gap between the Johnson and Kennedy factions.

The shock of the assassination led me to reflect on my personal life. My best friends in college had married the year after graduation but I felt less urgency to start a family, perhaps the result of growing up an only child. My professional life in the movies meant there was no shortage of inviting companionship, but the elevated divorce rate in the film world led me to conclude I wouldn't marry an actress. When I moved to Washington most of my new friends were couples with children, and I began to wonder if I had set some unrealistic standard for marriage and had missed the boat. I felt fortunate to be going out with Pamela Turnure. We shared professional interests and she was delightful company, but marriage seemed no more likely than in previous situations.

One weekend Pam invited me to join her in Virginia at the farm of Lily Polk Guest, the mother of her best friend. Lily Guest was divorced from the horse breeder, polo champion and businessman Raymond Guest, who President Johnson would soon name ambassador to Ireland. Pam and I arrived at Mrs. Guest's farm on the Shenandoah River, and when we entered the living room I saw a young woman in a beige cashmere sweater curled on a long sofa. Her modest smile was alluring, her beauty classic and refined, qualities that would for her prove timeless. This was Lily Guest's daughter Elizabeth. She had married some years earlier and was now separated and raising her four-year-old daughter Caroline. There were echoes of *Giant*, where Rock Hudson, the less cultivated westerner, visits a Virginia farm to buy a stallion and discovers the extremely beautiful daughter of the owner, a young woman of independent mind played by Elizabeth Taylor. Whereas a woman with a child might have seemed a complication at an earlier stage of my life, the idea of now coming together with this lovely woman and her young daughter grew on me. And in time it would make sense to her.

At USIA I found myself with a foot in two camps. I was working for President Johnson but my ties to the Kennedys were quietly maturing. In the aftermath of John Kennedy's death the family no longer had a government at their disposal so they called on friends for help. Jackie had moved with John and Caroline to a

Elizabeth Guest at the stable at Rock Hill Farm,
Front Royal, Virginia, 1964.

house on N Street in Georgetown, across the street from the Harrimans. She received eight hundred thousand condolence letters and was determined that each one be answered. A small group of her friends volunteered to assist, Elizabeth Guest among them.

Jackie decided to make a public expression of thanks and I was asked to organize it. I went to her house with a camera crew to film her response in 35mm color for distribution in theaters and on television. I was aware of the depth of her desolation, but she entered the flowered living room with a warm smile and greeted each of the crew in her soft and breathy voice. She then described on camera how the letters had sustained her. Mindful of the grace and courage she displayed only weeks before, I left deeply touched by her. Jacqueline Kennedy was not yet thirty-four.

Planning for the John F. Kennedy Presidential Library in Boston began immediately after the assassination. Arthur Schlesinger had asked for ideas and

I'd written to him describing the legacy of available film material and how it could enhance the library. The Kennedys were starting a fundraising campaign and a search for architects, and I was asked by Stephen Smith, husband of Jean Kennedy Smith, who managed Kennedy family business and political interests with discretion and Irish charm, to compile memorable footage of JFK for a presentation that would galvanize fundraising.

We met in the Georgetown living room of Senator Ted Kennedy and his wife Joan on a chilly February afternoon for a preview. I remember President Johnson taking his seat next to Mrs. Kennedy. Everyone was courteous, though well-meaning expressions of cordiality could not erase the tension. The members of the Kennedy family were younger than Johnson, and in the wake of the sudden shift of power the distance between Boston and Austin was palpable.

Bob Kennedy described the purpose of the library and spoke of fundraising goals. He introduced me. "George Stevens is going to tell us a little about the film and how film will be used in the Kennedy Library." Anxious that the gathering not be prolonged, he earned a laugh amidst the solemnity with his hint, "It will be very short."

The vivid color images of President Kennedy were so lifelike, the cadence of his voice so optimistic, that there was silence at the end. Spirits were suddenly lifted when the dashing and spirited Sargent Shriver burst through the front door with a twinkling smile and a box of cigars. He had come from the hospital where Eunice had given birth to the newest Kennedy, their third son. For a moment at least, Irish eyes were smiling.

I am often asked why the Kennedys had such loyal followers. A letter arrived that provides a clue.

Dear George,
I was extremely pleased when I saw the final version of the film, and the knowledge that it has touched so many people so deeply must give you a real sense of accomplishment.

The president's family and I will never forget your devotion to this project—which is so close to our hearts.

Sincerely,
Jackie

Arthur Schlesinger moved from the White House to a small office off Connecticut Avenue and on occasion invited me for lunch at Duke Zeibert's. "A

With Jacqueline Kennedy at 3017 N Street in Georgetown, filming her thank-you to
the American people, January 1964.

very dry Bombay martini," Arthur would instruct the waiter. Wishing to measure up, I would say, "The same." Conversation with Arthur was wise, witty and
wide-ranging, and when time came to order Arthur would ask for another martini and divide it between us. Afterward he would return to his office and write
a chapter of *A Thousand Days,* while I would spend a good part of the afternoon
sound asleep on my office sofa. Arthur enjoyed the uplift of luncheon martinis
with no diminishment of his intellectual acuity until his passing (while enjoying
a steak dinner in a New York bistro) in his ninetieth year.

Arthur announced he was moving to New York in April of 1964, so we organized a going-away party at a Georgetown University hangout called The Tombs.
The printed invitation was from "The Former Friends of Arthur Schlesinger," and
the theme of the evening was proclaimed in a banner over the door: "Forgotten
but not Gone." It brought out the full circle of Kennedy family and friends, the
first lighthearted gathering since November. The *Washington Star*'s Betty Beale
described it as a "gay, dancing, comical, celebrity-filled party . . . that looked like

a flashback to the Kennedy administration." Mary McGrory, the wise and spirited political essayist, labeled it "uproarious."

Art Buchwald, who moved from Paris to be humor columnist for the *Washington Post,* explained to the crowd that when someone leaves the White House the president writes two letters, one for publication and "one for the person being fired." He said Johnson's letter to Arthur began, "My Dear Arthur, Jack Valenti advises me that we are short on space in the West Wing of the White House. As you recall when I first became president I said I needed you very badly. Mr. Valenti advises me we need the space more." Midway through the evening Jackie slipped in quietly with her sister Lee Radziwill and joined Arthur at his table. When Arthur rose to speak, "The Eyes of Texas" blared on the loudspeakers and his "former friends" stood and cheered.

The Five Cities of June was nominated for an Academy Award, a touching requiem to President Kennedy's enthusiasm for the film. It was USIA's first nod from the academy and a great boost for the agency, even though a film about painter Marc Chagall won on Oscar night. Arthur wrote from Cannes, where he was serving on the jury and enjoying a three amigos relationship with fellow jurors Charles Boyer and Fritz Lang, commiserating over our Oscar loss, saying, "I couldn't have been sorrier about Monday night. I have not seen *Chagall* but (loyally) I have no doubt at all that the award should have gone to *Five Cities.*" He closed with a reflection on his farewell party. "It was wonderful to see all those N. Frontier faces gathered together—and a little sad. Will there ever be such days again?"

I headed the American delegation to the Karlovy Vary Film Festival in Czechoslovakia in July. Liz agreed to go with me and her charm and fluent French elevated my diplomatic game. We passed through the Iron Curtain driving from Frankfurt and pulled into the courtyard of the Grand Hotel Moskva Pupp. Emerging from another car was a lanky man with a familiar Carroll & Company black and red garment bag over his shoulder. Henry Fonda was arriving for a showing of the American political drama *The Best Man.*

There was an intense Cold War feel to this small Czech resort famed for its restorative baths. During the festival apparatchiks from behind the Iron Curtain and cinema intelligentsia from the West engaged in antagonistic seminars. I found myself the butt of accusations concerning the "imperialist intentions" of my father's *Gunga Din,* but the Czech filmmakers turned out to be a sprightly group who leavened events with rebellious humor, and presented a brilliant parody of American Westerns, *Lemonade Joe.* The Czechs delighted in observing Henry Fonda watching the movie's homage to the scene from *My Darling*

With Cliff Robertson and Henry Fonda at the Karlovy Vary film festival in 1964. Fonda holds the Special Jury Prize for *The Best Man,* in which he and Robertson portray rivals for the presidential nomination in a screenplay by Gore Vidal.

Clementine where, as Wyatt Earp, reclining on two legs of a four-legged chair on a hotel porch, he alternates balancing his boots against a post. Elia Kazan, earthy and feisty, brought his film *America America* with its signature scene of Greek immigrants seeing the Statue of Liberty and passing through Ellis Island.

One night Kazan, Cliff Robertson, also there for *The Best Man,* and Fonda joined Liz and me in the opulent suite allocated to the head of the American delegation to listen to the Republican Convention in San Francisco on the Voice of America. Through crackling reception we heard delegates jeering the moderate presidential contender Nelson Rockefeller, and listened as Barry Goldwater, the man Ralph Dungan had told me eight months earlier John Kennedy relished running against, captured the GOP nomination. We were a melancholy group that night on the far side of the Iron Curtain listening to what seemed like America unmoored.

The highlight of the trip for Liz and me was driving Henry Fonda from Karlovy Vary to beautiful Prague. He sat in the backseat with his feet propped against the window, telling stories of working for his old friend John Ford, including an account of the director on a bender during *Mister Roberts,* knocking on Fonda's door in the middle of the night and coldcocking him with a blow to the head. Ford was replaced by Mervyn LeRoy.

Liz and I were enchanted by Henry's modesty and easy companionship. He became our lifelong friend. A treasure on our library wall is a gift from Henry—the artist's proof of his exquisite watercolor of the three hats he wore in *On Golden Pond.*

29

The March

In 1963, before JFK's death, we had initiated what proved to be our most controversial film, and in my view one of our most effective. It would be years later before I understood the political subcurrents that affected the film.

I believed a documentary about the March on Washington for Jobs and Freedom, where Black and white Americans would rally together for equality, could serve as a counterweight to widely seen newsreel images of police dogs attacking Blacks and protesters being beaten. We engaged Hearst Metrotone News to have ten cameras cover the event for a thirty-minute film called *The March,* which begins with crowds arriving at the Lincoln Memorial to the song "Eyes on the Prize" and the gentle voice of director James Blue: "On the twenty-eighth of August of 1963, two hundred thousand Americans came to Washington to claim complete freedom for everyone. This is the story of that day."

Viewers around the world saw a diverse and committed throng transported by the voices of Marian Anderson, Mahalia Jackson and Joan Baez, and uplifted by the soaring eloquence of Martin Luther King, Jr.'s, "I Have a Dream" speech.

Historian Richard Dyer McCann compared *The March* to Pare Lorentz's classic of the Roosevelt era, writing, "It has something of the epic quality of *The River,* and in the manner of that poetic government documentary it reflects the sharp excitement of a great contemporary issue." However, when it came out in 1964 some thought the film brought unhelpful attention to an American problem. Clark Mollenhoff, a reporter who was a member of USIA's advisory commission, waged a vehement campaign against the film, telling members of Congress that "foreign audiences are not sophisticated and we should not advertise our problems." USIA sent cables asking US ambassadors to evaluate the film. The responses were largely enthusiastic but a few expressed concern that the marchers might be perceived as protesting against our government.

One morning I took a taxi to Capitol Hill to testify before the House Appropriations subcommittee chaired by John Rooney. Murrow having resigned and no replacement yet chosen, I was on my own. Rooney controlled USIA's budget and was a close friend of J. Edgar Hoover, whose FBI was wiretapping Martin Luther King.

We screened *The March* in the private hearing room. When it ended Rooney stared at me. "Did you ever think about asking for a security check on your star?" He was referring to Dr. King, whom he believed to be a communist. I thought back to the day USIA's general counsel warned Murrow that Rooney disapproved of our drawing attention to King. "Tell him to go to hell," Ed growled.

I didn't understand the heights to which the controversy had risen until a decade later when an investigative journalist sent me transcripts of secret recordings of President Johnson in the Oval Office. I realized then how naive I had been.

LBJ had decided to replace Murrow with Carl Rowan, an African American journalist and diplomat, and called his old friend John McClellan of Arkansas, chairman of the Senate Appropriations Committee. The Oval Office recorder captured the January 16, 1964, conversation, which turned to *The March*.

PRESIDENT JOHNSON. John, I've got a little problem. . . . Mr. Ed Murrow is dying with cancer of the lung. I've got to get me another man. I've got a good, solid man. . . . He's a good administrator and he'll listen to me—but he's a Negro. His name is Carl Rowan, he's Ambassador to Finland.

SENATOR MCCLELLAN. I doubt if I'm going with that. You do what you want to do.

PRESIDENT JOHNSON. I wouldn't expect you to endorse him, but I just wanted you to know about it because I didn't want to do it with you wondering why in hell your friend didn't tell you. . . . USIA is in your department on Appropriations and I don't want you to cut his guts out because he's a Nigra—and I've seen you operate with a knife and seen a few people get de-nutted.

SENATOR MCCLELLAN. I think they [USIA] are just throwing money away. . . . They took this picture, you know, of the mass demonstration here, March on Washington, and they've doctored that up and they're showing it all over the world, showing the worst side of America. God I'm against that sort of propaganda. I think it's more harmful than helpful. Ed Murrow's crowd has been doing that.

Johnson proposed they wait until Rowan arrived to discuss USIA's future. He then called the powerful Richard Russell of Georgia and appears to state our rationale for *The March*—before bringing up Robert Kennedy's name.

PRESIDENT JOHNSON. I looked at this movie last night that they published on the March to Washington . . . have been some hell raised about that. It's not a good movie, but it's not bad from the South's standpoint . . . it shows this march from Washington monument to Lincoln's tomb, and it shows that the Nigra has a right to be heard and has a voice and can petition—and doesn't get shot for doing it.

SENATOR RUSSELL. I had three Republicans talk to me about it and I haven't mentioned it to a living soul.

PRESIDENT JOHNSON. This damn sonofabitch, Mollenhoff, who's on the advisory board—Bobby Kennedy put him on there and he ain't worth a damn, and he's . . . called Fulbright [Senator J. William, Ark.], trying to get him to raise hell. . . . Lady Bird and I watched it, and she thought it could have been a better edited movie, but it was showing that . . . you do have the right of petition in this country, and by God they can come right up here, a hundred thousand of them and march down the street.

SENATOR RUSSELL. Damn sight rather they'd show that than show some of these things where they violate the laws by laying down in the road and all that stuff.

Don Wilson, acting director of USIA, called on February 4 to say Bob Kennedy was coming over to see *The March*. The attorney general was relaxed as we sat down in room 308, but he looked drawn. He seemed moved by the film but mentioned a shot of an attractive Black boy and a blond girl seated next to one another on a bus, saying it was an innocent image but that Southern senators might see it differently. I was encouraged by his overall reaction.

The White House log shows that at 6:10 p.m., just a few hours after Kennedy had seen us, LBJ called Secretary of State Dean Rusk.

PRESIDENT JOHNSON. I understand the Attorney General and Averell [Harriman] have been around looking at movies this afternoon and got all concerned about [*The March*]. Have you seen the picture?

DEAN RUSK. I have seen it and I talked to Averell and others about it. . . . It was made before November 22 and there's nothing in it about President Kennedy or your interest in Civil Rights. I think it's too bad that it be shown in its present form without being brought up to date. . . . I think we ought to have a chance to talk with you about it

PRESIDENT JOHNSON. I don't want it on my level. I don't want to be deciding on every damn movie is made. Clark Mollenhoff—now he's the one that started this. He's a vicious, mean man who said he's determined to destroy me, and I want it kept away from me just as far as I can. . . . I saw it with all the Negro leaders and their reaction was it demonstrated the right of peaceful petition. . . . I think that the moment you touch that film you're going to have all the Negro groups saying that here's a southerner [LBJ] suppressing it. . . . That's why I'm not going to get close to it.

DEAN RUSK. I think [for] audiences here who know the background it's a magnificent picture, but for audiences overseas who are very little informed, I'm concerned about it. I'll get into it further, Mr. President.

PRESIDENT JOHNSON. And we better get something for Averell and Bobby to be doing besides that.

There is no record in the White House phone logs of Robert Kennedy calling Johnson about *The March,* so some mystery attends this story. My focus was on protecting *The March.* I didn't realize that the film had become a pawn in the high-stakes game between the two men who regarded themselves as heir to JFK's legacy. Bobby and his inner circle thought Johnson should put him on the 1964 ticket as vice president at the August Democratic Convention. Johnson figured that he might need Kennedy to win but preferred to define his presidency independent of him.

When Carl Rowan took over USIA I was told that we were to film an introduction by Rowan to be attached to all prints of *The March.* Having no idea how many powerful voices were involved in this debate, I protested that the USIA director on camera telling the audience what the US government's intent was in making the film would undermine its persuasive quality. I was overruled, and from that point on *The March* would begin with Rowan explicitly stating the purpose of the film.

Our success at USIA had come from carefully crafting our films to contain messages that viewers could absorb visually without feeling they were being lectured to. Jim Blue and I wanted people overseas to see the uplifting story of Blacks and whites petitioning side by side for the redress of grievances and perhaps conclude that only a great nation would allow such a public protest to take place—and make a film about it. The Rowan prologue violated our cardinal rule of respect for the audience.

The March, presented without Rowan's introduction, earned grand prizes at the Bilbao Film Festival and Cannes, and nearly half a century later the "test of time" vote came in. The Library of Congress added *The March* to the prestigious United States National Film Registry—describing it as a film that ushered in "the Golden Era of USIA films."

For me the most enjoyable comment can be found in Ann Sperber's *Murrow: His Life and Times*. "I am unrepentant about *The March*," Ed wrote to Don Wilson after his retirement. "It's a good film and anybody, including Bob Kennedy and Rusk, who believes that every individual film must present a 'balanced' picture knows nothing about either balance or pictures."

30

Election Year

The Democratic Convention was approaching in August and all eyes were on Lyndon Johnson as he weighed his choice of a running mate. The Republican Party's recent nomination of far-right Senator Barry Goldwater had reduced the importance to Johnson of Robert Kennedy's popular appeal in the North. My friend Joe Kraft, the syndicated political columnist, invited me for a late July afternoon drink at his house in Georgetown, and as we chatted in his living room the doorbell signaled the unexpected arrival of Bob Kennedy. He was by himself, coming from a White House meeting with the president.

Bobby described how Johnson informed him he would not be his choice for vice president. LBJ explained gravely that he was removing his entire cabinet from consideration so they would not be distracted by politics—a list that, in addition to Bobby, included Dean Rusk, Adlai Stevenson, Robert McNamara and Sargent Shriver. Bobby related the grim encounter with rueful humor. He was, in the Washington tradition, getting his side of the story out to a friendly journalist. Kraft's subsequent column included Bobby's observation, "I'm sorry I took so many nice fellows over the side with me."

Two weeks later I was called out of a USIA screening to take a call from the attorney general. I made a note.

> This morning Bob Kennedy called from the Cape before going on his boat trip and asked for help. He said, "It looks like I am going to run [for the US Senate] in New York." He was serious but his sense of the absurd led him to add, "I really don't know why"—while knowing exactly why. Then he said that he thought a film was one of the most important things for him.

He asked if I would help with a documentary that could be shown to voters in his campaign against popular incumbent Republican senator, Kenneth Keating. I asked what he wanted the film to express. With a wry reference to two persisting criticisms, he said it would be helpful if it could convince people that he was not a carpetbagger and that he wasn't ruthless. Then he added, "Also, that I have experience and I used to be young." Before hanging up he asked if we could involve "the fellow [Bruce Herschensohn] you worked with on *The Five Cities of June.*"

I didn't realize at that moment that his request was a watershed in American politics. The country's most adroit political thinker, manager of his brother's winning campaign for the presidency, was gambling his own political future on a Senate run—and had determined that a film biography should be a key element of his campaign.

It was nearly fifty years later that an unexpected message from historian Michael Beschloss provided a clue to how Bobby's thinking had developed. Beschloss directed me to a newly released Oval Office tape recording from November 12, 1963, on the Kennedy Library website.

Sitting by myself at home I clicked on the link and heard John Kennedy's voice, clear and vibrant as if it were yesterday. He is in the Oval Office speaking with Bobby and brother-in-law Steve Smith about the 1964 Democratic Convention. He asks if they have seen *The Five Days* or *Cities of June,* and I hear my name. "Why don't you get it from George Stevens [and] look at it?" he says.

"I'll tell you," Bobby responds, "George did a number of those films . . ."

"Can't we get George Stevens to work on the films?" asks the president, before speaking with enthusiasm about the prospect of showing films at the convention. "Should they be made in color? . . . Probably a million people watching and it would have an effect." Then, after complaining about tedious convention speeches, he adds, "You'd have the film the first night, ahead of the keynoter."

It was stirring to hear John Kennedy's voice and discover he had decided to use films for his campaign—and that I was in his plans for 1964.

After Bobby's call that day in 1964, I reached Herschensohn in Los Angeles and proposed that he direct the campaign biography. To my surprise Bruce declined, saying he would prefer to continue making USIA films, so I called Charlie Guggenheim in St. Louis, who was enthusiastic. (Only later did Herschensohn tell me he voted for Goldwater in 1964. He eventually abandoned filmmaking to run twice for the United States Senate in California as a Republican.)

I took Charlie to the Justice Department and we met with the attorney general in his cavernous office with children's drawings pinned to the walls, and dodged his roving Newfoundland, Brumus. (When dining at Hickory Hill, the

Kennedys' house in McLean, Virginia, you had to take care lest Brumus snatch your steak.) Bobby was impressed, so with the election just ten weeks away Guggenheim went to work.

The Democratic Convention in Atlantic City in August was an event with Shakespearean overtones. LBJ saw the convention as his opportunity to finally put the Kennedys behind him and take full command of the Democratic party. Bobby was to speak in tribute to President Kennedy on Monday night, but Johnson, fearing that Bobby might stampede the delegates to choose him as vice president, ordered the JFK tribute moved to the closing night.

It was a shrewd move because when Bobby came on stage wearing a dark suit and a black mourning tie, the crowd began to applaud, then cheer and stomp. The ovation came in waves and continued for twenty-two minutes. Liz and I were standing together on the jammed convention floor looking up at Bobby, who appeared slight, almost frail, deeply moved by this declaration of love for his brother. At times he recognized someone and offered a wistful smile.

He then made the most stirring speech of the convention in memory of his brother, concluding with the words, "When I think of President Kennedy, I think of what Shakespeare said in *Romeo and Juliet*."

> When he shall die
> Take him and cut him out in little stars
> And he will make the face of heaven so fine
> That all the world will be in love with the Night
> And pay no worship to the garish Sun.

Liz and I were emotionally drained seeing Bobby the object of such ardor, and by our own conflicting feelings of sorrow and hope.

Senator Keating was leading in the polls in October, when we showed a fine cut of the campaign biography to Bobby, Ethel, Steve Smith and a scrum of advisors in a New York hotel suite. A conflict had developed between the ad agency buying television time for the campaign and Guggenheim and me. They argued that thirty-second commercials would win more votes than a thirty-minute film. We believed a full-fledged biography that gave insight into Robert Kennedy's human qualities would be more persuasive—and lead the viewer to positive conclusions, much in the style of our USIA films.

"Respectfully, sir," an ad agency man said as soon as the lights came up. "It's going to be very difficult to buy thirty-minute blocks of air time, and hardly anyone will watch such a long film."

Before anyone else could speak Bobby stood. "Let's buy as many half-hour television slots as possible for the last two weeks," he ordered. "I think this film can make the difference." And that was that.

The documentary blanketed television throughout New York in the closing days of the campaign. Bobby credited the film with closing the deal in his come-from-behind victory. He and Ethel asked Liz and me to join other supporters on stage when he made his election night acceptance speech. A boisterous audience provided a glimpse of the diverse constituencies required to get elected in New York. He closed with a quote from Tennyson that would become his calling card: "Come my friends, 'Tis not too late to seek a newer world."

When asked by a reporter what happens next, Bobby said, "Now I can go back to being ruthless."

31

In His Memory

Airports, highways, bridges and schools were being named for John Fitzgerald Kennedy in the wake of his assassination, and I found myself involved in three remembrance projects.

Congress had moved quickly to make the planned National Cultural Center a living memorial to the martyred president who had fostered it, and to name it the John F. Kennedy Center for the Performing Arts. Roger Stevens continued as chairman and in November of 1964 announced that opera, classical music, dance and theater would be featured in the building. Disappointed there was no provision for motion pictures, I wrote an op-ed for the *Washington Post* that they titled "A Case for the Cinema: Plans for the Kennedy Center Allow no Adequate Recognition of Film Art." I called for a theater that would show American classics, independent cinema and the best foreign films, in the spirit of my friend Henri Langlois and the Cinémathèque Française.

Two days later I received a call from Richard Coe, drama and film critic of the *Post,* who had learned that Roger Stevens was annoyed by my article. Coe, a peacemaker at heart, invited me to his small office to make my case. Roger, tall, bald and taciturn, listened silently during what was our first conversation. When I finished he said tersely, "If you want a film theater in the Kennedy Center, why don't you help me build it." At that moment began one of the most productive and enjoyable collaborations of my life. Roger Stevens and I were unrelated, but many people mistakenly assumed we were father and son.

At the same time Steve Smith had invited me to be an advisor to the John F. Kennedy Presidential Library project that he headed. It was stimulating to watch a new institution being conceived and to attend search committee presentations by the world's finest architects, including Philip Johnson, Louis Kahn, Mies van der Rohe and a lesser-known Chinese American, I. M. Pei, and to observe these masters articulate their concepts. Jackie Kennedy was attracted by Pei's creativity and personal magnetism. In the announcement of Pei's selection she described it as an emotional decision: "He was so full of promise, like Jack. They were born the same year. I decided it would be fun to take a great leap with him." Jackie's spirit and sense of history made her a joy to work with, and time spent with Pei was inspiring.

Earlier, on December 26, 1963, a month after the assassination, I had written to Arthur Schlesinger.

> There is more film on President Kennedy than on any other figure in world history. The moving image and likeness will provide an opportunity for future generations to sit in a darkened room and perhaps come closer to the Kennedy presence than has previously been possible with a historical figure.

We persuaded Pei to include a film theater, commissioned Charlie Guggenheim to make a biography of Kennedy for hourly showings, and prepared a collage of televised JFK press conferences that displayed his vision, verbal dexterity and sense of fun.

November 1964 marked completion of our USIA film *John F. Kennedy: Years of Lightning, Day of Drums*. It interwove the six faces of the New Frontier—the Peace Corps, Alliance for Progress, exploration of space, civil rights, freedom and peace—with striking footage of the funeral events in Washington. Color imagery intensified Kennedy's vitality and charm, as did touching home movies of him with John and Caroline. The resonant voice of Gregory Peck carried the narration and Bruce Herschensohn composed an affecting musical score.

The president's sister Pat Lawford came alone to preview the film on behalf of the family. It was an emotional experience for Pat, who requested just one change. Where Peck's narration explained, "The president failed at the Bay of Pigs," we changed "failed" to "was set back." A modest request from a bereaved family.

The first public showing was at the Department of State auditorium. Chief Justice Earl Warren, Secretary of State Dean Rusk, other JFK cabinet officers, members of Congress, Ethel Kennedy, New Frontier colleagues, political journalists and forty foreign ambassadors were present. Rarely had an audience been so directly linked to the subject of a motion picture. I could feel the film take hold of the audience, sober for the most part but laughing at lighter moments, as when a bemused Kennedy haltingly exchanges words in Spanish with a blissful crowd in Costa Rica.

"I have never seen an audience react so intensely to a film," began the review of veteran *New York Times* critic Bosley Crowther.

> There was scarcely a murmur or a rustle as its factual footage unreeled. Only sobs and sniffles—or occasionally ripples of laughter or indrawn breaths of admiration and pride at gallant passages—were heard.
> At the end, there was stillness and silence, then but a scattering of applause. The experience had been too deep and touching for the conventional appreciative response.

"Have you ever seen anything that tore your heart out so completely?" said Senator George McGovern to the *Washington Post*.

The most important reaction for me was from my father, who screened the picture at the Culver City Studio where he was editing *The Greatest Story Ever Told*. He told me how deeply moved he was, singling out the image at the end of the film of Kennedy's grave with the eternal flame coated with snow. Since so much of the sensibility that informed this film came from him, I was equally moved.

John F. Kennedy: Years of Lightning, Day of Drums premiered simultaneously in Rome, Beirut and Mexico City before opening in twenty-five other foreign capitals, soon to be seen in 114 countries. Bosley Crowther initiated a campaign for a domestic release, writing, "If it will inspire people in other lands, it should do it for us." Within weeks legislation was passed in Congress to permit showings in the United States. The major film companies were slow to step up because box office returns were uncertain, but Joseph E. Levine, the publicity-loving producer of *Godzilla* and *Hercules,* booked it in theaters across the country—giving a boost to USIA's prestige, especially when the National Board of Review selected *Years of Lightning* as one of the Ten Best Films of 1966.

Robert Kennedy continued to fight clouds of despair over the loss of his brother. His November 20 birthday fell two days before the anniversary of Dallas, and Ethel wanted him to have a good time. She invited friends for dinner and reminded us that the objective was to lift Bobby's spirits. Ethel kept Hickory Hill lively with unexpected guests, and on this night it was the young Russian poet Yevgeny Yevtushenko, tall and brooding with ash-blond hair and gray eyes, who at thirty-two had already appeared on the cover of *Time*.

He was seated on one side of the long table, with Bobby and Ethel at either end. Bob McNamara and his wife Margie, Averell and Marie Harriman, Steve and Jean Smith, and Eunice Shriver were there. The mirth and family teasing seemed to intrigue Yevtushenko, along with his fascination with the historic American documents framed on the walls alongside Kennedy family photos. There were a couple of cheerful birthday toasts and at our end of the table Ethel speculated on what game we might play after dinner. Suddenly the poet rose and stood waiting for silence. He began reciting in powerful tones an improvised ode to John F. Kennedy and the tragedy of his death. His words were as dark as the Soviet winter, and in conclusion he shattered his champagne glass in the fireplace.

Ethel clutched my arm, whispering, "That's *Waterford!*"

I'm sure Yevtushenko felt it was a necessary homage from a poet invited to the home of a family torn by tragedy.

My last memory of the evening was watching Bob McNamara, the man in charge of our nuclear arsenal, leading Yevtushenko down the front steps past a sign, "Beware of Dog—People Will Be Eaten," and showing him into the back-seat of the secretary of defense's armored limousine for a ride to his hotel.

In a generous parting gesture Ed Murrow had nominated me and I was chosen by the US Junior Chamber of Congress as one of the Ten Outstanding Young Men in the United States (changed in later years to Young Americans). It was bittersweet recognition coming just a year after the tragedy in Dallas. The 1964 class included Jim Whittaker, who climbed Mount Everest, Birch Bayh, senator from Indiana, Leon Higginbotham, a Philadelphia civil rights leader who would become a federal judge, and Zbigniew Brzezinski, who would head the National Security Council in the Carter administration.

I was pleased to be in such good company, perhaps feeling that I was moving beyond "the son of" label that had for so long been my companion.

32

LBJ at the Helm

Lyndon Johnson, savoring the distance the 1964 election had put between himself and the public's enchantment with John Kennedy, was preoccupied with Vietnam. Carl Rowan saw this as an area where USIA could demonstrate its value to the White House, leading his policy advisors to press me to produce a film explaining America's purpose in Vietnam.

I believed in our policy that South Vietnam should not have its government determined by the North Vietnamese, but I had failed to come up with a compelling film to support it. I met with Charlie Guggenheim, the most seasoned of our filmmakers, and we planned a documentary about the "strategic hamlet" program that would show South Vietnamese working to build a democratic society with assistance from American advisors while facing attacks by the Viet Cong.

I flew to Los Angeles in January and was greeted by a front-page Associated Press story, filed by a resourceful New Zealander, Peter Arnett, that described a USIA team from Guggenheim Productions filming a staged battle scene outside a Vietnamese village. When I arrived at the Beverly Hills Hotel I found a message from Rowan instructing me to return to Washington. When I walked into his office, straight off the red-eye, Carl complained that the story of faked battle scenes could compromise his initiative in support of Johnson's Vietnam policy. I acknowledged that it was an unfortunate story, but in defense of Guggenheim I pointed out that the great World War II documentaries supplemented combat footage with shots that couldn't be obtained during actual fighting. I explained that *Desert Victory,* the British classic of the North Africa campaign, included scenes shot at Pinewood Studios in England. But Carl wanted to stop the bleeding quickly so he issued a public apology and promised that the errant footage would be destroyed.

Night of the Dragon, absent the reenacted footage, turned out to be a tool that foreign service officers found useful when screened at embassies and forums.

USIA director Carl Rowan, Charles Guggenheim and Stevens show President Johnson the
Oscar for *Nine from Little Rock* in the Oval Office. April 18, 1965.

However, it was becoming ever more difficult to win the Vietnam argument and
the film never made it to my list of favorites. I discovered that the relationship
between reporters and government was rapidly shifting, as was confirmed soon
after when Peter Arnett won the Pulitzer Prize.

Ironically, on the heels of this embarrassment I received an April 6th "Dear
George" letter from the president of the United States.

> To you and all your associates in the Agency, I send you my delighted
> congratulations. The fact that the USIA film NINE FROM LITTLE
> ROCK won the Academy Award last night is both a precursor and an
> accolade. . . . This award points you to the future and urges you on
> to even higher levels of craftsmanship.

LBJ's delight that a government film on civil rights had been honored led to a
Hollywood on the Potomac moment when he beckoned Carl Rowan, Charlie

Guggenheim and me to the Oval Office for a photo. Oscar weighs in at eight and a half pounds and Johnson was surprised, saying, "That's a heavy little feller."

In April came the devastating news that Edward R. Murrow had died of cancer. He was just fifty-seven. I had seen him six months before on a sunny fall afternoon in his suite at the Jefferson Hotel when he was in Washington to receive the Medal of Freedom at the White House. He was with his wife Janet, relaxed, wry and in such good spirits that I left optimistic about his future. It was a shock to lose Ed just four months after John Kennedy. These were the two people in Washington I most respected—men of keen intellect and high purpose. Ed, like Kennedy, had self-deprecating humor that grounded him. "The fact that one's words can now reach to the other end of the continent instead of the other end of the bar," I remember him saying, "doesn't make them more worthy of hearing." For years to come when our country faced perplexing choices, I found myself asking, "What would Ed say?"

Later I saw a letter Jackie Kennedy had written to Ed just eight weeks after Dallas on her distinctive blue stationery.

> We saw *Five Cities of June* three nights in a row, because he [Jack]
> would ask in other people he wanted to see it. He was so proud of
> the music in the Pope's part—which he said you had especially
> commissioned for that film. This Christmas in Florida—with Jack
> no longer there—I watched it alone—and showed it to his father.

The idea of Jackie watching the film by herself spoke to the private loneliness that accompanied this very public national tragedy.

We initiated a film called *A President's Country*, in part a portrait of the Hill Country of Austin and part biography of Lyndon Johnson. Charlie Guggenheim was directing. I asked Dimitri Tiomkin, the Oscar-winning composer who I knew from *Giant*, to compose an original score, and Charlton Heston to narrate. Guggenheim and I flew to the LBJ Ranch with a camera crew.

Lady Bird Johnson was extremely hospitable, serving Charlie and me lunch before she joined us in Jeeps to do our filming. Michael Beschloss, who wrote two books about Lyndon Johnson, surprised me years later with a page from Lady Bird's diary. Dated Saturday, May 1, 1965, she recounts an appearance at Lyndon's boyhood home in Johnson City, and of "dispatching the lady press with a jug of Bloody Marys brought from the ranch."

> Then Simone [her aide] and I left with George Stevens of the USIA
> . . . and George's camera crew for the LBJ film. As we rode I gave a
> running commentary on the cattle and grasses and history of the
> ranch, the house where he was born, the schoolhouse, the graveyard.
> . . . They set up their cameras and shot and shot for the perfect
> picture. . . . At dusk we arrived at the Haywood, had drinks and
> barbecue out on the patio. . . . George Stevens is a personable,
> attractive young man. . . . I tried to elicit from A.W. [Judge A. W.
> Moursund] any extra local color that might help paint *A President's
> Country.* Then I went back to watch *Gunsmoke.*

Sadly Beschloss sent me this reference, one any mother would treasure, too late for mine to see it. I found Lady Bird Johnson inspiring. She was the gentle side of Lyndon, an early environmentalist who fostered change with her beautification program, removing billboards and junkyards from American highways.

LBJ had become impatient with Carl Rowan, who believed it important that he serve on the National Security Council, as Ed Murrow had. Carl pressed the point and was forced to resign. The next day Johnson announced that his successor was Leonard Marks, the lawyer who managed Lady Bird's radio and television properties in Texas. Marks was central to the creation of the Johnson fortune. When he died in 2006, his *New York Times* obituary headline was "Helped Lyndon Johnson Get Rich."

Marks had a jaunty enthusiasm but his lawyer's mindset wasn't in harmony with our filmmaking. Moreover his zest for Johnson's expansion of the war in Vietnam exceeded my own. Review screenings of our films were buffeted by conflicting opinions and the work suffered in the absence of Murrow's discerning decisiveness. Marks searched for efficiencies and decided to fold the Television Service into the Motion Picture Service, expanding my responsibilities and providing me one of the great offices in Washington. We moved to the landmark Old Post Office Building at the other end of Pennsylvania Avenue where the USIA television studios were located, and I was given the office built in the 1930s for Franklin Roosevelt's good friend, Postmaster General James A. Farley. It had a balcony with a vista overlooking the presidential inaugural parade route.

It was a great place to go to work in the morning but I was discovering that my way of making films was no longer in sync with USIA's leadership.

33

Kremlin Honeymoon

Liz and I were in love, and in 1965 decided to marry.

I was committed to head the American delegation to the Moscow Festival in July, so we decided to say our vows in London on the way to Moscow. Marie and Averell Harriman invited Liz and me for dinner at their house on N Street. Marie was wise and irreverent with a hoarse voice earned from too many cigarettes. I once observed her seated on her living room sofa when two women approached. One gushed, "Marie, Averell looks just wonderful!" "Toots," Marie replied, "you'd look pretty good too if all you did was play polo until you were forty." After Averell's triumphant test ban negotiation for Kennedy, LBJ had sidelined him as roving ambassador to Africa. Averell considered himself the best-informed member of the government on the Soviet Union and thought he could facilitate peace in Vietnam, so when Liz mentioned we were going to Moscow after our wedding, the Crocodile pounced. "Marie and I will join you on your honeymoon." And he meant it. Our honeymoon would be Averell's excuse to make an "unofficial" visit to the Soviet Union.

I made a quick trip to Los Angeles and was invited to a party where I found myself on a sofa talking with Sam Spiegel, the producer who won Oscars for *On the Waterfront*, *The Bridge on the River Kwai* and *Lawrence of Arabia*. Sam had left Austria in the late 1930s to become one of Hollywood's most skilled operators, initially using the name S. P. Eagle. He was known for his luxurious yacht *Malahne* that he kept in the South of France. Sam knew my parents but we had never met. When I mentioned I was getting married he asked, "Who's the lucky girl?" I told him and Sam lit up. "Oh, *Lizzie*. She is such a darling, elegant girl. You're a very fortunate young man." Then he knocked my socks off. "I want you and Lizzie to honeymoon on my boat." He pronounced it *bow—at*. I wondered if Sam might have had a few too many, but he seemed sincere and told me to call him the next day at the Beverly Wilshire.

When I awoke the next morning I concluded that I didn't have the chutzpah to call Sam Spiegel and say, "Remember Sam, you're giving me your boat for my honeymoon." That night I went to dinner with Hope Lange's brother, David, at Dominick's, a tiny place on Beverly Boulevard, one of those Hollywood spots that remained in favor for decades. In walked an exquisite raven-haired woman who eased down the narrow aisle past our table, confidently accepting the eyes of onlookers. It was Anouk Aimée, with Sam Spiegel in her wake. Sam looked at me sorrowfully and declared, "George, I'm disappointed. You didn't call me."

Sam and I connected later and he confirmed our cruise on the *Malahne,* then I ran into him on the street in New York and he insisted Liz and I come by for a drink. "Garbo will be there. You will enjoy her." I explained we were going to dinner with my father, and Sam rejoined, "You must bring George. I haven't seen him in too long."

Liz, my father and I walked into the lobby of Spiegel's Park Avenue apartment building, and as we approached the elevators the doorman stepped in front of my father. "We're here to see Mr. Spiegel," Dad said.

The doorman studied him before asking, "Whom may I say is calling on Mr. Spiegel?"

My father didn't hesitate. "Tell him it's Mr. S. T. Evens."

Liz was friends with many interesting people in the East, and while the movie world was new to her, she took everything in stride. But she did tell me that watching my father and Garbo, who had not met before, sitting on cushions on the floor, deep in conversation, was a treat. "Garbo seemed girlish and drawn to him," Liz said. "She asked him, 'How can it be that we never worked together?'"

Liz had to go in advance to London to qualify for a wedding permit, so our bright and assertive friend Dick Goodwin, who enjoyed the powers that came with writing speeches for the president, called Roy Jenkins, the British home secretary, an act of bravado that resulted in a reduced waiting period. Liz decamped to London and a group of friends organized a poolside celebration for me one warm June evening at David and Ann Brinkley's house. Many decades later Kay Evans, organizing the papers of her late columnist husband Rowland Evans, sent me onionskin copies of letters Rowly sent to Bob Kennedy, Joe Kraft, Art Buchwald, Averell Harriman and Roger Mudd to collect the shared costs of fifty dollars each for the party. Averell made a toast standing somewhat precariously on the diving board during dinner, reminding everyone how very fortunate I was to be marrying Liz.

After dinner, as we stood around the Brinkleys' pool, Rowly suddenly appeared next to me. He pointed to Arthur Schlesinger, saying, "Let's push him in." Rowly moved toward Arthur, and without a moment's reflection I joined in giving Arthur a shove. As he fell in the water I glanced toward the end of the pool where Bobby was standing on the diving board. He dropped his head, pressed his hands deep into his pockets and turned away, giving me instant feedback on the stupidity of our prank. Ethel and Bobby had given a festive party for John Glenn in 1962 after his orbit of the Earth that achieved some notoriety. They created a bridge spanning the Hickory Hill swimming pool from which Arthur fell, or was pushed, along with Ethel in a red evening dress. A *Washington Post* account of these New Frontier hijinks earned some chiding from President Kennedy.

A Thousand Days, the Pulitzer Prize–winning historian's account of the Kennedy presidency, was about to be published and Arthur wasn't in the market for publicity about a second dunking. He emerged from the pool dripping and displeased. I felt hugely foolish and dismayed. That night I wrote a letter of apology and slipped it under the door of Arthur's house on O Street. Sure enough, *Time* magazine got wind of the event, reporting that Schlesinger "took a swim up memory creek in Newsman David Brinkley's pool." The glib item was rescued by Arthur's verbal flair, bailing me out by attributing his dunking to an accident of "pre-marital exuberance on the part of George Stevens, Jr."

Our wedding party assembled at the Paddington Registry Office in London on the morning of July 5, after dinner and champagne at Liz's cousin Diana Phipps' house with friends who happened to be in "Swinging London," ranging from Cary Grant and the Gregory Pecks to our benefactor Sam Spiegel. My mother and father were standing side by side. Liz's mother was there, but her father, Raymond, who was serving as American ambassador in Dublin, had a horse running that day in the Irish Derby. Liz arranged for a distinguished stand-in, the brilliant and engaging American ambassador to the Court of St. James, David Bruce, to give her away. Ivan Moffat was my best man and Charles Guggenheim, informally and discreetly, acted as court photographer. My new daughter Caroline, and Alexandra Phipps, Diana's daughter, both six years old were flower girls. The ceremony was simple and intimate. Elizabeth was breathtakingly beautiful. Charlie captured an image of my father, the director of several of cinema's most deeply affecting wedding scenes, at the side of the frame, holding back tears.

From Paddington we repaired to the Moffat house on Tregunter Road for a cheery but brief reception, from which Liz and I went directly to Heathrow

At Paddington Registry, July 5, 1965. George Stevens, Sr., left.

Airport for the Pan Am flight to Moscow—with both of our mothers. Mine, an intrepid traveler, had planned a trip to Moscow even before Liz and I made plans to marry, and I decided that Liz's mother deserved equal time, so we made for a novel honeymoon quartet.

Esquire columnist, Helen Lawrenson, covered the Moscow Festival and assessed the American contingent:

> The American delegation was headed by George Stevens, Jr (son of the Hollywood director). He and his bride were on their honeymoon and their mothers were there, too. (Well, I guess they all wanted to see Moscow.) Her mother is Lily Guest, a very attractive woman with a casually elegant Southampton look that made her, in Moscow, stand

out like a creature from another planet. . . . The official American film entry was *The Great Race,* starring Jack Lemmon. When Jack arrived, his plane, for some reason came in at a different airport from the scheduled one, so no one was there to meet him. He and his wife and fifteen-year-old daughter waited for three hours. . . . Finally he got in touch with the American embassy, who sent a car. I admired his stamina; and I also had to give him credit just for showing up at the Festival, as lots of Hollywood stars won't go to Moscow, possibly through fear of sniping from the Ronald Reagan-Hedda Hopper-John Wayne axis.

English was spoken by very few and signs in Cyrillic script were indecipherable, so Cold War Moscow could be unsettling. Liz and I were registering at festival headquarters in the flag-draped but forbiddingly somber lobby of the Hotel Moskva when Jack Lemmon rushed up with a cheerful hug. His wife Felicia came next, and soon we were joined by Tony Curtis and his new bride (the second of six), actress Christine Kaufmann. Tony and Jack starred, with Natalie Wood, in *The Great Race.*

A black-tie audience of six thousand passed through the ancient Kremlin walls for the opening night ceremonies in the Palace of Congresses, Moscow's new marble, glass and concrete showplace. Fred Zinnemann had interrupted his preparation for *A Man for All Seasons* to fly to Moscow with his wife Renee to serve on the jury. The Zinnemanns, Lemmons, and Liz, with her mother and mine, were escorted to a special box for the American VIPs. I was taken to the front orchestra where delegation heads, predominately from countries in the Soviet orbit, were seated. I was directed to the third row, between Mongolia and Hungary, not far from Cold War favorites Cuba and North Vietnam. Two years earlier I sensed a measure of curious respect for my connection to the Kennedy world, but Lyndon Johnson's bombing of North Vietnam generated a less hospitable climate. I steeled myself for booing at my introduction.

The master of ceremonies stood on the stage before flags of all nations and began the roll call of delegates in Russian. The audience could choose from fourteen languages on earphones. When the host got to the American delegation he appeared to go off script, causing me some apprehension. Gradually it became evident that even Soviet apparatchiks maintained Old World sentimentality. He was telling the audience that the head of the American delegation had been married that morning in London and chose to bring his bride to Moscow for their wedding night. Then he gestured to the American box in the first tier and called on Liz to take a bow. She stood with a radiant but self-effacing smile as the applause built, with Jack Lemmon at her side wiping away tears. Soon the Kremlin Palace crowd was on its feet. Liz had joined the exclusive cohort of women who received a standing ovation from six thousand people on their wedding night.

A gala showing of *My Fair Lady* was planned mid-festival at the Kremlin Palace. Rex Harrison, Henry Higgins himself, was flying in with his wife Rachel Roberts. It turned out the Harrisons were arriving from London on the same flight as Averell and Marie Harriman. My interpreter, Angie, arranged a car to take us to the airport to meet the Harrisons, part of my official duties since he was the star of an American film. Angie persuaded an airport official to permit us to greet Rex on the tarmac, which would also give us a chance to say hello to the Harrimans. As the Pan Am flight taxied in, a black limousine with a small American flag flying above its right front fender parked on the ramp. Rex, wearing his signature fedora, was the first to emerge and stood at the top of the stairs with Rachel at his side.

There, an unfortunate misunderstanding occurred. Rex, having accommodated the eager photographers and seeing the limousine, strode toward the car under the mistaken assumption that it was for him. Averell then came to the top of the steps. Well-known because of his tour as Roosevelt's ambassador during World War II and his recent test ban success, he received applause and knowing shouts of "Garri-man" from the bystanders. By now Rex had been advised by the American ambassador's chauffeur that the car was for Governor Harriman. Rex retreated, and joined other passengers with their rucksacks shuffling toward the terminal.

Liz and I greeted an extremely disgruntled star, but she deployed her charm on the ride to the hotel, and by the time we arrived in the Harrisons' grand suite at the Moskva, Rex was chuckling about the inconveniences of Russia. I poured a Scotch for Rex, which he accepted with a rakish smile. There was time for the Harrisons to relax, bathe and dress for the screening of *My Fair Lady*. Then Angie barged in to the suite and confronted Rex with instructions. That might have been alright were it not for a linguistic slip that reversed Liz's restorative work. "Mr. Rex *Harriman*," Angie declared. "You will be downstairs at 7:30 for car to take you and Mrs. *Harriman* to Kremlin Palace."

The boulder was at the bottom of the hill again. Rex needed a couple of drinks to soothe his indignation and agree to appear at his movie.

My Fair Lady delighted the Soviet audience starved for popular American films, and Rex took his bows to an ovation from the thousands on hand. Liz and I were the only people Rex and Rachel knew in Moscow so we went together to

Liz and George arrive at Sheremetyevo Airport in Moscow on their wedding day, 1965.

the special rooftop bar at the Moskva where festival glitterati could drink. I ordered a bowl of caviar and a bottle of vodka, and together with Jack and Felicia Lemmon we had a spirited time. Rachel was every bit Rex's equal when it came to drinking, and Jack wasn't one to be left behind (until years later when he put the habit aside), so the vodka flowed and we had an enchanting evening.

When the bar closed at three we said our goodnights. Liz and I went to the large suite provided us by the festival with a grand piano in the living room. It had been a long day so she went directly to bed leaving me alone in the living room. Sitting in this baroque hotel suite I recalled the briefing given by security officers at the State Department who advised me that I was to assume that everything said or done in my hotel was being recorded by the KGB. The vodka that so lifted my spirits with the Harrisons and Lemmons now seemed to fuel my resentment of Soviet snooping. I set out to find the recording device that was invading my honeymoon privacy. I inspected the piano, examined the paintings on the walls, studied the floral arrangements, and stood on a table to check out a large chandelier. Finding nothing suspicious I went to the bedroom where Liz was sleeping and continued the search. I rolled back the carpet and under our bed found two wires bound together. I found a knife in the kitchen and sawed until I successfully severed them, then rolled back the carpet with care and re-placed the knife, even wiping the handle before climbing quietly into bed for a sublimely peaceful sleep.

I was awakened in the morning by Angie pounding on the door. I greeted her with sleep in my eyes. She declaimed reproachfully, "Mr. Stevens, you are to be downstairs at 8:30 to go to Soviet Cinematographer's Union." As I headed back to the bedroom to get ready she called after me. "Mr. Stevens, did you sleep well?" I turned and said, "Angie, I had the most peaceful sleep of my visit." Before closing the door she declared, "That is good. We worry that chandelier falling down last night in the suite below might have disturbed you."

The Great Race, the story of a daredevil car race across three continents, was the official American entry and drew a packed house at the Palace of Congresses. In the scene where the American racing cars arrive in wintry Russia the people in the streets greet them with stony silence, but when Natalie Wood's character speaks to them in Russian (she was fluent), they swarm forward and cheer her. The audience in the Kremlin Palace also cheered, providing a welcome emotional moment of goodwill as the festival drew to a close.

Liz and I flew from Moscow to Nice and took a short ride to the harbor at Monte Carlo, circling past glistening yachts to the prime berth at the end of the slip where we found Sam Spiegel's 165-foot *Malahne.* It was a dramatic change of ambience. *Malahne* had a luxurious grand salon, comfortable staterooms, a partially covered aft deck for seated lunches and dinners, and a crew of eleven. James Jordan, Spiegel's Bahamian butler, greeted Liz and me as we came aboard. Liz entrusted James with the one-kilo container of Beluga caviar we brought from Russia, to be enjoyed with blinis and sour cream.

My best man Ivan Moffat and his wife Kate arrived and we learned we were to be joined by another couple, Margot Fonteyn, the world's most admired ballerina, and her husband Robert "Tito" Arias, a Panamanian lawyer, diplomat and politician. Tito had become a quadriplegic confined to a wheelchair as a result of a political shooting in Panama. We cruised to Corsica and Sardinia off the coast of Italy. Margot was enchanting company, and Arias maintained a joie de vivre and a sly sense of humor. Each day at noon James would appear with Bullshots in chilled alabaster goblets. Swimming and waterskiing in the Mediterranean was refreshing, with high dives off the upper deck for the more adventurous, followed by cocktails in the lounge, then dinner in the soft air on the aft deck.

Liz and I returned to Washington stimulated by our experience behind the Iron Curtain, rested by a blissful week at sea, looking forward to married life.

34

The Arts and the White House

Eric Goldman, a history professor from Princeton appointed by Lyndon Johnson to be his special assistant for the arts, was assigned to broaden LBJ's connection to intellectuals from whom he believed he deserved greater support. Goldman seemed to have a good idea—a White House Festival of the Arts featuring painting, poetry, music, dance and theater. Sadly for Goldman, the June event came during Johnson's Operation Rolling Thunder bombing of North Vietnam, and some artists saw the White House event as an opportunity to protest the war. The poet Robert Lowell refused to attend, author John Hersey showed up and read from his landmark essay on the bombing of Hiroshima, and caustic *Esquire* film critic Dwight Macdonald scurried about collecting anti–Vietnam War signatures. President Johnson was furious. It was the dawn of a contentious time in Washington.

More and more I found myself standing up for motion pictures—for cinematic art—as equal to music, dance and theater. I pressed for a film program at the White House festival and was invited to produce one with my colleague James Silke. The White House named a panel of critics, including Bosley Crowther and Pauline Kael, who selected five American directors to be celebrated. We then chose scenes from Hitchcock's *North by Northwest,* Kazan's *On the Waterfront,* Wyler's *Friendly Persuasion,* Zinnemann's *High Noon* and my father's *Shane.* They were combined into a thirty-minute film presented by Charlton Heston. A White House curator told me it was the first time a film had been shown in the East Room since Woodrow Wilson screened D. W. Griffith's *The Birth of a Nation* in 1915.

All the directors except Hitchcock attended the ceremony, and the classic scenes drew prolonged applause. The recently deceased Gary Cooper appeared in *High Noon* and *Friendly Persuasion,* and as the lights came up Wyler said to his fellow directors, "It's a shame Coop couldn't have been here." My father waited a moment before saying, "Coop was here today, Willy."

It fell to President Johnson to appoint members to the National Council on the Arts that President Kennedy created by executive order, individuals who would govern the National Endowment for the Arts when its legislation passed Congress. I sent a note to Jack Valenti urging that film artists be included. He asked for suggestions and I gave him short bios of Stanley Kramer, Gregory Peck and Fred Zinnemann. Anxious not to misuse the opportunity I reluctantly omitted my father. Jack and I had no further discussion. When the White House announced the first members of the National Council, the motion picture appointees were Peck and my father, who Valenti had met and admired.

They were sworn in with a roster of creative pathfinders in the White House Cabinet Room, among them Marian Anderson, Leonard Bernstein, Agnes DeMille, Isaac Stern, Duke Ellington, Minoru Yamasaki, John Steinbeck and Ralph Ellison. Roger Stevens chaired a meeting of the Arts Council the next day where for the first time in American history artists met to determine how government should foster the arts. They agreed that support would go to symphony orchestras, dance companies and regional theaters, as well as to painters, poets and composers, but they were puzzled as to how to support film. As one member put it, "You can't give a grant to Warner Bros." They chose my father to head a committee that included Peck and council members William Pereira, a Los Angeles architect who had designed films, and actress Elizabeth Ashley, to study the question.

At USIA I had been advocating for film preservation, film education and opportunities for young filmmakers, and was pleased when Peck and my father asked my advice. I suggested that the National Endowment create an American Film Institute to address a wide range of motion picture projects. They took the idea seriously and formed an advisory committee to include film professionals and educators. I was invited to serve.

On September 29 President Johnson presided at a White House ceremony for the signing of the National Foundation on the Arts and the Humanities Act. The growing cohort of cultural leaders who enthusiastically supported the initiative was seated in the sunlight-bathed Rose Garden just outside the Oval Office. Johnson signed the bill before taking the podium with over 120 members of Congress standing behind him. He declared that art was the nation's most precious heritage, noting, "We in America have not always been kind to the artists and the scholars who are the creators and keepers of our vision." He drew laughter when he added, "The scientists always seem to get the penthouse, while the arts and humanities get the basement." The president thanked the National Arts

Council for having dreamed dreams and developed ideas, then became more specific, stating that a national theater would be created as well as a national ballet and a national opera company. He then described another idea in more detail. "We will create an American Film Institute, bringing together leading artists of the film industry, outstanding educators, and young men and women who wish to pursue the twentieth century art form as their life's work."

Sitting in the front row next to my father, taking care not to exchange a self-conscious glance, I felt a rush of adrenaline at this unexpected announcement. Here was the president of the United States declaring that there would be an American Film Institute, giving enormous weight to an idea that had only recently entered the conversation. How does something like this happen in Washington? One can only speculate, but my guess is that Johnson demanded that his speechwriters put some "meat on the bone" and Valenti plucked the American Film Institute from reports of Arts Council meetings.

No matter the means by which it landed in his text, it was now President Johnson's idea.

35

A Fast Moving Year

The important news as 1966 got under way and we settled into our yellow house on the corner of Twenty-Ninth and N in Georgetown was from Liz. I would be a father before the year was out.

It had been four years since I left Hollywood and my life had been productive and filled with discovery. Yet as I prepared to become a father, I still had misgivings about having left my own father in 1962 to manage the most arduous and challenging filmmaking venture of his life. *The Greatest Story Ever Told* had its premiere in New York chaired by Lady Bird Johnson for the benefit of the United Nations. Dad had shot in the dramatic landscapes of the American Southwest, encountering the first snowstorm in decades, leading to 201 shooting days that pushed the cost of the picture north of fifteen million dollars. He and I kept in close touch by letter and phone and the occasional visit, but I was pained that I couldn't be there to support him.

Dad enjoyed the irony of his flight to New York to show the completed film to his loyal partners Arthur Krim and Bob Benjamin, two esteemed Jewish lawyers who ran United Artists and had backed the most ambitious film ever made about Jesus. "Mr. Stevens, can I offer you a magazine?" asked a hostess as he sat down in the first-class cabin of American Airlines. "Thank you, do you have *Time*?" She handed him the magazine and went on her way. He settled back and stared at the cover. "Is God Dead?" The famous issue of *Time* reflected the troubled psyche of midsixties America that awaited the film's release. The *Greatest Story* received a raft of adulatory reviews and some scathing ones, but over time it has stood as a work of intelligence, humanity and uncommon beauty that cast aside the anti-Semitism too often baked into the story of Jesus. My father's biggest disappointment was that his friends at United Artists didn't recover their investment.

The White House was forming an advisory committee to guide planning for the John F. Kennedy Center for the Performing Arts. As the result of a delicate negotiation President Johnson would choose half the members and Jackie Kennedy the other half. I was thrilled with the unexpected news that I was among Jackie's choices and would be serving with Leonard Bernstein, Broadway director Harold Clurman, designer Oliver Smith and my friends Arthur Schlesinger and Dick Goodwin. Among Johnson's appointees were Supreme Court Justice Abe Fortas.

Schlesinger chaired the meetings in New York seated next to Roger Stevens, and Jackie's presence meant absenteeism was rare. It was fascinating to observe these imaginative men vie to impress the alluring widow, and inspiring to see fine minds working toward a common purpose. In our search for an artistic director we had lively interviews with Gian Carlo Menotti, Isaac Stern and Leonard Bernstein—exploring the goals of a national performing arts center. It was a masterclass in institution building, and I was beginning to see the connections between culture, government and politics. Jackie was animated and inquisitive, while being rigorous about a standard of excellence for her husband's memorial.

On St. Patrick's Day she and I left our meeting at 711 Fifth Avenue to find the parade in full swing. Jackie realized Bobby was marching so we crowded to the curbside for a view. The next day's *Daily News* had us on the front page wearing dark glasses. Jackie sent me the picture, inscribed "to my favorite secret service man."

Jack and Mary Margaret Valenti came to our house on N Street for dinner in early November. Jack had resigned from the White House in June to become president of the Motion Picture Association of America, the "movie czar" who lobbied Congress for the major film companies. Liz was cooking and Caroline was asleep upstairs. As we were about to sit down the phone rang—it was the White House looking for Valenti. Jack went to the phone in the kitchen. He came to the table to say that the president had just landed in Washington from Vietnam and wanted us to come to dinner.

We scrambled for a sitter to watch Caroline, then headed to the White House. I had never been to the family quarters upstairs where LBJ was holding forth. During cocktails he expressed his fury about a North Vietnamese offensive. "They attacked my generals," he said repeatedly. Hubert Humphrey was among a dozen guests, including the Johnson's daughter Luci and her husband.

The conversation shifted with Johnson's mood, as Humphrey sought to keep it positive. I decided to take the opportunity to inform the president that we were making a documentary about a trip he took as a senator during World War II during which a Japanese fighter attacked the airplane he was on. Johnson was awarded the Silver Star. I was rewarded for my solicitousness by the leader

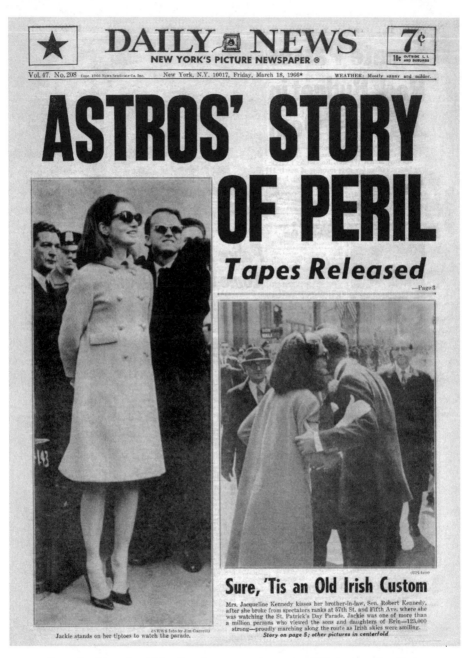

Jacqueline Kennedy with her favorite secret service man on Fifth Avenue, New York, St. Patrick's Day, 1966. At right she greets Robert Kennedy.

of the free world watching me expressionless through his rimless glasses while I labored on, then moving away to another conversation with just a nod.

I was seated one away from Johnson at the long family dinner table. He was served a bowl of peas, which he took in hand and ate with a spoon while keeping eye contact with those he was addressing. I noticed his eyes pan down in the direction of the PT 109 tie clasp I was wearing—a cherished JFK memento. It felt as if the little PT boat was sending out vibrations. He looked up past the peas, it seemed, to correlate my face with the offending tie clasp. Otherwise it was a lively and interesting evening, with Lady Bird serving as a vivacious hostess. It was typically gracious of Valenti to have invited us, but I sensed anew that night the power of the presidency and understood that I was a pawn in a tribal rivalry.

Liz and I returned to our house in Georgetown, an area LBJ described as the hotbed of "all those bomb throwing, ass kissing, fuzzy headed liberals." I knew that my best times in government were behind me.

LBJ's Rose Garden statement intensified thinking about the prospect of an American Film Institute, leading NEA's Advisory Committee to commission a feasibility study by the Stanford Research Institute. An article of mine, "The Mass Media in a Liberal Education," written in 1965 for the *American Council on Education Quarterly,* was part of the study. It called for eradicating the poverty of American film training and the creation of a national film archive. The committee would meet in January to consider next steps.

Ethel and Bobby sent invitations for a November party at Hickory Hill for Averell Harriman's seventy-fifth birthday. Ethel asked Art Buchwald and me to come up with some ideas. Playing off Bobby's political ambition, a huge "AVE IN '72 (SORRY BOBBY)" banner spanned the front of the house and blue and white "I CRAVE AVE." campaign buttons were handed out. The eighty guests ranged from Vice President and Muriel Humphrey to Alice Longworth, eighty-four-year-old daughter of Teddy Roosevelt. Guests were asked to dress in a way that reflected some aspect of Averell's life. Bobby donned a long black overcoat and diplomatic hat, and my Liz, days before she was due to give birth, wore a "Make Love Not War" poster. Bobby inscribed a photo of the two of them, "I will if you will."

Humphrey had assailed Bobby earlier in the year for proposing that Vietnam's National Liberation Front be included in the peace talks, saying, "That would be like putting a fox in a chicken coop." In a disarming toast in the Kennedy living room, Hubert said, "Tonight I feel like a chicken in a fox coop." Art Buchwald made one of his signature toasts, tracing the "rags to riches" rise of Averell. Then we drew back the curtains covering a bay window that looked onto a small terrace to reveal lifelike figures that Buchwald and I had liberated

Guests were dressed to represent phases of Averell Harriman's career.
I came as a "dove" and Bobby wore a diplomat's hat and
Chesterfield overcoat.

from Washington's Wax Museum. It was a rousing moment when the guests
saw Churchill, Roosevelt and Stalin seated as they were at the Yalta Conference
in which Averell participated as ambassador to Russia. Averell's friends stood
and cheered him and his departed friends.

At midnight, five nights after the Harriman birthday, Liz asked me to take
her to the George Washington Hospital where at 7:20 a.m. she gave birth to a
7 pound, 2 ounce boy. It was the greatest thrill of my life. Liz was so beautiful,
and the baby was healthy. My father flew to the bedside. Always on the cutting
edge of photography, he unveiled a new Polaroid camera to take the first pictures of his first grandson and the radiant mother. Having gambled the family
destiny on me, an only child, Dad was now assured that the Stevens name would
carry on.

Liz and I had still not settled on a name, and after three days my father
joined me in a small sitting room at our house. For a man who was so formidable
at work and at war, he had the most gentle and reassuring manner. He offered
a quizzical smile. "Are you planning on naming this boy?" "Sure we are, Dad,"
I replied hastily. Seeing the opportunity for a trial balloon, I added, "What
would you think if we called him George?" My father pondered, before testing
the phrase, "*George the third.*" And then with Stan Laurel timing, "I think that's

why we left England." In one stroke my father saved this fine child from going through life as Georgie Triple Sticks.

Liz and I soon agreed the boy would be named Michael Murrow Stevens.

Robert Kennedy and Alice Roosevelt Longworth with Liz at Hickory Hill, November 1966.

PART FIVE

AN AMERICAN FILM INSTITUTE

Roger L. Stevens, Founding Chairman of the National Endowment for the Arts;
George Stevens, Jr., Founding Director of AFI; Gregory Peck, Founding Chairman of AFI;
Sidney Poitier, Founding Vice-Chairman of AFI. September 26, 1969.

36

A New Adventure

It appeared that my ideas about what an American Film Institute might be, combined with my experience at USIA, had made me first choice to head the new organization.

Liz and I were facing questions of what kind of lives we wanted to live, and how to raise our children. I now had a family to support and a decision to make between heading the new nonprofit institute in Washington or returning to Hollywood to resume a moviemaking career. Liz and I had a lovely house in Georgetown and a host of friends who were guided by good purpose, but should I choose moviemaking, she was prepared to go west. The prospect of starting something new did fire my imagination, especially after my recent involvement in the planning of the Kennedy Center and the Kennedy Library.

Gregory Peck would be the American Film Institute's first chairman. In January of 1967 he and Roger Stevens held a meeting of the NEA Advisory Committee in New York to select its leader. They took me to lunch the next day and offered me the job. Roger explained that the National Endowment would provide an initial grant of $1,300,000, with the requirement that it be "matched" three times. He was confident that the Ford Foundation would provide $1,300,000 for a program to train filmmakers, and that the seven major motion picture companies would contribute an equal amount. The AFI would be responsible for raising $1,300,000 for a total budget of $5,200,000 for three years. I said it was important to be assured of long-term government support before we embarked on such an ambitious venture, and Peck agreed. On February 16, 1967, Roger wrote to Peck on National Endowment for the Arts letterhead:

Assuming that the American Film Institute achieves the purposes for which it is being formed and the Board of Trustees and management are successful in achieving contemplated goals, it is reasonable to expect that approximately ten percent of the available Endowment funds would be available to aid the Film Institute.

Roger's assurance that AFI could expect a percentage of the NEA budget—which would grow each year—gave me confidence in the proposed public–private partnership. I signed a three-year contract to serve as director and chief executive officer of the American Film Institute at a salary of $75,000. A June 5 announcement was planned in Washington.

Peck came to our house on N Street the afternoon before, a glorious spring Sunday with dogwood in bloom. Greg had become a friend as a result of his narration work on USIA films and the planning of AFI. We sat in Liz's garden near a bassinet holding Michael Stevens, now six months old, as we shaped the announcement of AFI's purposes and initial programs.

My cherished memory of that day is Gregory, standing tall, in Atticus Finch mode, looking down at the sleeping baby and declaring, "My, what a fine looking lad."

It was a time of new beginnings.

Roger, Greg and I presided at the press luncheon at the Madison Hotel. We announced that AFI would preserve America's film heritage, train and support new filmmakers, and foster the study of motion pictures. President Johnson clarified the concept in a letter to Roger:

> I think your organization approach is a sound one. Operating as a
> private nonprofit, nongovernmental corporation supported by funds
> from the National Endowment for the Arts, and private monies, the
> American Film Institute will have the necessary support as well as
> the essential freedom of action which a creative venture of this kind
> requires.

The National Endowment appointed twenty-two individuals to be trustees. They mirrored Johnson's 1965 statement in the Rose Garden when he spoke of "bringing together leading artists of the film industry, outstanding educators, and young men and women who wish to pursue the twentieth century art form as their life's work." Included were a new young screenwriter who would soon become a director, Francis Ford Coppola, cinéma vérité pioneer Ricky Leacock, actress Elizabeth Ashley, and senior figures who shared progressive views about the future of film: Sidney Poitier, as vice-chairman, directors George Seaton and Fred Zinnemann, and screenwriter Daniel Taradash. Arthur Knight, David

Mallery and US Commissioner of Education Francis Keppel were our outstanding educators.

We embraced President Johnson's view that a nonprofit organization supported by a combination of government and private funding would provide stability and freedom to innovate. It was a different model than our European counterparts, which were funded entirely by the state. I defined our role this way:

> The American Film Institute is concerned with the motion picture in American life—in theaters, homes, libraries, classrooms, or on a television set—wherever films are found. To bring cinema to its fullest stature in the country of its birth; to preserve, stimulate, enrich and nurture the art of film in America—these are the Institute's goals.

I knew that building a new institution would be challenging, but I expected AFI to be greeted as a progressive force. I didn't yet recognize how rapidly the country was changing from Kennedy-era optimism to a period of division and unrest. There was swelling opposition to the Vietnam War and "burn baby burn" was the cry in American cities. A counterculture—sex, drugs and rock 'n' roll—was spreading. Young people didn't trust anyone over thirty—and I had just turned thirty-five.

The first signal was a banner headline in *Variety* that appeared a week before AFI was announced: "INSTANT HOOT AT NEW INSTITUTE: GEORGE STEVENS JR. FACES UPROAR." *Variety* quoted "film society leaders" complaining that AFI board members were too industry oriented and lacked appreciation for the art of film. In fact, the trustees firmly believed in art and in change, while also having the stature to generate financial support. Robert Landry, *Variety*'s New York editor, wrote a sidebar.

> Almost nothing is heard of late about the Institute assuming any responsibility for creating film archives, which many consider a desperate neglect in this country. . . . As an easy forecast the expected selection of George Stevens, Jr. as director of the Institute will not comfort these malcontents, Stevens being born and bred of the industry.

On the day after our announcement I was less concerned with comforting malcontents than I was about facing my "What do I do now?" moment. I walked over to the Dart Drugstore on Pennsylvania Avenue and bought a box of #2 pencils and a dozen yellow legal pads with which to define the tasks at hand and first steps to be taken. I settled into a small room that Roger Stevens offered me in offices where he was planning the Kennedy Center, while also running the National Endowment. In addition to providing an office, Roger offered his example. He was forging ahead to build the Kennedy Center in the face of opposition and apathy.

37

Two Tracks—Old and New

There were the old films—hundreds of them, perhaps thousands, missing or lost.

I was determined to make the preservation of our country's film heritage, contrary to the forecast in *Variety,* the cornerstone of AFI. "Film is the only art in which the United States has made a real difference," wrote Arthur Schlesinger, Jr. "Strike the American contribution from drama, painting, music, sculpture, dance, and the world's achievement is only marginally diminished. But film without the American contribution is unimaginable."

Yet in 1967 fewer than one-tenth of the two hundred thousand motion pictures produced in the United States since 1894 were properly stored in film archives.

After that morning in 1962 when Henri Langlois cornered me on the Croisette at Cannes, I learned that black-and-white motion pictures made before 1950 were filmed on highly flammable nitrocellulose stock which is likely to decompose over time, leaving nothing but a pile of odorous powder. This fragility was compounded by the indifference of producers who demonstrated little or no interest in safeguarding their films, some even melting down their negatives to recover the silver content. Our mission was to locate missing films and transfer them to the nonflammable acetate film stock that was introduced in the 1950s and store them in refrigerated vaults.

Since 1870 book publishers had been required to deposit copies of copyrighted works with the Library of Congress, resulting in a comprehensive collection of American books. In 1894 Thomas Alva Edison submitted for copyright a five-second, black-and-white, moving picture of his assistant, Fred Ott, pinching snuff and sneezing. With *Fred Ott's Sneeze,* Edison initiated the concept of motion picture copyright. Nitrate, however, posed the risk of fire and explosions, so between 1912 and 1942, the flowering era of American movies, the Library accepted only thirty feature films.

I knew that AFI would never have sufficient funding to construct storage vaults and employ the staff required to restore the endangered films, so on a fall afternoon in 1967 I entered the magnificent marble and granite Thomas Jefferson Building across from the Capitol, passing a display of the Gutenberg Bible, which stimulated my preservation buds.

I sat down with the librarian of Congress, Dr. L. Quincy Mumford, and said, "The art of motion pictures is one of America's principal twentieth century achievements, and unless we do something this cultural legacy will be lost to future generations." It was evident that books, not motion pictures, were Dr. Mumford's passion, but he listened politely before telling me that the library was strapped for funds and had other urgent priorities. I pressed him. "Would you consider a collaborative program in which AFI took responsibility for tracking down the missing films and delivered them to the library for restoration and preservation?" I pointed out that his motion picture section had only five employees, before asking, "What if AFI were to provide funds for seven new positions for film preservationists?"

This opened the door, and we worked out a partnership in which AFI allocated $1,210,000, nearly a quarter of our three-year budget, to pay for the exacting work of transferring films from nitrate to acetate stock. Ours was a strategy of getting the library a little bit pregnant, to trigger growth in its film preservation program. Dr. Mumford agreed that the films we brought to the library would be known as the American Film Institute Collection.

We were fortunate to enlist Sam Kula, a thirty-four-year-old Canadian who had been deputy curator at the British Film Institute, to head AFI's archive activities. Sam formed an advisory committee that included the two institutions that pioneered film preservation in the United States—the Museum of Modern Art and George Eastman House. MoMA started a film library in 1935 headed by a devoted film scholar, Iris Barry, and Eastman House was established in 1945 under James Card. Card and Willard van Dyke, Barry's successor, joined the committee along with Dr. Edgar Breitenbach and Dr. John Kuiper from the Library of Congress. They used their encyclopedic knowledge of cinema history to develop a rescue list of film treasures that were lost or missing.

Kula hired two intrepid young film sleuths, David Shepard and Larry Karr, who coined the term "Nitrate Won't Wait." They met with private collectors and old-time projectionists and sweet-talked their way into studio archives. They located missing gems and negotiated with copyright holders. Paramount's archive of silent films, the RKO library and Mary Pickford's Biograph films from 1909 to 1913 were handed over to the library. By 1972 there were ten thousand negatives of classic motion pictures in the AFI Collection in the Library of Congress, with thousands more to come.

In Europe motion pictures were meticulously catalogued but in the United States records were sparse. We initiated what would become a three-decade project to assemble cast and crew information, story synopses and production data on feature motion pictures. The first edition of *The American Film Institute Catalog of Feature Films Made in the United States* (1921–1930) was published in two handsome red volumes in 1971. This painstaking work continued into the digital age, so that today the authoritative *AFI Catalog* covers the twentieth century, and is available online to scholars and the general public.

While AFI archivists were on the road searching musty vaults for rusty cans of nitrate, I was meeting scores of young men and women who turned to AFI seeking support for their filmmaking ambitions. Motion pictures had long been the province of major studios but the sixties unleashed a wave of young filmmakers who wanted to tell their own stories free from the restraints of the commercial system. They struggled because their tools were more costly than the novelist's pen or the paint and canvases of visual artists. We developed a two-tiered approach—announcing a program of AFI grants to support independent filmmakers, and making plans for a conservatory in Los Angeles that would serve as a bridge between the study of filmmaking and the profession.

Aspiring filmmakers were invited to apply to this AFI Independent Filmmaker Program for grants ranging from $500 to $15,000. Toni Vellani, who had joined me at USIA to supervise documentary production after he finished work with my father on *The Greatest Story Ever Told,* headed the program, establishing an evaluation process that was open and professional. We received hundreds of applications and made twenty-two grants in the first year. The filmmakers were pleased that they retained creative control and ownership of their films.

Storm de Hirsch, a New Yorker in her mid-fifties, received a grant to film her poem *The Tattooed Man.* "I wanted badly to make an animated short and had no camera available," she said. "I did have some old, unused film stock and several rolls of 16mm sound tape. So I used that—plus a variety of discarded surgical instruments and the sharp edge of a screwdriver—etching and painting directly on film." Robert Kramer was a politically active twenty-eight-year-old who received a grant for *Ice,* his contentious feature-length film about urban guerrillas in the United States. It was an early indicator that AFI would not turn away from strong content.

Other grantees included Jimmy Murakami for a 35mm animated film *The Good Friend,* Nell Cox for a documentary about a girl growing up in rural

Kentucky, and John Korty for a portrait of the photographer Imogene Cunning-ham. Stan VanDerBeek, a visionary of the avant-garde, received support for exper-imentation with color videotape. We also made grants to student filmmakers, among them David Lynch, a twenty-two-year-old painter from Philadelphia, who received $2,000 for a combined animation–live action film, *The Grandmother*.

Barbara Kopple was awarded $10,000 for her feature film about striking miners in Appalachia, *Harlan County, USA*. "The AFI money was vital," she said, "but the idea that an organization so respected had seen the footage, and wanted to support the film, gave me the confidence to push on and finish it." Barbara would take home an Academy Award for Best Documentary Feature.

Tom McDonough, a hardy New Yorker who received funding for a film about the Brooklyn Bridge, had an apt description of the AFI program. "It's a way for the performer—the independent film worker—to get his horn out of hock."

We were at the center of a decade of change. Motion picture cameras—long harbored in Hollywood studios—were gradually becoming more accessible, and young men and women with the urge to create were turning to film.

38

Bobby

Liz and I enjoyed life among friends from journalism, politics and show business, and I adored being the father of a baby boy and introducing Caroline to school. Moreover, we received from a deposed suitor of Liz's a glorious hundred-pound Great Pyrenees called Nuage, who brightened our life and tested our stamina.

We spent a good deal of time with Bobby and Ethel. Liz and Kay Evans, the wise and witty wife of columnist Rowland Evans, were close to Ethel and helped with her projects. Ethel was feisty and vivacious and devoted to making life on Hickory Hill's six acres enjoyable for her husband and ten children (and counting). She was always ready to laugh and good humor in the company of friends muted the still-lingering ache of the assassination.

Robert Kennedy had become the most active of United States senators, yet he made time for each of his children—quarterbacking touch football, playing in the tree house, riding the "slide for life" that was strung from a great oak next to the house, and making certain that history and world affairs were discussed at the dinner table. He seemed to enjoy the parade of politicians, reporters, entertainers, astronauts and athletes who streamed through the house. Ethel built a screening room next to the swimming pool and I was in charge of finding movies for Friday and Saturday nights. The audience age ranged from six to eighty. A film would begin with the Kennedy kids on the floor in front, but if a scene would become steamy everybody would look at the children, then at me. "George!" The children would be hustled off to bed, several in tears. I soon retired as programmer.

Bob Kennedy was one of the most extraordinary individuals I would know. Time spent with him was always interesting, often great fun, and frequently focused on issues of the day. He showed sound judgment and a capacity for making tough decisions at his brother's side, and his campaign for the Senate

Caroline and George at Rock Hill Farm, Virginia.

proved his political prowess. He was evolving in the wake of his brother's death. Rather than clinging to certainties as most people do as they grow older, he was shedding them. He was just forty-three. I had no doubt he was the person best equipped to lead our country.

I continued to serve on the advisory committee in the search for a leader for the Kennedy Center. Two years had passed without a decision, and when we met in January of 1968 at Arthur Schlesinger's office at City University in New York, several members had become impatient at the lack of resolution. At one point I was asked to leave the room, returning minutes later to be informed by Chairman Roger Stevens that the committee had decided that *I* should be director of the Kennedy Center. This was a reassuring sign of respect from such a distinguished group, but very surprising. I was just six months into the job of creating the American Film Institute and my instinct was that the idea of heading both organizations was impractical. Roger Stevens brushed aside my attempt to question the proposition.

I took the afternoon shuttle to Washington, assessing whether there was a way to manage these two exciting jobs. Liz and I concluded that both positions were highly demanding and that my full commitment must be to AFI. We decided the best way not to disappoint Roger would be to come up with an alternative. On our way to Hickory Hill for dinner that evening Liz said, "What about Bill Blair?" Bill was in his last year as ambassador to the Philippines. He wasn't experienced in the performing arts but was widely respected for his good judgment.

The next day I explained my misgivings to Roger. I told him that Liz had discussed the prospect of Bill Blair with Bob Kennedy and he seemed receptive. I knew Roger would be partial to a name welcomed by the Kennedy family. In fact Roger asked Bobby to call Bill Blair, and his appointment as director of the Kennedy Center was announced six weeks later.

Roger had slain many dragons in his ten-year quest to build the Kennedy Center, and I believe it was always his intention to run it himself. Why didn't he make his thinking known to Jackie and the committee? I suspect it was pride—he didn't feel he should have to ask for the job. So he sat stoically through two years of interviews, then accepted Bill Blair, just as he apparently was prepared to accept me. What he didn't want was an arts personality who could usurp his authority. Blair served ably as general director of the Kennedy Center for three years, but it was Roger, as chairman, who called the shots—and would do so for years to come.

By the fall of 1967 the protest movement against the war had widened and speculation grew that Bobby might challenge Lyndon Johnson. He was initially hopeful that Johnson would find his way out of Vietnam and believed his own time would come later. But as the war escalated and the situation deteriorated, people pressed him to run. His confidants weighed the pros and cons. Ted Kennedy and Ted Sorensen were opposed, believing that 1972 would be his year, while Arthur Schlesinger and Dick Goodwin were convinced that Johnson was not going to end the war and had to be challenged. Bobby knew that taking on a sitting president risked splitting the Democratic Party and giving the White House to the Republicans. Or, should Johnson prevail, it might strengthen his resolve to continue the war. He was on the record. "I intend to support Lyndon Johnson's reelection in 1968."

Bobby and Ethel invited Liz and me to join them on a Labor Day cruise in Maine. We flew from National Airport on the *Caroline,* the plane that John Kennedy used in the 1960 campaign, to Brunswick Naval Air Station. Nearby we boarded the *Palawan,* the sleek sailing yacht that Tom Watson, the modest and engaging chairman of IBM, had offered the Kennedys for the holiday. We were joined by John and Annie Glenn, Andy Williams and his wife, singer Claudine Longet, Rowly and Kay Evans, Bobby and Ethel's fifteen-year-old son Joe, and his guitar-playing chum Chuck McDermott.

We set sail near Bath and headed north toward the Penobscot Bay. Watson's captain, a lean crew-cut German named Paul, was autocratic and given to stern instructions, including a warning that survival time in Maine's frigid waters was short. Should anyone stumble overboard at full sail it would be difficult to turn about in time for a rescue.

I emerged from below deck on the *Palawan* in seafaring gear, just before we took a tender to shore. Shipmates, from left: Andy Williams, Rowly Evans, Kay Evans. Behind Kay, from left: Liz Stevens partially hidden, Ethel Kennedy, Claudine Longet. Rear: Annie Glenn partially hidden, John Glenn, Robert Kennedy and his son Joe. Labor Day, 1967.

At sunset we approached an island bluff near North Haven topped by the Watson's two-story house. Tom and his wife Olive provided a feast of mussels and clams and fresh corn on the cob, and organized a lively game of charades before bed. Bobby was relaxed and playful away from the Washington grind.

We cruised all the next day, landing at dusk at Dark Harbor on Islesboro, the island where Liz's mother Lily had a summer cottage. She put up part of our group, and Douglas Dillon, the patrician Republican who served as JFK's secretary of the treasury, hosted the others. The Dillons gave a moonlit dinner party at their cottage overlooking Penobscot Bay, and the predominantly Republican island turned out. Curiosity about Bobby overcame partisanship, and everyone was thrilled to meet America's favorite astronaut and hear Andy Williams croon "Moon River."

On Labor Day John Glenn deftly built a bonfire on a rock formation for a picturesque luncheon picnic, then plunged into the frigid water (he *was* a Marine Corps colonel), followed by his competitive host, obliging the rest of us self-respecting males to follow. Bobby and John compounded our inconvenience by pretending the water wasn't cold.

John and Annie Glenn were marvelous companions and became lifelong friends. He radiated decency and went on to serve in the United States Senate and run for president. Annie, overcoming a persistent stutter, worked on behalf of the disabled throughout their seventy-three-year marriage.

Bob Kennedy and I were on deck as we cruised south on the dark blustery afternoon. In his search to come to terms with his brother's death he had taken to reading poetry, and from time to time would lower Edith Hamilton's *The Greek Way* and say, "Listen to this," then read a passage. Folded under his head was a leather jacket with the presidential seal. At one point he sat up and a sudden gust swept the jacket overboard. He was over the stern in an instant swimming after the jacket. Our German captain began maneuvering a 180-degree turn. When we reached Bobby he was treading water, clutching his brother's jacket, looking as blue as the Maine waters. His lack of hesitation was a reflection of his nature. He loved whitewater rafting and had climbed the previously unscaled, newly named, Mount Kennedy in the Yukon in tribute to his brother, accompanied by Mount Everest conqueror Jim Whittaker. Bobby was, as much as anyone I have known, fearless.

Robert Kennedy's dismay over the direction of the war was growing by 1968. Johnson had half a million men on the ground and had dropped more bombs on North Vietnam than fell on Europe during World War II. The prospect of victory was remote, yet Johnson assured American troops at Cam Ranh Bay that we would "nail that coonskin to the wall." Bobby was certain that peace talks would go nowhere unless the opposition was offered a role in governing South Vietnam, but Johnson saw that as a betrayal of American interests.

Katharine Graham came for dinner one night, her first outing after an illness. "Bobby Kennedy started arguing with me about the *Post*'s position on Vietnam, about how hopeless the war was and why didn't I do something about it," she revealed in her memoir, *Personal History*. "He was perfectly pleasant, but my head started pounding and I felt that I might faint." Kay told Bobby she was terribly sorry, but she had to go. She wrote him a note the next day saying she hadn't wanted to end the conversation about the war but felt ill. "I hope you are feeling better," Bobby replied. "I often have that effect on people—but they recover rapidly."

When Senator Eugene McCarthy announced he would challenge Johnson in the New Hampshire primary it led to more speculation over Bobby's future. I knew Senator McCarthy and didn't see him as a man who could solve the big problems and heal our wounds, though I did admire his decision. The first time I raised what by then we were calling "Topic A" with Bobby was in January 1968. He was in New York to present the best picture award to *In the Heat of the Night* at the New York Film Critics awards. Afterward a group of us met at the King Cole Bar in the St. Regis. I was sitting next to Bobby and quietly asked, "Do you know what you're going to do?" Often accused of being obsessed with the White House, he said, "You know, I have ten children and I could spend time with them. We could do interesting things. I don't have to be president." It was defensive and authentic—and touching.

Allard Lowenstein, the shrewd and idealistic New York political activist, had implored Bobby to run and failed, so he joined McCarthy's campaign, as did Dick Goodwin. Bobby saw no constructive option for himself, though he told one friend that when he woke up at five in the morning, he would ask himself whether the country could stand four more years of Johnson.

Late February, three weeks before the New Hampshire primary, was Ethel's annual fundraiser for Junior Village, an organization that cared for homeless children. This year she wanted to raise enough money for a swimming pool. Imaginative and irrepressible, Ethel decided to put on a telethon, and persuaded the manager of Channel 5, the local Metro-Media affiliate, to give airtime on a Saturday night. She secured the auditorium at George Washington University and wrote letters, each personalized with a witty postscript, asking her show business friends to appear. Ethel felt that if just a few of them accepted it would be a success. She expected Andy Williams, but then came Perry Como, Tony Bennett, Eddie Fisher, Bobby Darin and the psychedelic rock group Jefferson Airplane. In the end no one refused her. Television star Jack Paar was a close friend, but along came Woody Allen and the Smothers Brothers. Then Carol Channing, Lauren Bacall, Herb Alpert, Connie Stevens and Skitch Henderson answered the call, along with Stan Musial, Roosevelt Grier and Joe Namath.

Liz and Kay Evans were bright and resourceful but they had never produced a telethon. One Sunday Ethel called Liz saying that Bobby wanted to talk, so we drove to Hickory Hill. Bobby extracted himself from a touch football game and the four of us walked in the woods. He gently explored the scale of the telethon and the importance of controlling costs, then grinned before suggesting that there must be a way to build a swimming pool for Junior Village without putting an early end to his political career.

Bobby called the next day and asked if I would look after the production. I had never produced a telethon and had a full-time job, but it was hard to say no to Bobby. Concerns rose about the cost of bringing so many celebrities to

For Liz, Who ran such a happy Benefit. With so much love, Ethel. (inscription) Onstage during the Junior Village Telethon: Jack Paar, Ethel Kennedy, Claudine Longet, Liz, George, Robert Kennedy. March 1968.

Washington, fueled by memories of gigantic bills for hotels, meals and liquor for the JFK inaugural gala. The solution was a "welcome" letter from Art Buchwald on Ethel's behalf, advising the stars that a famous singer (by implication Frank Sinatra) had come to Washington with his posse and run up a tab that amounted to drinking two orphanages and an old lady's home, so we hoped they would understand that the hotel would not be filling room service orders. The celebrities gracefully accepted the rules.

We had three hours of program time on a local station and enough talent for two days of entertainment. Everyone was happy to fit in where they could. Bobby's long hair had been a hot topic in the press, including references to him looking like a fifth Beatle, so Ethel arranged for his mother Rose, who thought his hair should be shorter, to donate $500 if Perry Como, who started out as a barber, would cut Bobby's hair. The senator agreed but as the hour drew near his aides persuaded him that the images would be played over and over, a red flag for those who suspected he was a dangerous radical. At the last minute Tommy Smothers agreed to step in, which solved the problem but wasn't as much fun.

Marie and Averell Harriman gave a party for the cast at their N Street house. Sandy Vanocur, the veteran NBC political correspondent, recalled standing with a drink in the entry hall admiring a priceless Monet when Governor Harriman came down the stairs in a burgundy dinner jacket just as the front door opened and Jefferson Airplane entered in their hippie regalia. Averell's patrician manners were on display as one by one he shook hands with the stoned musicians.

The telethon was evidence of what would later be called "convening power." Bobby and Ethel's magnetism drew in extraordinarily accomplished people, and he had a way of mixing gravitas and humor. Everyone had a good time, Junior Village took in a record haul, and the senator's political career survived.

With the distraction of the telethon behind me I looked forward to total concentration on AFI's challenges, yet politics remained in the conversation. Liz and I went up the street to have dinner with Marie Harriman one night when Averell was in Florida. We were in the living room when the phone rang. Marie took it in the small adjoining bar. She signaled that Averell wanted to speak with me. When I took the phone he was in "crocodile" form.

"What's going on with Bob Kennedy?" he shouted. "I want you to tell Bob Kennedy he has no business running for president. He will tear the Democratic Party apart."

"I'm counting on you," Averell said before hanging up. He had tremendous respect and affection for Bobby, but this was a matter of their agendas diverging. Averell was hoping that Johnson would appoint him to negotiate an end to the war, a deed that would crown his public career.

I did not deliver his message to Bobby.

39

Into the Breach

On March 12 Gene McCarthy captured 42 percent of the Democratic vote in the New Hampshire primary to Johnson's 49 percent, a sobering rebuke to the incumbent president and one that posed a new reality: there would be a fight for the Democratic nomination.

We had accepted an invitation for dinner and a movie at Hickory Hill on the Friday after New Hampshire, and Ethel called that morning to tell Liz and me that Bobby had decided to run. He would announce on Saturday in the Senate Caucus Room. Ethel's dinners were informal but I put on a blue suit to respect a friend who was now running for president. When we went through the door at Hickory Hill, Bobby was standing there in khakis and a bright green sweater.

Regular pals like Art Buchwald and mountain climber Jim Whittaker were on hand, but Bobby's change of heart meant his political advisers soon arrived— the Young Turks on Bobby's staff, Adam Walinsky, Peter Edelman and Jeff Greenfield, followed by his senior adviser Fred Dutton and press secretary Frank Mankiewicz, and JFK aides Ted Sorensen and Arthur Schlesinger. During dinner Bill vanden Heuvel arrived from New York. The Jack people, Teddy people and Bobby people were there. Ted had flown to Wisconsin, the site of the next primary, to propose a joint effort with McCarthy.

Dinner was served in the living room at three round tables, as dogs and children wandered about. The political types were impatient, eager to sit down with the candidate and work on his speech. I sat next to Allard Lowenstein who told me he had committed to McCarthy and there was no turning back, before looking across the table at Bobby and reflecting, "That man should be president of the United States."

After dinner a number of us gravitated to the white-shuttered sitting room. Bobby slipped in and sat on a deep cushion sofa with a draft of his speech.

Arthur Schlesinger wrote in his journal: "Finally around 10:30 we (Dutton, Sorensen and vanden Heuvel) settled down with Bobby for a serious talk, along with Adam Walinsky, Allard Lowenstein, a bright fellow named Greenfield from Bobby's office and George Stevens, Jr." There was talk of the joint effort (which McCarthy would reject), then a detailed discussion of two drafts of the speech.

Kennedy friends, relatives and children were out in force in the Senate Caucus room on Saturday morning, along with an energized press corps. Bobby stood where Jack had eight years before and declared his candidacy. America, he said, was mired in war and riven by racism, but we must "stand for hope instead of despair." Then he headed to New York to march in the St. Patrick's Day Parade. His aides remained in Washington to put together a presidential campaign on the fly, setting up headquarters in a vacant building on L Street. Liz, seven months pregnant, was there every day, organizing surrogates and celebrities. I was locked into duties at AFI but remained an avid observer.

On Sunday, March 31, two weeks after Bobby's announcement and three days before the Wisconsin primary, where McCarthy was polling ahead of Johnson, Liz and I finished dinner and sat down to watch LBJ address the nation from the Oval Office. He spoke of progress in Vietnam and his desire for peace, before declaring to everyone's astonishment that he would neither seek nor accept the Democratic nomination. Liz and I were shaken as we walked across the street to see our good friend Senator John Sherman Cooper of Kentucky. We sat with John, his wife Lorraine, and their dinner guest, writer and hostess Evangeline Bruce, all of whom were seasoned political observers. They too were in shock. It was a political earthquake.

Three days later, April 3, was my thirty-sixth birthday, and Liz gave a party at our house. It was animated by the energy of the campaign. Bobby had returned to Washington from stumping in Indiana to court DC voters and have what he described as an unproductive meeting with Lyndon Johnson. The same day Averell Harriman was named US negotiator for Vietnam peace talks in Paris. Bobby called after dinner and said he and Ethel would like to stop by. They arrived with my friend Don Wilson from USIA days, who left *Life* magazine to join the campaign as head of media.

When Bobby walked into our living room he saw Averell, who because of his senior role in the administration had not endorsed him. It was a touching encounter because no one doubted their deep affection. At one point Bobby guided me and Wilson to a sofa. He explained that Jack Paar, the host of the popular *Tonight Show* on NBC, was the interviewer he felt most comfortable with, and he was going to sit with Paar for an on-camera conversation that he hoped would produce effective material for television commercials. "Can you meet us in Indianapolis and direct the interview with Paar?" he said. Flattered and eager to be of service, I said yes without hesitation, failing to calculate that some AFI supporters might object to me engaging so directly in the campaign.

Don Wilson and I met Jack Paar the following evening in a sparsely occupied Indianapolis hotel dining room while we waited for Bobby to arrive from campaigning upstate. Our main course had been served when a young woman came to our table with tears in her eyes. "Dr. King's been shot in Memphis," she sobbed. We sat silently absorbing the shock. At a nearby table we heard laughter and a derogatory remark about King. It was no time for midwestern warfare, so we went upstairs to the senator's suite.

Bobby learned that King was dead only after landing in Indianapolis after dark. He was scheduled to address an African American audience in the inner city at Seventeenth and Broadway. The chief of police warned him not to go but Bobby insisted, and the police escort left him on his own as his car neared the area. Climbing onto a flatbed truck wearing his brother's overcoat, he learned that the crowd of mostly young men didn't know that King had died. "I have bad news for you, for all of our fellow citizens, and people who love peace all over the world," he said. "And that is that Martin Luther King was shot and killed tonight in Memphis, Tennessee." He paused while cries of disbelief rang out, then spoke for the first time in public of his brother's murder.

> For those of you who are black and are tempted to be filled with
> hatred and distrust at the injustice of such an act, I can only say that
> I feel in my own heart the same kind of feeling. I had a member of my
> family killed, but he was killed by a white man. But we have to make
> an effort in the United States, we have to make an effort to
> understand, to go beyond these rather difficult times.

He urged the crowd to go home and "say a prayer for understanding and compassion. And to say a prayer for our country and for our people."

Riots broke out in dozens of cities across America that night, but there was no violence in Indianapolis. The wound Robert Kennedy felt from his brother's death allowed him to identify with others in pain. Many tough-minded political reporters were beginning to see in him qualities that might heal the country's divisions. Richard Harwood of the *Washington Post*, a marine who had been wounded on Iwo Jima, called Ben Bradlee and asked to be taken off the campaign. "I'm falling in love with the guy," he confessed.

Ethel was pregnant so Bobby had her taken to the hotel suite where campaign aides were considering what the candidate should do next. Once he arrived Bobby listened to opinions and decided to go ahead with his scheduled speech in Cleveland the next day, then suspend his campaign. He called Coretta Scott King and arranged a plane to take her to pick up Martin's body in Memphis.

Jack Paar was in the crowded suite, unnerved and perplexed. I thought Bobby would cancel the taping, but he decided to go through with it. We went to the studio at 7 a.m. Jack's questions were lengthy and he interrupted Bobby's responses, as television hosts do. We needed complete statements for television spots. I don't believe any footage was seen on television, but there was a sobering moment when Paar asked Bobby what his reaction was to King's assassination. "More and more people are turning to violence," he replied softly. "And in the last analysis it's going to destroy our country."

Washington was a city under siege the following night. There were fires and looting on Fourteenth Street and fourteen thousand National Guard troops and thousands of DC police were patrolling the area. The White House received a report that Stokely Carmichael was organizing a mob to burn down Georgetown. My only amusing memory of that awful night was friend and LBJ aide Joe Califano telling us that when Johnson read the report he said, "I've been waiting thirty years for this day."

Liz and I were driving to Hickory Hill for dinner. When we got to Georgetown's Key Bridge we were stopped by troops in riot gear and told there was a curfew and that the bridge was closed. I explained where we were going and after some checking they let us pass. We had a subdued dinner and discussed the course of the campaign in the wake of King's death. In Indiana Bobby was facing Democratic governor Roger Branigan, standing in for Vice President Humphrey, as well as Eugene McCarthy. Knowing that a loss there would be devastating, Bobby doggedly wooed voters, campaigning in a convertible. His only security was his unarmed bodyguard Bill Barry, a cadre of robust linemen from the Los Angeles Rams, and Olympic decathlon champion Rafer Johnson. Jack Newfield, the gifted *Village Voice* columnist, compared his hands, bruised and swollen after a day of greeting supporters, to those of middleweight Tony Zale after a fifteen-round bout. Bobby gained the crucial Indiana victory, then headed to Oregon for another tough fight with McCarthy.

At two in the morning on May 22 I drove Liz to Sibley Hospital where she gave birth to David Averell Stevens. She had worked in Bobby's campaign headquarters up to the last minute. A playful telegram from Oregon was delivered to her hospital room.

Dear Liz.
I heard the wonderful news about the birth of your son David.
Can you arrange for Gregory Peck to be at my rally in Eugene tonight.
Love Bobby.

We were thrilled to have our fine new son David, and with eyes on the future we placed a down payment on a larger house on R Street for our growing family.

McCarthy won in Oregon, the first political defeat ever for a Kennedy. Maybe Bobby really did need Gregory Peck. The California primary was next and Bobby campaigned sixteen hours a day, determined to win the state's huge slate of delegates. Tom Wicker recorded the intensity of Bobby's visit to the streets of Oakland's inner city for the *New York Times*. "The crowds surge in alarmingly, children leap and shriek and grown men risk the wheels of Kennedy's car just to pound his arm or grasp his hand."

On the evening of June 4 Liz cooked dinner at home in Georgetown and we watched the early returns from California. Liz, caring for two-week-old David, went up to bed at eleven with exit polls showing Bobby winning. I dozed off waiting for final returns and awoke in a fog. The screen showed chaos in a passageway of the Ambassador Hotel with screaming crowds and reporters. The unthinkable had happened. I saw Rafer sheltering Bobby's prone body in a pool of blood. I watched through the night as Frank Mankiewicz appeared at the Good Samaritan Hospital with terse reports on his condition.

I waited till morning to tell Liz. We went to Hickory Hill and spent the day fielding calls and trying to make ourselves useful, hoping against hope. It was after midnight when a ravaged Mankiewicz came before the cameras and delivered the dreaded news with resigned precision.

"Senator Robert Francis Kennedy died at 1:44 a.m. today, June 6, 1968. He was forty-two years old."

My father called from Los Angeles. He was a strong and compassionate man, but I sensed his helplessness, in this, our second assassination conversation in five years.

Liz arranged care for the children and we flew to New York for the requiem mass at St. Patrick's Cathedral. Ethel arrived from Los Angeles accompanied by

Jackie and Coretta King. Ethel was heroic, a grieving pregnant widow, comforting everyone around her. The mass for four thousand people, a funeral train to Washington, and the burial at Arlington National Cemetery had to be organized in twenty-four hours. Campaign aides and a legion of accomplished friends were now using their talents to produce a funeral.

Some of us were asked to stand watch during "the vigil"—shifts of six, three on either side of Bobby's flag-draped casket in the nave of St. Patrick's. Standing in silence alongside friends provided an eerie solace, as more than fifty thousand anguished mourners filed past.

There was a frisson the following morning when Lyndon Johnson entered St. Patrick's with Lady Bird. Then Jacqueline Kennedy and Coretta King were seated. Ted Kennedy gave a heartrending eulogy, his voice cracking at the words, "My brother need not be idealized, or enlarged in death beyond what he was in life, to be remembered simply as a good and decent man, who saw wrong and tried to right it, saw suffering and tried to heal it, saw war and tried to stop it." Ethel asked Andy Williams to sing "Battle Hymn of the Republic," and he, who was accustomed to television studios with teleprompters, fretted about remembering the words. But when the moment came Andy's lone voice coming from the choir loft was at once angelic and majestic, reverberating in the vaulted cathedral.

Liz and I crowded into a funeral limousine headed for Grand Central Station with Rowly and Kay Evans and Dave Powers, the Boston Irish newsboy who became President Kennedy's closest aide. Someone asked, "What will we do for four hours on the train?" "Don't worry about that," Powers said. "You'll be wishing it never ends."

The twenty-one-car funeral train, with the casket visible in the final car, left the station in the simmering one o'clock heat carrying a band of people that under any other circumstances would have the makings of an incomparably festive party. Bright and engaging figures from politics, entertainment, journalism and sports joined together for what became an eight-hour ride to Washington. This moment of profound grief became the ultimate Irish wake as we walked among the cars, talking, drinking and reminiscing. Through the windows we saw the tableau of mostly working-class Americans on both sides of the tracks bowing their heads or saluting as the senator's casket rattled by—more than a million people, who reflected the diversity of Bobby's following.

Ethel spent time with her rosary beside Bobby, and then with her son Joe, in an act of grace and fortitude, walked the entire length of the train thanking the mourners.

The journey ended in the darkness of Washington's white granite Union Station, where we debarked into a moonlight motorcade that circled the Capitol,

June 8, 1968.

passed by the Department of Justice, which would later carry Bobby's name, the Lincoln Memorial, and across the bridge to Arlington National Cemetery. The casket was carried up the hill to the open grave by Bobby's pallbearers, including his son Robert, brother-in-law Steve Smith, and friends Rafer Johnson, John Glenn and Jim Whittaker. In the crowd holding twinkling candles that provided illumination were many of the same people who five years earlier had stood on this ground to bury Jack.

I believe Robert Kennedy would have been elected president and that he was the only person who could have brought together disenchanted young people, the working class, and minorities. Jack Newfield said it best. "Anyone who rode his funeral train and looked out at the rows of wounded black faces that lined the poor side of the tracks knew what might have been. The stone is once again at the bottom of the hill and we are alone." My lingering memory of the dark blustery afternoon the next day at Hickory Hill was sitting with friends while children ran about, watching as Ted Kennedy swam alone in the pool, back and forth under the water.

Liz and I had rented Jackie Kennedy's house in Hyannisport for August. It was next door to Ethel's, so Bobby's absence weighed heavily. The Cape was beautiful, there was tennis and sailing, and Caroline, Michael and our new baby David gave us comfort and love. Yet the cloud of desolation lingered.

One last duty remained. Charlie Guggenheim was producing a Robert Kennedy tribute film to be shown at the Democratic Convention. Ethel had her heart set on Richard Burton as the narrator. It fell to me to arrange it. Richard agreed on the condition we come to Long Island where he was vacationing. Charlie and I drove to Quogue and found Richard and Elizabeth in a relatively modest rental house. Richard's voice was a magnificent instrument and he nimbly recorded his piece in our improvised studio in the living room. Elizabeth was airily displaying her recently acquired ring with the 33-carat Krupp diamond, said to be the world's largest. The ambience around the world's most famous couple was at odds with what for Charlie and me was a solemn final act for Bob Kennedy.

Hubert Humphrey received Johnson's support at the Democratic Convention in Chicago, even though the majority of primary voters had opposed the war. There was an effort to draft Ted Kennedy, who evaluated the situation at his Squaw Island house up the road from us in Hyannis. Teddy, conscious of the strain his entering the race would place on the extended family that was now his responsibility, took his name out of consideration. There was, as well, the unspoken thought that in these fractious times another Kennedy race could mean another Kennedy funeral.

We returned to our N Street house and prepared to go forward in what felt like a different world, negotiating a withdrawal from our contract to purchase the house on R Street. It was a time for healing. The aftermath of Bobby's death drew us closer to Ethel and the friends who rallied around her. The Irish penchant for smiling through tears kept everyone looking to the future. On the twelfth of December Ethel gave birth to hers and Bobby's eleventh child. She called Liz at home to tell her the baby's name—Rory Elizabeth Katherine Kennedy. The Elizabeth for Liz, the Katherine for Kay Evans.

Liz kept a special place in her heart for Rory as she grew to be a remarkable young woman, and we took pleasure that this scion of America's foremost political family became a filmmaker, creating works that affirmed her legacy, a commitment to social justice.

40

Epitaph for Georgie

There was another death in 1968, the quiet passing of my grandmother Georgie Cooper Stevens, at the age of eighty-six in her house in Glendale. My mother was a devoted daughter-in-law and, as was so often the case in our family, she stepped forward.

My father had recently arrived in Paris to film *The Only Game in Town*, a return to his roots in romantic comedy with Elizabeth Taylor and Warren Beatty. Before leaving Los Angeles he called to tell me he was going to marry Joan McTavish. Joan had been his companion for years in a rather private relationship. I suspect my father held off marrying until my life was settled. I sensed it was a long-contemplated decision and knew my encouragement was important to him, and I provided it.

It fell to my mother to call Dad and tell him of his mother's death. She knew he was shooting six days a week and was determined to shoot *The Only Game in Town* expeditiously. However Elizabeth had insisted on shooting the story set in Las Vegas in Paris to be near Richard Burton who was working there. The production faced delays because of Elizabeth gaining weight, calling in sick, and living the high life with Burton, which included bringing the Duke and Duchess of Windsor to the set for an extended lunch. My mother knew Dad would feel he should come home to respect his mother, but she persuaded him it was in no one's interest for him to disrupt production and fly back to California. His mother, she assured him, knew he was devoted to her, and she was at peace.

My mother once told me a story that is a fit epitaph for my extraordinary grandmother.

Georgie called her early one morning with a question. She asked whether the Burbank Theater, where she made her debut at age seven as Little Lord Fauntleroy, was still standing. My mother said she believed it was. Georgie told

Georgie Cooper Stevens in a portrait taken by her son.

her she had a dream about the theater and longed to see it again. She had by all accounts been a distinctive Lord Fauntleroy, as noted in an 1890 review of a performance in New Orleans: "For nearly three hours last night little Georgie Cooper held one of the largest audiences ever assembled in the Grand Opera House perfectly spellbound. Clever as performances of this bright little creature have been, last evening she fairly outdid her previous efforts."

My mother picked Georgie up in Glendale, drove downtown to Los Angeles, and parked on Main Street across from the theater—no longer Dr. Burbank's vision of a palace for fine plays but a burlesque house featuring striptease dancers. The two ladies surveyed the old theater from across the street. "Do you think we can go inside?" asked Georgie. My intrepid mother, standing just under five feet tall, led Georgie across the street to the box office and bought two tickets, earning a skeptical look from the wizened attendant. They went inside and found seats among the scattering of men, some wearing raincoats on a sunny Los Angeles day. The theater was handsome but sorely neglected, and on the stage a shapely brunette with "pasties" on her breasts was removing garments to the "rat tat ta boom" of a small house band. Georgie gazed at the walls and studied the balcony friezes. It moved her to be in the seats from which fashionable theatergoers had once watched her and her mother. After a while she nodded to my mother and they made their way out into the sunshine of Main Street.

My mother turned toward the parking lot but Georgie stopped her. "I wonder if my dressing room is still there?" My mother hesitated, but seeing resolve in the older woman's eyes turned and led Georgie to the stage door, and together they stepped into a dim passageway. A dancer rushed by and, confounded by the sight of two nicely dressed older women, stopped. "This lady played Little Lord Fauntleroy when this theater opened seventy-five years ago," my mother explained. "She wonders whether her dressing room is still here." Other girls had gathered in their flimsy garb. One of them took Georgie by the arm and led her through the darkness to stage left and the dressing rooms. My grandmother walked closer and with her actress bearing gestured, "This was mine. The large one was mother's."

Georgie turned, thanked the girls, and shook each one's hand. She had closed the circle, reclaiming memories of her mother, who made her stage debut in San Francisco during the Gold Rush and provided her daughter a life in the theater and nights at the Academy Awards with her son. Then to the car and back to the freeway with my mother, on their way to Hollywood Boulevard and lunch at Musso & Frank.

41

A Bridge for Filmmakers

AFI's biggest challenge was ahead—the creation of the Center for Advanced Film Studies. I knew many of the most accomplished filmmakers in Hollywood and envisioned a conservatory where aspiring directors, writers and cinematographers would learn from the masters.

My own film education—watching at my father's side as he made three films widely regarded as masterpieces—provided me with a point of view about what AFI might achieve. UCLA, USC, NYU and several other universities offered motion picture programs as part of an overall university education. Our plan was for an intense two-year conservatory approach that explored screen storytelling in all its dimensions and provided a bridge from the study of filmmaking to the profession.

This venture would demand most of my attention, so Liz and I decided to live in Los Angeles during 1969 and 1970 and do our commuting in the other direction. Liz, effortlessly, it seemed, organized three successive rental houses, found a preschool for Michael, and enrolled Caroline in the Westlake School.

The first challenge was to find a home for the center (which a decade later would be renamed the AFI Conservatory). We didn't have money for a capital investment and rental opportunities were scarce, but a providential call came from writer-director and AFI trustee George Seaton. George reminded me that his wife Phyllis was mayor of Beverly Hills, and explained that the city was deciding on the best use for Greystone—the sixteen-acre estate above Sunset Boulevard built in the 1920s by oil magnate E. L. Doheny for his son. The perception of a nonprofit organization housed in a lavish hillside mansion had downsides, but the substantial benefits included 44,000 square feet of usable space, and the price—one dollar a year.

Greystone offered a tale of intrigue worthy of a campus for storytellers. The elder Doheny was the centerpiece of one of America's greatest political scandals, Teapot Dome, when he was secretary of commerce for Warren G. Harding in the 1920s. His son died in what was believed to be a murder-suicide with his secretary-chauffeur in the bedroom that became my office.

We encountered delays when Beverly Hills neighbors questioned the desirability of having students, a good portion of whom bore a passing resemblance to Che Guevara, coming and going in their quiet neighborhood, but after hearings at city hall we negotiated a ten-year agreement with rules to curb inconveniences to neighbors.

I wanted to know more about the highly regarded European film academies, so Liz and I flew to Poland to see the school in Łódź, where young Roman Polanski cut his teeth. I spent time with Stanislaus Wohl, a veteran cinematographer who had decades of experience making films as well as years of teaching, a combination rarely found in the United States. Stanislaus agreed to join us and organize our program for cinematographers.

This was 1968, the year of the Prague Spring in Czechoslovakia when President Alexander Dubček enacted "socialism with a human face." He abolished government censorship and promised democratic elections. The Soviet Union cracked down, sending in two hundred thousand Warsaw Pact troops, seizing control of radio and television stations and killing over a hundred civilians. Liz and I arrived in the old city of Prague to find Soviet tanks standing ominously in the streets, a chilling sight in contrast to spirited conversation we enjoyed with writers and directors in the café of FAMU, the state film academy. The school had fostered a new wave of Czech filmmaking led by Oscar winners Ján Kadár (*The Shop on Main Street*) and Jiří Menzel (*Closely Watched Trains*), alongside Věra Chytilová (*Daisies*) and Miloš Forman (*Loves of a Blonde*)—an extraordinary crop for a tiny country.

Frantisek Daniel, head of the screenwriting program, gave us an illuminating tour of the school, centered on a hands-on approach to learning the various facets of screen storytelling. Liz and I had dinner the next night with Frank, as he was called, his wife Eva and their two young boys. Frank had a strong grasp of screenwriting. On a foggy night beyond any listening devices he and I went for a walk and I asked if he would join us in Hollywood at our new conservatory. His manner was indirect, a symptom of the political atmosphere in the Communist state. "We can explore it," he told me, pointing out it would be difficult to get out of Prague with his family.

In Washington I discussed the situation at the Department of State and succeeded in gaining permits for the Daniel family to board a flight out of Prague.

We structured an admission process and recruited staff in advance of a September opening. I persuaded Jim Blue, my colleague from USIA who was a graduate of the French film academy, to join us. Once Frank Daniel arrived he and Jim and I interviewed the three hundred who applied for admission as "fellows," a term we chose over students to reflect the advanced nature of the program. Filmmaking skills were helpful, but we were more interested in individuals with intellect and life experience that would equip them to tell interesting stories once technique was mastered. One of the first to come to Greystone for an interview was an Oklahoman who had graduated from Harvard, worked as a correspondent for *Time* in Latin America, and was now teaching existential philosophy at MIT. Terrence Malick was the only applicant who showed up for his interview in a jacket and tie. He looked more like a linebacker than a philosopher, and combined intellectual heft with a wry humor. All he had to show was a short he made in Boston for $750, but it was apparent that he had stories to tell.

We accepted fifteen filmmaking fellows and three research fellows, the latter to fulfill an idea of mine that blending scholarship and criticism with filmmaking would be stimulating. It turned out that the aspiring critics and historians resented the substantial spending on film production and the filmmakers were unenthusiastic about theoretical discussion, and the research program was abandoned after three years. The backgrounds of the fellows varied. Tom Rickman was a struggling novelist from Paducah, Kentucky; Jeremy Paul Kagan had made clever short films at NYU; Matthew Robbins from San Antonio had gone to graduate school at Johns Hopkins; Caleb Deschanel was a USC graduate with a cameraman's keen eye; and Frank Dandridge was a *Life* photojournalist who covered the 1964 Harlem riots. Paul Schrader, a midwestern Calvinist keen on Japanese cinema, enrolled as a research fellow.

July of 1969 was a month of intense planning, with the occasional intrusion of high drama. On a Saturday morning the phone rang at the small house we were renting in Stone Canyon. John Chancellor was on the line from his anchor desk at NBC News in Rockefeller Center. John was a good friend, but a call from him on Saturday was not the norm. "I thought you should know," he said, "we have a bulletin about your friend. He drove his car into the water on Martha's Vineyard and a girl drowned." It took a moment for me to realize he was talking about Ted Kennedy. From John's lips I heard for the first time the name Chappaquiddick.

The next day Terry Malick, his wife Jill Jakes, and director Arthur Penn came for dinner. We discussed Chappaquiddick before sitting together in front of the television to watch Neil Armstrong step off the landing module and become the first human to set foot on the moon. Just eight years earlier we had heard John Kennedy, his voice soaring, commit America to "landing a man on the moon and returning him safely to Earth before the decade was over." It was stimulating to share the astounding images from the moon with creative minds like Arthur and Terry. The landing was a fulfillment of JFK's optimism and vision, dimmed only by his absence.

Days later another early morning call, this one from Averell Harriman, who had heard news in the East before we did, telling us that Sharon Tate, eight months pregnant with Roman Polanski's child, had been murdered by the Manson Family. The normally suave statesman expressed alarm about the grisly tragedy that took place in a rental house half a mile from ours. He urged us to return to Washington.

My calendar shows days filled with organizing a new school and stimulating evenings during which I spread word about AFI to the Hollywood community: "Dinner at the Pecks—Mr. and Mrs. Jean Renoir, Omar Sharif and Barbra Streisand; dinner at home—John Huston and Shirley MacLaine; dinner at Danny Kaye's with Pecks and Isaac Stern; dinner at George Englund's w/Warren Beatty, Paul Newman, Robert Towne."

I explained to the brilliant Billy Wilder our concept for this new Center for Advanced Film Studies. "Ah," Billy said. "What you're doing is teaching new dogs old tricks."

Mr. Doheny's old mansion was pulsing with energy on September 23, 1969. Equipped with state-of-the-art projection rooms, sound and editing facilities, the Center for Advanced Film Studies was ready for its close-up. In a morning welcome with the fellows and faculty I described our concept. "While it may not be possible to *train* people to make films, it *is* possible to create a climate in which people can *learn* to make films, where aspiring artists can absorb, in a relatively short period, insight that other people have wrested from the experience of an entire career." I explained that there would be the opportunity at AFI to examine the great works of world cinema, and that "film structure"—the engine that keeps an audience engaged with a motion picture—would be at the heart of the program.

On this opening day we initiated what we hoped would become a tutorial tradition where accomplished filmmakers would share their knowledge—beginning with an afternoon seminar on the Greystone lawn with Elia Kazan. Gadge, as he was called, was earthy and magnetic and his nonconformist nature

On the set of Terrence Malick's 1970 AFI thesis film, *Lanton Mills*. Cinematographer Caleb Deschanel kneels at center, Harry Dean Stanton behind him. Malick at right.

meshed with the spirit of the AFI fellows. Most young filmmakers lacked experience working with actors. Here was Kazan, America's master of the Stanislavski method, who introduced Marlon Brando, Karl Malden, Eva Marie Saint and James Dean to the screen. "I'm not afraid to make demands on actors," he told the fellows. "I reach into them for more. Power is an ugly but necessary tool. Your own power to say, 'My dear, this is the way it's going to be.'"

That evening we lightened up with a screening of a vintage print of Harold Lloyd's silent classic *Kid Brother*. The director-comedian, then in his seventies, seemed more like someone's cheerful uncle than a moviemaking entrepreneur who ended up owning his films, enabling him to build a forty-four-room house in Beverly Hills with a hundred-foot waterfall and a nine-hole golf course. He brought along his neighbor, King Vidor, director of fifty-six films including *The Crowd*, *Our Daily Bread* and *Duel in the Sun*. Tall and dignified in a tailored suit, Vidor was there to celebrate the occasion. Lloyd spoke about his concept of gags in film comedy, how to provide a "topper" for a gag, and the need to have a topper for the topper.

David Lynch on his first day as a fellow at
the AFI Conservatory, September 25, 1970.
At left, Robert Mundy.

The harmony across generations that evening reassured me. The idea of filmmakers coming to Greystone to pass on their wisdom was going to work. Lloyd said he was honored to be at what he called "the initial shove off." A founder of the Academy of Motion Picture Arts and Sciences, he quipped, "If your institute gathers momentum you may outdistance the Motion Picture Academy." The old master was placing our young organization, however tentatively, in the continuum of American cinema history.

The casting of that opening week signaled the variety of tutorial talent: writers Ray Bradbury and Dalton Trumbo, directors Sam Peckinpah and Rouben Mamoulian, and composer Henry Mancini. Ever since that day in 1969, every session of the Harold Lloyd Master Seminar series has been recorded and transcribed for use by students and historians.

The heartbeat of the conservatory was the screening of films in the Great Hall, the former Doheny living room, and a smaller projection room that replaced the bowling alley. In those days, long before the advent of home video, DVDs and streaming, it was next to impossible to see classic films, but the studios loaned 35mm prints to AFI which we screened day and night. When Frank Capra or Jean Renoir was scheduled for a seminar, we would show their films in advance. The faculty would analyze them from a creative—as distinct from a critical—standpoint, exploring storytelling structure. David Lynch, who arrived at AFI in year two and spent several years making *Eraserhead* in the Doheny stables, recalled his arrival.

The day I got to Los Angeles—in this bright, beautiful sunshine, and walked up Sunset Boulevard to Greystone—I thought for sure I'd died and gone to heaven. At AFI, all day the greatest cinema played in the Great Hall. George brought foreign voices along with powerful American voices to enrich American cinema.

Another hallmark was filmmakers in residence who came for an extended period. Roberto Rossellini from Rome was brilliant and spontaneous, and native New Yorker John Cassavetes was intense and irreverent. The fellows' avid interest in foreign auteurs was rewarded with seminars from François Truffaut, Ingmar Bergman and Satyajit Ray. Local directors defined American cinema—Ford, Walsh, Lang, Wyler, Stevens and Huston. It was a continual feast, with actors, writers, cinematographers, art directors, editors and composers adding to the mix.

Improvisation was a buzzword among many of the fellows—the practice of allowing actors free rein to reshape scenes and create dialogue. To some it suggested originality and freedom from constraint, a belief that ideas emerging from the "moment" would produce a bolder cinema. The faculty felt that while improvisation could on occasion be useful, we had a responsibility to address screenwriting as the backbone of quality films.

It was an exciting night in 1970 when Federico Fellini walked into the Great Hall, smiling like a champion. He was accompanied by his wife and muse, Giulietta Masina, who had given unforgettable performances in *La Strada* and *Nights of Cabiria,* and Anthony Quinn, who played the brutish circus performer Zampano in *La Strada.* The fellows had watched *Fellini Satyricon* earlier in the day and a full menu of his work the week before. Word of the great man's appearance spread around town, and Jack Lemmon, Shirley MacLaine, Billy Wilder, Sidney Poitier and Sam Fuller found seats.

Quinn sat beside Fellini and I moderated the discussion. An interpreter was nearby but Fellini spoke in English. Shortly after the seminar began a fellow from New York stood, saying, "I've read that you often come on the set with the actors not knowing what's going to happen during the day's shooting. Is it true that you do a great deal of improvisation?" The students and faculty sensed that this was a moment of truth—word was about to come down from the mountain. Fellini turned to Anthony Quinn for clarification.

"Improvistore?"

Quinn nodded. Fellini frowned.

"No, it's absolutely impossible to improvise," he declared. "Making a movie is a mathematical operation. It is like for you Americans sending a man to the moon. It isn't improvised."

Federico Fellini, left, Anthony Quinn and George Stevens, Jr., in AFI's Great Hall,
January 1970.

This was a crucial moment for our new academy. The conservatory was there to advance the principle that creativity goes hand in hand with craftsmanship and discipline, and that night the man who was arguably the world's most imaginative director spoke up for preparation, calculation and structure.

42

Nixon in Charge

The tumultuous year of 1968 ended with the election of Richard Nixon. He defeated Hubert Humphrey, whose alignment with Johnson on the Vietnam War cost him support, while touting a secret plan to end the conflict. We could only hope that Nixon did indeed plan on ending it.

The American Film Institute was off to a strong start and well into its second year when Nixon took office. The arts were bipartisan and we looked forward to a smooth transition at the National Endowment for the Arts. It was widely expected that NEA chairman Roger Stevens, the prime architect of the organization who was just two years into his term, would be asked to continue, but Nixon appointed Nancy Hanks, who had worked at the Rockefeller Brothers Fund. She was politically adept and less deferential to members of the arts council than her predecessor, and decided to change course with AFI.

Hanks set up a Public Media Program within NEA that would support programs in film similar to AFI. It would have its own director, as well as a Public Media Panel, a small body of advisers akin to AFI's board of trustees that would approve projects and funding. NEA would retain for its Public Media Program the lion's share of the funding that Roger Stevens assured AFI it could expect, and when AFI applied for funding, our proposals and performance would be judged by the NEA Public Media staff and panelists, our new competitors.

AFI had initiated major programs in preservation, cataloging, and support for independent filmmakers, as well as establishing the Center for Advanced Film Studies. We made those commitments based on the assurance of stable funding from the National Endowment. NEA had created AFI on the premise that a nongovernmental organization would have a capacity for creativity and innovation that a purely governmental program would not. We were suddenly swimming against the tide.

The chairs of the arts-related committees in Congress, Senator Claiborne Pell of Rhode Island and Representative John Brademas of Indiana, were believers in AFI, as were many others on both sides of the aisle. As Hanks' intentions became clear they weighed in, urging her to support AFI in the fashion originally contemplated, but Hanks stood her ground. At one stage Brademas and Pell introduced legislation that would separate AFI from the endowment and fund it directly by Congress—similar to the National Gallery of Art and the Smithsonian. Brademas, a Rhodes Scholar who would one day become president of New York University, shepherded the legislation in the face of NEA resistance. The bill fell short of the votes necessary.

"Film as an art form had a golden opportunity to move on to the national level," said Brademas' legislative aide Jack Duncan. "By bickering they gave it up." Brademas did broker a slightly improved budget process for AFI, but it was clear that NEA would not live up to the original long-term funding pledge. We had no choice but to cut back our programs and double our fundraising efforts if we were to survive. It was said that AFI was speeding at two hundred knots and taking on water.

A rational response might have been to face the fact that the premise of the new national institution secured by dependable government funding was no longer a reality, and make a graceful exit. But I was young, perhaps naive, and convinced that the NEA Public Media Program lacked a coherent vision and would never achieve what AFI set out to do, so my instinct was to keep moving forward. Forced to make budget cuts and suspend pay raises, I asked the AFI board to reduce my $75,000 salary to $60,000, where it remained for the rest of my time at AFI.

Gregory Peck decided that after two years he was ready to retire as chairman, leaving a vacuum at a challenging time, and I am forever grateful that Roger Stevens understood our predicament. He was angry that Nancy Hanks had turned her back on the plan for AFI that he and the National Council on the Arts had put in place, so he stepped up and took over as chairman, while simultaneously bringing the Kennedy Center to life. Roger was calm and intrepid, and having him at my side inspired confidence.

Nancy Hanks called one day in response to the prodding of Pell and Brademas with an offer of a $500,000 matching grant. This was no substitute for dependable annual funding but it was an offer we couldn't refuse, so I began contemplating how to find half a million dollars on top of the money we were already raising. I had "matching grant, matching grant," going round and round in my head—then a lightbulb flashed. *Cary* Grant. Three decades after my childhood visit to the set of *Penny Serenade,* Cary became—at least in my imagination—the solution to our matching grant problem.

I put in a call ready to explain my purpose to his secretary. After a few rings I heard the soothing and unmistakable voice.

"*Hel-lo.* Who is calling?"

"This is George Stevens . . . Junior."

"Why *George,* how *nice* to hear from you."

Cary sounded pleased so I felt emboldened. I told him that his career was so rich and distinguished that the American Film Institute wanted to celebrate it at an event at the Kennedy Center where we would show scenes from his movies and invite guests to salute him. At the time this was a new idea, unlike today when retrospectives dot the landscape. I explained that AFI would use the money raised to preserve endangered films. "Oh, George, that's a *lovely* idea," he enthused, before adding one caveat. "I'm employed by Fabergé and there must be no conflict."

Energized, I placed a call to Bob Wood, the president of CBS, who agreed to see me in New York. I rode the elevator to the top of Black Rock, the concrete and glass Eero Saarinen skyscraper on Fifty-Second Street. Mr. Wood offered me a seat in front of his desk with a panoramic view of the city. I launched into my presentation—the first of many I would make to networks through the years. Bob Wood wasted no words. "CBS will do this."

I danced into the elevator, elated that my first network pitch was a home run. I called Cary Grant the next morning to discuss dates, proudly advising him that the Tiffany Network (Cary liked quality) would broadcast his tribute from the Kennedy Center. I felt something inauspicious in the pause that followed.

"George, are you speaking about *telly*-vision?"

"Yes, Cary, it will be extraordinary."

"Oh, George, that's out of the question. I never do *telly*-vision."

I'll never know whether I failed to make clear in our first conversation that television was central to the idea (but why then was he concerned about Fabergé?) or whether Cary just didn't absorb it. Or whether he changed his mind. Either way my "matching Grant" brainstorm was dead.

We found another way to match Nancy Hanks' money, but the concept of celebrating great careers in American film stayed with me. It grew from the idea instilled in me by my father that the important films were the ones that stood the test of time. If there was religion in our family, it was this idea of quality and excellence—values at the heart of AFI's purpose.

43

A Place to Stand

One of John F. Kennedy's favored quotes was from Archimedes: "Give me a place to stand and I will move the world."

The steel superstructure that was to become the president's national memorial was rising along the Potomac. One day Roger Stevens called with an invitation to visit the site. We donned hard hats and plodded gingerly through debris, riding freight elevators to see the Opera House, the Concert Hall and the Eisenhower Theater, and we renewed our discussion of building a motion picture theater.

Earlier I had mentioned to Roger how AFI's search for permanent office space in Washington had been stalled by NEA budget cuts. As we approached an elevator to take us down to ground level, Roger surprised me. He pointed to the corridor above where his own third-floor offices were being constructed, and said matter-of-factly, "Well, if you're going to be responsible for movies in this place, you might as well be in the building." This game-changing opportunity meant that the American Film Institute, the new kid in town, would have a base of operations in our national cultural center, giving us new stature and a prestigious mailing address. A place to stand.

I watched Roger manage a decade-long crusade to build the Kennedy Center in the face of opposition from Congress, business interests and the press. His resolve was inspiring. Not long after the groundbreaking in 1964, Wolf Von Eckardt, the influential *Washington Post* architecture critic, savaged architect Edward Durrell Stone's design, calling it "a folly that would plague us for the next 100 years," claiming that a "spaghetti of access ramps" would largely obscure the Kennedy Center from view. The American Institute of Architects seconded the complaint, and in one congressional debate Republican Frank Bow of Ohio feverishly called the Kennedy Center "a national disgrace" and "a beautiful morgue," before fainting on the House floor.

With two great ladies of the screen, Lillian Gish and Cicely Tyson.

Roger's critics called for a review, but he believed that stopping to reconsider would halt momentum and sink the project. He called a press conference at the construction site on a grassy strip beside the Potomac and declared: "We are going ahead. I won't stop until I produce a building for you." Roger's determination and resilience inspired me to push ahead with AFI in the face of what seemed like daunting obstacles.

Roger invited me back to the center six weeks later and showed me a rectangular space on the ground floor behind the Eisenhower Theater. "If you can make this work," he said, "here's a space for your film theater."

I was acquainted with Malcolm Holzman, one of a trio of outstanding young architects at Hardy Holzman Pfeiffer who were building a reputation in performing arts design. "We require perfect sight lines and a screen that fills the fourth wall," I told Malcolm, before adding, "Our funds are limited." Malcolm came up with an elevated grid to accommodate 224 seats—a forerunner to stadium seating in multiplexes that would become popular decades later.

AFI was responsible for the cost of the theater, so when Jack Warner, now retired from Warner Bros., came to Washington, Roger and I met him in his suite at the Madison Hotel. Dapper in a plaid suit with his waxed mustache,

Warner was no longer in power but trying to stay in the game. He liked the idea of being associated with the Kennedy Center and appeared to have forgotten our differences on *PT 109*. He agreed to donate $250,000 to build the AFI Theater.

In 1970, while the Kennedy Center was being completed and the AFI Theater constructed, we presented programs of movie classics at the National Gallery of Art, building a membership of three thousand film enthusiasts. The association with the august National Gallery reinforced the premise that AFI was concerned with the *art* of film.

I wanted the opening of the AFI Theater in the Kennedy Center in April of 1973 to have the same sense of history that Harold Lloyd provided to the opening of the conservatory, so we invited Lillian Gish, then eighty, to appear with D. W. Griffith's *Broken Blossoms* from 1919. She was there at the birth of an art form and became the greatest actress of the silent era. Miss Gish was extremely gracious with everyone she encountered, except for one unfortunate photographer who was determined to get a low-angle shot of her. "Get up from there! Get up!" Miss Gish protested. "If God had wanted you to shoot me from that angle, he would have given you a camera in your belly button." She then smiled and explained, "Mr. Griffith always said, 'Shoot from above for an angel, shoot from below for a devil.'"

44

Come Home America

The quadrennial election process was becoming a staple in our Washington lives, and as 1972 approached Democrats were looking for a candidate. Ted Kennedy inspired hope among many but recognized he was compromised by Chappaquiddick and that this was not his time. Senator Ed Muskie of Maine, Hubert Humphrey's running mate in 1968, was the frontrunner when George McGovern, a plain-spoken liberal from South Dakota, decided to enter the race. Bobby had described McGovern as the most decent man in the Senate and Liz and I respected his integrity and opposition to the Vietnam War. He was at 2 percent in the polls when Liz decided to join his "Come Home America" campaign, working closely with our friend Frank Mankiewicz, the campaign director, and thirty-six-year-old Gary Hart from Colorado, a precocious policy and political thinker, who was campaign manager.

Frank and I shared Hollywood roots. He was the son of *Citizen Kane* scenarist Herman Mankiewicz and nephew of writer-director Joe Mankiewicz. Frank fought in the Battle of the Bulge and, as an idealistic young lawyer, left Hollywood to serve in the Peace Corps before becoming Bob Kennedy's quick-witted Senate press secretary. Frank and Gary ran a lean grassroots campaign.

McGovern, whose wardrobe reflected his Sioux Falls upbringing, mentioned over lunch in Los Angeles that he admired the suits I wore. He was contemplating an upgrade for presidential politics, so I took him to Carroll and Company, a low-key haberdashery in Beverly Hills, after alerting the owner Dick Carroll, a former Warner Bros. publicist who had such an acrimonious time with Bette Davis he gave up on the movie business and opened a clothing store. Dick showed McGovern a wide selection of suits, but George continued browsing. I looked up and saw that he had found the only electric blue suit I ever saw at Carroll's. We guided him toward selections more suited for high office,

Presidential candidate George McGovern meets with women leaders to commemorate the
fifty-second anniversary of women's suffrage on August 25, 1972. To McGovern's right,
Elizabeth Stevens. Front row, left to right: Anne Martindell, Shirley MacLaine, Bella Abzug,
Anne Wexler. Rear, left to right, three unidentified. Next to McGovern, Jean Westwood,
chair of the Democratic National Committee.

and George chose two smart suits that served him well, and which resulted in a
Washington Post story on his new threads. I stopped by the store later. Dick was
glowing. "Do you think I might become haberdasher to the president?" he asked
with a smile. "Dick," I said, "this is a small campaign and you're in on the
ground floor. Don't rule out secretary of state."

Terry Malick called as Liz and I were packing to fly to the Democratic Convention in Miami. He was preparing his first feature film. I had met his young
lead actors, Sissy Spacek and Martin Sheen, when they auditioned at his house
near Greystone. Terry had raised $300,000 for *Badlands* and was in South Dakota
ready to begin shooting, but during the conversation he revealed that an investor
had dropped out and he was $15,000 short. It was evident that he hoped I might
fill the void. Terry was like an uncle to our boys and I teased him.

"Are you saying you think that it's more important that you make your film
than Michael goes to college?"

Terry, straight-faced, said, "I guess that's what I'm saying."

I sent Terry a check before going to the airport. A year later he called with the good news that Warner Bros. was going to buy *Badlands*. Soon after I received a check from Terry, and on the line where you write "groceries" or "auto repair," he had put, "Go, Michael, Go!"

McGovern staked his campaign on opposition to the war and a belief that ending it would revive the American economy and reunite the country. He surprised Muskie with a strong showing in New Hampshire, followed by other primary successes, and won the nomination, but the Miami convention was a disaster. A protracted vice presidential nominating process delayed his acceptance speech until nearly three in the morning and he chose Indiana senator Thomas Eagleton as his running mate, only to face reports three days later that Eagleton had undergone electroshock therapy for depression. Eagleton withdrew and was replaced by Sargent Shriver.

Meanwhile, our Georgetown neighbor Bob Woodward was investigating the burglary of the Democratic National Committee headquarters in the Watergate with his colleague Carl Bernstein. The burglars were employed by Nixon's Committee to Re-elect the President (which bore the delightful acronym CREEP), though the accumulating evidence of White House involvement in the "third-rate burglary" seemed to be having little impact on voters. Nixon had won in 1968 promising "peace with honor" in Vietnam, but four years later the war was still raging. This time, one week before election day, Secretary of State Henry Kissinger declared, "We believe that peace is at hand. We believe an agreement is within sight." Nixon won in a landslide.

I have been asked how I retained my admiration for McGovern, who lost every state except Massachusetts and the District of Columbia. It was because of his character and integrity. He volunteered for the Army Air Corps after Pearl Harbor and piloted a B-24 heavy bomber on dozens of missions over Germany, earning the Distinguished Flying Cross. During the campaign Nixon exaggerated his own modest record in the navy and scorned his opponent as weak on defense, but George refused to campaign on his war record because his greatest generation mindset saw that as boasting. He was soft-spoken and a gentleman, but late in the campaign a Nixon supporter kept railing at him during a speech. Afterward McGovern called the heckler over and was heard saying, "Listen, you son-of-a-bitch, why don't you kiss my ass?" Some feared a backlash if this leaked to the press, but free spirits in the campaign ordered "KMA" buttons that were worn by McGovernites at the next night's rally.

Frank Mankiewicz, who considered his place on Nixon's notorious Enemies List a badge of honor, later wrote: "I never apologize for that campaign. All we did was lose an election. We didn't go to jail—none of us. No perjurers, no conspiracies to obstruct justice."

Twelve years later Walter Mondale was routed by Ronald Reagan by the highest electoral vote margin in history, 525 to 13. He went to see George McGovern.

"Tell me how long it takes to get over a defeat of this kind?" he asked.

"I'll let you know," was the reply.

45

The Test of Time

Not long after my failed courtship to honor Cary Grant, we obtained funding from the California Arts Commission to produce *Directed by John Ford,* the first feature-length documentary about an American filmmaker, directed by Peter Bogdanovich. At a preview at the Directors Guild on Sunset Boulevard, Hollywood's foremost directors watched classic scenes from Ford's career unspool. There was laughter and tears and a palpable sense of shared pride on the part of Ford's peers.

I was touched by my father's emotional response to seeing this summing-up of his colleague's half century of filmmaking. It harked back to the night we were riding home from the 1951 Academy Awards, an Oscar for *A Place in the Sun* on the seat between us, and he said, "We'll have a better idea what kind of film this is in about twenty-five years." The audience response at the Directors Guild spoke to the test of time. It clarified in my mind the idea of honoring American filmmakers —not for a popular film of a certain year but for a lifetime of enduring work.

Leonard Garment was an unusual figure in the famously unfriendly Nixon White House. He was an affable and shrewd New York lawyer who once played tenor sax in Woody Herman's band, and advised Nixon on many matters, including the arts. I went to see him to propose that the president participate in honoring an American filmmaker at a fundraising tribute at the Kennedy Center. I said we were thinking of John Ford. No one was more deserving, and Ford just happened to be a Republican from Nixon's home state. Garment, who was aware of our funding struggle with Nancy Hanks, liked the idea but made no promises. One day shortly after Nixon's second inauguration, Garment called.

"You have him in Los Angeles on March 31."

"Thank you, Leonard," I said, "but the idea is for a tribute at the Kennedy Center."

"The president will participate on March 31 in Los Angeles," he said firmly. "That's what we have."

The cachet of an AFI event with a president participating was a bird in the hand—a big one. I revised my thinking. A trustees meeting was scheduled in Los Angeles on February 27, five weeks before the March 31 date. I wrote selection criteria for what we would call the AFI Life Achievement Award, so we could present the idea to the board, select John Ford, and honor him on March 31 at the Beverly Hilton with the participation of President Nixon.

Charlton Heston had succeeded Roger Stevens as chairman because Roger had to focus his attention on the opening of the Kennedy Center. Chuck was intelligent and public-spirited and had always been ready to help when I was at USIA. And at AFI, when I asked him to come to Washington to testify before Congress, he would buy his own ticket on the red-eye and do a full day's work persuading legislators of AFI's virtues. Chuck was a good citizen whose late in life enthusiasm for guns baffled his friends.

The trustees gathered in the stately Doheny mansion and unanimously approved a resolution that began, "Great accomplishments of the past must be recognized so that the masters of film may take their deserved place in history beside leaders in other arts." The vote to select John Ford was unanimous. Paul Ziffren, a prominent movie lawyer, argued that five weeks wasn't sufficient to mount an event of this scale. A number of trustees joined Ziffren in proposing that we ask the White House for a later date.

I saw our bird in the hand flying out to sea and suggested a recess. I guided Heston to the sunlit terrace with its majestic view of Los Angeles and the Pacific Ocean beyond. "Chuck, the odds of us getting another date are long."

He pondered, Moses like, before intoning, "Dammit, let's go for it!"

Heston called the meeting to order and made the case for seizing the opportunity. Displaying more self-confidence than I felt, I assured the trustees we could have everything ready by March 31. Heston then telephoned John Ford in Palm Springs. Ford was deeply moved and said he would accept the AFI award. I called Leonard Garment and the date was confirmed.

Only because of AFI trustee Jack Schneider, who had succeeded Bob Wood as the top decision maker at CBS, were we able in short order to get approval to present *The American Film Institute Salute to John Ford* on television as a ninety-minute special. The contract provided money to stage a show to which we could sell tickets and raise funds for AFI. Warner Bros. chairman Ted Ashley rallied Hollywood to fill the Beverly Hilton ballroom. As executive producer I worked with Jim Silke of the AFI faculty and producer Carolyn Raskin. We laid out the Beverly Hilton ballroom with a head table and large movie screen to present Ford's films. A televised retrospective of a film career was new territory in 1973.

Having promised CBS a star host, Ted Ashley arranged dinner at Danny Kaye's house. Dinner with Danny was always a performance. He cooked Chinese with dramatic flair, telling rapid-fire stories and waiting for his laughs. Ted made our pitch. Danny was voluble, full of ideas, elusive and noncommittal, until Ted said, "The host is the one who introduces the president of the United States." Danny stopped talking. "I'm in," he said.

The event at the Beverly Hilton marked the beginning of AFI's national visibility. Nixon flew in from Washington on Air Force One, going directly to the Beverly Hilton, where he greeted guests at a VIP reception. Gregory Peck, whose name had appeared on Nixon's Enemies List, was first in line as AFI founding chairman. The president greeted Peck with a smile and surprising enthusiasm. "I'm a great admirer," Nixon said. We were off to a good start. Then the president spoke of William Wyler's film *Friendly Persuasion.* "You were excellent in that," enthused Nixon. "I've seen it twenty times." Warming to his theme, he continued, "Jessamyn West, the author of the book, is a distant cousin. It's my favorite film." Gregory managed a deep-throated, "Thank you, Mr. President," before moving quickly to the ballroom—wondering why, after twenty viewings, the president hadn't noticed that Gary Cooper was the star of *Friendly Persuasion.*

I shook the hand of Richard Nixon, the third president I had met. I was aware of the irony that this man, whose views and values were distant from mine, was enabling the event that was vital to our organization's future. H. R. Bob Haldeman, my onetime Toluca Lake neighbor and company commander at Harvard School, was the president's chief of staff. When the Nixon crew first arrived in Washington and I saw Bob at the British Embassy, I expected a bit of old school bonhomie, but he looked at me with cold eyes. My history as a Kennedy man had severed our school ties.

Hollywood turned out in full force for John Ford. I was in the lobby and noticed confusion at a desk where table assignments were provided. The imposing figure of Walter Matthau was holding forth. Next to him stood my diminutive mother. There was a mix-up with her seating. I heard Matthau take charge with his brew of gruffness and charm. "If it wasn't for this lady there wouldn't be any show tonight," he growled, taking her arm. "You'd better give her a good seat." Just then Cary Grant approached with that enchanting smile. "George," he said, "this is a *magical* evening." As we shook hands (hugs and embraces had not yet taken hold among men in Hollywood), I whispered, "Cary, this was meant to be your night." He stood straight, eyes moistening, and clasped both my hands. If he had second thoughts, it was only for an instant.

The ballroom was packed with Ford pals—Pat O'Brien, Frank Capra, Walter Brennan, Fred Astaire, Rosalind Russell, Bob Hope and California's governor, Ronald Reagan, as well as younger admirers like Roddy McDowall, Robert Wagner, Clint Eastwood and Charles Bronson. At a table close to the stage in the well of the ballroom were prominent members of Nixon's inner circle—Haldeman, Henry Kissinger, John Ehrlichman and our patron saint, Leonard Garment. The United States Marine Corps Band played "Ruffles and Flourishes" and "Hail to the Chief" as the president entered with Mrs. Nixon, alongside John Ford in a wheelchair, his signature black patch covering his left eye. Hollywood cheered.

After dinner Danny Kaye presided, introducing Ford veterans John Wayne and Jimmy Stewart, along with Jack Lemmon from *Mister Roberts,* whose stories blended accolade with humor, finding fun in the director's autocratic behavior. Kaye told of the studio head who sent an assistant to tell Ford he was a day behind on his shooting schedule. Ford, sitting in his director's chair, chewing his pipe, asked the young man how many pages he was supposed to shoot in one day. The lad replied nervously, "About eight, sir." Ford took his script, leafed the pages counting to eight, tore them out and handed them to the young man. "Tell your boss we're on schedule."

Ford's colleagues called him Pappy or Admiral, but the red-maned Maureen O'Hara saluted him as Sean Aloysius Kilmartin O'Feeney before singing "Isle of Innisfree" from *The Quiet Man.* This song and another from Leslie Uggams were the result of CBS insisting on two musical numbers. Television executives were convinced that ratings for variety television depended on "entertainment," which they defined as music. For the rest of my career I tussled with network programmers to avoid unnecessary songs.

The transcendent moment was when the room went dark and projected on the screen was a medley of memorable Ford scenes—my idea of entertainment—from *Young Mr. Lincoln, Stagecoach, The Searchers, The Man Who Shot Liberty Valance,* and ending with Henry Fonda's powerful, "Wherever there's a cop beating up a guy, I'll be there" soliloquy from *The Grapes of Wrath.* In that darkened ballroom the range of Ford's work was mesmerizing, bringing the audience to its feet.

I had asked Katharine Hepburn, who was close to Ford, to present the award, but she was busy in New York. I decided that the recognition should properly come from the American Film Institute, so I presented it myself. I gave

President Nixon presenting the Medal of Freedom to John Ford at the first AFI Life
Achievement Award. Charlton Heston, right. March 31, 1973.

AFI's pledge to preserve for all time the surviving works of John Ford, and quoted another New England Yankee, Henry Adams: "He too serves a purpose who only stands and cheers," then invited the audience to stand and cheer John Ford.

Ford rose from his wheelchair and walked toward me with a stub of a cigar in hand. He accepted the first AFI Silver Star trophy and said he was overcome with gratitude for what he called "a momentous occasion in the annals of motion pictures."

Charlton Heston then mistakenly returned to the stage and introduced President Nixon. Danny Kaye sat apoplectic. Ted Ashley hurried over to calm Danny as Nixon walked on stage and surprised Ford by presenting him with the nation's highest civilian honor, the Medal of Freedom. Ford stood as Nixon placed the laurel around his neck, then offered what he said was "not an original prayer, but one that is spoken in millions of American homes today—it's simply, 'God Bless Richard Nixon.'" With those words (a prayer not equally embraced by everyone in the audience), the president departed and flew to San Clemente for a meeting with President Thieu of Vietnam.

We would only discover much later that there was a dramatic subtext to the AFI's John Ford dinner. It was only after Nixon and his senior staff left the White House and boarded Air Force One to fly to Los Angeles that his trusted counsel John Dean took the opportunity to meet with Judge John Sirica and began spilling the inner secrets of Watergate that would scuttle the Nixon presidency. By the end of the month Haldeman and Ehrlichman were fired and both would go to prison. On two occasions twenty years apart I asked Henry Kissinger if he remembered the John Ford dinner. Both times he smiled ruefully and uttered the same phrase, "Oh yes . . . the last of the happy days."

It was a "last hurrah" for John Ford and a turning point for AFI that would not have happened but for my futile pursuit of Cary Grant, teaching me that even rejection can reap rewards. The Life Achievement Award would become my companion for twenty-five years. Writing and producing these shows provided a much-appreciated creative dimension to my AFI life, respite from the managerial charge that was part and parcel of building a new institution.

46

A Capital Life

The term "bicoastal" came later, but from the time I moved to Washington in 1962 it described my life. Now, with AFI a major presence in Hollywood and Washington, plus a small office on Fifty-Sixth Street in New York, my world had become triangular. I enjoyed air travel, finding the five-hour flights between coasts valuable for thinking and writing. Liz and I were a young couple with growing children and relished our stimulating friendships. She was known and admired in Washington, and I carried a show business connection that was rare in the city.

Senators and members of Congress were ingrained in the life of the capital in those days, neighbors who lived with their families in the city and suburbs of Maryland and Virginia, sharing responsibilities on school boards and seeing one another at church and children's sporting events. It was much later that politicians, yoked to fundraising and fearful of being identified too closely with Washington, left their families back home and spent just three days a week in the city. Liz and I enjoyed the company of political figures from both parties, and it was fun waking up to the *New York Times* and *Washington Post* after having discussed the front-page story with participants the night before.

Part of Washington's charm in those days was that people weren't preoccupied by money. Yes, Averell Harriman and Douglas Dillon and others had lots of it, but it didn't determine one's standing. People were measured by their ideas, interests and accomplishments. Wealth didn't get you to the table, nor was it flaunted and rarely was it the topic of conversation.

Art Buchwald, with his thrice-weekly column syndicated in five hundred newspapers, and his sad-sack cigar-smoking man of the people personality, was a source of joy to everyone not the target of his pen. He would show up in the morning at his office in the *Newsweek* building, sit at his typewriter, and within

Art Buchwald and Stevens. Lunch at the Sans Souci.

an hour had knocked out a sparkling column which he messengered to his editor. Then he would stroll down the hall to the office where columnists Rowland Evans and Bob Novak were just beginning a long day of calls to political sources for their own syndicated column. Art would announce cherubically that *his* work was done and sit down to chat.

Our bistro of choice was the Sans Souci on Seventeenth Street, just a block from the White House. Art and I had a regular table. We enjoyed friends passing by with gossip or a jibe of some sort. Artie would begin our lunch by asking me to bring him up to date on what was going on at AFI. I would give him a couple of sentences, after which he would sit back and declare, "Good. Now lunch is deductible."

On other days we would get together with Ben Bradlee and Edward Bennett Williams, each one talented and irreverent. Reporting was in Bradlee's blood—and he had swagger. As executive editor of the *Post* during Watergate he relished the idea of subscribers opening their front door, unfolding the paper and saying, "Holy Shit!" Ben lived to produce those editions. Ed Williams, at the peak of his illustrious career as a defense attorney, became managing owner of the Washington Redskins and hired George Allen as coach. When the Redskins won on Sunday Ed showed up for lunch on Monday exclaiming, "Joy, joy, joy!" When the Redskins lost he arrived glum, ordered two martinis and ranted about his stubborn coach. "I gave George Allen an unlimited budget, and he exceeded it." Later Ed would get rid of the Redskins and buy the Baltimore Orioles baseball team, explaining that football didn't provide sufficient occasions for agony. "In football you only have sixteen vulnerable days for depression. In baseball it's practically every day." Between Buchwald's permanent grin, Bradlee's dirt from the *Post* newsroom, and Williams' stories from courtroom to gridiron, lunches were priceless.

Dinner parties were the social engine of Georgetown. Katharine Graham, Joseph Alsop, the Harrimans, and Evangeline and David Bruce were frequent hosts. You could count on excellent food, fine wine, interesting company and informed, sometimes contentious, conversations. Hostesses knew how to cast an enjoyable dinner—mixing a cabinet officer or two, a Supreme Court justice, an ambassador, legislators, and journalists of the Walter Lippmann, Scotty Reston caliber, or, as television took hold, David Brinkley or Tom Brokaw.

Liz had a gift for entertaining and did so with understated elegance. We would sometimes have one round table, or on special occasions two or three. Our honeymoon on the *Malahne* led to a close friendship with Sam Spiegel. He arrived in town for the premiere of *The Night of the Generals* and brought along stars Peter O'Toole and Tom Courtenay, and director Anatole Litvak. There was a growing affinity between Washington and show business. And when stars and directors brought their new films to Washington under the auspices of AFI, it expanded awareness of the organization.

Averell Harriman came to the Spiegel dinner. Although heir to the Union Pacific fortune, he had a reputation for being frugal. Instead of bearing the cost of a chauffeur in Washington, he got a good deal on a New York Checker Cab, had it painted black, and on occasion drove it the three blocks from his house to ours. These taxis had a notoriously wide turning ratio and after dinner a few of us were on the front steps to observe Averell climb into the Checker Cab with his wife Marie, and, using the sturdy hands of an eight-goal polo player, deftly maneuver a U-turn on N Street for the return trip home, drawing applause from the movie crowd.

When District of Columbia Stadium was built in 1961 on ground owned by the National Park Service, it became home to the Washington Redskins. On January 18, 1969, in the waning hours of Lyndon Johnson's presidency, seven months after the assassination of Robert Kennedy, Secretary of Interior Stewart Udall, a Bobby admirer appointed by John Kennedy, used his authority to rename the field. He earned Johnson's undying enmity by calling it Robert F. Kennedy Memorial Stadium. Ed Williams called Ethel to say a box was available to her for all Redskin games as long as he was in charge.

On Redskin Sundays it would often fall to me to drive our Chrysler station wagon to Hickory Hill where it was filled with picnic baskets and as many human beings as could be sardined inside, including Kennedy children and our Caroline, Michael and David. The children issued challenges. "Drive to RFK Stadium without stopping the car!" At moments when I slowed down, the chant of "Go, Go, Go, Go!" boomed in my ears. The urge to please the kids was powerful so I learned how to get off crowded roads, occasionally going up onto sidewalks. After a time, as a safety measure, Ethel hired a driver with a small bus.

Officially there were twelve seats in Ethel's box with an open window looking out to the field. Provided with twelve tickets and a parking pass, she would walk up to the ticket taker with twenty-odd friends and children in her wake, smile, hand him the twelve tickets, then stand and chat as her party streamed in bearing baskets and thermoses. The ticket man understood that counting the passersby wasn't a good career move. There were never happier times at football games than in Ethel's overflowing box, and we even traipsed with Eddie to Los Angeles to watch his Redskins lose to Miami in the 1973 Super Bowl.

Ethel was the driving force behind the Robert Kennedy Memorial, which addressed Bobby's concerns by assisting disadvantaged youth. She was an avid tennis player and organized a pro–celebrity tournament as a fundraiser at Forest Hills, the site of the US Open. Ethel persuaded Roone Arledge, the originator of *ABC's Wide World of Sports,* to broadcast it, and crafted seductive letters to invitees. ("It's hard to believe that your backhand could give a kid on an Indian reservation a better life.") Acceptances came from Hall of Famers Don Budge, Pancho Gonzales, Althea Gibson and Rod Laver, along with current champions Arthur Ashe, Chris Evert and Jimmy Connors. Decathlon champions Rafer Johnson and Bruce Jenner joined basketball legends Elgin Baylor and Julius Erving, and show business favorites Clint Eastwood, Elton John, Dinah Shore, Sidney Poitier and Andy Williams.

The first RFK tournament was in August of 1972 and Ethel was at the center of a spirited Friday night dinner at the Rainbow Room at Rockefeller Center, making each player feel part of the work being done in Bobby's memory. Dustin Hoffman and Davis-Cupper Erik van Dillen won the championship before fifteen thousand fans and ABC's cameras.

The next year celebrities jockeyed to be paired with a pro who would enhance their prospect of winning. Ethel, overlooking my subpar celebrity quotient, invited me to play. To no one's surprise my partner was an unknown tour rookie. "Hi, I'm Raul," said a tall twenty-year-old Mexican with a mustache when I showed up in the bright sunlight at Court 19. He and I were to play the New York Knicks Hall of Famer Bill Bradley and the South African ace Cliff

Drysdale in our first of five qualifying matches. Raul and I won, and I realized that he was by far the swiftest person I'd ever shared a court with. Waiting for our next match I gave him some inside information. "Do you know, Raul, the winning pro gets a new car?" His dark eyes lit up. "Seriously?" I looked him in the eye. "Yes, sir . . . a Ford convertible." We won our next four matches with Raul poaching like a panther to swat away the celebrities' cross-court returns of my serve, and sprinting to track down well-placed lobs, moving us to the quarterfinals on center court in the stadium where thousands filled the bleachers, and celebrities and legions of Kennedy children sat in a small covered grandstand.

Our quarterfinal match against Senator Ted Kennedy and French champion George Govan was a close contest but once again Raul delivered in crucial moments. Roone Arledge cared about ABC's ratings, so I took no offense when he complained that he would have preferred not having Teddy eliminated. Raul and I won our semifinal match which took us to the finals. But first there was an exhibition match between rivals Arthur Ashe and Stan Smith that Raul and I watched courtside in our perspiration-stained shirts. Observing their power and finesse at close range gave me second thoughts about my presence in the stadium. Then our opponents walked out in fresh attire, matching tee shirts with shamrocks: James Caan, Oscar nominee for *The Godfather,* and Tom Gorman, USA's Davis Cup captain. The fans signaled their pleasure to these confident and well-turned-out stars. As I scanned the towering grandstand it occurred to me that my previous experience playing before spectators topped out at fifteen.

There is an odd psychology that takes over in events like these. The ego of celebrity amateurs drives us to want to excel and to succeed in the spotlight, sometimes losing sight of the colossal disparity between our skills and those of the professionals. Jimmy Caan opened the first game with a hard serve that was long. Raul whispered with a puzzled grin, "I think he's trying to ace me." Jimmy followed his second serve to the net and Raul pounced, striking it with topspin at Caan's feet to win the point. The next thing I knew I was serving for the match. No one then knew that my unheralded partner, Raul Ramirez, would go on to stardom, capturing doubles titles at Wimbledon and the French Open. Soon Ethel and Teddy were presenting Raul and me handsome bronze busts of Robert Kennedy. But best of all, Ethel handed Raul the keys to a bright red Ford convertible.

Coming from a family where pictures count it was perhaps not surprising that my father was at home with his newest Polaroid camera photographing the ABC telecast off the screen. He sent a framed set of color shots that had the Stevens touch—the yellow ABC chyron legend displayed over Forest Hills center court: "Stevens–Ramirez 6 . . . Caan–Gorman 4," and next to it my mustachioed partner—his head thrown back in victory with me smiling at his side.

Art Buchwald, left, interviews the RFK champions at Forest Hills.
Raul Ramirez, center. 1973.

I reminded myself that I must be discreet and modest about my good fortune. I keep one memento that speaks to my failure to meet that goal—a tee shirt with blue lettering that Tom and Meredith Brokaw sent me that reads: "Hi, Have I Told You Lately How I Won the RFK in 1973?"

In my calendar for that year I made two notes on Saturday, October 20. "12 noon. Cox spoke on television." And below: "6 pm. Art Buchwald Birthday Tennis Tournament."

The "Cox" was Archibald Cox, who had been appointed special prosecutor by Attorney General Elliot Richardson to investigate the Watergate break-in. After Cox subpoenaed the Oval Office tapes, a US court of appeals ruled that Nixon had to turn them over. The White House said it would only provide "internally created summaries." Cox called a press conference at noon where he surgically dismantled the White House refusal to obey a court order, citing the law and the Constitution. He was standing his ground and Nixon was infuriated.

I have a vivid recollection of driving with Liz and Kay Graham at sunset toward the Watergate Hotel to pick up screenwriter Peter Stone and take him to Art's tennis party. Kay, with inside knowledge as publisher of the *Washington Post* confided, "We're going with a story that Nixon called Elliot Richardson to the White House this afternoon and they had a shouting match."

There was a bar and buffet at the Buchwald gathering at the Arlington Y, where journalists and members of Congress were discussing the crisis as play began. For a time reporters would run to the pay phone in the hallway, but before long most departed to cover the story. The rest of us served and volleyed and received word that Richardson had refused to fire Cox, leading General Alexander Haig, Nixon's chief of staff, to call Richardson's deputy, William Ruckelshaus, and give him the same order. Ruckelshaus boldly refused, saying he could not fire Cox without cause.

The next morning we got the full story in Mrs. Graham's Sunday *Post*: "NIX-ON FORCES FIRING OF COX. RICHARDSON, RUCKELSHAUS QUIT." The story contained a weighty statement from Cox: "Whether ours shall continue to be a government of laws and not of men is now before Congress and ultimately the American people."

This event led to Nixon's downfall and became known as "the Saturday Night Massacre." A reporter tracking the origins of the phrase decades later heard that it was born at the Arlington Y tennis party. He asked Buchwald's son Joel if it was true that his father coined the term.

"It sounds like something that my dad would have off-the-cuff quipped," Joel said, mulling the possibility. "I can't with 100 percent certainty say it was him. But I *can* with 100 percent certainty say that he would be happy to claim credit."

Buchwald's October 20 birthday became an annual event called the Saturday Night Massacre Tennis Party.

47

Honor Catches Up with a Fugitive

James Cagney stepped out of the public eye in 1961 after appearing in sixty-two films, and in 1974 was dividing his time between his farm in New York and a house on Martha's Vineyard. The news that he was to receive the second AFI Life Achievement Award and would be returning to Hollywood to accept the honor was greeted with surprise and enthusiasm.

Cagney arrived by car from Martha's Vineyard with Billie Cagney, his former vaudeville partner and wife of fifty years. Henry Mancini, whom I got to know when I was directing *Peter Gunn* and he was writing its signature musical score, and his wife Ginny invited Liz and me and the Cagneys for dinner. Jimmy, at seventy-three, stood straight and square-jawed at five feet six. I was struck by the bright blue eyes and gentle manner. Ginny served dinner in a cozy area next to the kitchen and I watched Cagney, who considered himself a "listening actor," as he displayed that quality in discussing gardens and horses with Liz.

Jimmy and I talked briefly about the show, and as he was leaving he said, "George, I'm going to need a 'getavasia.'" I was left with a blank look. "It's a vaudeville term," he whispered. "When you leave the stage, you do a little something extra, so they remember you." As he went out the door he tapped out a graceful little step.

If the John Ford Life Achievement Award dinner with President Nixon on hand was a state occasion for the movie capital, the 1974 Cagney dinner was a love fest. Paul Keyes, a genial silver-haired writer from *Rowan and Martin's Laugh-In,* joined me as producer of the show and enlisted Frank Sinatra as host. The old guard was out in force, but so too was the young set who normally avoided industry functions. Ali McGraw and Steve McQueen bought nine tickets (Paul Newman, Joanne Woodward, Cicely Tyson and Clint Eastwood were at their table), and John Lennon and Mick Jagger came to salute the reclusive star. The orchestra brought Cagney into the ballroom with George M. Cohan's *The Yankee Doodle Boy.* The infectious tune had the crowd on its feet as he entered with his straight-legged forward-tilting stride. His friends—Joan Blondell, George Raft, Loretta Young, Ralph Bellamy and Mae Clark—were clapping in time as the music took Cagney to his seat between his wife and Governor Ronald Reagan.

After dinner Sinatra took the stage and spoke with good-natured ease. "I guess it's no secret that the reason we've pulled the world together tonight is to honor a great motion picture star—James Cagney the actor. And we're here to pay tribute to a wonderfully warm and sensitive human being—Jim Cagney the man—poet, painter, farmer, conservationist and humanitarian." The show blended scenes from Cagney films presented on the big screen with tributes from his friends, including his beguiling costar from *Love Me or Leave Me,* Doris Day, who was rarely seen at industry gatherings. Bob Hope, Jack Lemmon and Shirley MacLaine had their say, then a scene from *Boy Meets Girl* showed Reagan in 1938 playing a perplexed announcer interviewing Cagney at a movie premiere. Reagan stood at his table and praised AFI's film preservation effort, noting that *Boy Meets Girl* was among those pictures being saved. He asked for one favor: "I hope they forget that scene I was in. Heaven only knows *I've* been trying to forget it."

The final scenes displayed Cagney's range: the compelling tough guy roles ending with the powerful vision of Cagney walking in the rain toward the camera in *Public Enemy,* the scintillating soft-shoe duet on a banquet table with Bob Hope in *The Seven Little Foys,* topped by his performance in *Yankee Doodle Dandy.*

In presenting the award I made a nod to Cagney's reclusive tendencies. "There's an old saying that honor follows him who flees it," I began. "Tonight honor catches up with a fugitive. James Cagney has made his mark on the mosaic of American character as few others have . . . as he sang, acted, danced and machine-gunned his way into our hearts."

Cagney bounced to his feet and strode briskly through the crowd to the podium, where, written in block letters on cardboard that came back with his shirts from the laundry, was his speech. He accepted AFI's Silver Star, exhaled and drew understanding laughter with the words, "I'm a wreck."

He complimented AFI for its efforts to establish film firmly as an art, then offered his own definition.

> Art is life plus . . . life plus caprice. Where the simple declarative sentence becomes a line of Shakespearean poetry. Where a number of musical notes strung together become a Beethoven sonata. Where a walk done in cadence by a Freddy Astaire or Edward Villella or Patricia Farrell becomes an exciting dance. That's art.

James Cagney accepts the second AFI Life Achievement Award March 13, 1974.

"Why don't we just say for now that I'm merely the custodian of this award," he said, "holding it for all those wonderful guys and gals who worked over the years to bring about this night for me." He called out his leading ladies and male stars, acknowledged Frank Sinatra "as one of the neighbor's children," then gave a nod to his old boss and antagonist who was seated close to the stage. "Jack Warner gave me a name I shall always cherish— 'The Professional Againster.' But we're old now and full of understanding and that's water over the dam."

And then, for his getavasia, Cagney chose to reflect on his boyhood on the streets of New York, looking to the audience with a twinkle.

"The names . . . the names of my youth," he said, "Loggerhead Quinlaven, Picky Houlihan, Artie Kline, Jake Brodkin, Brother O'Meara. . . . They were all part of a very stimulating early environment which produced that unmistakable touch of the gutter without which this evening might never have happened at all."

48

Shaping AFI

The CBS broadcast of the Cagney show drew a phenomenal 49 percent share of the primetime audience, thirty-eight million viewers, providing a priceless national platform for AFI that spurred our fundraising and brought me my first Emmy.

Civil rights was on the national agenda when AFI was launched, so we sought diversity in our programs. In the summer of 1968 I sat down with Cliff Frazier, a bright-eyed New Yorker with infectious idealism who, after Martin Luther King, Jr., was assassinated, put aside his acting career and dedicated himself to King's vision of a "beloved community" free of racism and violence. Cliff had ideas about how AFI should encourage minorities, so we provided a $50,000 grant to create the Community Film Workshop Council in our New York office, with Cliff as executive director. Paul Heller, producer of the well-received independent film *David and Lisa,* joined the effort as pro bono chairman, and Sidney Poitier and Ossie Davis became board members.

We were able to secure a $675,000 grant from the Organization for Economic Opportunity, the jobs-related agency of Johnson's Great Society, to enable CFWC to set up independent programs to provide film and television training and identify job opportunities for minority young people in Chicago, New York, Philadelphia and Atlanta, with rural projects in Whitesburg, Kentucky, and Jackson, Mississippi. Cliff Frazier guided all the projects and at the end of the first year every trainee received a job at a television station. The Community Film Workshop programs planted roots and thrived, and Cliff went on to devote his life to supporting minority training and employment in the media.

We were less sensitive to the needs of women. Our independent filmmaker grantees included Nell Cox, Storm De Hirsch and Barbara Kopple, but only three of the three hundred applicants to the conservatory in its first year were

Maya Angelou at the AFI Directing Workshop for Women; editor Miles Watkins, right. 1975.

women and none were chosen. The industry's track record of hiring women directors was dismal, with only Lois Weber and Dorothy Arzner of the silent and early sound era and Ida Lupino in the fifties sustaining important careers. Studios rarely considered women for directing jobs, succumbing to Cecil B. DeMille's warning that women would "crumple from the strain" of eighteen-hour days.

In 1973 Mathilde Krim came for a visit to the Kennedy Center. Mathilde was a vivacious woman who was trained as a biologist in Geneva and would become a leader in the crusade to combat AIDS. Her husband Arthur was the head of United Artists and she was on the board of the Rockefeller Foundation. Over lunch we discussed the limited opportunities for women directors. Toni Vellani was now associate dean at the conservatory, supported by Jan Haag, who managed independent filmmaker grants and administered the admissions process. They came up with the idea of creating a directing workshop for women, modeled on the workshop Toni had initiated for the fellows. Jan took a proposal to Mathilde Krim and the Rockefeller Foundation made a $30,000 grant to AFI for a pilot project.

The Directing Workshop for Women began in 1974 with a class that included the poet Maya Angelou, producer Julia Phillips, and actors Ellen Burstyn, Lee Grant, Margot Kidder and Lily Tomlin. The wave of applicants signaled the unquenched appetite for women to be storytellers in charge of their films. Budgets were small but the money went a long way because fellows from the conservatory collaborated as cinematographers, production designers and editors, and the new medium of videotape was much less costly than 35mm film. The women directors brought a new dimension to Greystone and a year later Rockefeller renewed its grant, sponsoring a class that included Anne Bancroft, Dyan Cannon, Marilyn Bergman, Carole Eastman and Randa Haines. Cannon's short film, *Number One,* received an Oscar nomination, stimulating interest in the program. Joanne Woodward, Cicely Tyson, Marsha Mason and Candice Bergen joined the program in succeeding years.

AFI was criticized because so many actors were accepted, but they brought years of firsthand experience working with and observing directors on the set. Writers, editors, cinematographers and musicians also thrived. Maya Angelou— who was an early AFI trustee—sent a note of appreciation after directing her short film, *All Day Long*: "I am proud of the American Film Institute," she wrote, "for what it has done for me and others who would never have had the delicious experience of saying 'action' and 'that's a wrap.'"

I was stretched thin running AFI on both coasts, so in 1974 I enlisted my friend Martin Manulis, the producer of *Playhouse 90* during New York's golden age of television, to a new position as director of AFI West. Martin was in his late fifties and once explained his success managing the live dramas at *Playhouse 90* as being "mother, wet-nurse and psychiatrist," qualities that seemed pertinent to the challenges at Greystone. Martin's long association with many of the actresses in the Directing Workshop was a timely asset.

Frank Daniel had been promoted to dean a year earlier and in June he surprised us with a proposal that the conservatory should become a separate operation under his direction with financial autonomy and its own board of trustees. The concept was ill-considered, and Frank, whom we valued as a teacher, escalated the situation by submitting his resignation. The matter became public and *Variety* labeled the uproar that followed "AFI's Summer of Discontent." Several members of the executive committee held meetings with Frank and concluded there was no way to meet his requirements, so we accepted his resignation six weeks before the beginning of the school year.

The Daniel matter was disruptive in the short term but his departure became a catalyst for the conservatory's defining era. Toni Vellani took over as director and he and Martin Manulis managed to start the school year on time. Toni began clarifying the method by which AFI would help young people become filmmakers. He had spent three years at my father's side as associate producer on *The Greatest Story Ever Told* and had a keen understanding of classical drama, literature and art. Despite being very close to Toni, I didn't fully anticipate how skilled he would be at communicating the principles of storytelling.

Toni placed narrative structure—"action and conflict"—at the heart of the program. His approach to writing a screenplay began with the filmmaker asking one question, "What is the premise?" That one-line premise, he explained, "will tell you what happens with every one of the scenes. It becomes your overall touchstone for the film." Toni considered that the storyteller's primary job was to engage the viewer's attention. "Let us understand at the beginning what your character wants, what his goal is, and what the obstacles are to that goal," he

Welcoming new fellows at the Conservatory in September 1976. Jan Kadar, Filmmaker in Residence, seated center in plaid shirt; to his left, Dean Toni Vellani and Martin Manulis, director of AFI West.

said. "If the audience knows what the character wants they can begin to wonder if he or she will ever get it. And if they begin to wonder, you've hooked them."

Marshall Herskowitz, who with fellow 1975 graduate Ed Zwick formed a successful filmmaking partnership, credits Vellani for priceless guidance. "Toni taught us that filmmaking is a Samurai job, a Captain down-with-the-ship job. Every scene is opening night—mess it up and it will be that way in the film forever."

AFI's summer of discontent was stressful, but it was a turning point that secured the future of the conservatory.

49

Maverick

AFI was fending off critics who claimed the institute was just a farm system for the Hollywood industry, while receiving little acknowledgment for our deep-rooted dedication to creating artistic opportunities for young filmmakers and preserving America's film heritage. The selection of the 1975 Life Achievement Award recipient offered an opportunity.

The board of trustees seized it by putting aside chronology and selecting Orson Welles ahead of older future recipients like Frank Capra, Jimmy Stewart, Bette Davis and William Wyler. Orson, who arrived at the RKO Studio at age twenty-four to make *Citizen Kane* and said, "This is the greatest electric train set any boy ever had," proceeded to make a masterpiece that led every international poll as the greatest film ever made. Welles lived in Europe and was out of fashion with the Hollywood studios, but we decided it was important that we honor an innovator with a reputation for independence.

I spoke with Peter Bogdanovich, who was close to Orson. He reached him in Paris and Orson agreed to come to Hollywood in February to accept the award. The announcement of Welles' selection was widely praised as a deserving and bold choice, but there was a backlash, with complaints that thirty-five years had passed since *Citizen Kane* and that Welles owed money around town.

All my dealings with Orson would be conducted through Peter, whom I came to refer to as Orson's "medium." Peter parceled out nuggets of information like gems from Tiffany & Co. "Orson will not ascend or descend any steps in his walk to the Century Plaza ballroom stage." "Orson requires a super-sized black leather chair at the head table to accommodate his girth, and he insists that a scene be shown from his film in progress, *The Other Side of the Wind.*" Each request was a demand, with the implication that a denial would lead to Orson bowing out.

I am generally an optimistic person, but in honoring a maverick who thrived on unpredictability, one corner of my brain was contaminated with the prospect that this self-dramatizing genius might demonstrate his contrarian nature by not showing up. His personal finances were in disarray and he had been warned that a tax agent might use his appearance to deliver a subpoena. This seed of doubt was still with me two days before the dinner, when, after delivering two first-class TWA tickets to Orson in Paris, we sent a small welcoming committee to meet him. While they were waiting at Los Angeles airport Peter called. "George," he sighed, "Orson lost his tickets." He assured me Orson would fly the next day if we replaced the tickets, and sure enough he did. (I cultivated my ignorance as to whether AFI succeeded in recovering the first pair.)

Late that evening my phone rang at home and I heard Orson's resonant voice brimming with charm. He was looking forward to the "grand compliment" we were paying him the following night. He then asked for assurance that host Frank Sinatra would provide a proper setup to the scene from *The Other Side of the Wind,* the film Orson had been working on for several years in which John Huston plays a director seeking money to finish a film. It occurred to me that I was speaking with a director seeking money to finish his film, who was looking forward to displaying his wares to a captive audience that included film financiers. I said we would welcome his suggestions, reminding him "respectfully" that Frank would be reading from cue cards and had a short attention span.

Orson sent over a text that ran four minutes for a spot where thirty seconds would be normal. We trimmed it to fit our time structure and what was manageable for Frank. At the dress rehearsal on Sunday, Chuck Heston was sitting with me at the producer's table preparing to run his opening welcome when Sinatra arrived. Sammy Cahn had written special lyrics for a Rodgers and Hart standard, retitled *The Gentleman is a Champ,* for Frank. There was concern that Nelson Riddle's orchestra was positioned too far from the podium where Frank would be singing. Nobody wanted to give him the news so I went over and said hello. "Ah, young 'Jaw-dge,'" was Frank's greeting. "I'm afraid the only spot for Nelson's orchestra is over there," I said, pointing. "I hope that will be all right for you." Sinatra paced from the podium and leaned around the corner in the direction of the musicians. I awaited his verdict. "Don't worry, 'Jaw-dge.' I used to sing on fuckin' second base at Ebbets Field with the orchestra in the bleachers."

A stage manager interrupted saying I had a call from Mr. Welles. Chuck Heston was watching as I picked up the phone at the producer's table in the center of the ballroom. Orson started slowly. "My spies tell me that my script has been truncated." I explained, "We worked to keep the essence, but time would not allow its entirety." Orson took it up a notch, causing my fear of a rebellious no-show to creep back into my head. "You are honoring me, I believe, for my work. At the heart of my work is my writing and you have elected not to use what I have written, preferring it seems, the work of your TV writers."

Heston, showing concern, leaned in closer. Posed, it seemed, between Moses and Macbeth, I searched for the proper words. At that moment the room went dark. Lights, cameras, phones—everything crashed, bringing to mind a thunderous Wellesian climax in *Chimes at Midnight.* I was left standing in the darkness with a dead phone, thinking, "Now we're cooked." When the lights came on we had a hurried conversation about Orson's intentions and our next move. The blinking light on the phone signaled an incoming call. It was Peter, speaking in a tone of weary disappointment. "George, why did you hang up on Orson?"

It seems the power outage had led me inadvertently to call Orson's bluff. Peter told me solemnly that I must make amends to Orson that evening. The great man *was* coming!

I greeted Orson that night. He was magnificent in a tuxedo with a flowing black cravat for a tie, a neatly trimmed gray beard, a beaming smile, booming voice and boisterous laugh. He had come to town to let the world know that he was not a reclusive director on the edge of retirement. I showed him the stage bedecked with towering black-and-white portraits of his signature roles— Charles Foster Kane looking from stage left across to Harry Lime, Othello and Macbeth. He beamed his approval.

Stars entering the ballroom with high expectation ranged from veterans Rosalind Russell, Ingrid Bergman and Joseph Cotten to new faces like Jack Nicholson, Faye Dunaway and Ryan O'Neal. Directors turned out in force, among them William Wyler, Frank Capra and my father. One of the photographs to keep from that night was of Orson and my father, two formidable men sharing a fraternal moment, Orson perhaps reminding George that his mentor had been George's uncle Ashton.

I know my father was proud of my work. But only later, once I understood what it was to have children spreading their wings, did I contemplate the pressures he must have felt as he watched me bringing the American Film Institute to life with its alternating controversies and successes. During the afternoon rehearsal I spotted him in a doorway to the ballroom. He had come to discreetly appraise the situation. I went over and we hugged. Knowing how much we cared for one another, words were unnecessary.

When the overflow crowd found their tables the announcer's voice signaled the entrance of the guest of honor: "Tonight the American Film Institute honors a director . . . an actor . . . a writer . . . a producer . . . and here they are . . .

Lions. George Stevens, Sr., and Orson Welles at 1975 AFI Life Achievement
Award Dinner. February 9, 1975.

Orson Welles!" The orchestra played the theme from *The Third Man,* the center
doors opened, and Orson strode in with alert eyes and stopped—a massive figure in the spotlight, drawing applause and cheers. He surveyed the crowd, eyes
widening as he recognized friends, raising his hand and smiling as the ovation
crested. He glided nimbly for such a large man to the head table.

Sinatra teased Orson about his portentous introduction, saying, "He came
to my house for dinner one night and we had to do the same thing to get
him from the den into the dining room. Luckily, Nelson Riddle and the guys
were in the neighborhood." Orson looked on in delight, cigar in hand, clench-
ing it in his teeth in order to applaud. Sinatra introduced a selection of Welles'
films: *Citizen Kane,* where in the stunning scene with Ruth Warrick the course
of an entire marriage is revealed in three minutes of screen time, glimpses
from *Touch of Evil* with Marlene Dietrich, Rita Hayworth among the mirrors
in *The Lady from Shanghai,* the battle scene from *Chimes at Midnight,* and the
classic portrait of a midwestern town in *The Magnificent Ambersons.* This was

followed by *The Other Side of the Wind*, which was warmly, if not enthusiastically, received.

In presenting the award to Orson Welles I spoke of how he had advanced the art of film like few others, noting that too often a film was measured by its bank account. I quoted John Ruskin's observation that many of the most enduring works in art and literature are never paid for. "How much do you think Homer got for his Iliad? Or Dante for his Paradise? Only bitter bread and salt and walking up and down other people's stairs."

"So tonight," I said, "we measure Orson Welles by his courage and by the intensity of his vision. Let us call him forth with the purest definition of a great man. 'A great man never reminds us of others.'"

Orson got to his feet. Because of his demand that there be no steps on his path, he had to circle the expansive seating area, like a locomotive, steaming past the cheering crowd. As he arrived at the stage Sinatra met him, taking his arm and guiding him toward the podium, where Orson arrived just a touch out of breath.

"My father once told me that the art of receiving a compliment is of all things the sign of a civilized man," he began. "And he died soon afterwards leaving my education in this important matter sadly incomplete. I'm only glad that on this, the occasion of the rarest compliment he ever could have dreamed of, that he isn't here to see his son so publicly at a loss."

"This is Samuel Johnson," he continued, "on what he calls contrarieties: 'There are goals so opposed that we cannot seize both, and in trying fail to seize either. Of the blessings set before you, make your choice. No man can at the same time fill his cup from the source and from the mouth of the Nile.'"

Orson then explained how this choice of contrarieties had led him to stray so far "from this home town of ours."

> Not that I am alone in this or unique. I am never that. But there are just a few left in this conglomerated world of ours who still trudge stubbornly along the lonely, rocky road. And this is, in fact, our contrariety. What we come up with has no right to call itself better. It's just different. If there is any excuse for us at all, it's that we're simply following the old American tradition of the Maverick—and we are a vanishing breed.

He surveyed the audience and said, "This honor I can only accept in the name of all the Mavericks." After applause, he added, drawing laughter, "And also as a tribute to the generosity of all the rest of you—to the givers—the ones with fixed addresses."

Orson elaborated on his maverick nature. "A maverick may go his own way but he doesn't think it's the only way—it's just that some of the necessities to which I am a slave are different from yours. As a director, for instance, I pay myself out of my acting jobs. I use my own work to subsidize my work. In other words I'm crazy."

He enjoyed the roar of laughter before continuing, "The truth is I don't believe this great evening would ever have brightened my life if it weren't for this—my own particular contrariety." Applause again filled the room leading him to propose a toast:

> Let us raise our cups then, standing as some of us do, on opposite ends
> of the river, and drink together to what really matters to us all—to our
> crazy and beloved profession. To the movies—to *good* movies—to
> every possible kind.

Orson had knocked it out of the park. And his toast to the movies echoed the spirit of the American Film Institute.

There was a lively after-party upstairs following the dinner. Orson and Sinatra got on an elevator together, and as the doors were about to close a man in a tuxedo reached inside and slapped a subpoena on Orson's chest. As the doors closed, Orson, in all his majesty, calmly stuffed the paper in his pocket and resumed his conversation with Frank.

A great man never reminds us of others.

50

A Giant Oak

George Stevens has died—from politeness, I should imagine: thoughtfulness about others, generosity, and all of the other decencies than any man may be permitted to believe he can acquire, and a few men have no way of thrusting out of themselves."

That was William Saroyan, responding to the March 8, 1975, wire service report.

My mother-in-law Lily Guest came to our house in Georgetown early Sunday morning with the news. Liz and I had enjoyed a late night at what was then the trendy, pre–hostage crisis Iranian Embassy and our phone was turned off. It was just four weeks since the Welles dinner. The photograph of my father with Orson was the last in a life of picture making.

We'd had a scare four years earlier. Dad and Joan were visiting King Vidor and actress Colleen Moore at their ranch in the central California hill country. Dad called me in Washington to tell me he was having emergency heart surgery. He expected to be fine but asked if I would watch after Joan if something went wrong. I assured him I would.

Liz and I had a bleak cross-country flight to the Paso Robles Hospital where he was being cared for by a fine surgeon, James R. Spencer, who told us he expected my father to recover but that he "wasn't out of the woods." When Dr. Spencer left I stayed at my father's bedside, machines above him squiggling their graphic indicators. Although asleep, he began to speak his first words since my arrival. "Keep your cover . . . Jerries on that bluff." Then words came slowly, dreamlike, not every word distinct—names of his wartime comrades. "Mellor . . . Morse . . . Moffat." Then "Malmedy . . . Krauts . . . Panzers." He was back in the snow of the Ardennes Forest at the Battle of the Bulge. Dad's reverie of combat thirty years past was stirring but unsettling.

Michael Murrow Stevens and David Averell Stevens with
their grandfather, 1971.

The next morning he was alert and the Stevens humor was back. He smiled through his tubes and told me that when he and Joan arrived at the hospital she had apparently asked for a priest. When the priest turned up she was nowhere to be found, so the obliging fellow found my father's room. Dad, half-conscious and fighting for his life, sees the priest walk in. "I figured that was it," he said. "I'd seen too many of those damn Leo McCarey movies."

My father recovered and had four good years enjoying his life with Joan, considering film projects, doing seminars with the fellows at AFI, remaining a sage at the Directors Guild, and savoring occasional visits with his grandsons. One day we were having breakfast in the Polo Lounge and Dad asked how

Michael, then eight, was doing. "He's not doing great in school," I replied. "The only thing he wants to read is the *Washington Post* sports page." I can still feel my father's pause, the little smile, and then, "He's interested in *something*. It will lead to other things." Although he knew his grandchildren for just a few years, they held him in their hearts throughout their lives, coming to know him better through his films.

It was a fatal heart attack that took him on a weekend visit with Joan to Palmdale outside of Los Angeles. It was unexpected and we had given no thought to a funeral for the man who in *Shane* and *Giant* created two of cinema's most memorable burial scenes. Nor did he indicate any preferences. There were just three days to put together a fitting service for the father I adored.

A story from Ivan Moffat came to mind. When the brilliantly observant *New Yorker* writer Lillian Ross came to Hollywood she was wined and dined, and told Ivan she would like to have dinner with my father. To Ivan's dismay Dad invited Fred Guiol, his outdoorsman pal from the Roach days, a Colonel Ross, his transportation officer in the war, and Charlie Peckham, his chum who sold fishing gear at Kerr's Sporting Goods. Ivan told Dad he thought it was ridiculous, that Lillian had nothing in common with those men. "The conversation was hesitant and stiff as dinner began," Ivan recalled, "but by the time it was over Lillian had a marvelous time, and she concluded that George was a man's man, a man of the people, which was exactly what he had in mind."

Liz went with me to Forest Lawn. We selected the lovely Old North Chapel and a hillside gravesite not far from his mother and father overlooking the San Fernando Valley. The lugubrious Forest Lawn salesman was pushing elaborate coffins, but we found the closest they had to a plain pine box, not too dissimilar from Stonewall Torrey's, to be draped with the American flag. In a coincidence of timing the twenty-fifth-year reunion of the Special Coverage Unit was scheduled that week and the Stevens Irregulars had arrived from across the country. They came in force to Forest Lawn to bid farewell to their Colonel.

His director friends King Vidor, Rouben Mamoulian, William Wyler, Henry King, Stanley Kramer, Robert Wise and Robert Aldrich were pallbearers. Vidor read "When the Earth's Last Picture is Painted" by Rudyard Kipling, whose poem "Gunga Din" inspired Dad's high-spirited film. The Reverend Dean S. Collins spoke of "George Stevens' deep awareness of beauty and awe which left a mark in his pictures, and showed an integrity that he would not compromise."

The bereaved, who overflowed the four-hundred-seat chapel, moved to chairs in a clearing among the trees on a green hillside for the burial. An army bugler sounded taps and military aides folded the American flag and presented it to

Michael Stevens, nine years old in his blue blazer and tie. My friend from Robert Kennedy's presidential campaign, John Stewart, once of the Kingston Trio, was a tall, boot-wearing songwriter/guitarist with a touch of the poet. John concluded the service with an extraordinarily simple and stirring rendition of *America the Beautiful*. As we started down the hill Willy Wyler caught up with me. "That's the way George would have staged and shot it," he whispered hoarsely.

As days of mourning went on I kept near me a quotation from Aristotle that President Kennedy was fond of. "Everything dies, but the reverberation of his works in the lives of others gives his life great amplitude."

51

1976

AFI had long contemplated launching a national magazine, an intellectually sound and stylish publication that covered cinema in its broadest dimension. I asked Hollis Alpert, a witty and venturous New Yorker, the respected film critic of the *Saturday Review of Literature,* to be our editor.

The first issue of *American Film,* published in October of 1975, featured a color cover with Dustin Hoffman and Robert Redford in *All the President's Men,* and articles by Sam Fuller, Larry McMurtry and Arthur Schlesinger, Jr. The November cover featured a striking Erich von Stroheim in costume for his "mangled masterpiece" *The Wedding March.* Together these two issues reflected the range of the magazine. The base of our circulation was the AFI membership of forty thousand, but soon *American Film* was reaching a quarter of a million readers. Hollis enlisted writers ranging from Molly Haskell to Stephen King and put together a lively and well-informed publication. We wanted *American Film* to further our educational mandate and be a foundation for a national constituency.

The 1976 election looked like a good opportunity for a Democrat, with Gerald Ford vulnerable after his controversial pardon of Nixon. Liz and I were friends with several of the prospects but we hadn't committed to anyone. She agreed to host a dinner to meet Georgia governor Jimmy Carter, the peanut farmer and former submarine captain who had announced a long-shot campaign for the nomination. Governor Carter arrived at our house by himself, a reflection of his low-key manner that saw him toting his own suit bag onto airplanes. Liz, deciding that one table of twelve would give everyone a chance to listen and ask questions, invited Frank Mankiewicz, Joe Duffy and Ann Wexler, he a professor, she a political operative and lobbyist, and Richard Holbrooke. Dick made an impression on the candidate, who was then polling at 4 percent among Democrats. Carter was soft-spoken and encouraged others to speak. He had a keen intellect and was prepared on every topic.

Toward the end of the discussion Liz asked the southern governor with some intensity about civil rights and, in passing, mentioned Robert Kennedy. Carter said he was aware of the strong feelings in the room for Kennedy, leading to an uneasy silence that foreshadowed a tension Carter would face as a Washington outsider. We were impressed with him and his strategy for the primaries. I flew to California the next morning and Liz was out when Carter called to thank us. Ten-year-old Michael Stevens answered the phone and reported to us that he had a nice conversation with Governor Carter. That sealed it.

Liz went to work full time for the campaign, concentrating on enlisting support among members of Congress. Carter's team had figured out how post-McGovern changes in the Democratic nominating system could work in their candidate's favor, so he entered every primary and caucus. I was at a party at Averell Harriman's the night of the New Hampshire primary when Carter startled the nation with an upset victory over seven contenders, causing dismay in the faces of leading Democrats. Carter won the nomination and party leaders scrambled to be at his side. With Walter Mondale as his vice president he defeated the Gerald Ford–Bob Dole ticket.

I was at Greystone in April of 1976 when I received a call from Fred Roos, who was in the Philippines working with Francis Coppola on his Vietnam war saga *Apocalypse Now*. Francis and I knew one another from when he served on the AFI board. Fred surprised me by saying that Francis wanted me to play a role in his film. My only previous screen appearance had been the one with Spanky McFarland in an *Our Gang* comedy when I was a toddler. Fred explained that the actor who was supposed to play a brief but pivotal role couldn't get the necessary shots to travel to the Philippines, and Francis was convinced from our time together at AFI that I could handle the part. I told Fred how busy I was but he persisted. "Francis wants me to send you the scene so you can read it and make a decision." Then came his closer. "It's a scene that can't be cut from the picture."

The script arrived the next day. The scene *was* pivotal. The character orders the lead character, a young Captain Willard, to go north, find Colonel Kurtz, played by Marlon Brando, and "terminate him with extreme prejudice." I went to the full-length mirror and tested that termination line a few times, warming up to the idea of flying to Manila to work with Francis. He sent word that I should bring one of the light tan suits from Carroll and Company that I wore on occasion at AFI meetings, to give the aura of a high-ranking civilian in government service—read CIA.

I landed at Manila Airport and was ferried by helicopter directly to the set. We fine-tuned my wardrobe and makeup and hair people did their thing. Francis invited me to dinner at his sprawling house. The Doors' "Come on baby, light my fire" shook the walls. The brilliant cinematographer Vittorio Storaro, who Francis brought from Italy with his camera retinue of relatives, cooked fabulous pasta. There was a fine Montepulciano and the scent of other substances. Francis was behind schedule and over budget, leading to a conversation about other ambitious epics like *The Bridge on the River Kwai* and *Giant.* "Does every director wake up at four in the morning with nausea on these pictures?" he asked.

I found myself working with some first-rate actors, including Harvey Keitel, who played Captain Willard. I assumed Francis would break up our scene into different shots so he could work around my lack of acting experience, but he had become fascinated with the long continuous camera moves favored by Storaro. I struggled a bit, but when the moment came for me to instruct the young captain to find Colonel Kurtz and terminate him, it seemed to hit home. Francis wrangled a bit with Keitel but after two days the scene was complete. He was generous with praise and warm in his thanks for me flying to Manila.

I was proud to be part of Francis' ambitious epic and back in Los Angeles received an enthusiastic letter from Fred Roos. "We have now seen the dailies," he said, "and I can honestly report that you were terrific. We think it will be a very good and unusual scene." Ten days later I picked up *Variety* and saw a front-page story: "COPPOLA LOSES HIS BEARD, 38 POUNDS, AND STAR KEITEL." No, it never occurred to me that the tensions I saw on the set would result in the leading man being fired and replaced by Martin Sheen (or that Francis would shave, and wean himself off Storaro family pasta). Francis reshot the scene with Sheen, changing my role to an army colonel and using another actor.

It was an invigorating adventure and I don't for a minute regret having gone to Manila. Three years later at the Ziegfeld Theater in New York I went with my son Michael to see *Apocalypse Now* and felt a slight pang of envy watching veteran actor G. D. Spradlin (supported by a junior officer played by a young Harrison Ford) instruct Martin Sheen how to deal with Colonel Kurtz—in a film that would stand the test of time without me.

The year 1976 brought an enhancing change in the life of the Stevens family. On a Saturday morning Liz and I walked to Q Street with David, now eight, on his bicycle, and up a driveway to a gate by a tennis court. There stood Cuthbert Train, an agreeable gentleman in his seventies from an accomplished Washington family, wearing khakis and tennis shoes. His 1805 farmhouse stood above the court, with its large southern porch looking south toward the Potomac. Mr. Train had to give up tennis and his house was for sale. I longed for a tennis court, which were few and far between in Georgetown.

Mr. Train invited us to inspect the house by ourselves—three drawing rooms, a dining room and kitchen on the main floor, and four bedrooms and a small office above. As we walked out on the porch to rejoin Mr. Train, I said to Liz, "I think this is the one." She nodded. I decided not to kick the tires. "Mr. Train," I said, "we'd really like to have this house." He smiled, then Liz mentioned that she loved the mantelpiece in the living room. "That's my father's mantel," he replied. "I'm so glad you like it." He volunteered that the head of the Securities and Exchange Commission, a lawyer from California, had been to see the house eight times and didn't like the mantel. I took care not to betray my California roots and said we would be in touch.

I called my business manager in California who happened to be in his office on Saturday. He said it was a bit of a stretch but he thought we could make it work, even considering my relatively modest AFI salary. He suggested we make an opening offer. That evening Liz and I dropped our proposal off for the broker on Wisconsin Avenue on the way to a party for Fritz and Joan Mondale. I remember sitting on a sofa talking politics with my friend John Chancellor of NBC when Liz came over smiling.

"It's ours," she said. "They accepted the offer."

Apparently Mr. Train wanted the beautiful girl who liked his father's mantel to have the house. Liz soon applied her taste and decorative skills, giving us French doors, comfortable rooms, a glorious garden and a swimming pool—and the Stevens family had a delightful house that would be a foundation for an active life in Washington, a home that would last a lifetime.

52

The Stars Salute

The year 1977 signaled the tenth anniversary of the American Film Institute, and once again a Democrat was in the White House. I had devoted a decade to AFI, much longer than intended, and was feeling the world passing me by. I was determined to solidify the organization so I could give up its directorship and move on to projects of my own.

The anniversary was an opportunity to advance that goal. Liz and I had attended the Kennedy Center's first fundraising gala in the Opera House. Remembering the excitement that could be generated in that grand hall, I thought it would be an ideal setting for an AFI celebration. Jerry Rafshoon, one of Jimmy Carter's inner circle of Georgians, who had once worked for 20th Century Fox, became a friend during the campaign, so I explored with him the possibility of a White House reception celebrating AFI's anniversary. The closest the motion picture community had come to a White House event was the luncheon that was canceled in the wake of the JFK assassination.

Ambitious ideas invariably have a chicken and egg factor where several elements are required and each depends upon the other. We needed a White House commitment, a deal for a network television special, and a mutually acceptable date in the Kennedy Center Opera House. Rafshoon succeeded in getting the Carters to agree to a black-tie White House reception on November 17, CBS accepted my proposal for a two-hour special, *The Stars Salute America's Greatest Films,* and the ever-reliable Roger Stevens made the Opera House available.

We put in motion an *American Film* poll of AFI's quarter million members to select America's greatest films, and a fund-raising committee went to work selling the two thousand seats in the Opera House. AFI members surprised us by voting for nine hundred different films, with a second ballot narrowing it down to the top fifty—a palette for a gala show at the Kennedy Center. Larry McMurtry, author of *The Last Picture Show* who lived down the street from us above his antiquarian bookstore, agreed to write the show.

AFI's travel budget was limited, but we hoped that an invitation to the White House would be an incentive for the stars and writers and directors of the fifty top films to make their own way to Washington. A wave of acceptances and rumors of a big turnout of stars spurred ticket sales. Olivia de Havilland, having returned from a trip to America to her home in Paris, and finding her invitation, told a reporter, "I turned right around and flew back."

President and Mrs. Carter, standing in a receiving line between portraits of George and Martha Washington, cheerfully greeted four hundred guests, ranging from eighty-four-year-old Lillian Gish, who made her first movie in 1912, to Steven Spielberg and George Lucas, age thirty and thirty-three, whose *Jaws* and *Star Wars* were shaking up Hollywood. When Carter came to the microphone in the East Room he was facing a group that included Jimmy Stewart, Henry Fonda, Lauren Bacall, Sidney Poitier, Rosalind Russell, Tennessee Williams, George Cukor, Gordon Parks and Andy Warhol.

"I am honored to welcome a group of people who have contributed so much to our nation," Carter said, "what it is, what it stands for and the image of it around the world." He was proud, he said, to meet these famous people. "I've had a chance to put my arms around Olivia de Havilland and Lillian Gish and many others whom I have loved from a great distance." Carter grinned as he told the guests that in the South, "We date life either before *Gone With the Wind* and after *Gone With the Wind*," saying one of his favorite scenes "was the burning of Schenectady." (Carter blunted the joke a bit by adding "New York." My pal, playwright Peter Stone, who wrote it, complained, "Writing jokes for politicians is better when they're Irish.")

Carter concluded with a nod to the American Film Institute for taking "14,000 films that are in the Library of Congress and restoring them and preserving them for the future."

I watched the video of the 1977 CBS broadcast of *The Stars Salute America's Greatest Films* for the first time in forty years and was pleasantly surprised by the emotional quality of the evening, and touched to see in full flower artists who became lifelong friends and colleagues. The Carters and the Vice President and Joan Mondale were in the Presidential Box and entertainment figures were seated amid senators, members of Congress and cabinet officers. "It was Hollywood West meeting Hollywood East last night on the grandest stage of all," said the *Washington Post*. "As turnouts go, even in Hollywood East, it was something more than spectacular."

The only star who didn't have to fly in for the occasion was my new neighbor Elizabeth Taylor, who had moved to a house a block away from ours in Georgetown after marrying Senator John Warner. Elizabeth entered in a violet gown and presented Gene Kelly joyously dancing in the rain, which caused Elia Kazan, a director known for gritty drama, to tell the *New York Times*, "That *Singin' in the Rain* number hit me so hard I was bawling." When time came for the greatest film, Olivia de Havilland, its only surviving star, entered in a flowing white gown to represent *Gone with the Wind*. Olivia reminded the audience that Scarlett said, "The South will rise again." Then gesturing to the Presidential Box, added, "And it has."

The White House reception and the Kennedy Center gala provided public validation for AFI, as did the two-hour telecast on CBS. The nation's leaders and top figures in motion pictures saw moviemaking at its best and learned how this new institution was preserving America's film heritage.

53

Honors

Leonard Bernstein had ideas about creativity and the circuitry of the human brain. "Every once in a while there is a short circuit when those strands cross and electrify each other, and set off something called an idea," he used to say. "Something new is born. This is the most exciting moment that can happen in an artist's life."

I was standing on the Opera House stage during rehearsal for the AFI gala looking at white cards in the rows of seats, each bearing the name of the VIP soon to be sitting there. As I glanced up to the box tier I saw the card that read "President Jimmy Carter," and one of those short circuits occurred.

On the morning after the show I said to Roger Stevens, "Last night was a great success for AFI, but the Kennedy Center should have its own show."

"Got any '*eye-dees*'?" was his reply.

I reminded him of the John F. Kennedy quote engraved on the center's marble façade: "I look forward to an America which will not be afraid of grace and beauty . . . an America which will reward achievement in the arts as we reward achievement in business or statecraft."

"The Kennedy Center," I said, "should have an annual celebration to honor artists for lifetime achievement with the president attending."

Roger Stevens had a quality that set him apart from many other powerful men—he didn't tinker or second-guess. He was a real estate investor and Broadway producer who made decisions and rolled the dice. "I like it. You should go to work on it."

Once again, we needed the participation of the president and a television broadcast. A White House reception and the commander in chief in the President's Box would attract artists, the telecast would provide visibility, and a network license fee would pay for a crowd-pleasing show to which the center could sell tickets. We had a leg up because the Carters so enjoyed the AFI event. We knew the commercial networks had an aversion to opera, ballet and classical music but we met with CBS and proposed a show called "America Salutes the Performing Arts," convincing them that we could enlist stars and produce an entertaining special. The network understood that the event could provide unique access to the White House and Congress.

The Carters signed on and soon after CBS confirmed their interest, insisting on a first negotiation/first refusal contract that would assure them continuing rights to the show if it proved successful.

Roger suggested I seek the advice of Isaac Stern. I remember walking into the virtuoso violinist's apartment on New York's West Side. He greeted me with an engaging openness, his reading glasses perched on top of his head. He was enthusiastic about the idea and his wisdom and easy irreverence would lift me going forward. We wanted to differentiate our program from the awards shows that dotted the television landscape and agreed that the title submitted to CBS fell short, so I tried out a new one on Isaac—"The Kennedy Center Honors."

Isaac reacted quickly. "It has grace."

Roger and I had agreed on criteria for selecting honorees that was approved by the Kennedy Center trustees: "To provide recognition to individuals who throughout their lifetimes have made significant contributions to American culture through the performing arts. Achievement in dance, music, theater, opera, motion pictures and television will be considered. The primary criterion is excellence."

Isaac and I reviewed a list of accomplished artists in the various disciplines, testing combinations of five, eventually coming up with a slate we recommended to Roger and his board: African American contralto Marian Anderson, ballet's foremost choreographer George Balanchine, the composer of forty-three Broadway musicals Richard Rodgers, Polish-born classical pianist Arthur Rubinstein, and the movies' premier dancer Fred Astaire. Isaac likened the process to seating an elegant dinner table.

There was the lingering question of what the Kennedy Center could present to our honorees that would be distinctive. I met with an innovative young designer, Ivan Chermayeff, and asked for something elegant that would be recognized on television. Ivan produced seven brightly hued ribbons held together by three brass clasps, on which were engraved "The Kennedy Center Honors," the name of the honoree and the date. He called it a "laurel," to be clasped over the shoulders and rest on the honoree's chest.

I realized this ambitious show called for a two-person effort, so I enlisted Nick Vanoff, producer of *The Hollywood Palace,* who had started out as a classical dancer in Martha Graham's company and had an avid appreciation for the arts. Our first step was to create an Artists Committee, which became the foundation of the Honors. We sent telegrams to a hundred performing artists, describing the new recognition and the names of the first recipients, inviting them to attend the gala at the Kennedy Center with an alert that a White House invitation was on its way. Responses poured in from Edward Albee to Vera Zorina, giving us knowledge of where America's most prominent performers would be on the weekend of December 3. If Beverly Sills had a concert in Vienna we knew she wasn't available. If Lucille Ball was in Palm Springs, she might be. And there were surprises: "Miss Aretha Franklin's attendance may depend on whether seven family members can join her." This was just the first of Aretha's extravagant requests through the years, but each time she appeared she provided full value. Artists on the "attending" list were a pool of talent that, as Nick put it, we could press into service. Or, as our shorthand developed, "Aretha's in the elevator."

We produced five-minute biographical films that became a unique and defining element of the Honors. Filmed in 35mm and projected on a mammoth screen in the darkened Opera House, they revealed each honoree's creative journey, marked by obstacles and triumph, accented by luminous artistry. Audiences were moved and enlightened, ready for the spoken tributes and performances that followed. Charles Guggenheim came on board to direct the first Honors films, and Sara Lukinson's writing elevated them.

I had hoped that Walter Cronkite, who held the sobriquet "the most trusted man in America," would be our host, but CBS News, drawing a sharp line between news and entertainment, wouldn't let him appear. We turned instead to the most gifted and charismatic of classical musicians, Leonard Bernstein, who became a spirited collaborator.

The night before the Sunday gala there was a dinner at the Kennedy Center. We turned to Liz Stevens to organize an intimate gathering of the Artists Committee and Kennedy Center trustees where the laurels were bestowed on each recipient followed by witty and touching toasts from colleagues. The honorees were not asked to speak or perform during the weekend—no singing for their supper. In succeeding years the dinner was hosted by the secretary of state in the State Department's historic Benjamin Franklin Room. Limited to two hundred guests and marked by Liz's refined good taste, the artists dinner became the most sought after invitation of Honors weekend.

The White House seemed especially majestic on Sunday night with the United States Marine Corps Band in their scarlet dress coats playing melodies associated with the five honorees. Scores of the nation's leading artists were in

Liz Stevens and Kennedy Center chairman Roger L. Stevens presenting the first Honors laurel to Arthur Rubinstein, who observed that it made him look like a "prize bull." December 2, 1978.

the East Room when the honorees were announced one by one wearing what the *New York Times* described as "their rather avant-garde medal with its garland of seven ribbons in brilliant hues." Each was escorted by a military aide to a small stage, after which "Hail to the Chief" sounded and President and Mrs. Carter were introduced.

The president spoke with modest authority in his gentle southern accent. "These five people, Americans, great, beloved, recognized—come here tonight to be honored through the auspices of the Kennedy Center. But as a matter of fact, they come here to honor us and all the people of the world."

Nick Vanoff and I watched, awestruck, as the Opera House began to fill with creative leaders. We saw Gian Carlo Menotti and Sara Caldwell from the world of opera; Lionel Hampton and Count Basie from jazz; Jerome Robbins, Alicia Alonso, Maria Tallchief and Twyla Tharp from dance; Alan Jay Lerner, Stephen Sondheim and Elia Kazan from Broadway; Lillian Gish, Ginger Rogers and Gregory Peck from movies. "One became convinced that footlights across the country must be dimmed—and Broadway dark," the *Times* reported the following day. "For the entire performing arts community appeared to have gathered for one momentous sentimental evening under one roof."

Whereas television productions commonly treated audience members like "dress extras" to serve the needs of the producers, we were determined to respect our audience by disguising cameras, keeping technicians out of sight, and avoiding stage waits. We didn't provide a program listing performers and succeeded in making each one a surprise when announced.

The first *Kennedy Center Honors* began with a bow to freedom of expression. Mstislav Rostropovich had recently fled the Soviet Union to become conductor of Washington's National Symphony. He strode to center stage as the Opera House orchestra was revealed. The honorees, standing side by side in the box next to the president, included Rubinstein, who was born in Poland, and Balanchine, born in Russia. The most recent Soviet émigré, proud of his heritage but mindful of his new artistic freedom, conducted America's national anthem.

"You can imagine how deeply touched I am to be standing here with the signal honor of introducing these festivities," said Leonard Bernstein, standing center stage wearing a black velvet tuxedo jacket. "This homage takes the form of what will henceforth be known as the Kennedy Center Honors, to be presented annually to individuals who throughout their lifetimes have made especially significant contributions to American culture through the performing arts." After applause he added, "I think you will agree that this first group of artists constitutes a glorious beginning to this new form of national tribute."

The first song performed in the Opera House was "A Simple Song," the hymn from Bernstein's *Mass,* at the Kennedy Center opening four years earlier. "Tonight," Bernstein said, "the hymn will be sung by Jon Rubinstein, son of Arthur, lending a heartwarming sense of continuity to this evening's proceedings." He had chosen Jon, who had won a Tony for *Pippin,* over several opera stars to sing the classical piece to surprise his ninety-three-year-old father. My mother-in-law Lily Guest, seated in the honorees box as the guest of her longtime friend Fred Astaire, sent me a note the next morning. "If you could have seen up close Marian Anderson singing the 'Star Spangled Banner,' then the expression on Rubinstein's face watching his son, you might have offered to put the whole show on again tonight."

Harry Belafonte presented what became the traditional spoken tribute to an honoree, describing Marian Anderson "as an artistic pioneer who truly overcame, and gave to the world a voice that Maestro Toscanini said 'is heard only once in a hundred years.'" The lights dimmed to black and a movie screen filled the proscenium as Belafonte narrated the first of our biographical films: "She was poor, she was black, and her dreams of becoming a concert singer seemed as bleak as the Philadelphia streets she grew up in." The audience heard Anderson's soaring voice and learned that after being refused at Constitution Hall because of the color of her skin, she was invited by Eleanor Roosevelt to sing on the steps of the Lincoln Memorial on Easter Sunday. Photographs of Miss Anderson and the crowd of seventy-five thousand filled the screen as we heard her soulful rendition of "My Country 'Tis of Thee, Sweet Land of Liberty." When the lights came up the audience—moved by her artistry and courage—rose as one and turned to give Marian Anderson a sustained ovation.

We hadn't anticipated such a reaction to the films. It was an ovation that would be accorded all future Kennedy Center honorees.

Aretha Franklin, her seven relatives seated in the third row, concluded Miss Anderson's tribute by singing her favorite, "He's Got the Whole World in His Hands," joined by the Howard University Choir.

Mary Martin, who created lead roles in *The Sound of Music* and *South Pacific,* assured Richard Rodgers that he was the one person she would never, ever wash out of her hair, and introduced a musical bouquet of Rodgers' songs featuring John Raitt, Tony Bennett and Florence Henderson.

Balanchine protégé Edward Villella described his mentor as having revolutionized classical ballet around the world, and introduced Suzanne Farrell and Peter Martins, Balanchine's stars from the New York City Ballet, who danced his virtuoso *Tchaikovsky Pas de Deux.*

"I do not think there is a single musician alive today," said Isaac Stern, "who in his inner ear does not carry the sound and the influence of Arthur Rubinstein." In the film biography, Rubinstein describes receiving his American naturalization papers in 1937, saying, "I am prouder of this document than all the decorations bestowed on me by foreign governments." Stern introduced a sublime Leclair violin duet with the young Itzhak Perlman: "If I dare say it . . . yes, I dare say it—a chocolate Leclair to Mr. Rubinstein."

Douglas Fairbanks, Jr., described his old friend Fred Astaire as "the magical embodiment of all that is best in the performing arts," and the film displayed his singular artistry, drawing cheers for his dazzling "Puttin' on the Ritz" solo from *Blue Skies.* The entire company of *A Chorus Line,* winner of nine Tonys and the Pulitzer Prize, entered onto a mirrored set in their shimmering top hats and gold spangled outfits. A chorus boy looked up to the box, calling out, "Mr. Astaire, do you have the faintest idea how hard it is to follow that act?" On the downbeat the dancers began "One . . . Singular Sensation." Fred watched the showstopping number for the first time with unassuming delight—as an homage to himself.

"I think it is the best thing that has happened in the arts in this country," Alan J. Lerner, Tony and Oscar winner for *My Fair Lady,* told the *Times.* "You can be knighted in England and they have the Légion d'honneur in France, but this is the first time we have had national recognition for excellence in the arts in this country."

Mary Martin sent a handwritten note in red ink about the telecast. "I arrived in *cold* Palm Springs just in time to see it. Everyone was filled with admiration. Janet Gaynor [the winner of the first Oscar for Best Actress] called to say it had more entertainment in *good* taste than anything she has seen! It was truly an Enchanted Evening!"

CBS faithfully presented classical ballet, grand opera and a violin duet to their prime time audience on Tuesday night. The *Washington Post* dedicated its lead editorial to the Honors, stating that there was a rare coherence to the event. "It occurred to no one to ask: Is this high art or popular art? It was and is art, the best we have, pure and simple, and magnificent."

For Nick and me and our collaborators it was, indeed, an enchanted evening. For Liz and me it was the beginning of a long and happy tradition. We had no way of knowing that eleven of the artists who appeared on the stage that night would themselves receive a Kennedy Center Honor, or that out front in that distinguished audience were twenty-one others who would one day sit in the box as honorees.

Lenny Bernstein was right—something new being born can be one of life's most exciting moments.

54

I Love Tiananmen Square

Buoyed by the success of the first Kennedy Center Honors, Liz and I flew with our Caroline, Michael and David to Barbados for Christmas where I had a New Year's Day 1979 call from Jerry Rafshoon at the White House. Jerry confided that President Carter had decided to normalize diplomatic relations with Communist China. He said that Vice Premier Deng Xiaoping would be the highest ranking official to visit the United States since Madame Chiang Kaishek in 1943. Jerry explained that rather than having the customary entertainment for two hundred guests at the White House after the state dinner, Carter, inspired by the Kennedy Center Honors, wanted to entertain the vice premier in the Opera House.

"The president would like it to be televised and hopes you will produce it," he said. As we talked I became excited about the concept, even suggesting that we try for a satellite broadcast to China. I asked Jerry about timing, expecting a date sometime in the spring. "January 29," was the reply. I looked out at the shimmering blue Caribbean waters, calculating that was just four weeks away. Jerry then added, "And we have to find the money for the production." As we used to say in JFK times, "Ask not!"

The task was to celebrate the embrace of two major powers that hadn't spoken to each other for three decades. What would the show be? Who would broadcast it? Who would pay for it? Roger Stevens solved one problem by providing us a forty-eight-hour window in the Opera House during the transition between two Broadway shows. CBS, NBC and ABC had immovable commitments on their prime time schedules on January 29 so we turned to PBS. They agreed to present the show but could not fund it, so we had to find $500,000.

Jack Masey, head of design at USIA, was about to retire, and in need of a coconspirator I enlisted him as a creative consultant. We sketched out a plan for the show, and after many rejections submitted a sponsorship proposal to ARCO, the Atlantic Richfield Corporation.

We had set a drop dead date of January 19, ten days before the state dinner, to conclude negotiations with an underwriter, based on deadlines with contractors and production crew. That morning ARCO's vice president called to say that they could not underwrite the show. Masey and I sat in my office trying to come up with another idea before pulling the plug. After lunch Jack confronted me. "You have to call Robert O. Anderson." Anderson was the founder-chairman of Atlantic Richfield. I reminded Jack that it was bad form to go over the head of the person you're dealing with, and that CEOs avoided such calls.

"This is a one-time opportunity. You have to stand up!"

I dialed the ARCO number in Los Angeles and asked for Robert O. Anderson. I told his secretary I was calling about the Kennedy Center program for Deng Xiaoping. She said she would give Mr. Anderson my message. At 5:30 my assistant came in—just like in the movies—and said, "Mr. Anderson from Atlantic Richfield is calling." Masey jumped to his feet. I picked up the phone and Anderson was on the line. "Mr. Stevens, we've had a change of thinking here at ARCO about your Kennedy Center program for the Chinese premier. We will underwrite it." Our line producer Jack Seifert began confirming performers and deals with equipment suppliers. Seifert got rid of his Mobil credit card and switched to ARCO.

We had been inquiring about Deng Xiaoping's interests, hoping to spark an idea for a performance that he would enjoy. "Deng likes bridge and basketball" was the recurrent reply. We decided to have a choir of fifty Washington children learn a song in Mandarin and selected the popular "I Love Tiananmen Square." Four days before the show I received an urgent instruction from the White House National Security Council that it would be inappropriate to sing "I Love Tiananmen Square." I was told that Deng Xiaoping had been humiliated in Tiananmen Square when he was purged by the Red Guards and would be offended. I went to see Jerry Schecter, press spokesman for NSC head Zbigniew Brzezinski, and explained that fifty Washington schoolchildren had been working for two weeks mastering the lyrics in Mandarin and we were depending on this for our closing number. He was unyielding. The China experts feared Deng would walk out of the performance.

I arranged to go to the Chinese Chancery with Masey to see Chai Zemin, the head of the Chinese mission in Washington. Speaking through an interpreter, I described the show and then asked if the minister knew the song "I love Tiananmen Square." Jack and I studied his face, but Chai replied in the affirmative without expression. We concluded, optimists that we were, that if the song

Vice Premier Deng Xiaoping and Jimmy Carter in the Presidential Box at the Kennedy Center
as the United States and China establish diplomatic relations. At left, Zhuo Lin, Deng's wife.
At right, Rosalynn Carter. January 29, 1979.

was a problem the diplomat would have said something. I let the White House
know we were going ahead with the children's song. The implication was that if
the song went away, I went away.

When the two leaders entered the Presidential Box in the Kennedy Center
Opera House satellites were beaming America's first live broadcast to China.
Deng, seventy-four, just five feet tall but confident in manner, and Jimmy Car-
ter, smiling with pride, were embracing the future.

The Broadway company of *Eubie,* featuring the music of ragtime pioneer
Eubie Blake, got the show off to a rousing start with a sizzling tap ensemble led
by Tony winner Gregory Hines and his brother Maurice. Architect I. M. Pei
spoke to the vice premier from the stage in Mandarin of his own excitement
about the historic changes taking place, and introduced piano virtuoso Rudolph
Serkin who played a sublime Schubert impromptu in F minor.

Senator John Glenn told of first seeing the Great Wall of China from the
window of *Friendship Seven* at an altitude of 165 miles. Then relying on our

limited knowledge of Deng's interests, he introduced the Harlem Globetrotters, which led the vice premier to stand and clap in time as they executed their famous "Sweet Georgia Brown" warm-up—dribbling, passing and lofting trick shots to an on stage backboard and basket.

After Shirley MacLaine presented the Joffrey Ballet performing Agnes DeMille's "Saturday Night Dance," from *Rodeo* to Aaron Copland's music, John Denver took the stage joined by the fifty schoolchildren who had mastered "I Love Tiananmen Square." The boys and girls were angelic and the Chinese guests appeared to be touched by their command of Mandarin. Jack Masey and I had our eyes on the close-up camera trained on Deng Xiaoping. We were more than relieved when he produced a bright smile.

President Carter then escorted the vice premier onto the crowded stage as the orchestra played "Getting to Know You" from Rodgers and Hammerstein's *The King and I*. Deng moved among the cast, leaning over to greet the children, kissing some on the head. Then, seeming to gaze at the sky, he shook the hands of the Harlem Globetrotters.

Jimmy Carter recorded in his diary that when he walked on stage with Deng and his wife Madame Zhou Lin, Rosalynn and Amy, there was a genuine sense of emotion. "The newspapers said that men in the audience wept." Ever alert to political implications, the president added, "Senator Laxalt [Republican from Nevada], who has been a strong opponent of normalization, said that we had them beat; there was no way to vote against little children singing Chinese songs."

55

A New Direction

The January 1979 broadcast of the Deng Xiaoping show meant that in fourteen months I had written and produced three two-hour television specials at the Kennedy Center, as well as the AFI Life Achievement award for Henry Fonda in Hollywood. The AFI tribute to Alfred Hitchcock was five weeks away. These productions were invigorating, and working on the stage with so many extraordinary artists on the Honors reminded me that I was drawn to a creative life. I was confident the American Film Institute was now on solid ground and the baton could be passed, so I opened discussions for recruitment of a new director and a year-end transition.

I was delighted AFI was honoring Hitchcock. He was a master storyteller, and on a personal level had trusted me when I was twenty-seven to direct *Alfred Hitchcock Presents.* I went to see Hitch for lunch at Universal in the same bungalow he occupied when I worked for him in the sixties. He was fastidiously dressed in a dark suit, white shirt and tie, his face pink and full, his staid demeanor punctuated with quick conspiratorial smiles. At seventy-nine he showed a boyish enthusiasm for the upcoming dinner, but the strain of passing years was evident when he rose from his chair and moved his portly frame across the room.

A special pleasure of Hitch's tribute was working with Ingrid Bergman, who starred for him in *Spellbound, Notorious* and *Under Capricorn,* and agreed to come from London to be our host. She arrived two days before the dinner and checked into the Beverly Wilshire Hotel. We had met only briefly when she appeared at the Orson Welles tribute, so I was pleased when she called and asked "if it would be too much trouble" for me to stop by and see her. She welcomed me into a small but stately junior suite where she had been unpacking, and a few items were scattered on the bed. Her blue eyes, for all her self-assurance, radiated great warmth. She listened attentively as I described the show. Then, smiling as though she was guarding some secret, she went to a dressing table and picked up something. "Don't you think this would be nice?" she said, before telling a story and revealing the object in her hand. She had come, as artists often did, with an idea we would never have thought of.

Ingrid took the stage on Thursday night at the Beverly Hilton and explained with a flirtatious air that she had come from London to give her director her love and affection, calling him "an adorable genius." Hitch was seated at the head table between his wife and "toughest critic," Alma Reville, and Cary Grant. When he accepted AFI's Silver Star, mocking stealth, he tried like a burglar to conceal it in his tuxedo jacket, before saying, "It would tax your endurance and mine to recite the names of those thousands of actors, writers, editors, cameramen, musicians, technicians . . . [then, ominously] *bankers and exhibitors,* and a variety of other criminals who have contributed to my life." He asked permission to mention by name only four people who had given him the most affection and encouragement and constant collaboration. "The first of the four is a film editor, the second is a script writer, the third is the mother of my daughter Pat, and the fourth is as fine a cook as ever performed miracles in a domestic kitchen. And their names are Alma Reville." Alma, seated on his right, seemed both surprised and touched.

"Had the beautiful Miss Reville not accepted a lifetime contract—without options—as Mrs. Alfred Hitchcock some fifty-three years ago, Mr. Alfred Hitchcock might be in this room tonight . . . not at this table, but as one of the slower waiters on the floor. I share my award, as I have my life, with her."

Ingrid returned to the stage and asked her director if he recalled the magisterial shot in the famous party scene in *Notorious,* when his camera tracked from the ceiling to a close-up of her hand holding the silver key.

"Well, you know what? Cary stole that key after the scene. Yes, and he kept it for about ten years, and one day he put it in my hand and he said, "I've kept this long enough. Now it's for you, for good luck." I've kept it for twenty years and it has given me a lot of good luck. And now I'm going to give it to you, with a prayer that it will open some very good doors for you too." She then walked down the steps from the stage to Hitch's table. She stood between him and Cary, both seated—the three together for the last time—and placed the key in Hitch's hand. She leaned over and kissed him, and as they parted she placed her hands on his cheeks, bringing forth a cherubic smile.

Just three weeks later an event in Washington reflected the variation in Liz's and my bicoastal lives. We were invited to the ceremony on the North Lawn of the

Alfred Hitchcock conceals his trophy. Alma Reville, seated. Stevens, Jr., and
Cary Grant standing. March 7, 1979.

White House where Menachem Begin and Anwar Sadat were to sign the peace
treaty negotiated at Camp David the previous September. The last treaty between the people of Israel and Egypt was in the time of King Solomon. It was a
windswept spring day and we could see sharpshooters with binoculars on the
White House roof surveying noisy protesters on Lafayette Square.

President Carter quoted the prophet Isaiah. "Nations shall beat their swords
into plowshares and their spears into pruning hooks. Let us now lay aside war.
Let us now reward all the children of Abraham who hunger for a comprehensive
peace in the Middle East." The leaders then affixed their signatures to the documents as the bells of St. John's Church across the square pealed resoundingly.

That night the Carters held a dinner for the two leaders in a tent on the
South Lawn. I had the presence of mind to ask our table partners to sign the
printed program that noted Leontyne Price and Itzhak Perlman as entertainers.
The signatures suggest the lively conversation we enjoyed—Katharine Graham,
publisher of the *Washington Post*; Jim Hoagland whose byline led the *Post*'s front-
page story on the signing ceremony; James "Scotty" Reston, *New York Times*

pundit; Pete Peterson, Nixon's secretary of commerce; Barry Diller, then chairman of Paramount Pictures; and Jerry Rafshoon, Carter's media man with his new bride, Eden.

The irrepressible Art Buchwald was wandering with his small flash camera taking pictures of everyone in sight, and I chastised him for this breach of protocol at a state dinner. Art ignored me and went about his business. A few minutes later I saw my Elizabeth, looking radiant, in conversation with President Sadat. I raced across and snatched Art's camera, then snapped a flash picture of the two. I would receive prolonged abuse from Buchwald for my hypocrisy.

A mob stormed the American Embassy in Iran in November and took fifty-two hostages. As a result of the crisis, Jimmy Carter did not appear at the 1979 Kennedy Center Honors. Instead Rosalynn Carter welcomed honorees Aaron Copland, Ella Fitzgerald, Henry Fonda, Martha Graham and Tennessee Williams to the East Room. "This is the greatest honor I've ever received," said Williams. "I'm not normally very gregarious and like small parties by candlelight, but if it's a big party, I like it in the White House."

At the Kennedy Center CBS correspondent Eric Sevareid took the stage with dignified authority. "Consider their origins and the different paths their lives have taken to bring them together here tonight," he said, looking to the honorees in the box tier. "An actor from Grand Island, Nebraska. A dancer from Allegheny, Pennsylvania. A playwright from Columbus, Mississippi. A singer from Yonkers by way of Newport News, Virginia. A musician from the borough of Brooklyn. We all live in their debt."

Leonard Bernstein spoke of the way Copland captured the texture of the American experience in his music, and Peggy Lee described Ella Fitzgerald as "the standard by which all of the rest of us are measured." Elia Kazan said of Williams that "No one in our theater has created a world of people to compare with Tennessee's characters—they will live in our memories as long as we live." Of Martha Graham, Gene Kelly said, "We all regarded her with wonder and respect, as someone who led a revolt against all the conventions of dance." Alan Alda, then television's young star of *M*A*S*H,* described Fonda as an actor who "set a standard in our profession that we admire and reach for, but that precious few will ever match."

The honorees received performance tributes, the most touching of which was the last. Henry Fonda served as a lieutenant in the navy during the war, then spent three years on Broadway playing the first officer of a navy vessel in the hit *Mister Roberts.* The midshipmen of the Naval Academy Glee Club performed a medley of *Anchors Aweigh, The Red River Valley* and *America the Beautiful,* after

With Liz Stevens, honoree Henry Fonda and Alan Alda at the
Kennedy Center Honors. December 2, 1979.

which an African American cadet stepped forward, snapped a salute, and addressed the honoree. "Thank you, Mr. Roberts."

The lean actor stood in the box, smiling through tears and waving at the cadets as they exited up the aisles. For a second year millions of Americans saw a celebration of the arts on CBS.

A week later I received a handwritten letter.

> Dear George
> We saw the Kennedy Honors show in Denver with a lot of family around and the place was awash with tears. I am, maybe more than anyone, aware of your enormous contribution to the dignity, the taste, the surprise elements, and the emotion of the evening. And this is to try to convey my heartfelt gratitude.
>
> Love, Hank

At year-end a committee of AFI's board recommended Jean Firstenberg to be our new director. Jean was an executive at the Markle Foundation who previously headed the communication office at Princeton University. Charlton Heston informed the committee he would be shooting three consecutive films abroad and agreed to continue as chairman if I served as cochair with him. I would continue producing the annual Life Achievement Award shows, a responsibility I welcomed.

As my AFI "getavasia" I wrote an article for Arts & Leisure in the Sunday *New York Times* that they titled "The Founding Director Grades the Film Institute at age 12 1/2." I noted that in his 1965 speech in the White House Rose Garden, President Johnson had called for the creation of a national opera, a national theater and a national ballet company, as well as for an American Film Institute—and that AFI was the only one to be realized. I expressed the hope that we had built "an institution that would continue to serve as a rallying place for Americans who want to see the film medium grow and change and meet its full promise."

PART SIX

A CREATIVE LIFE

George Stevens, Jr., on the Supreme Court steps directing Sidney Poitier as Thurgood
Marshall, *Separate But Equal,* 1990.

56

1980

In 1980 I went off the AFI payroll. I would never again be a salaried employee. I held public service jobs from age thirty to forty-eight, normally optimum earning years, but from now on I would be working for myself. Ideas became the engine for my professional pursuits and my earnings—nothing would happen unless I initiated it. I named my production company New Liberty Productions, a tip of the hat to my father, Capra and Wyler—the three colonels who formed Liberty Films after the war.

In February my friends and colleagues held a black-tie dinner in the elegant Benjamin Franklin Room at the State Department where the Kennedy Center Honors dinners took place. Richard Holbrooke, who had precociously risen to be Carter's assistant secretary of state for Pacific and East Asian Affairs, was the host along with Roger Stevens and Charlton Heston. It was an important night for AFI because Livingston Biddle, the new head of the National Endowment, was there, as was John Brademas, chair of arts policy in the House of Representatives, along with half a dozen United States senators. This was an opportunity for AFI's new director Jean Firstenberg to meet them. I was seated between the Elizabeths, my wife and Miss Taylor. My mother came from California and Cicely Tyson, Tom Brokaw, Ben Bradlee, Gary Hart and Jack Valenti joined in.

Art Buchwald held forth as master of ceremonies for what was more roast than tribute. Art framed the occasion as bidding farewell to "Pop" Stevens, the Grand Old Man of the American Film Institute. "It's hard to believe we will no longer see the familiar figure of Pop in his baseball cap and torn cardigan sweater," said Art, "running up and down the hallways trying to squeeze another dollar out of Congress." He declared that the score was in—"AFI $25,000,000—taxpayers zero." It was a night of sentiment and laughter that tied a ribbon around my twelve years as AFI's founding director.

At home on Avon Lane I relished my role as a father. Caroline thrived at Sidwell Friends, volunteered at the Kennedy Center, and went on to Tufts University to earn her degree in English. She worked as a waitress at Howard Johnson's to pay for a car, spent an inspiring summer at a kibbutz in Israel, and began to seek opportunities in film. Michael and David, now fourteen and twelve, were blessed with wit and generous hearts, brightening my days. They loved sports and I enjoyed coaching them as my father had me. Caroline's Shih Tzu Mao, Michael's Springer Spaniel Yo Yo, and David's Abyssinian cat, Shane, were all in residence. I knew that without the children my professional life would be hollow.

Washington offered unique learning opportunities. Michael, a sophomore at Landon School, was writing a paper on the controversy over Sony's new Betamax video recorder that was destined to change how we watched moving images. Universal and Disney sued Sony to block the device they claimed threatened their copyrighted movies, and the case went to the Supreme Court.

I called Byron White, my friend from the Kennedy years who was now a Supreme Court justice. He invited Michael and me to the argument, and to his chambers beforehand, where sandwiches and soft drinks awaited. Byron "Whizzer" White had been an All-American halfback at the University of Colorado, and after a year as a Rhodes Scholar led the NFL in rushing as a rookie with the Pittsburgh Steelers. Footballs and sports memorabilia dotted his office. Byron, warm and wise, drew Michael out about his life at school. Afterward we walked down a corridor and the justice opened a door that led up a dark stairway. At the top was a small gym where he hung his blue suit jacket on a chair, picked up a basketball, made a swift pass to Michael, who shucked his blue blazer—and the two passed, dribbled and shot baskets.

"Time to go to work," the justice said after ten minutes, and led us to the courtroom. It was stirring to sit beside my son in that historic chamber with its marble columns, brass railings and heavy red draperies, and hear the justices receive and challenge arguments. When we left Justice White shook hands with my son. "Michael," he said, "tell the boys at Landon that you played on the highest court."

Ted Kennedy decided to challenge Jimmy Carter in the 1980 Democratic primary. Polls showed him as much as forty points ahead of the incumbent president. He was urged on by congressional Democrats who feared a ticket headed by Carter would be a drag on their own races, but Ted's campaign was marked by missteps, and Carter used the power of incumbency to mount a strong campaign and secure the nomination.

Honoree Leonard Bernstein responds to ovation at the Kennedy Center Honors.
December 7, 1980.

It was a stinging defeat for Ted, but after conceding he appeared at the convention in Madison Square Garden. Liz and I watched his speech that was interrupted fifty-one times by applause followed by a thirty-minute ovation, a scene the *New York Times* described as "one of the great emotional outpourings of convention history." Teddy closed by saying, "For me, a few hours ago, this campaign came to an end. For all those whose cares have been our concern, the work goes on, the cause endures, the hope still lives, and the dream shall never die." In defeat he was speaking to the progressive ideals of the Democratic party and America's highest aspirations. Liz and I were brought into politics with Jack's presidency and had watched Bobby inspire the convention in 1964. We clung to that idealism. Going forward Teddy would devote himself to the United States Senate, and the Kennedy name would no longer be a factor in White House futures—but we remained on the lookout for the leader who could restore the dream.

Ronald Reagan carried forty-four states in November and became the first candidate in nearly a hundred years to defeat an incumbent Democratic president, so the 1980 Kennedy Center Honors was Jimmy Carter's last. We bade an affectionate farewell—Carter made the Honors possible with his decision to participate in 1978, an act for which the Kennedy Center and the nation will be ever grateful.

Leonard Bernstein and James Cagney were honorees along with three formidable female artists, Agnes DeMille, Lynn Fontanne and Leontyne Price. At the end of his ovation Lenny flung his arms open in joy and gratitude, a gesture that became an enduring image of the Honors through the years.

My father was never far out of mind. The only time he had spoken to me of his mortality was a few days before I moved to Washington. We were driving on Ventura Boulevard to a storage vault he kept at Bekins Storage. "If something happens to me," he said, "all that stuff in Bekins goes to you. Don't let it become a burden to you the way it has been to me." Then he turned to me with a smile. "You can throw it all in the L.A. River as far as I'm concerned."

Now I decided to address the situation, taking the master key and opening the forty by forty foot storage room. It was packed from floor to ceiling. There were rows of filing cabinets, photographs he took as a child, Laurel and Hardy scripts, stacks of film cans and World War II mementos—a Schmeisser MP 40 submachine gun he had liberated from an SS captain, and the wood-handled stamp he took from the post office at Dachau. One eight-foot-high rust-colored cabinet was filled with shimmering trophies that he chose to keep out of sight, including Oscars for *A Place in the Sun* and *Giant*.

I recalled the phrase "let something of me survive," attributed to the cave dwellers who carved the first pictures on the ancient walls at Altamira, realizing that this room contained the evidence of a man's life.

It was certainly *not* headed for the L.A. River. One of my responsibilities going forward was to shepherd my father's legacy, and as a first step I donated his archive to the Academy of Motion Picture Arts and Sciences, where they initiated an annual George Stevens Lecture to explore his life and films.

A publisher was encouraging me to write a book about my father, and on impulse I ordered a rusty can of film labeled "D-Day" to be sent to the Kennedy Center. One Friday afternoon I sat alone in the AFI screening room and watched vivid color images fill the screen—a gray sky at dawn with warships tossing on a blustery blue sea, under massive oblong barrage balloons tethered by mile-long cables to deter low-flying aircraft, and sailors busy on the deck of HMS *Belfast,* the flagship of the invasion fleet. This was D-Day, and I realized that my eyes were the first other than those who were there in 1944 to see this fateful day in color. An officer wearing a helmet and flak gear comes around a bulkhead

The room at Bekins Storage in North Hollywood where my father kept his belongings.

moving toward the camera. It is my father, grave and handsome, still shy of his fortieth birthday, headed for the Normandy beaches.

Never had I been touched more deeply. Decisions can be made by analysis and calculation, or by instinct. In that moment I knew I would not write a book about my father—I must make a film.

57

Hollywood on the Potomac

The year 1981 brought Ronald Reagan to Washington. He would usher in a new era, and he and his wife Nancy arrived in town with a band of dedicated conservatives. I had met them when they attended the John Ford and Jimmy Cagney AFI dinners but did not know them.

Nick Vanoff did know the Reagans, and he and his wife Felisa were invited to a reception at the White House the day after the inauguration. Nick surprised me by saying that he had arranged for Liz and me to attend. It didn't feel quite right but everyone likes to be where the action is, so Liz and I went with the Vanoffs. It was a big crowd and at one point Nancy Reagan came over to our group. It may have just been my own sense of not belonging at their celebration, but I read her expression as, "What the hell is he doing here?"

The older, socially active Reagan crowd could not have been more different from the laid-back Carter contingent. Kay Graham had a dinner for the Reagans that quickly made them part of the Washington scene in a way that had eluded the Carters. The Kennedy Center Honors depended upon participation by the president—the Reagans would decide if this new national tradition would continue. "There's nothing in the Constitution that says the president of the United States has to show up at the Kennedy Center Honors," I reminded colleagues. The glass-half-empty side of my brain worried that the name Kennedy in the title, the preponderance of liberal-leaning individuals among the most deserving honorees, and perhaps even my own identification with Democratic politics might dim their enthusiasm. The optimistic view was that the Reagans came to Washington with an affinity for show business.

Nancy appointed Muffie Brandon, a New Englander with ancestors who arrived on the *Mayflower*, as White House social secretary. Muffie was a surprising choice because she was a Democrat. She was also a good friend of Liz's and

Three masterful dancers come together at *The AFI Salute to Fred Astaire.*
Mikhail Baryshnikov, Astaire and James Cagney. April 10, 1981.

mine and enthusiastic about the Honors and the AFI. I took Muffie to lunch
after which she presented the Kennedy Center Honors proposal to the Reagans.
She called two days later with the good news that they would hold a White
House reception and attend the performance at the Kennedy Center.

Fred Astaire received the AFI Life Achievement award in April of Reagan's
first year. It was a special treat for me to work with Fred because he and my
father had made two pictures together, *Damsel in Distress* and the gem of the
Astaire–Rogers collaborations, *Swing Time.* Fred's lifelong pal David Niven
came from Switzerland and was a captivating host, and *Funny Face* costar Audrey Hepburn also came from Europe. "I experienced the thrill that all women
have at some point in their lives dreamed of," said Audrey, "to dance just once
with Fred Astaire."

One treasure of that evening is a photograph of Fred and two fellow dancers
who came to honor him, James Cagney and Mikhail Baryshnikov.

The shocking assassination attempt on Ronald Reagan in April led to the
Astaire event in Hollywood being postponed for three days. The president recovered after saying to his surgeons at George Washington Hospital, as the anesthe-
sia was taking hold, "I hope you're all Republicans." During the aftermath his
secretary of state, General Alexander Haig, blotted his copybook by declaring at

the White House, "I am in charge," blind to the constitutional role of Vice President George Bush.

The fully recovered Ronald Reagan proved to be perfect casting for the Honors. The recipients in his first year were Count Basie, Cary Grant, Helen Hayes, Jerome Robbins and Rudolph Serkin. We knew Cary avoided television at all costs, but the stature of the Honors and our rule that recipients do not have to speak or perform made him amenable. At the White House Ronnie and Nancy greeted the world of show business with winning smiles. He thanked the honorees for "the pure pearl of tears, the gold of laughter and the diamonds of stardust they spread on what otherwise might have been a rather dreary world." I used to muse that nothing Reagan did as president exceeded his skill at presiding at the Honors.

Cary Grant's seat next to Reagan in the Opera House box gave an opening to Art Buchwald in his remarks from the stage. "Just think, Mr. President, if you had not decided to go into politics," he said, "you might be sitting in the chair that Cary Grant is in right now . . . and Al Haig would be sitting in yours." The forty-carat smiles and laughter of Grant and Reagan were a sight to behold.

Walter Cronkite became our host after retiring from CBS News. His gravity, wit and sense of history made him ideal for the role. New stars Meryl Streep, Richard Chamberlin and Donald Sutherland were there for Helen Hayes, and icons Rex Harrison and Audrey Hepburn saluted Cary, she with a poem she had written for him. There were glorious performances for Basie, Serkin and Robbins.

But one moment stood out.

Soon after Leontyne Price agreed to be an Honoree the previous year, her manager Hubert Dilworth called. "What would you like Miss Price to sing?" he intoned in a resonant baritone. "Mr. Dilworth," I explained with assurance, "it is one of the traditions of the Honors that the recipients are not asked to speak or perform." The deep voice resumed more insistently. "Mr. Stevens, what would you like Miss Price to sing?" Leontyne was just fifty-four, appearing with honorees in their seventies and eighties, and Dilworth wanted the public to see her as an artist in her prime. It took me several nervous weeks to persuade him to accept our premise.

Leontyne adored her experience as an Honoree. An elegant set of recordings, *Leontyne Prima Donna,* was on my desk the morning after, with a handwritten note in green ink. "Dear George Stevens. Thanks from the bottom of my heart for everything. You run the tightest ship I've ever known. Bravo! Let me know if there is ever anything I can do for you."

I take some pride in not being a total opportunist, yet I quickly dialed the Ritz Carlton Hotel and invited Miss Price to come back to sing at the next Honors. "I shall be there," was her reply.

Honoree Cary Grant with Ronald Reagan, Barbara Grant and
Nancy Reagan at the Kennedy Center Honors. December 6, 1981.

Six months later I heard from Mr. Dilworth. "Mr. Stevens," he began. "I believe Miss Price promised that she would sing at the Kennedy Center Honors on Sunday, December sixth. It turns out she has a performance of *Aida* in San Francisco on December fifth."

Appreciating his problem, I interrupted. "Mr. Dilworth, we understand. These things happen."

"No, Mr. Stevens, you do not understand. Miss Price gave you her word."

On Saturday night December 5, 1981, Leontyne Price sang a triumphant *Aida* with the San Francisco Opera, put on her fur coat, walked out of the theater without removing her makeup, and was driven to the airport for a flight to Chicago, where she changed planes to Washington in midwinter cold.

I arrived at the Kennedy Center at 7:30 Sunday morning prepared for a bracing day of rehearsals and entered the Opera House through the Grand Foyer. The hall was empty and silent, the stage dark except for the single "ghost

Leonard Bernstein congratulates fellow honoree Leontyne Price. Honorees Lynn Fontanne, Agnes DeMille and Kennedy Center chairman Roger Stevens in background. December 7, 1980.

light" that remains on overnight, an old theater tradition. I saw a figure in a long fur coat standing alone on the stage. Then I heard a sound of angels, the rich soprano of Leontyne, still in her *Aida* makeup, singing her Puccini aria for that night. Never have I been more moved by a song. Here was a professional artist, unconcerned about sleep or resting her voice—but intent on keeping her word.

Twelve hours later Walter Cronkite opened the Honors with a simple introduction, "The magnificent Leontyne Price."

She entered in a deep-purple sequined dress bowing her head to Basie, Grant, Hayes, Robbins and Serkin in the box tier. "One year ago when I sat where you are, I hadn't in my wildest dreams thought that I would be able to perform for you this evening," she said. "I would like to dedicate "Vissi d'arte"—*my life is art*—from Puccini's *Tosca* to this year's Honorees."

It is a thrilling aria and Miss Price *was* magnificent. There were bravas, cheers and tears. The artistry and the professionalism she displayed became for me a talisman of the Honors tradition, and Leontyne herself became a radiant and abiding Honors presence, showing up yearly to express her respect for the generation of artists to follow.

58

Dodger Blue

Then a voice from the past. Al Horwits, the former Philadelphia sportswriter who introduced me to Connie Mack as a boy and now headed publicity at Columbia Pictures, called to propose that Michael and David and I join him at a Dodgers game when next in Los Angeles. Washington had no team so In the summer of 1980 my baseball-starved lads were thrilled to walk into Dodger Stadium for a game under the lights, after which Al said, "Let's say hello to Tommy Lasorda." We were soon in the Dodger manager's office under the stadium, a room brimming with photos and mementos.

Tommy Lasorda's gift for gab is legendary and he had a straightforward way of talking to children. "David, say hello to Reggie Smith," he said, as his All-Star right fielder entered carrying his black Louisville Slugger. "Reggie, David doesn't have a good bat. Can he have yours?" David was wide-eyed as Smith somewhat reluctantly handed over a treasure that would one day pass to a next generation. Then Tommy led us down a corridor, and coming in the other direction was the six-foot, five-inch left hander Jerry Reuss.

"Hold up, Jerry! This is Michael Stevens from Washington DC," Tommy proclaimed. "Michael's a pitcher. Do you have any pointers for him?"

Reuss looked down, making eye contact with the fourteen-year-old. "Michael," he said. "Never put your hands in dishwater."

As we were leaving Dodger Stadium, Tommy said, "Look us up when we're on the road back East."

The next June on a Friday afternoon Michael, David and I landed in St. Louis—my first glimpse of the city since Dad took me to the All-Star game in 1948. Now I was walking with my sons toward Busch Memorial Stadium, passing the bronze statue of Cardinal legend "Stan the Man" Musial, whose autograph I secured at that All-Star game. We found Lasorda's office in the visitors' dressing room where he greeted the boys and introduced us to Joe Amalfitano and his other coaches. The players were getting dressed nearby when suddenly Tommy, pointing to Michael, called to the equipment manager:

"Louie! Michael Stevens is my batboy. He needs a uniform."

This amazing prospect had never occurred to us and Michael disappeared, soon to return in a gray and blue Dodger uniform with "BAT BOY" displayed on the back. Still wearing his brown loafers, he whispered, "Dad, would you mind going to the hotel and getting my sneakers?"

"Saxey," Tommy called out to second baseman Steve Sax. "You've got extra shoes back there. Give a pair to my batboy."

Before long I was in the left field stands with my Leica documenting Michael shagging fly balls under the bright lights with the Dodger's playful Mexican pitching star Fernando Valenzuela, who had induced "Fernandomania" in Los Angeles. Of his Rookie of the Year, Lasorda complained, "We worked like hell to teach Fernando English, but the only word he learned was 'million.'"

Michael acquitted himself well during the game and Tommy took us for an Italian dinner afterward. David, just twelve, was seated in his Dodger Blue jacket next to Steve Garvey, the movie-star-handsome first baseman. The personable slugger confided to David that he had started out as a batboy with the Brooklyn Dodgers. Just then Lasorda spoke up. "David—tomorrow night you're my batboy." The younger son pulled off his big league debut on Saturday night with aplomb.

We had father and son batboy excursions to New York, Philadelphia, Montreal and Chicago, each one an adventure for the boys and an opportunity for me to hang out with the irrepressible Dodger manager. David remembers an afternoon game at Chicago's Wrigley Field where Tommy made both Michael and David batboys. David was sitting beside his brother on the bench with the Cubs at bat when their shortstop Shawn Dunston hit a ground ball, took off like a rocket, and beat it out for a base hit. Dodger coach Joe Amalfitano began hollering at the Dodger players. The Stevens boys—in this pre-*Sopranos* era—had a circumscribed vocabulary and stared wide-eyed as Amalfitano roared, "Did you see that motherfucker run? If you cocksuckers got off your fuckin' asses and ran like that we'd win some ball games." Observing his Dodger veterans looking absently at the sky mulling their dinner plans, Tommy shouted, "Joey . . . only *two* people in this dugout are listening to ya."

Two years later in Chicago on a Saturday afternoon, Michael, nearing sixteen and tall for his age, was fielding fly balls before the game in the Wrigley Field outfield with its ivy-covered walls, and I was paternally taking more pictures than necessary. I noticed three young girls watching from the bleachers

David Stevens, Steve Garvey and Michael Stevens in
Tommy Lasorda's office, Dodger Stadium, 1980.

above the players and overheard one call out, "Hey batboy, what's your room number?"

This seemed a propitious time to conclude our traveling life with Tommy Lasorda, but our friendship continued. I invited him to the 1981 Kennedy Center Honors, the year his Dodgers won the World Series. From backstage before the show I spotted Tommy walking down the aisle of the Opera House in his tuxedo with a large bag, not an easy maneuver in a restricted security area. I watched as he placed two new Rawlings fielder's gloves on Michael and David's seats. Tommy always came through for kids.

59

The Christmas Spirit

Each New Year's Day, when I revised my notebook of goals for the coming year, one idea kept recurring: a Christmas concert for families in Washington. The success of the first Reagan Honors weekend emboldened me to ask for an appointment with Michael Deaver, an architect of Reagan's political career and now his deputy chief of staff. One of his special talents was creating visual situations that displayed Reagan to advantage. In his office next to the president's I described my notion of an annual Christmas concert for which we would enlist leading musical artists and choirs—a televised fundraiser for a worthy charity. I proposed that the president and Mrs. Reagan be honorary sponsors, that they appear at the concert, and Mrs. Reagan designate the beneficiary organization. Deaver was a political animal and I wondered how our differing views would affect his receptivity.

He asked just a few questions before saying, "I think the president may like this. I'll get back to you."

Three days later Deaver called. "We want to do this," he said. "Nancy would like Children's Hospital to benefit and our only condition is that I approve the television sponsors. We don't want defense contractors or other companies that might send the wrong message."

This was a "bird in the hand" similar to the one Leonard Garment handed me in the Nixon White House that spawned the AFI Life Achievement Award. I had been discussing projects with Perry Lafferty, a senior program executive at NBC, and flew to Los Angeles to see him. "This could work," he enthused.

I was looking for a distinctive setting for the show, and a friend who had a keen sense of history took me to see the Pension Building, an out-of-service red brick Civil War structure on Fourth Street that was about to be restored and become the home of the National Building Museum. It had a five-story open interior where soldiers used to collect their pensions, even, according to legend, riding their horses into the building. With its eight Roman-style columns, taller even than those at Baalbek, I considered it a "found object"—a splendid setting for a television event.

There was one obstacle. Because NBC wanted the broadcast to be one week before Christmas, the optimum date to tape the concert was the second Sunday in December—just seven days after the Kennedy Center Honors. This led me to enlist Gary Smith and Dwight Hemion, a successful producer and director team, as partners. I would serve as executive producer and cowriter, jiggering my time between the two shows.

We needed a star to get this show off the ground. I called Dinah Shore, who lived just behind the Beverly Hills Hotel where I stayed when I was on the West Coast. Dinah, a vivacious vocalist of the big band era known for her southern charm, was one of television's brightest stars. Also one of its nicest people. She managed to make me feel like a hero for inviting her. With Dinah as our anchor, we rounded out the cast with Diahann Carroll, Ben Vereen, Debby Boone, John Schneider and the United States Naval Academy Glee Club.

Children's Hospital was thrilled to be the benefiting charity. Invitations to the show were for parents and their children, with each family asked to bring a gift for a child at Children's Hospital. Nancy Reagan agreed to visit the hospital to give the presents to the children.

The Reagans were enthusiastic front-row participants. Mike Deaver shaped Reagan's onstage remarks at the end of the show to be a holiday greeting to the American people—a practice repeated by his successors that solidified the program as a national tradition. Parents and children seated together in this festive setting in Washington, and families watching together across the nation on television, were moved by the glorious and unifying sounds of the season. Moreover, Ronnie and Nancy remained onstage with the cast, choirs, orchestra and the US Herald Trumpets for a rhapsodic presentation of "Hark the Herald Angels Sing," which became the eagerly anticipated finale each year.

My mother used to tell me that busy people got more things done, and I found that producing the Kennedy Center Honors and *Christmas in Washington* on successive weekends was stimulating. Casting, writing, rehearsing and problem solving for the two shows became adventurous at times, but working with established stars and new artists renewed old friendships and created new ones. For the next thirty-two years—through five presidencies—with an array of the most popular stars of the era, and the regular participation of the men and women of the Naval Academy Glee Club in their dress blues—*Christmas in Washington* shined a light on Washington's magnificent Children's Hospital.

60

Homage

"Life is a journey, and it's most interesting when you're not sure where you're going." These words which I found in my father's wartime diary became the touchstone and opening narration for a film.

I wrote a ten-page treatment in June of 1981 for what I called "George Stevens: American Filmmaker." The title didn't survive but the themes were defined. I was inspired not only by the cache of personal history that my father had tucked away in the Bekins storeroom—which became the setting for the opening scene—but also a book Warren Beatty gave me, *Renoir, My Father,* in which Jean Renoir, the director of *Grand Illusion* and *Rules of the Game,* tells the story of his father, master impressionist Pierre Auguste Renoir.

I plunged in and hired Susan Winslow, who had done excellent work on the AFI shows, to be editor and coproducer, and my daughter Caroline, newly graduated from Tufts, who brought knowledge of George Stevens to the task of gathering research, viewing prints of twenty-five feature films, and organizing photographs, audio recordings, press clippings, interviews—everything available on his life and career. I rented a two-story townhouse on Washington Circle not far from my Kennedy Center office and equipped it with two Steenbeck editing tables.

I had no studio or sponsor and distribution opportunities for a film about a filmmaker were slim to none. I was able to get a couple of small grants to defray some costs, but soon realized that this was a labor of love. I was paying for it myself with money I earned producing television shows. I recalled Orson Welles accepting the Life Achievement Award. "As a director, for instance, I pay myself out of my acting jobs. I use my own work to subsidize my work. In other words I'm crazy."

Moreover, it was sobering to realize I was putting my father's reputation on the line as well as my own. The film had to rise to his standards, which meant it had to be shot in 35mm so scenes from his movies would be presented with fidelity. This was cause for anxiety as I watched costly Eastman Color negative speeding through cameras while Dad's friends told their stories. Over the next year we filmed Jimmy Stewart, Joel McCrea, Ginger Rogers, Fred Astaire, Douglas Fairbanks, Jr., Rock Hudson, Elizabeth Taylor, Warren Beatty, and directors John Huston, Fred Zinnemann, Joseph Mankiewicz and Frank Capra. We interviewed Irwin Shaw and others who served with the Stevens Irregulars. And, of course, my mother.

Cary Grant and Katharine Hepburn each made three pictures with my father but both presented challenges.

Cary cheerfully agreed to an in-person conversation, so Susan Winslow and I went to his house above Beverly Hills with its view of the Pacific Ocean. Cary, astonishingly fit and handsome at eighty, in a bright red sweater and cream colored trousers, opened the door. I watched Susan blink in awe. She and I sat on a sofa with Cary across from us and I put a recorder on the table. "Oh please," Cary said, "we mustn't do that." I turned it off and put it beside me. He regaled us for an hour with stories, even getting to his feet to act out memories of *Gunga Din,* concluding, a bit teary, "I think we all loved each other, in a manner we couldn't possibly express. My God, we were so young."

I confess that partway through, in the interest of history, let's say, I unobtrusively switched on the recorder.

Your father had a very serious exterior—with a great deal of humor.
He had a loose fan going on behind him. He struck me as a one
purpose man. Now, he might permit you to believe that you were
doing it your way but you weren't at all. 'What do you think, fellows?'
he'd say. But he already knew what we were going to do.

Cary said something nourishing to the younger man sitting across from him, who may have appeared more confident than he was.

You're rather like that, yourself, George. You generally do what you
want to do. And if others don't conform, then you charm them into
wanting to do what you want them to do. That's you—you're just like
your father—you know that?

"Cary," I said, as we were leaving, "we'd like to make a date to film a few of your stories."

"I'm sorry, that's not possible," he said firmly. "If I were to do it for George, I'd have to do it for Hitch, for Hawks and the others." I had been in this place before with Cary, but this time I intended to press on. It was for my father after all.

When I spoke with Hepburn she was direct. "I adored your father and I will do this, but I'm not well just now—you'll have to wait." Six months later we set a date, but soon after I read that she had driven into a telephone pole in Connecticut and fractured her foot. She was essential to the movie so I kept in touch.

The film proved to be more daunting than I anticipated. Having written and produced successful AFI tributes to directors Ford, Capra, Wyler, Hitchcock and Huston, I assumed this would be similar, before realizing it wasn't a television tribute—it was a motion picture. I was telling the story of my father's life, and a solid structure was required to engage an audience for two hours.

Susan assembled a cut of the film that included irresistible scenes from every one of my father's pictures. It ran nearly four hours. One drawback to a son making a film about his father emerged. If I decided, for example, to remove the scene from *Annie Oakley* or *Penny Serenade,* it felt like I was consigning one of my father's films to the dustbin of history. We moved forward, paring and cutting the film to two and a half hours. Shaping so many disparate elements into a coherent story was a challenge, and I admit to wishing at times that I had never undertaken it.

I gave the film a new title, *George Stevens: A Filmmaker's Journey,* and as 1983 came to an end I was keen to finish it so it could receive consideration by film festivals—yet I still hadn't corralled our two elusive stars. When I called Cary for what must have been the fourth time, he surprised me. "Barbara and I are coming to Washington for a meeting of the Princess Grace Foundation," he said. "You can record my voice as long as there is no photography." We agreed that I would pick him up on Friday at the L'Enfant Plaza Hotel and take him to our production office.

I had turned over my aging but safe Volvo sedan to my son Michael and was using a decrepit ten-year-old Subaru that my mother-in-law kept on her farm. I decided not to be self-conscious about the old Subaru and drove to the hotel entrance which was jammed with limousines, Prince Rainier himself having just arrived. I saw an open spot and leaned out the window to explain to the doorman that I was there to pick up "Mister Cary Grant" and would be just a few minutes. He glared. "Okay. Five minutes." I rushed inside and called Cary's suite.

"Oh George . . . *do* come up. Barbara and I have coffee and pastries for you."

Cary greeted me at the door in a dark chalk stripe suit and dark-rimmed glasses, exuding charm. I restlessly sipped coffee and conversed, visualizing the doorman raging at my Subaru, until Cary got to his feet. "*Well,* Barbara . . . George and I *must* go now and do our *bis-i-ness.*"

I decided neither to apologize for nor explain our mode of transportation. The doorman smiled nervously at his honored guest as he led Cary to the Subaru sitting in a row of limousines. I got in the driver's seat and Cary settled on the passenger side, his long legs forcing his chalk stripe knees tight against the glove box. I shifted gears and drove off. Cary reached for the window knob and jiggled it to no effect. I kept my vow not to explain. It was minutes later when he spoke.

"George," he said. "The only *other* man I knew who had a car like *this* was *Howard*."

He was speaking of his friend—the eccentric billionaire Howard Hughes.

Then came a call from Katharine Hepburn telling me I should have a camera crew at her brownstone in New York City the following Friday at ten. I called her from home the night before to confirm. "What are you doing in Washington?" she complained. "I'm here in New York ready to be photographed tomorrow morning." I assured her that I was taking a seven a.m. flight and everything would be fine. When I arrived at the American Airlines counter I was told my flight was canceled. I pictured the punctual actress waiting in her parlor with my film crew as I ran to the other end of the terminal, crowded onto the seven-thirty Eastern flight, landed at La Guardia, and rushed outside to a taxi.

"I'm in a hurry," I called out. "244 East Forty-Ninth."

The elderly driver nodded approvingly. "Oui. . . . *Miz Kass-er-een Hepburn!*" said the French cabbie—a former Manhattan tour guide.

Dressed in black slacks, a white turtleneck and a dark blouse, Miss Hepburn had selected a tall chair backed with red fabric that set off her face. She began by describing with self-deprecating humor her first encounter with my father at RKO when she was choosing a director for *Alice Adams.*

> I was sitting in the car lot with Charles Boyer—flirting I'm afraid
> —when all of a sudden your father's face came into view this close to
> mine and said, "I'm George Stevens." And I said, "Oh for heaven's sake!"

Her phrase "your father" neatly let the audience understand that this was a son telling his father's story, even though, except for a few photographs, I would not appear on-screen. She spoke with relish about doing a scene they thought was terrific and going across the street to Lucey's Restaurant to have dinner and celebrate. Her recollection introduced a theme of the film.

> And someone, who was a good friend of mine, came in and sat down
> and talked about a deal he made for someone, and millions of dollars

and this and that, and money and money and money, and he left.
George looked at me and he put his arms around me and gave me a
big kiss. And I said, "George!" And he said, "Money, money, money.
I can't bear that talk." That was sweet, you know. And he said, "It's
what we *do* that's so great, isn't it?"

After thirty minutes, she turned to me. "You are a very fortunate man, and I've
told you more than you need to know."

The crew started removing equipment and she asked me to come upstairs.
Kate sat on her bed and I in the chair at her side, and her assistant served tea. She
spoke of the parlor downstairs.

> I was throwing logs on the fire one night when there was this terrible
> roar and I said, "George, the chimney is on fire. I'm going upstairs
> to make sure the roof doesn't catch fire. You go to the kitchen, fill a
> saucepan with water and put the fire out." There was pounding on
> the front door and your father goes downstairs. He's standing there
> with the saucepan and two huge firemen came in shouting, "Where's
> the fire?" He answered perfectly honestly with that deadpan look,
> "In the fireplace." They pushed him out of the way, thinking, "Wise
> guy." One fireman found me on the roof, and I said, "Look out,
> you're awfully heavy, you may fall through the ceiling," and the
> man jumped up and down to prove me wrong. I told this to George
> afterwards. "Wouldn't it have been funny," he said, "if I was standing
> with that goddamn saucepan in the middle of the living room,
> and that fireman had come right through two stories and landed
> in the pan."

Kate looked at me, moved by her own story. It seemed she wanted me to know
how close they had been. As I got up to leave, she said, "He was a funny man,
you see. A darling human being."

Susan Winslow and I were sparring over choices in the editing. She had spent a
year on the project and had strong views. Yet the story was personal to me. I had
placed the final scene from *Shane* at the end of the film in the original treatment.
Susan wasn't keen on the idea, so one evening I asked Cathy Shields, her young
assistant, to splice in the scene where Shane dispatches the Ryker gang in the
shootout in Grafton's Saloon. Young Joey is waiting when Shane exits through
the swinging doors and rides off into the Tetons, calling after him, "Shane, come

back . . . come back, Shane." My father had created my ending—a scene of a boy comprehending loss. I loved it.

I asked Toni Vellani to come to Washington. Toni sat at my side behind Susan as she operated the editing table. About three minutes into the first reel Tony snapped his fingers—"I already know that!" He was referring to a still photograph that had been repeated. We went through the film with Toni making precise comments, essentially speaking the language of my father, from whom we both learned. He broke the logjam. Susan decided she couldn't continue, but her contribution had been substantial. Cathy and I proceeded to finish the film. I have no affinity for the clairvoyant, yet more than once, alone at the editing table, I felt my father over my shoulder.

"George, Orson Welles here," intoned a voice on the phone. "When I came to RKO at twenty-five your father treated me as a friend. If my voice will help your film, I'm ready to repay the favor." It was a call from the blue. I knew that a famous narrator would make the film more salable. I had Gregory Peck and Warren Beatty in mind, and now Orson added his magnificent voice to the list. Toni Vellani posed another view. "This is your story. It should be your voice." Toni was right. The voice of the son gave the story unique perspective.

I previewed the film just once, for a handful of friends, and felt its power for the first time. Scenes I had been looking at day after day suddenly came to life in the dark in the presence of lively minds. Our structure placed my father's remarkable color film of World War II at the midpoint, after his brilliant but lighthearted prewar films. The audience witnessed his life-changing experiences from D-Day to the horror of Dachau, then learned about his deep and powerful postwar films.

A large orchestra was beyond our budget, so we tried licensing existing music, but nothing fit. An original score was essential to bind the film together. Earlier that year I enlisted Carl Davis, an American composer living in England, to compose music for the silent films of Lillian Gish at her AFI tribute, and to conduct it live with an orchestra. It was a triumph. I sent Carl a videotape of *A Filmmaker's Journey* and he called from London to say he loved the film and could produce something that would fit our tiny budget.

I flew to see him at his house outside of London, where we "spotted" the film, deciding at what points original music was required. Carl had a sunlit workroom with shelves laden with recordings. He took a ladder and removed a Shostakovich quintet which he played for me. The idea of five musicians made budgetary sense, but I said, "It's too European, Carl. My father was a man of the American West." We looked at one another in silence. Carl went back to the shelves and chose another disk. A stirring sound came forth. It was a 1944 recording of the debut performance of Aaron Copland's *Appalachian Spring* in the small chamber at the Library of Congress, the size of which limited the ensemble to a dozen. I idolized Copland, whom we had recently honored at the Kennedy Center. Carl composed a Stevens theme in the spirit of Copland. His evocative score fused and elevated the film.

Then came a providential call. Ruda Dauphin, director of the prestigious annual Festival of American Films at Deauville, a seaside town on the Normandy coast, asked to see *A Filmmaker's Journey*. She was so taken with it that she scheduled it for the Friday night of the festival's closing weekend, to be preceded by a week of George Stevens films. Also premiering at Deauville were *Indiana Jones and the Temple of Doom, Splash, Gremlins* and *The Natural*. We pressed ahead to produce a French-subtitled version of our film.

Liz, Caroline and I arrived at Deauville's Hotel Royal in early September. (Michael had been invited but felt obliged to stay in Washington's August heat for football practice.) I hadn't seen the subtitled print so I found a place to stand in the side aisle at the international press preview, where I could watch both audience and screen. I felt the film take hold. There was stillness and laughter. During the World War II section the French saw for the first time in color the D-Day landing on nearby Normandy beaches and the stirring scenes of Paris being liberated. I glanced to a row of French women in their thirties and saw their tears reflected in the light from the screen—and savored the marvel of how pieces of celluloid could be joined together in a way that so affected the hearts of strangers.

The night before the premiere the porter at the front desk handed me a cable signaling a change of heart. "Dad. I belong with you. Arriving on early a.m. flight. Love Michael"

Caroline, Michael, Liz and I were joined on the red carpet by Rock Hudson and Shelley Winters, who appeared in the film. Sam Spiegel came from London and my faithful ally Toni Vellani flew in from Los Angeles. The American ambassador, the mayor of Bordeaux and my New Frontier pal Pierre Salinger, now a correspondent for *L'Express,* spoke briefly before the film. Pierre had obtained an advance copy of the influential *International Herald Tribune*'s review by Thomas Quinn Curtis, which began: "The Deauville Festival offered a choice selection of US films. The occasion's most imposing and memorable event was the world premiere of *George Stevens: A Filmmaker's Journey*." Stunned, I scanned the first paragraph as we were walking to our box in the center of the first balcony.

His son has drawn the portrait of a man of fierce convictions and unyielding integrity, an artist whose keen observation and quick imagination made it possible for him to set millions laughing at human absurdities and also to instill in his audiences a profound sympathy for human sorrows. The younger Stevens in his film biography has mastered the communicative magic of his father.

The lights went down before I could absorb the significance of this first critique.

The Deauville onlookers were engaged throughout, and at the end, when Shane rides into the mountains with young Joey calling after him, applause began and built to an ovation when the lights came up. The spotlight centered on our box. I got to my feet, warmed by the approving faces below. Then I glimpsed my son Michael two seats away, tears streaming down his cheeks—not the way a six-foot-two football player might want to be seen. I turned back to the audience acknowledging their appreciation, then felt Michael embracing me. I was surprised and profoundly affected—father, son and grandson bound together in so personal a way. The scene of little Joey calling after *Shane* had touched a nerve. That moment alone justified my three-year journey, yet I didn't foresee that Michael's deep response was one step on the road to his becoming the Stevens family's fifth generation in show business.

I returned to the United States buoyed by wonderful reviews to face a sobering reality. Our film didn't fall into normal categories for distribution in theaters or on television. It was a tremendously busy fall with the *Kennedy Center Honors* and *Christmas in Washington,* and by mid-December there were no offers.

I turned to the smartest entertainment person I knew, Barry Diller. We met for lunch at the Russian Tea Room in New York. He wasn't optimistic but promised to screen the film. Three days later he called, as always getting directly to the point. "It's superb." Then the words I was longing for: "This film deserves to be seen in theaters, but it requires special handling. I've sent it to Julian Schlossberg of Castle Hill Films." Two nights later the phone rang at home. It was Julian, a genial go-getter, bursting with enthusiasm after just seeing the film. We made a deal and he organized a plan to distribute the film theatrically in the United States, with premieres in Hollywood, New York and Washington.

Family, friends and stars turned out in April at the Motion Picture Academy's thousand-seat Samuel Goldwyn theater in Beverly Hills. Colleagues of my

With Millie Perkins and Warren Beatty at Academy screening of
George Stevens: A Filmmaker's Journey.

father were introduced, ranging from ninety-three-year-old Hal Roach to Jimmy
Stewart, Cary Grant, Fred Astaire, Shelley Winters and Millie Perkins.

Warren Beatty, notoriously elusive when asked to speak publicly, came to
the microphone.

> I always called George Stevens the "Superchief." We have George
> Sr. to thank for the feeling that there need not be limits to our
> aspirations, and that movies have a higher calling than simply the
> gross theatrical film rentals. [laughter and applause]
>
> The film tonight is unique not only because I'm in it for fifty
> seconds—which constitutes my entire body of work for the past few
> years [laughter]. It's unique because of the testimony of a son's love
> and respect for his father. I think how proud George Sr. would be to
> know that his own qualities of generosity and protectiveness toward
> his fellow filmmakers would now be best embodied in his son. And
> of the contribution George Jr. has made to the elevation and the
> preservation of film—how proud he must be that his son picked up
> the baton and didn't go just for the money.

I saw *A Filmmaker's Journey* hundreds of times through the years, but this night at the Academy, of which my father was once president, in the company of his collaborators, was unmatched. Cary Grant, seated directly behind me, was emotional as the applause died. He took my right hand in both of his before saying, "Oh, *George*. I *should* have let you *photo*-graph me." Jack Lemmon was standing next to Cary. "My father made donuts in Boston," he sniffed. "Can't we make a nine-minute film about him?"

"We've never heard or seen prolonged applause and a standing ovation to match that given *George Stevens: A Filmmaker's Journey,* Wednesday night," was Army Archerd's lede in *Variety.* The reviews said everything a filmmaker could wish for. *Time* made it personal: "George Stevens, Jr has his father's sharp eye . . . the perspective is both judicious and adoring, as if he were young Brandon de Wilde to his father's *Shane.* The old pro taught the boy how to shoot and, as this moving biography proves, how to say goodbye."

The film played in theaters across the country and later on the ABC television network. It would be seen widely overseas and through the years on Turner Classic Movies, on DVDs and streaming. Most satisfying to me is that *George Stevens: A Filmmaker's Journey* is still being shown today, meeting my father's standard—the test of time.

61

Guess Who's Coming to Dinner

Lena Horne, Danny Kaye, Gian Carlo Menotti, Arthur Miller and Isaac Stern were recognized at the 1984 Kennedy Center Honors. We liked to close the shows with an uplifting and inspiring tribute, and Danny Kaye presented that opportunity. He combined his show business life with his role as ambassador at large for the United Nations Fund for Children. We arranged for the hundred-member United Nations Children's Choir to pay tribute to Danny. Wearing resplendent clothing of their countries they joined soprano Roberta Peters of the Metropolitan Opera and the Washington Choral Arts Society in "Let There Be Peace on Earth," a hymn to world harmony and understanding.

The children were bewitching and it was a stirring finale, earning a standing ovation and sending people home inspired and happy on Sunday night.

However, on Monday we heard rumors about discontent at the White House. It was hard to pin down but we were told Mike Deaver was irate. Nick and I decided to address it head on and asked to see Deaver. Mike, usually cordial, gestured to two chairs, remaining at his White House desk when we arrived.

"We know what you guys were doing," he said. "You were sticking it to the president."

Nick and I sat in puzzled silence.

"The president knew he had to be the first one on his feet," he continued.

"Mike," I said. "I don't know what you're talking about."

"Jim Baker got it," he went on, referring to the chief of staff. "I talked to him and Mrs. Reagan this morning."

Deaver was convinced that "Peace on Earth" was meant to embarrass Reagan, seemingly because the president was pro-war.

"Mike," I said. "Can you honestly believe that the two of us, whose mission is to have the Kennedy Center Honors become permanent, would set out to publicly embarrass the man who is essential to its future?"

We got nowhere. Nick and I, shell-shocked, stood and said goodnight. Deaver was one thing, but Nancy Reagan was part of the conversation and she was Ronald Reagan's most zealous defender. *Christmas in Washington* was the next Sunday and we had scheduled a pretaping with her at the White House. I sent a handwritten letter with some carefully chosen flowers to the White House.

> Dear Mrs. Reagan,
> Once again you and the president provided a most gracious setting for the Kennedy Center Honors. It was much easier to write a note of appreciation last year. Let this one be an expression of gratitude as well as an apology for any discomfort that may have come to you.
>
> Of greater concern is the thought that the final production number was misunderstood. Our idea was that it would be touching and inspiring to have 100 children from many nations singing "Let There Be Peace on Earth" and sharing it with the man who carries on his shoulders our nation's quest for peace.
>
> You and the president have been friendly to me personally and trusting of me professionally. I would not think of responding by offending you. On our team Nick Vanoff is the musical one and I am the verbal one—so please accept these words as our shared apology for any discomfort we may have caused.
>
> George Stevens, Jr.

On Friday morning we set up our lights and cameras and I waited for the First Lady to come down the staircase from the family quarters. Nancy Reagan's wide eyes dominated her face and I was studying them as she approached our small group. She came over, looked at me directly, with just a hint of emotion. "Thank you for the *lovely* flowers," she said, then smiled. She was persuaded.

I got to know Mike Deaver and we became friends. Hard times came when a *Time* magazine cover showed him as a lobbyist in a chauffeured car heading to the Capitol, and soon after he was convicted on perjury charges. The son of alcoholic parents, he admitted his own addiction and went on to lead a life of helping others. I suspect his then secret addiction led to our Honors crisis.

Two years later in the spring of 1986 I was at my desk around seven p.m. on the balcony above the Kennedy Center's Eisenhower Theater when I noticed outside my door a secret service agent with an identifying earpiece. He asked if I would be leaving soon, explaining that President Reagan was coming to see the

With Nancy Reagan in the White House Library.

performance of *The Caine Mutiny Court Martial.* This reminded me that Charlton Heston had told me he was coming to Washington to play Captain Queeg and I promised that Liz and I would have him for dinner. It sparked an idea. I dialed 456-1414 and asked for Linda Faulkner, Nancy Reagan's social secretary. "Linda, do the Reagans ever go out for dinner?" I asked. "Of course," she replied, defensively, "they were at the British Embassy last Friday." Awkwardly and hesitantly I explained that I had promised to have Charlton Heston for dinner and it occurred to me the Reagans might enjoy seeing him (realizing as I heard my own words that the Reagans had sundry means to achieve such an outcome). "I see," Linda said. "I'll put your request in the proper channel." I went home feeling foolish and decided to make no further mention of it.

The next morning the phone rang at home and a secretary announced that Mr. Jack Courtemanche, the First Lady's chief of staff, was calling. "Mr. Stevens, did you invite the Reagans for dinner?" I began to backpedal. "Well, it happens Chuck Heston's in town, and I was thinking about . . ." He interrupted. "Would Monday night be convenient?" This was Thursday. "I think so," I said, "but I should check with Mrs. Stevens."

My wife was off for a busy day of meetings at the Women's Campaign Fund, her husband having neglected to mention to her, an ardent Democrat, that he had invited the Republican president to dinner. When I finally reached her, she listened to my story with incredulity. True to her nature, she quickly turned to practical questions. How many people, who, what to serve, etc. There had been no discussion with Mr. Courtemanche about numbers. We could put a tent on the tennis court and invite two hundred people. "The Reagans are always at big dinners at separate tables," Liz said. "I think they would enjoy one table of ten." And so it would be.

The Reagans and Stevenses were four. Pierre Salinger's wife Nicole was coming from Paris to stay with us, that's five. Heston and his wife Lydia make seven. Andy Williams was in town for a concert at Wolf Trap, that's eight. And we invited John Guare, our gifted playwright friend, and his talented and beautiful wife, Adele Chatfield Taylor, director of Design Arts at the National Endowment. We received visits from the White House secret service detail. The young agent in charge was at once stern and personable. He resisted Liz's desire to serve cocktails outside on our porch overlooking the garden, but Liz stood her ground, and after some adjustments he agreed. Finally he showed us the arrival procedure, in which the motorcade would come down our narrow mews-like street and stop in front of our small courtyard, and the president and Mrs. Reagan would walk from the car to the front steps and enter. This, he said, was the most vulnerable moment and stressed to Liz that we must remain inside the front door.

The second of June was a glorious spring day with roses and clematis blooming. Nicole Salinger arrived in the afternoon and was staying in David's room. She was taking a shower when the secret service agents, unaware of her arrival, conducted their "sweep" with two black and tan Belgian Malinois. It seems one of the canines caught scent of a banned substance and entered David's bathroom, startling Nicole. The agents were repentant.

Our friends came at six-thirty in advance of the Reagan's arrival at seven. We gathered on the porch, joined by sons Michael and David, enjoying the balmy spring weather and catching up with one another, including complimenting John Guare on the success of his *House of Blue Leaves* at the Tonys the previous night.

"They're five minutes away," said the lead agent, beckoning to Liz and me. We stood in the hall inside the open front door and heard the sound of sirens. Then we saw the first elements of the motorcade come through our tiny alleyway. Motorcycles, black sedans, an ambulance, more cycles, and then the Cadillac Fleetwood with the small American flag flying at the right front. It rolled past our entrance. Before I could accuse Liz of giving the wrong address, another set of motorcycles, sedans and another ambulance came along, then the bona fide presidential limousine came to a stop (the decoy carried the president's doctor and is known as the "toast" car, as in what it would be if the worst happened). Neighbors were watching discreetly as the president and First Lady stepped into the sunlight and walked toward us. Liz, with her beautiful manners, found it unseemly to remain inside and have the Reagans approach an unwelcoming front door. She stepped out to the landing and I followed. As they neared the front steps smiling, he in a blue suit with his head cocked to the side, she in a blue silk summer dress with a jacket, the lead agent moved in front of them. Had Liz and I not retreated we would have been steamrollered. The Reagans entered and we exchanged warm greetings. It seemed like they came to have a good time.

Liz and George welcome the Reagans at Avon Lane. June 2, 1986.

"Five Tonys!" exclaimed the president to John Guare (whom he had never met), as he stepped onto the porch, lifting the spirits of all. He and Nancy were happy to see their Bel Air neighbor Andy Williams, and Heston, his fellow former Screen Actors Guild president. Reagan sipped a glass of Tang provided by the White House and talked about movies, leading Adele Chatfield Taylor to say, "Mr. President, can you tell us how fights are staged?" He seemed pleased. "Chuck, you say, 'Ugghh' when I throw a punch and Mr. Guare you make a loud clap." He then turned to Adele, the subject-to-be of the blow, asking her to toss her head back when he threw a simulated punch, to give the appearance of it landing. He kept directing Heston and Guare until they succeeded in synchronizing their claps and "Ugghhs." The result was one of the more unusual photos ever captured by a White House photographer.

A white tablecloth and spring bouquet from our garden adorned the round table in the dining room. Conversation was halting at first and I was feeling a sense of unease, but then Guare, effervescent, and sitting higher than the rest of us at six foot four, spoke to the table.

"Isn't it wonderful that George and Liz brought us all together," he proclaimed. "Isn't this lovely?" Nancy looked to him wide-eyed, then smiled, and we were off to the conversational races. John told Nancy that his uncle, Billy Grady, was in the casting department at MGM when she was starting out (not mentioning that his uncle was part of the red-baiting clique with Adolphe Menjou and Ward Bond), and they got along like a house on fire. Reagan talked to

Cradling his Tang in his left hand, the Gipper tosses a punch. Left to right: Ronald Reagan, Charlton Heston, Adele Chatfield Taylor, David Stevens (partially hidden), George and John Guare.

Liz about her garden, and she with him about his ranch, but then she asked which president he most admired and we had a disquisition on Calvin Coolidge. He said he had read a lot about "Silent Cal" and felt he was underrated. He and Coolidge shared a belief that small government (which Reagan pronounced dismissively with the "r" silent) would assure industrial productivity and prosperity. He said his own firing of the air traffic controllers, a defining act of his presidency, was inspired by Coolidge's tough stance on striking Boston policemen. I quickly asked Andy about his concert tour and he told a hilarious story of locking himself naked out of his hotel room (don't ask).

We enjoyed a champagne toast and after dinner spent half an hour talking in the living room, then the Reagans said their goodbyes and walked to the motorcade, waving to the neighbors. They were off on the ten-minute ride to 1600 Pennsylvania Avenue and would be in bed before ten.

Looking back from the tribal Washington of the twenty-first century makes me long for evenings where people of different beliefs enjoyed one another's company without a hint of conflict.

The 1988 Kennedy Center Honors was the last of the Reagan era. Ten days after the telecast a distinctive blue envelope arrived at Avon Lane. Following the events of November 1963, Jackie Kennedy had chosen to avoid public life in Washington and never attended the Honors. I often wondered whether she watched the show on CBS. Her handwritten letter answered the question.

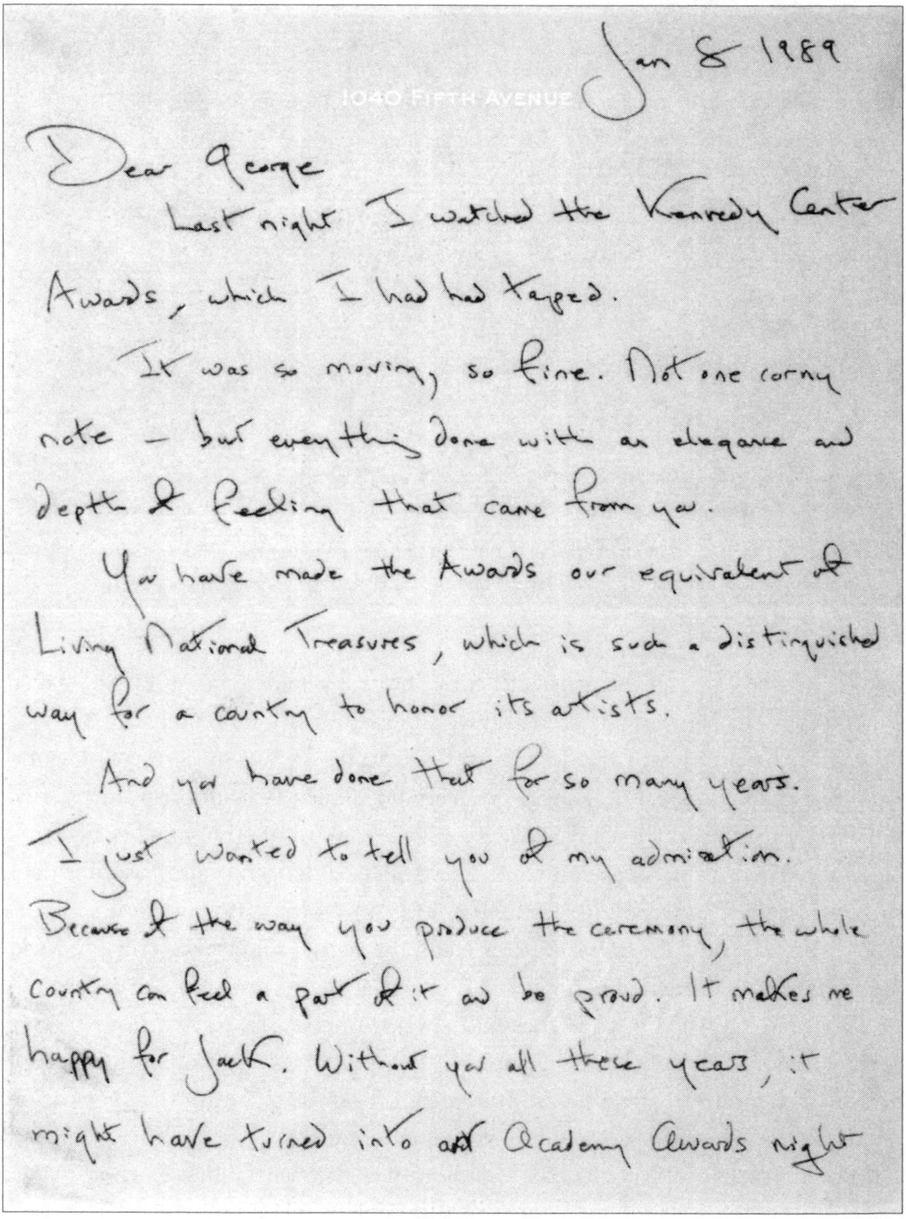

Jan 8 1989

1040 FIFTH AVENUE

Dear George

Last night I watched the Kennedy Center Awards, which I had had taped.

It was so moving, so fine. Not one corny note — but everything done with an elegance and depth of feeling that came from you.

You have made the Awards our equivalent of Living National Treasures, which is such a distinguished way for a country to honor its artists.

And you have done that for so many years. I just wanted to tell you of my admiration. Because of the way you produce the ceremony, the whole country can feel a part of it and be proud. It makes me happy for Jack. Without you all these years, it might have turned into an Academy Awards night

And I saw your film about your father.
How proud he would be of you. What a magnificent
thing to have done for him, for everyone —

All my happy new Year wishes and love to
you and Lizzie —

Jackie

Letter from Jacqueline Kennedy. January 8, 1989.

January 8, 1989

Dear George,

Last night I watched the Kennedy Center Awards, which I had had taped.

It was so moving, so fine. Not one corny note—but everything done with an elegance and depth of feeling that came from you.

You have made the Awards an equivalent of Living National Treasures, which is such a distinguished way for a country to honor its artists. And you have done that for so many years. I just wanted to tell you of my admiration. Because of the way you produce the ceremony, the whole country can feel a part of it and be proud. It makes me happy for Jack. Without you all these years, it might have turned into an Academy Awards night.

And I saw your film about your father. How proud he would be of you. What a magnificent thing to have done for him, for everyone.

All my happy new year wishes and love to you and Lizzie.

Jackie

62

Telling a Story

Ｈow do you get a movie made?" is an oft-asked question. Or "How do you sell a story to television?" The answer then and now is, "It ain't easy."

David Lean once told me that the hardest part of making a movie is finding a story you fall in love with. I had set my heart on filming Edmund Morris's Pulitzer Prize–winning biography of Theodore Roosevelt's early years, when as a young politician he returned from Albany to his house in New York and found that his mother and young wife had died the same night. This led to young Theodore going west and making himself into a man of the outdoors. Unfortunately Morris had sold the rights to a novice New York filmmaker for $25,000 on terms that gave him perpetual control of the property. After a year of fruitless attempts to work with him or to acquire it, I gave up. It has never been filmed. I would do it tomorrow if I could.

Billy Hale, my air force colleague and traveling companion to Cuba, had become a successful television director and told me about an historic 1915 trial that was known in legal circles as the American Dreyfus case. A thirteen-year-old girl named Mary Phagan was murdered in a Georgia pencil factory, and Leo Frank, the New York–born Jewish manager of the factory, was tried and convicted of the crime, and later lynched. It was a fascinating story with compelling twists. In April of 1982 I presented it to Perry Lafferty at NBC.

"Let's get a script," he said.

"Oh, this is easy," I thought.

NBC provided $60,000 to finance a screenplay for a two-hour movie and placed a young executive, Allen Sabinson, in charge. Billy and I did comprehensive research of court records and newspapers; then I asked my novelist neighbor Larry McMurtry to write the screenplay.

By the time we delivered the script early in 1983 there was an executive over Sabinson named Steve White. NBC asked for revisions, which we gave them in

June, then awaited approval to start production. Steve White called on July 13. "NBC is going to pass on the Leo Frank story," he said cheerlessly. "We need contemporary stories—we're making a movie about Yoko Ono."

"We owe you one" was Steve White's puzzling greeting when he called two years later in July of 1985. "We have decided to contract with another producer for a four-hour movie on Leo Frank." He explained that Orion Pictures had made a "pitch" on the Leo Frank story and NBC preferred their approach. White's solution was to offer me a deal to develop another project—a way of buying us off that would waste more of our time.

Networks have layers of program executives in whom I have found two common qualities: they lack storytelling skills and are afraid of being fired. White's position was brazen. We had brought them the idea, contracted for and delivered a screenplay that they decided wasn't timely. They send us away and two years later decide to make the same story with another producer. I called Brandon Tartikoff, the reigning head of the network, who did not return my calls.

Grant Tinker, producer of the *Mary Tyler Moore* show and other hits, had been named chairman of NBC. It was rare for a creative producer to hold such a job. It occurred to me to appeal to him but I hesitated because we had *Christmas in Washington* at NBC and going over Tartikoff's head was known to be hazardous. But I couldn't sit back in silence, so I called Tinker's office and was given an appointment in New York at NBC's Rockefeller Center headquarters. It was the busy week of the Kennedy Center Honors but I couldn't be choosey. "I've come for advice," I began, and proceeded to recite the chronology, concluding, "NBC now plans to produce our idea with Orion Television." My presentation had been earnest and complex. His response was relaxed and simple. "I don't know all of the nuances here," he said, "but I would think we'd want someone with your reputation for quality producing the movie." I didn't know where he was headed but his words of respect meant the world to me.

"Why don't you state your case in a letter to Brandon Tartikoff," he said. "You can copy me."

I found time between Honors chores to write a four-page letter to Tartikoff. Letter writing was becoming one of my weapons.

I brought the Leo Frank story to NBC along with a highly talented creative team. We developed a screenplay which NBC chose not to put into production in 1983 because the story was viewed by management as untimely. In 1985 it is viewed, once again, as timely. We believe, and I hope you agree, that legally and ethically NBC's obligation must be to the party that brought you this story and developed it in the first instance. Since I've had a conversation about this with Grant, I am sending him a copy.

I returned to producing the *Honors* for CBS, wondering what kind of firestorm I may have unleashed at NBC and if I might be the one incinerated.

A week later, on December 11, 1985—three and a half years since my initial meeting with NBC—Steve White was on the phone. "I want you to know we've had a change of thinking," he said. "We would like you to produce the Leo Frank story as a four-hour miniseries."

So, how do you sell a movie to television? I suggest patience and thick skin. If I had been a producer with the Leo Frank story as my only project I would have starved. I suspect Grant Tinker never said a word to anyone. My letter to Brandon with his name at the bottom was all it took.

New Liberty Productions joined forces with Orion Television, previously our competitor, who provided completion financing. I served as producer-writer and Billy Hale was the director. Orion proved to be a good partner. The expansion to four hours gave us the time to tell a more complete story and aspire to make a distinguished film. I suggested to Jeffrey Lane, a gifted young man with whom I had been cowriting AFI shows, that we collaborate on the expanded screenplay, using the solid foundation created by McMurtry, who was by then busy writing *Terms of Endearment.*

We called it *The Ballad of Mary Phagan.* The story of a man who is lynched by the Ku Klux Klan may seem a dreary topic, but we saw the governor of Georgia, John M. Slaton, as the protagonist. He was a favorite to run for the US Senate and touted as a prospect for the White House. A problematic trial led to Leo Frank being convicted of murder by a jury and sentenced to hang. Governor Slaton initiated an investigation. Convinced of Frank's innocence, he pardoned him, inciting outrage in Georgia and sacrificing his political future.

I hoped to persuade a movie star to play Slaton and sent the script to Jimmy Stewart, who I felt would be compelling as the conscience-driven governor. I went to see him and had the only uncomfortable moment in my years of knowing him. "Why would I want to do this?" he asked, seeming annoyed. I should have anticipated that the role wouldn't align with Jimmy's conservative views. Hale and I reviewed NBC's list of prospects at breakfast, none of which excited us. I had a date to play golf at Hillcrest with Jack Lemmon. "Could you see Jack Lemmon in this part?" I asked. "He would be amazing," said Billy, "but like most movie stars he won't do television. Agents tell them it will ruin their careers."

I was walking alongside Jack late in our round. "I have a script with a wonderful role, a man who does the right thing at a time of moral crisis," I said. "We think we can make a great film but it's for television. Will you read it?" "Sure kid," he

On the set with Robert Prosky, who played populist Georgia senator Tom Watson, and Jack Lemmon, Governor John Slaton, in *The Murder of Mary Phagan,* 1987.

said in his agreeable manner. "Send it up to the house." Six nights later I was sitting at home in Washington when the phone rang. "You wrote a helluva script and that's a helluva part," said the unmistakable voice. "Now, you're gonna have to deal with Lenny Hirshon," he said referring to his agent. "Lenny's an asshole, but he's my asshole. He'll tell you I don't do television, but you have to press him."

NBC was delighted to have a two-time Oscar winner and they paid Jack a million dollars, a new high for television. He was about to do O'Neill's *Long Day's Journey into Night* on the stage in pre-Broadway previews at Duke University, where my son Michael was now a student, and then at the Kennedy Center.

Michael and I went to see *Long Day's Journey* at Duke. Peter Gallagher, playing the elder son, Edmund Tyrone, was a good prospect for Leo Frank. I still recall the entrance from stage right of the actor playing the younger brother Jamie Tyrone. There was a stage presence and mysteriousness conveyed just by his movement that took my breath away. It was Kevin Spacey in one of his first roles. We cast Peter as Leo and Kevin, just twenty-six, as a jaded reporter in his forties. We rounded out a sparkling cast in New York with new actors who would go on to important careers, including fourteen-year-old Cynthia Nixon (one day a candidate for mayor of New York), Charles M. Dutton, Dylan Baker, William H. Macy and Rebecca Miller, daughter of Arthur Miller and Inge Morath, in her screen debut.

We decided to shoot the entire picture in Richmond, Virginia, and assembled an outstanding team, including my daughter Caroline as a resourceful and well-organized associate producer. Production designer Penny Hadfield created imaginative sets that matched the Georgia settings we required, making use of Virginia's historic state capitol and the governor's mansion. I asked a director friend of mine about Nic Knowland, a cinematographer from England who had been recommended. "He's Storaro without the baggage," he said, referring to my brilliant friend from *Apocalypse Now* and his posse of family members. Nick lit the scenes, operated the camera himself, and provided a look that was at once elegant and authentic.

When we began shooting in May we had one imperative. Screen Actors Guild negotiations were under way so we had a hard deadline to complete all shooting before a likely strike on July 1. We had a productive first six weeks, then one afternoon I was standing at the back of the set where Lemmon, as Governor Slaton, was questioning two witnesses. After a take I hear Billy Hale's deep baritone, in the presence of cast and crew: "Please don't give me any more of that Jack Lemmon stuff." He was addressing our star, a disciplined performer, a gentleman and my good friend, who had accepted Billy on my word. They did another take and Hale, now aware of my presence, printed it without further comment.

It was an early hint of a growing crisis. Apparently Billy, whose wife and two infant children were with him on location, had, unknown to me, suffered from depression and was taking medicine for a bipolar condition. Or, more to the point, he had stopped taking it. A couple of days later he was directing a crowd scene on a street with a bullhorn. "If we can arrange for the producer to leave the set," he announced, "I will be able to shoot this scene." He repeated it, then went to his trailer. I had known Bill for twenty years. He had spent Christmases at our house; I was his friend and ally. In order not to waste a day with a hundred extras on the set, I quietly drifted away. The next day Billy strode over to Caroline Stevens. "You're the associate producer. Will you see to it that your father leaves the set." Disturbing episodes became more frequent and Lemmon's concern grew. He frequently had to remind Hale of key shots that were required. Billy's behavior became more erratic and NBC raised questions from Burbank about missing coverage. We knew we had to make a change, but because of the SAG deadline there was no time to stop and take even a day to regroup.

Facing a July first train wreck, I was distressed about disappointing people who had put their trust in us. The company was shooting at night in the Virginia State Capitol, and I was pacing in the basement near a pay phone when it rang. Daniel Petrie—a respected director who I had met when he volunteered at AFI—was returning my call. "What are you doing in Virginia?" he asked. "I'm shooting a movie," I replied, summarizing the story and describing our cast. Dan interspersed, "Oh, Jack's great," "Rebecca Miller is so interesting," before asking how it was going. "Dan," I replied, "not as well as we hoped." I explained that we had a talented and dedicated team that needed help. "I hope you will read the script and join us the day after tomorrow." A day later after work the president of Orion Pictures and I assumed the unpleasant task of advising Billy Hale he was being replaced. Petrie took over and led the cast and crew skillfully through the final three weeks. We finished on schedule. The breach with Hale never healed.

Normally the director and editor shape a first cut, but in Hale's absence I worked with our editor John Martinelli. Toni Vellani agreed to pitch in and Caroline was a steady presence. Our task was to edit two two-hour movies that would be shown on consecutive nights. By the time we completed a fine cut I realized our story would fill five hours. Brandon Tartikoff agreed, though he thought the title was "soft" and believed he could advertise it more effectively with the more lurid title *The Murder of Mary Phagan*. Brandon had given me free rein in the editing and an extra hour of air time. Appreciative of his trust, I agreed.

Mary Phagan needed a vibrant score. I had recently seen David Lean's *A Passage to India,* for which Frenchman Maurice Jarre won an Oscar (to accompany two others for *Lawrence of Arabia* and *Doctor Zhivago*). I didn't know Jarre but I reached him by phone in Malibu and told him the story. He was surprised when I explained it was for television, but he agreed to look at the film. Three days later we sat together in his house spotting *Mary Phagan*. Unlike some composers who want music in every scene, Maurice required justification for its every use, and two weeks later he played two marvelous themes on his piano—not the sweeping majesty of his movie scores but a leaner style that was both poignant and stirring. Jarre's music lifted our story and to this day I am moved by his artistry and generosity of spirit.

The miniseries was shown over two nights in January 1988, nearly six years from the day I proposed the idea to Perry Lafferty. It attracted a huge audience for NBC. "*The Murder of Mary Phagan* is exactly what television should do more of—history with nuance, the sociology of culture," said the heading above John Leonard's review in *New York* magazine. It is "uncommonly scrupulous and affecting," he wrote, calling Jack Lemmon perfect as John Slaton. *Newsday* called it a masterpiece, but especially pleasing was the *Christian Science Monitor*: "*The Murder of Mary Phagan* is not merely entertainment television at its best: it is contemporary cinema at its best."

It received five Emmy nominations, including ones for Outstanding Miniseries, and for Lemmon for best actor. Liz and I went with Jack and Felicia to the ceremonies where Jack lost out to Jason Robards in *Inherit the Wind*. I felt bad for Jack—but he did have Oscars at home to keep him company. *The Murder of Mary Phagan* won as Outstanding Miniseries and I accepted the Emmy. It was a resounding tribute to our great cast and production team and a splendid reward for years of patience.

We dodged the big party afterward. Jack took Felicia, Liz and me for a quiet celebration dinner at Chasen's. It was a joy to be with this dear and modest friend, a major star who said yes to scripts about ideas, and in this case took a chance on television.

63

Paris

I took a break from editing *Mary Phagan* to fly to Paris with Liz to join friends for the one-hundredth anniversary celebration of the *International Herald Tribune* in October of 1987, hosted by its joint owners the *New York Times* and the *Washington Post*. It started with a festive Thursday night dinner at Versailles, where it seemed as if most of my friends had gathered. The French government had decided to present me with the Légion d'honneur at a Friday morning ceremony at the Ministry of Culture. We were joined by Ethel Kennedy, Nicole Salinger, Arthur and Alexandra Schlesinger, and Art Buchwald, known as America's most famous expatriate when he was Paris humorist for the *Herald Tribune*. Minister of Culture Jack Lang draped the French laurel around my neck, while Buchwald made certain I couldn't take myself too seriously.

Both Michael and David at different times worked as interns at the *Herald Tribune* with the encouragement and assistance of Sydney Gruson, the fabled *Times* foreign correspondent who later supervised the international edition. Sydney became a wonderful friend and golf buddy. He insisted I bring my clubs to Paris so he could take me to the famous Saint-Cloud Golf Club. On Friday afternoon he got word we couldn't play Saint-Cloud because of a tournament. He was furious and pledged he would find me a golf game. I said not to worry, but Sydney was famously persistent.

That night Liz and I took the Buchwalds, the Bradlees and Gruson for a spirited feast at Chez Ami Louis. Late in the meal Gruson announced his solution. "Guy de Rothschild has invited us to play at Ferrières." Buchwald shot back. "Tomorrow is Yom Kippur. Guy will not be playing golf on our holiest day."

The next morning Sydney and I climbed in a sedan in front of the Ritz and rode east for a spell before turning onto a winding private road and suddenly coming upon Baron Guy de Rothschild's small private course. It had three greens that could be played from different teeing grounds to provide a nine-hole experience. We put our bags on two pull carts and teed off in a serene gray fog. At the third tee a man approached in a khaki jacket and trousers with a light golf bag on his shoulder. "Guy!" Sydney called out. Their greetings suggested a fond friendship. Guy, a war hero, sportsman, champion amateur golfer and patriarch of the Rothschild banking dynasty, joined us for six holes of light conversation and relaxed play. He had donated the celebrated Ferrières Chateau to the French government, and built for himself in the forest an unpretentious chalet with a wood-shingled roof and plantation shutters, where he offered us baguettes, cheese, sausages and an exemplary Chateau Lafitte Rothschild. During lunch we discussed World War II in which Guy had earned the Croix de Guerre, so later I sent him an inscribed copy of *Victory in Europe,* a book composed of color photos from my father's World War II footage.

We saw Buchwald that evening and I recounted our day. "Guy de Rothschild did not play golf on Yom Kippur!" he said emphatically. The topic was becoming contentious so we decided to agree to disagree. At home in Washington I received a warm thank-you note for the book: "How very kind of you indeed. I very much enjoyed our 'clandestine' round of golf. Very Sincerely, Guy."

I had Baron de Rothschild's letter framed and sent it to Buchwald saying, "Documentation is not normally required between friends, but I want you to have this."

"Dear George," began Art's gracious reply. "I don't want this junk in my office."

64

Separate but Equal

I clipped an opinion piece from the *Washington Star* entitled "25 Years after Brown" which quoted historian J. Harvie Wilkinson III on the 1954 Supreme Court decision on *Brown v. Board of Education*: "Brown may be the most important political, social, and legal event in America's twentieth-century history. Its greatness lay in the enormity of injustice it condemned . . . in the intensity of the law it both created and overthrew. The story of Brown is the story of revolution."

My choice of material for films had long been shaped by my experience in Washington. Two of our most effective USIA films were *The March* and *Nine from Little Rock,* and here was an opportunity to explore social justice on a larger canvas. After investigating Thurgood Marshall's role in challenging the 1896 *Plessy v. Ferguson* decision that made segregation legal in America, I outlined a narrative centered on one of the five cases that made up *Brown v. Board.* In South Carolina, Harry Briggs, Jr., the son of an auto mechanic, was forced to walk five miles to school on dusty roads because white school administrators refused to provide a bus for the Scotts Branch School. Reverend J. A. Delaine, who taught the Negro children in the one-room schoolhouse, agreed to work with Marshall to bring the case—*Briggs v. Elliot*—that climaxed with the argument in the Supreme Court between Marshall and the man known as the "lawyer's lawyer," John W. Davis.

I went to see William Self, an erudite CBS executive. "That's a terrific story," he said, "but you have one major problem."

"And what is that?" I asked.

"Who can play Thurgood Marshall and attract an audience for two nights of commercial television?"

"Sidney Poitier could certainly do it."

"We've gone to Sidney for twenty years," Self said with a knowing smile. "He doesn't do television." Seeing my disappointment, he added, "If you come to us with assurance that Sidney will read a script, we will pay for it."

Two days later Sidney Poitier showed me into his large and comfortable living room at his house on Cove Way in Beverly Hills and listened as I described my plan to make a miniseries recounting Thurgood Marshall's quest to end legal segregation. I told him the story before saying, "I know you're reluctant to do television, but in order to dramatize this complex history we need the four hours television can provide." Sidney sat straight on his sofa, silent, organizing his thoughts. "I do not . . . I have not done television," he said deliberately. "Because it is you, and because Thurgood Marshall means a great deal to me, if a powerful script comes to me I would want to do it."

Sidney's clarity was magnetic, and I was stirred driving down to the Beverly Hills Hotel—determined to pursue this, knowing that I was sentencing myself to write a screenplay, the value of which would depend entirely on one man's opinion.

A Writer's Guild strike went into effect during which members were permitted to write their own projects so long as they were not connected to a studio or network. Had I gone back to CBS and taken a fee for writing, I wouldn't be able to begin until the strike ended. Moreover, by writing it on "spec" I would control the project and avoid debilitating "development" memos from network executives. Like "the crazy man" Orson Welles, I was once again spending what I earned on other shows to do this one. I hired my daughter Caroline and a young scholar, Julie Goetz, to research court records and press reports and interview participants in the case.

I had become friends with the lawyer and civil rights leader Vernon Jordan. He became my rabbi on the project, introducing me to civil rights pioneers who worked on the *Brown* case. I sat with historian John Hope Franklin on his porch in North Carolina; listened to the powerful voice of Constance Baker Motley, now a judge, in her New York chambers; and heard William Coleman, who planned strategy for Marshall and went on to become secretary of transportation for Gerald Ford, emphasize, "These weren't the smartest *Black* lawyers in America, these were the smartest lawyers in America."

The *Plessy* decision stated that segregated public facilities, including public schools, were lawful, so long as the segregated facilities were equal. This established the "separate but equal" doctrine that provided the title for our film. I rose early every morning for three months to write a narrative that I hoped would be true to history and engage an audience.

At year's end I sent a screenplay to Sidney.

"You wrote this?" he said on the phone a week later. "You really are into this, aren't you?"

"Yes," I replied. "I hope you will be too."

"I want to do it. There are a few complications. Marty Baum will call you."

"You must've written a hell of a script," said Baum the next day. He had been Poitier's agent since *Blackboard Jungle*. "I've never been able to get him to do television but he wants to do this. He has a Bill Cosby film to direct first, so you'll have to wait a year."

The mills of the gods grind slowly. Once again, patience was called for.

I flew to Detroit to present the project to executives at General Motors who supported *The Kennedy Center Honors* with its Mark of Excellence campaign. They loved the screenplay and agreed to be sole sponsor of the miniseries. I intended to direct *Separate But Equal* and knew that network executives would favor a more established director, but Sidney's confidence in me and the backing of General Motors meant there was no pushback. We made a deal at ABC, and the revolving doors of network television meant that Allen Sabinson, the original executive on *Mary Phagan*, was our liaison. I hired television veteran Stan Margulies to serve as co-executive producer.

I had tried without success to discuss the project with Thurgood Marshall, now sitting as an associate justice on the Supreme Court. This was now a problem because ABC was concerned about proceeding without his consent. Liz and I were invited to dinner at a friend's house where I met eighty-six-year-old Justice William Brennan, an Irish Catholic with twinkling eyes, known for his progressive decisions. After dinner I mentioned the film. "I'm so glad to hear that," he said. "Thurgood doesn't appreciate the enormous change he's brought. A good film will lift his spirits." I pondered the justice's comments overnight and placed a call to him at the court the next morning.

"Mr. Justice," I said, "I have been unable to get a response to my project from Justice Marshall and would prefer to proceed with his consent. Sidney Poitier will play him, and we plan to start shooting in eight weeks."

"Here's what I would do," Brennan said. "Send the script to his chambers by messenger and let's see how he responds."

"I worry, Mr. Justice, that if I send the script and hear nothing, we will be stalled."

There was a long silence, a judicial mind at work. "Mr. Stevens, why don't you just go ahead and make your film."

And that's what I decided to do. I wrote to Justice Marshall informing him that Sidney Poitier was going to portray him and would appreciate the opportunity to meet him. Soon thereafter Thurgood Marshall invited Sidney to what proved to be a harmonious lunch at the Georgetown Club.

There were seventy-seven speaking parts in *Separate But Equal* and New York casting director, Alixe Gordin, was so effective that she received a special prime-time Emmy for her work. Richard Kiley brought strength and humanity to the crucial role of Chief Justice Earl Warren. New York actors with little fame but great gifts filled the other parts. John W. Davis, described as a man "whose sturdy figure seemed to personify the spirit of constitutionalism," was the hardest to cast. Davis had been the Democratic nominee for president in 1924 and argued more cases before the Supreme Court than any other lawyer. I felt an unknown actor, however skilled, matched against Sidney, an iconic star, would lead audiences to assume Sidney would prevail. Two weeks before we started shooting I wrote to Burt Lancaster.

"Burt read your script," his agent advised me four days later. "He understands John W. Davis and wants to be part of this." Burt saw this as an important story of justice and accepted what for him was a modest fee. His star quality opposite Poitier took our film to another level. The last part to cast was Julia Davis, the daughter of John W. Davis, who urged her father not to take the *Brown* case. My Liz's grandfather had been Davis' law partner and she arranged for Caroline to interview Julia Davis Adams, then ninety, who gave us priceless insights. Hallie Foote, daughter of writer Horton Foote, played Julia.

I brought back Nic Knowland as cinematographer and Penny Hadfield as production designer based on their outstanding work on *Mary Phagan.* They shaped a visual framework ranging from the bare-bones Legal Defense Fund offices in New York to South Carolina's actual federal courthouse. I knew that a realistic Supreme Court set—the site for *Separate But Equal*'s "chariot race"—was pivotal to telling the story, but its cost exceeded our budget and ABC was unwilling to provide the additional $440,000. When I arrived in South Carolina in late July to start shooting I repeated my plea to Allen Sabinson, to no avail.

Vernon Jordan called to check in on a rainy Friday afternoon. We had a long talk during which I mentioned my dilemma. We signed off and an hour later Vernon called back.

"Dan Burke [president of Capital Cities/ABC] is driving to Maine for the weekend," Vernon said. "He promised he would call you from a pay phone between four and five o'clock."

Unselfish helpfulness, I would learn during a thirty-year friendship, was Vernon's DNA. Once again I was violating the rules by going over the heads of Sabinson and his boss Bob Iger.

"George Stevens?" the voice on the phone said after I picked it up on the first ring. "This is Dan Burke."

I thanked him for taking time to call me, described our aspirations for a miniseries of consequence, and explained that scenes in the Supreme Court were crucial. "Mr. Burke," I said, "I expect we'll have a premiere of *Separate But Equal* next year at the Kennedy Center, and that Justice Marshall and his colleagues will be present. I'm hoping ABC will provide an additional $400,000 so that the Supreme Court will look like the Supreme Court when you see it at the Kennedy Center." I pictured the head of Capital Cities/ABC standing in a phone booth in the rain.

"Your project is important to ABC, but I'll have to speak with my colleagues in Los Angeles," he said over the traffic noise. "I tend to leave these matters in their hands."

At noon on Monday Allen Sabinson was on the phone from Hollywood. "George, we've done some digging on our end. We found money for the Supreme Court set."

We began shooting at the one-room wooden schoolhouse—they were called "doghouse schools"—that Penny Hadfield erected beside a dusty road outside Summerton, South Carolina. The tiny structure, with its American flag on the wall and authentic cast of schoolchildren, set us on a sound path. Knowland's muted color photography gave scenes the feeling of real events. We shot the scene of Harry Briggs, Jr., trudging away from school as a yellow school bus passes, obscuring him in dust. Sidney did his first scene at night in Reverend Delaine's small church where he starts the wheels of justice turning. "What happened to Harry Briggs happens everywhere we go," he said to the members of the parish. "If there are twenty people here in Summerton who are willing to sign a complaint against the school board, we will take your case to the Supreme Court."

Our partner, Republic Pictures, imposed a penalty clause which meant I was financially responsible for cost overruns, adding to the day-to-day pressure I felt trying to keep on schedule while seeking a high-quality result. I hadn't directed actors on a movie set since my work on *Alfred Hitchcock Presents* thirty years earlier, but was enjoying the process and the cast appeared to have confidence in me. We moved to the set for the Legal Defense Fund offices. In the first scene Thurgood returns to New York late at night from South Carolina and finds his colleagues with drinks, playing poker. He sits in. Sidney was playing the scene a little broad, looking for humor. I hadn't seen the comedies he made with Bill Cosby—my frame of reference was his quiet restraint in *The Defiant*

Ones and *In the Heat of the Night,* so I took Sidney aside and we ended up in a dark equipment room.

"Sidney, I'm not sure we have the right tone yet in this scene."

There was silence, his luminous dark eyes focused on mine. "Why don't you just tell me what you want," he said.

It seemed like a minute passed. I felt my relationship with the actor cracking. "I think of Thurgood Marshall as a man with secrets," I said.

Another silence, then Sidney ended the conversation. "When that is what you want, just say that word. And that is what you will get."

Sidney and I went back to work—and from that moment on it was smooth sailing. My occasional requests for "secrets" brought Sidney's moral authority to the screen.

Burt Lancaster, long devoted to progressive causes, took the role of John W. Davis even though his character was arguing to retain segregated schools. Now seventy-eight with white hair, Burt retained his formidable persona. I was in my fifties but Burt had known me years before as a young guy in Hollywood, so he would respond mischievously to my direction. "If that is what pleases our young director," he would say, "I'll try it." Burt had a reputation for being difficult and was having trouble remembering his lines. There were explosions of Irish fury whenever he faltered in a scene. "I used to stay out all night," he told me in frustration after a difficult scene. "The script girl would hand me four pages in the makeup chair and I'd know my lines in thirty minutes." The Supreme Court speeches were lengthy and demanded accuracy, so remembering Jack Webb's technique on *Dragnet* I cautiously suggested we employ a teleprompter, an idea that Burt embraced. Sidney was fine with whatever helped his costar, but was no fan of the device. Burt, making deft use of the monitors, was vigorous and affecting in his Supreme Court argument. The next morning Sidney whispered, "Can we put my stuff on those screens?"

Separate But Equal was Burt's last performance. He was a warm and witty man behind all that strength, and I remember him for his great heart and talent.

The United States Supreme Court that Penny Hadfield designed provided an august setting for the climax of the film. The courtroom, offices, conference rooms and hallways were stately and the fine actors playing the nine justices were distinct from one another, giving power and clarity to the drama of Richard Kiley, as Chief Justice Warren, working to unite the court for a unanimous verdict to overturn *Plessy.*

The world premiere of *Separate But Equal*—the showing I described to Dan Burke when pleading for money—took place at the AFI Theater in the Kennedy

Justice Thurgood Marshall, seated front right. Left to right: Richard Kiley, who portrayed Chief Justice Earl Warren, Sidney Poitier, Tom Murphy of ABC and Stevens, at Kennedy Center premiere of *Separate But Equal,* 1991.

Center. Burke was there with Capital Cities/ABC CEO Tom Murphy. After invitations were mailed we waited anxiously for a response from Thurgood Marshall. One morning his wife Cissy called saying the justice would attend and asking if they could bring nine people. Justices Brennan, David Souter, and Sandra Day O'Connor also came, along with civil rights leaders, and ninety-three-year-old Julia Davis, daughter of John W. Davis.

The film, running three hours and eleven minutes, played beautifully on the big screen. Thurgood sat in the front row and enjoyed the prolonged applause at the end. At supper upstairs word circulated that he was pleased. People were touched when he and Sidney embraced. "You were better than I was," the justice said, "but you also made more money." I was beckoned over at one point and kneeled beside his formidable frame. "Whiskey! Cards!" Marshall thundered, referring to the poker scene in the Legal Defense Fund office. "Yes, sir," I said meekly. "Never at the office!" he said.

ABC drew a huge audience on Sunday and Monday, April 7th and 8th, and scores of letters came to our office. I especially appreciated this from one of America's foremost historians, David McCullough.

> I find this morning that I am still thinking about the past two nights
> that you've given the country. *Separate But Equal* was superb—
> powerful, intelligent, and beautifully filmed and performed, an
> important event for everyone who saw it. You have made a magnificent
> film and I can't let the day go by without writing to say so.

"For once, commercial television has lived up to its mighty potential to define and enrich our national heritage," said the *Washington Post.* And from the *Wall Street Journal,* "This film is that rare thing—a drama about race relations not given to caricature or homily."

Stan Margulies and I accepted Emmys for the year's Outstanding Miniseries. But the icing on the cake for this long journey was a report from a friend that Thurgood Marshall was seen in his chambers at the court hunched over two Betamax video recorders, making a copy of the videocassette we had sent over— for him a rare flirtation with lawlessness.

65

George and Barbara

Liz and I knew and liked George H. W. and Barbara Bush. Arriving at the White House as America's forty-first president and First Lady, they enthusiastically adopted *The Kennedy Center Honors* and *Christmas in Washington* traditions. Barbara could be warm as well as crusty, and George was open and engaging.

The Bushes were especially enthusiastic when they presided at *Christmas in Washington,* arriving at the festively decorated National Building Museum with their children and grandchildren. Barbara was an ardent supporter of Children's Hospital, going there to read to the patients and deliver presents that concert guests brought for them. She invited performers back to the White House for supper and caroling after the shows—Diahann Carroll, Vic Damone, Olivia Newton John, Reba McEntire, John Denver and James Galway among them. In 1990 Aretha Franklin, encouraged by President Bush, memorably sat down at the Steinway grand piano in the East Room and played and sang Christmas music to her heart's—and our hearts'—content.

Harry Belafonte was recognized at the Honors in 1989, the Bushes' first year, for his extraordinary musical career, which also encompassed his lifelong commitment to human rights. Harry was a friend who hosted our AFI Life Achievement Award to Sidney Poitier, and Sidney paid homage to Harry at the Honors, harking back to their first meeting as young men in a cramped storage area of the American Negro Theater. "I am glad to have made that journey with such a man, such an artist, such an activist, such a father, such a friend," he said. "Harry B, my old young friend," he added as their eyes met. "I am proud to see you honored by your country—which speaks volumes for you and volumes for your beloved country."

Walter Cronkite's mix of gravitas and warmth marked the next introduction. "Ladies and gentlemen, he arrived just hours ago after a long journey from

Aretha Franklin playing the Steinway grand piano that was given to President Franklin Roosevelt in 1939. The gilded mahogany legs are carved as American eagles. From left, Barbara Bush, Reba McEntire. Center, Barbara Hendricks and Liz Stevens. December 9, 1990.

South Africa—the Archbishop of Cape Town, the Most Reverend, Desmond M. Tutu."

The small upright man in clerical collar, a purple vest beneath his pectoral cross, entered from upstage center and walked to the footlights. There had been Honors moments of unexpected elation when an unexpected star like Ray Charles or Robert Redford was announced, but the surprise and the awe and reverence for this man surpassed the others. The depth of feeling in Harry's eyes spoke to a story of determination and triumph.

"My friends, such as they are," said Archbishop Tutu with a benign smile, "won't believe that I came 10,000 miles and actually made a speech that lasted only two minutes. They will say the age of miracles has not ended." He looked to the Honor box. "What a privilege to be part of this glittering tribute to a truly great man. You have worked with a consistent zeal in your opposition to the madness of apartheid. And when the history—the true history—of South Africa is written, your name will appear in letters of gold. Harry, we salute you."

Each year members of the Artists Committee would send recommendations to guide the selection process. Katharine Hepburn, whose sense of privacy led her not to accept any of her four Oscars in person, annually led the list. The usually persuasive Roger Stevens spoke to her over two successive years without any luck, so we enlisted her close friend Garson Kanin to coax her. She was emphatic in relaying her lack of interest. One Sunday evening in August 1990, as we were wrapping up the selection process, I watched a television special that led me to call Miss Hepburn in New York.

"Every year your name is at the top of the list of suggested recipients for the Kennedy Center Honors," I said to her the next morning. "Artists come to the Honors and ask why have we never honored Katharine Hepburn, and we explain that you are a very private person and would be uncomfortable at an event like this."

"That's true," she interrupted. "I rarely even go out for dinner."

"Last night," I continued, "I was watching something on ABC called *Alexander Cohen's Night of a Hundred Stars II,* and who do I see striding across the stage of the Radio City Music Hall with the orchestra playing, but you, all in black. What will I say to those artists this year when they ask where you are?"

"Oh," she said, "you're a very fine young man and I loved your father, but you must understand that appearing at an event like yours would be just too painful."

I stressed that we would take care of her and make the Honors weekend a pleasing experience. Then, perhaps just to get me off the phone, she said, "I'm busy now, why don't you call me on Wednesday. But don't get your hopes up."

The conversation on Wednesday was much the same. Eventually, with some annoyance, she said, "You don't understand. It would be too much pressure, simply too difficult."

"Miss Hepburn," I said in a voice that felt like it was coming from another planet. "We've been reading for many years about that Yankee fiber of yours. Why don't you just summon some of that Yankee fiber and say yes?"

There was silence. Then she growled, "All right . . . Yes!" And hung up.

Kate turned out to be a captivating Honoree, appearing in good spirits at the various events. When the Honorees walked into the East Room she wore her trademark black turtleneck and a white scarf. I was sitting on the aisle so couldn't help but notice, peeking from beneath her black trousers, a pair of polished black Reeboks. After shaking hands with President Bush in the receiving line, the always candid Kate whispered to Barbara Bush, "How can you let him be against abortion?"

There was a prolonged ovation in the Opera House following the biographical film of her career that included scenes with Spencer Tracy, ending with *Guess Who's Coming to Dinner.* As the applause subsided she leaned toward the

Katharine Hepburn at 1990 Kennedy Center Honors. She was,
on that night, first among equals.

audience below, her bright blue eyes shining, her head shaking slightly, and became the only Honoree ever to speak from the box.

"I'd never seen that scene with Spence before," she said. "It was a privilege to work with such wonderful actors. I was very lucky."

George and Barbara Bush came to *Christmas in Washington* in 1992 with their daughter Doro and four grandchildren, just six weeks after losing a bruising election. They were in good spirits and invited Julie Andrews and Neil Diamond back to the White House, where President Bush took time to show us the rarely visited rooms in the family quarters upstairs, including the Lincoln Bedroom. Neil, Julie and Liz and I walked across the hall to the Queens' Bedroom where Churchill stayed when visiting Roosevelt during the war. The shades were down on the windows looking out to Pennsylvania Avenue. When Julie walked to the window President Bush noticed her interest and graciously lifted the shade.

KATHARINE HOUGHTON HEPBURN

XII - 4 - 1990

Dear George Stevens and Nick Vanoff -

Just a word of thanks for

your very sweet - generous - and

extravagant handling from the

ungracious, difficult, terrified

Creature that this particular

customer turned out to be -

Kate Hep

The last bit even
DREW a tear from
my cold eyes

Handwritten note: "The last bit even drew a tear from my cold eyes."

Looming on the White House front lawn were bleachers under construction for Bill Clinton's inaugural parade. After an uneasy moment the president smiled. "Dinner's on the table," he said, taking Julie's arm and leading us to the family dining room where we enjoyed his and Barbara's good company in one of their last nights in the White House.

66

The Man from Hope

Few anticipated that William Jefferson Clinton would be the Democratic Party's nominee for the president in 1992, but early favorites Senators Jay Rockefeller and Al Gore chose not to challenge George H. W. Bush, who was enjoying an 89 percent approval rating following the success of the 1991 Gulf War. Clinton saw his opening, captured the nomination, and with Gore as his running mate defeated Bush and ended a twelve-year reign of Republicans in the White House.

Bill Clinton tells the story of his having been elected governor of Arkansas in 1978 at the age of thirty-one and two years later being defeated for reelection, becoming, as he joked, the youngest former governor in history. He recalled walking the streets of Little Rock and seeing people cross over to avoid him, then one day receiving a call from an acquaintance in New York. "Fix some grits," said Vernon Jordan, "I'm coming for breakfast tomorrow." Vernon offered encouragement to the downcast Clinton and they became fast friends, and it was Vernon who during the campaign introduced me to his candidate. People running for president meet hundreds of new people every day, and the most one should expect is a smile and a perfunctory greeting. I remember shaking hands with the tall southerner and being immediately taken by his vitality and charm. The next time I saw Clinton was weeks later in Los Angeles at an event at power-broker Lew Wasserman's house. I was surprised when he called me by name before dazzling the group with his mastery of detail on policy questions. He was, at forty-six, a prodigious political talent.

Bill and Hillary Clinton's debut on the Washington scene two weeks after his election wasn't at the residence of a traditional Democratic hostess but at an energized and buoyant dinner at the house of Vernon and Ann Jordan. It was without question the most racially mixed gathering ever to welcome a new president to the nation's capital, and in time some would be calling Bill Clinton America's first Black president. He chose Vernon to be cochairman of his transition, a pivotal responsibility in forming his government. Having spent most of his life in public service, and having survived an assassination attempt, Vernon wasn't interested in a position in the administration. He assured the president he could be more helpful on the outside, and managed his status as "first friend" with discretion and a light touch.

One Sunday morning Vernon picked me up at home in his red convertible and we drove to the southwest gate of the White House with our golf clubs in the trunk. As we approached, a stern uniformed officer impatiently signaled to what he assumed were two sightseers to make a left turn and clear the area. Vernon, who as a son of segregated Georgia had borne more than his share of rebukes, carefully and slowly kept on course. As we neared the gate the annoyed officer and a sidekick came close and glared.

"Good morning, sir. My name is Vernon Jordan and this is Mr. Stevens. I believe the president is expecting us."

A hurried check with the guard shack led them to lower the concrete barrier, open the iron gates, and wave us through. We circled the South Lawn drive to the Diplomatic Entrance where the presidential motorcade was lined up. We were directed to park to the side and our clubs were moved into what is called the Beast, then a Cadillac Fleetwood. Minutes later the president walked out of the South Portico carrying his hat.

This was five days after the suicide of his close friend, Deputy White House Counsel Vince Foster, a tragedy for the Clintons that led to lurid press speculation, and the week he announced his controversial "Don't ask, Don't tell" plan under which gays could serve in the armed forces as long as they didn't expose their sexual identity, a reversal of his campaign promise to overturn the military's ban on homosexuals. Senator Sam Nunn, chairman of the Armed Services Committee, with the backing of General Colin Powell and the Joint Chiefs of Staff, was advancing legislation that would reinforce the Pentagon's existing policy, and the new president was forced to settle for what he could get. On the hour-long ride to the Robert Trent Jones golf course in Virginia he dissected the opposing views, the political complexity and power dynamics that forced him to accept a bruising compromise. It was an early and sobering setback.

Sunday on the golf course was a respite. The president was a congenial and voluble companion, and I soon forgot about the armed secret service agents in the trees on either side of the fairway. Waiting for Vernon to tee off on one hole I found Bill Clinton leaning on my shoulder, whispering commentary on his friend's swing. Yes, he did have a practice of dropping a second ball after a bad

With Vernon Jordan and President Clinton at Robert Trent Jones Golf Club, Gainesville, Virginia, July 25, 1993.

shot to try for a better result, but he was the scorekeeper and he signed the card for me as a souvenir. He hadn't lowered his score with any of those mulligans.

Riding back to Washington I was on the "jump seat" facing to the rear toward Vernon and the dozing president, ruddy after an afternoon in the sun. As we neared the White House there were scatterings of people on the sidewalks watching the president's limousine and its train of SUVs and motorcycles, all with sirens off. Clinton opened his eyes and gazed out the window. The onlookers were subdued, with little waving or cheering. "You can tell how you're doing by the crowds on the streets," he mused, as his week of controversy neared its end.

My son Michael came to me with an idea called *The Great Ones,* a television special that would celebrate accomplished figures in sports. Vernon arranged a meeting with White House chief of staff, Mack McLarty, which led to Clinton supporting the project. The result was a festive weekend that included a Saturday dinner at the Smithsonian and a Father's Day golf tournament featuring President Clinton and Arnold Palmer. "I have to say that of all the perks that have come along with being president of the United States," Clinton said at the White House reception that evening, "the best one was being able to play eighteen holes with Arnold Palmer this morning." Earning a laugh, he added, "I glad I didn't have to play one-on-one with Kareem or go fifteen rounds with Muhammad Ali to justify that round of golf."

Ali, Palmer, Kareem Abdul Jabbar, Wilma Rudolph and Ted Williams were the Great Ones, honored for their contributions to American life at a star-studded show at Constitution Hall that was televised on NBC. Tom Brokaw, with his prominent role as anchor of NBC Nightly News and his affinity for the sports world, was the ideal host. Jack Lemmon, Sidney Poitier and James Garner from the movie world and sports figure Chris Evert and Senator Bill Bradley gave tributes. Champions Joe Frazier and Archie Moore were feisty in presenting the award to Ali, who stole the show with his mischief and humor.

President Clinton capped the evening with an emotional posthumous presentation of the Presidential Medal of Freedom to the late Arthur Ashe for his tennis career and bold initiatives for racial justice. His wife Jeanne accepted the honor. It was an inspiring night and our first opportunity to discover Bill Clinton's enthusiasm for the sidebar events of his presidency. We hoped that the National Sports Awards might become an annual event but, alas, were unable to secure continuing sponsorship.

The National Holocaust Museum opened in Washington during Clinton's first year. A representative had met with me earlier to discuss my father's color film

Ali stole the show at the National Sports Awards. I regard Muhammad Ali
as one of the great men of the twentieth century.

of World War II. Liz and I attended the opening and we were deeply touched to discover that arriving visitors entered an austere metal elevator and were deposited on a landing to face a screen showing harrowing color film of emaciated prisoners, and bodies stacked like cordwood in the concentration camp at Dachau. A small plaque rests beside the screen.

> A special film team headed by Lieutenant Colonel George Stevens entered the Dachau concentration camp in early May 1945, just days after its liberation. Stevens and his men shot this film as a record of what they encountered. One of America's leading film directors, Stevens went on after the war to direct *The Diary of Anne Frank* and other films.

The Dachau film has been seen by over forty million museum visitors and remains in place to this day.

The three hours of unique color footage shot by the Stevens Irregulars during the war in Europe was donated to the Library of Congress in 1981, waiving any rights so it could be used without charge by producers of documentaries about the war. In 2008 the Library's film board voted to include *George Stevens' World War II Footage—1943–1946* in the prestigious National Film Registry which enshrines our country's most historic and culturally significant motion pictures. I wish my father could have known that the wartime work of the men in his Special Coverage Unit has a place on the honor roll of America's great films, which also includes six of his own feature films.

I had a related rite of passage with my sons when I traveled to Europe to record the score for *Separate But Equal*. Michael and David were both studying in Paris and they flew to Germany to join me and observe sessions with the Munich Symphony Orchestra. Early the following morning we rented a car and drove to Dachau. It was a solemn but memorable day as a third generation of Stevenses walked the grounds and saw firsthand the notorious camp that they had first been exposed to through their grandfather's pictures.

67

The Thin Red Line

In 1995 Mike Medavoy, who had been Terry Malick's agent in the AFI days, was launching Phoenix Pictures and surprised me with an offer to become head of production. I felt I would serve Mike and myself better as an independent producer, so we worked out a deal for me and my son Michael to develop films for his new company.

When my father was making landmark films like *Shane* and *Giant* he provided hands-on experience for his son. A generation later my daughter Caroline made substantial contributions to *A Filmmaker's Journey* and *The Murder of Mary Phagan* while learning at my side. Michael worked with me on the AFI Life Achievement Award shows honoring Jack Nicholson, Steven Spielberg, Clint Eastwood and Martin Scorsese, proving to be a diligent and imaginative collaborator.

Terry Malick, after placing himself in the front rank of new directors with the release of *Days of Heaven* in 1978, moved to Paris and mysteriously disappeared from the moviemaking scene for nearly twenty years. Our friendship continued, and one day Terry reappeared in Los Angeles. He had written a script based on *The Thin Red Line*, James Jones' novel of the battle for Guadalcanal. Terry insisted he didn't want to direct it but Medavoy and I felt he might be more interested than he let on, and after several months he committed. Phoenix had a partnership with Sony Pictures, but they turned down the project doubting that Terry could make the picture on the proposed $50,000,000 budget, so Terry, Mike and I met with Laura Ziskin and Bill Mechanic at Twentieth Century Fox. They were keen on having the Malick film and agreed to put up $39,000,000 if we delivered five name actors from an approved list of ten. A Japanese partner and Phoenix raised the total to $51,000,000.

Despite Terry's twenty-year sabbatical, or perhaps because of it, actors were keen to work with him. Sean Penn was the first to commit, followed by Woody

Harrelson, Nick Nolte and John Cusack. Then George Clooney and John Travolta came on board in cameo roles to support Terry's comeback, assuring a green light from Fox.

The production was of a scale and ambition beyond Terry's previous experience, and Fox wanted to safeguard its investment in a film that would be shooting in the Australian rainforest eight thousand miles away. They asked that I be on the set as executive producer for the entire five months of shooting. I saw my relationship with Phoenix as an opportunity to make my own films, but my role on *The Thin Red Line* was to facilitate Terry making *his* film—an echo of our early experience at AFI. I would have to straddle the line between being the director's friend who believed in the importance of directorial authority and the person the studio expected to keep the production on the rails.

Terry held a fondness for Michael Stevens well before the day he wrote "Go Michael Go" on the check returning my investment in *Badlands,* and he asked Michael to be associate producer, offering the prospect of a rich father–son experience. That sealed it for me.

Michael and I flew to Sydney on May 31, 1997, then took a short flight north to Cairns and a car ride to Port Douglas, the small town near the Great Barrier Reef in Queensland where the production was based. Except for a one-week trip back to the US, this would be home base until the end of October, where in addition to producing the movie I would orchestrate *The Kennedy Center Honors, Christmas in Washington* and the AFI Life Achievement Award show—all by phone, fax and something new called E-mail. Grant Hill, a cool and capable Australian, signed on as line producer.

The Thin Red Line is an experience laced with happy memories along with the expected tensions, crises and strains of madness that color location shooting. It was also for me a clarifying experience about the nature of filmmaking. "Take me by the lapels if you need to," Terry said, looking me in the eye, on the first day of shooting. It was his way of encouraging straight talk.

Terry assured Fox and Phoenix that he would rewrite and shorten his 192-page screenplay, but didn't get around to it during preproduction in Hollywood. He promised to do it in Australia before shooting began, but the final shooting script was shortened by just five pages. This was no act of deception—for the first time Terry was adapting a novel, and he wasn't inclined toward conventional character development. The script was a blueprint that attracted resources to make a movie—a legion of fine actors, a dedicated crew that included his steadfast friend and production designer Jack Fisk, who resourcefully created sets in the Daintree Rainforest, and the soft-spoken and brilliant two-time

Oscar-winning cinematographer John Toll. Shooting involved grueling twelve-hour days in the jungle, six days a week. On occasion when a scene was rehearsed and ready to shoot, Terry would spot an animal or an exotic bird and set off with Toll and his camera. It often seemed arbitrary and random, but many of these shots became integral to the finished picture. Terry was making a big Hollywood war movie while ruminating cinematically on life, death and creation.

We had a gifted band of young performers, including John C. Reilly, Ben Chaplin, Adrien Brody, Tim Blake Nelson, Dash Mihok, Jared Leto and Jim Caviezel. I wrote occasional "Letters from Port Douglas" to our colleagues at home. One described their welcome to Australia, a "boot camp" that involved six nights sleeping on the ground in the jungle.

> In the middle of the second night they were surprised by an attack of mortars and automatic weapons and Japanese voices crying out in the darkness. Tim Blake Nelson, a playwright who has just directed his first film, called it the transforming experience of his life—being under the absolute control of others in conditions he never had encountered. I asked if during the darker moments he thought about saying, "Screw it." Tim said he has dreamed about being part of *The Thin Red Line* for so long that that was never a consideration.

The boot camp was a defining moment. From then on the actors were the men of Charlie Company.

Terry inspired and, on occasion, confounded his actors with metaphor and allusion. A few, including Bill Pullman, Lukas Haas and Mickey Rourke, were put through rigorous paces but ended up on the cutting room floor—not for faulty performances but because the length of the film left no room. Adrien Brody, who played Fife, one of the leading characters in the novel and the script, appeared at the New York premiere to discover he was left with only a couple of lines and five minutes of screen time.

We filmed a hundred days in Australia before a smaller unit went to Guadalcanal for twenty four days. In total Terry accumulated twelve hundred thousand feet of film. Billy Webber, his editor on *Badlands* and *Days of Heaven,* joined him to wrestle a five-hour first cut into a finished film over the next year. Terry refused to look at dailies during production in Australia, nor would he look at a cut of *The Thin Red Line* until editing was complete because he wanted to wait and see the film with fresh eyes. This frustrated his colleagues because he seemed to be flying blind, but Terry was dogged in his attention to detail, combing through bins to find just the right shot, experimenting with voice-over narration, and trying countless music concepts with composer Hans Zimmer. The finished film, at two hours and fifty minutes, was as Terry intended—a fully immersive experience.

The contrasting response to *The Thin Red Line* was nowhere better demonstrated than by the reviewing team of Siskel and Ebert. "The actors in *The Thin Red Line* are making one movie, and the director is making another," wrote Ebert. "This leads to an almost hallucinatory sense of displacement, as the actors struggle for realism." Siskel, on the other hand, declared it "the greatest contemporary war film I've seen." He described Malick's "almost unmatched eye for the landscape and for storytelling through pictures. There are so many indelible images in *The Thin Red Line* that it almost defines what moviemaking is about." The film earned the admiration of leading filmmakers—Martin Scorsese ranking it the second-best film of the nineties and Christopher Nolan declaring it one of his favorite films of all time.

Steven Spielberg's *Saving Private Ryan* also came out in 1998, giving the public a choice of two equally ambitious but very different war films, and at Oscar time both received multiple nominations, including best director and best picture. Spielberg won for directing and *Shakespeare in Love* was the surprise choice for best picture—but *The Thin Red Line*'s seven nominations along with strong reviews triggered a successful international release.

The film is memorable because of Terrence Malick's distinct point of view. It wasn't his nature to write a crisp 120-page script with a beginning, middle and end, then shoot it methodically. One of the young actors Dash Mihok said much later, "I was hired to shoot a war film. Now, I don't think it's a war film—it's an amazing poem about the beauty of life."

I treasure the association with Terry and the dedicated band of Aussies and Americans who emerged from the Queensland jungle with a film of distinction.

68

Impeachment

President Clinton won a decisive victory over Senator Bob Dole in the 1996 election. He and Hillary continued stewardship of the Kennedy Center Honors and *Christmas in Washington*, bringing their vitality and appreciation of the arts to the President's Box. Bill Clinton displayed an uncanny familiarity with every piece of music performed, and proved to be the most avid consumer of popular entertainment of any president.

Liz and Richard Holbrooke started "home and home" annual birthday parties for Dick's wife Kati Marton and me, alternating between Washington and New York. Kati and I were both born on April third, though she, understandably, made certain that guests knew it wasn't the same year. We had a roster of stimulating friends from our shared worlds. At the 1997 party Arthur Schlesinger arrived from New York to stay at our house, found the front door open, and walked in. "I found Liz talking to a couple of people whom she introduced as Secret Service," Arthur recorded in *Journals 1952–2000.* "I then understood the Clintons were coming and thought to myself how easy it would have been for assassins to enter the house as I had just done."

President Clinton had torn a tendon in his knee on a visit to golf legend Greg Norman in Florida the previous month, so he arrived on crutches, as did Holbrooke who, having successfully negotiated the Dayton Peace Agreement in Ohio, had less success negotiating an icy slope in Telluride. Holbrooke and Clinton, standing on their crutches, with all guests hoping for a few words with the president, created a jam. Arthur recounted in his diary that he spoke with Clinton, "who didn't seem to have a care in the world," about Boris Yeltsin, John Major and Tony Blair. "He wanted to talk about foreign policy—ironical in view of his preference for domestic policy; but foreign affairs are traditionally the

Richard Holbrooke experiments with POTUS's crutches at the Stevens' house. Standing,
left to right: Stevens, General Chuck Boyd, Eileen James, Kati Marton, Hillary Clinton,
Liz Stevens, Arthur Schlesinger, Jr., Maxine Isaacs, Holbrooke.

escape hatch for presidents blocked and frustrated at home." Arthur addressed
the matter of crutches with a historian's yen for detail: "Dick had the old-
fashioned crutches fitting in the armpits, Bill has new crutches that you grip in
your hand, so they went into specialized discussion on the merits of the respective types." Arthur noted that at dinner he sat next to Madeleine Albright, who
had just eight weeks earlier prevailed over Holbrooke as Clinton's choice for
secretary of state—a setback for Dick in his quest for the post for which he had
fervent ambition and substantial credentials.

Clinton did name Holbrooke to be ambassador to the United Nations, and
the Ambassador's Residence at the Waldorf Astoria became the setting for the
next of our annual parties. Dick discovered that the charismatic secretary general
of the United Nations, Nobel Prize winner Kofi Annan, had an April birthday
five days after Kati's and mine, and he concluded the discrepancy was within the
margin of error, so Kofi became a third celebrant. Sidney Poitier came from Los
Angeles, joined by our Broadway friends. These stimulating gatherings reminded

me of the life enhancement that comes from having accomplished friends of good purpose.

I was starting to think about the millennium, which was two years away. One evening Vernon and Ann Jordan had the Clintons for dinner and asked Liz and me to join them. I was seated next to Hillary, who was always spontaneous and engaged. She agreed that the millennium was an important opportunity and we discussed different ways in which it might be celebrated.

Six weeks later on January 21, 1998, the earth turned in Washington. Liz and I watched in disbelief as reporters on television discussed the breaking *Washington Post* story that President Clinton had had a sexual relationship with White House intern Monica Lewinsky. I thought it was the end, that senators would come down from Capitol Hill and insist, as they had with Nixon, that the president resign, but Clinton's answer to Jim Lehrer's question at a White House media event—"I did not have sexual relations with that woman, Ms. Lewinsky"—seemed to buy time. Kenneth Starr's year-long investigation proceeded slowly, to Clinton's advantage.

The scandal touched people close to Clinton. Vernon Jordan had helped Lewinsky find a job in New York and Starr called him to appear before the grand jury. Driving to work the next morning I heard on the radio that Vernon was holding a news conference at noon at the Park Hyatt Hotel, where we often had breakfast. I left my Kennedy Center office and drove to the hotel. I hadn't been invited and wondered whether it was my place to be there. I saw Vernon standing near microphones waiting to address a noisy room jammed with reporters and cameras. He saw me off to the side and nodded. He then stated unequivocally that he did not tell Lewinsky to lie and that she told him that she hadn't had a sexual relationship with the president. It proved a costly ordeal for Vernon, having to appear five times before the grand jury, but leading to no action on Starr's unsupported charges. There were reports that during those five days he made a strong impression on the jury. A final question was posed by the panel's forewoman.

"If ever any of us need a job, Mr. Jordan," she said, "can we feel free to come to you?"

"Madam Forelady," Vernon replied, "my door swings back on welcome hinges to anybody in this grand jury."

I learned something from my spontaneous appearance at the Hyatt. Vernon never forgot my presence that day. It was a lesson in the importance of standing up for friends you believe in, not waiting to be asked.

Starr's investigation continued through the November election in which the Democrats—defying Speaker Newt Gingrich's prediction that the Republicans would gain up to thirty house seats—picked up five. The House of Representatives voted to impeach the president on charges of perjury and obstruction of justice on the afternoon of Saturday, December 19th, just five hours before the Clintons' annual black-tie Christmas celebration.

The White House was decked out with a festive Winter Wonderland motif and the large gathering was in surprising high spirits, considering that the host had just become the first president to be impeached since Andrew Johnson in 1868. When we went through the receiving line Liz asked Hillary, "How do you account for the cheerful mood on such a dismal day?" Hillary answered with resolve, "It's because we're fighting back."

The impeachment proceedings in the Senate began in January. The Clintons seemed to keep life during the trial as normal as possible. Our friend, playwright Peter Stone, had done a revised book for a revival of *Annie Get Your Gun* starring Bernadette Peters that was previewing at the Kennedy Center. Hillary accepted an invitation to come to dinner at our place on Avon Lane with Peter and his wife Mary, then to go on to the show. Hillary's mother Dorothy Rodham and Melanne Verveer, her policy aide and close friend, came with her. We were enjoying a pleasant dinner kept light by Peter's Broadway stories when the doorbell rang. I received a nod from a secret service agent and went to the door. There, unexpected, was William Jefferson Clinton. Liz made an additional place at the table and he joined us, cordial but somewhat subdued. Soon he was quizzing Peter on the history of *Annie Get Your Gun.*

When we entered the Kennedy Center and took our seats in the President's Box, a buzz started as the audience became aware of the Clintons' presence and some stood to get a better look. They began to applaud, and when the president rose and took Hillary by the hand, the entire audience was on its feet, the applause growing into a rousing and prolonged ovation. In the wake of the House vote to impeach him, Clinton's approval rating had jumped ten points to an all-time high of 73 percent.

The next week Capricia Marshall, a bright young lawyer who served as Hillary's social secretary, called with a surprise invitation to Camp David for the weekend. The wooded retreat in Maryland's Catoctin Mountain Park is an hour and a half drive from Washington. The easygoing atmosphere belied the reality that the first presidential impeachment trial in over a hundred years was under way in the Senate. The president was relaxed, holding forth in the informal living room of Laurel Cabin, while Hillary was fully engaged with each one of their guests, including White House Counsel Lloyd Cutler and his wife, painter Polly Kraft, singer-songwriter Carly Simon, Ann Pincus with her husband Walter Pincus of the *Washington Post,* and investment banker Steve Rattner and his wife

Maureen White, who was Clinton's representative to the United Nations Children's Fund. We were together for each meal, movies were shown in the screening room, laughter was abundant, and impeachment never entered the conversation. It was a master class in Bill Clinton's ability to compartmentalize.

Two weeks later, Liz and I watched on television as the Senate voted to acquit President Clinton on all charges, falling well short of the sixty-seven votes needed to convict. Relieved but not surprised, we both thought back to Hillary's comment at Christmas about fighting back.

An hour later the phone rang. It was Terry Malick calling from the Berlin Film Festival. "*The Thin Red Line* won the Golden Bear, the top prize!" he said with unaccustomed zeal. My two worlds continued to intersect.

69

America's Millennium

In April of 1998 Hillary asked me to meet with her, Capricia Marshall and other aides in the Map Room of the White House—the large parlor on the ground floor where Franklin Roosevelt consulted maps tracking progress during World War II. Hillary wanted the White House to be a focal point of a millennium celebration. I had sent her the first chapter of *The Rise of Theodore Roosevelt* in which Edmund Morris describes the New Year's celebration in 1907. "Roosevelt may be the fastest handshaker in history (he averages fifty grips a minute)," Morris wrote, "but he is also the most conscientious, insisting that all citizens who are sober, washed, and free of bodily advertising be permitted to wish the President of the United States a Happy New Year."

Hillary led an animated discussion during which I proposed a starry show steeped in history leading to the midnight transition to the new millennium. Hillary said there should be a White House dinner before the gala and a party afterward. "I plan to dance all night," she enthused as I was leaving.

Capricia called later to say, "Hillary wants you to produce the Gala." Then six weeks later another call. "How would you feel about working with Steven Spielberg and Quincy Jones?" she asked. I replied with a question, "How would Steven and Quincy feel about working with me?" "They're fine with that," she said quickly. The die was cast for what turned out to be an invigorating shotgun marriage. Steven and I were friends but I knew Quincy only in passing.

The next Saturday Liz and I boarded Air Force One at Andrews Air Force Base and flew to Long Island with the Clintons, followed by a scenic chopper ride to East Hampton. There the presidential motorcade took us to Spielberg's house for a meeting with my new coconspirators. Steven, Quincy and I sat in the garden with Hillary for a spirited conversation, lively minds putting ideas in play. The president dropped in, a few minutes here and there, but it was

Hillary's project. We agreed that we would produce a sparkling entertainment that celebrated American history with a bravura climax to take us into a new century and new millennium.

The next week in Los Angeles we made a plan. Steven preferred that Quincy and I produce the show and he concentrate on making *The Unfinished Journey*, a seventeen-minute film that celebrated the American experience, for the broadcast. Quincy and I developed an easy working relationship that was marked by us rarely using the other's proper name. He was one of the few who remembered that Kingfish, the leading character on the *Amos 'n Andy* radio show, was George "Kingfish" Stevens. Henceforth I was Kingfish and Quincy was "Q."

Spielberg asked Michael Stevens to be his right hand as producer of *The Unfinished Journey*. After *The Thin Red Line*, Michael, determined to make his own mark, had produced and directed an independent film based on Tim Willocks' novel, *Bad City Blues*. He raised the money, enlisted a young team, and shot the film in New Orleans and Los Angeles. He cast it with unknown actors—except for one bow to continuity. Michael asked Dennis Hopper to take a role. "I learned more than you can imagine from your grandfather on *Giant*," Dennis responded generously. "Just give me the script and tell me where to show up."

Michael's work was sure-handed and had the family stamp of respecting the audience. Watching my son become a third-generation film director—I know of no others—brought me pleasure beyond reckoning.

We organized research which included a session with historians Doris Kearns Goodwin, David McCullough and Michael Beschloss, and began putting together the small army that would be needed in Washington on the night—still eighteen months away. A *Variety* story in October, speculating about a "lavish millennium celebration," mordantly observed that the president would have to survive impeachment in order to be in attendance.

In March 1999, after the Senate voted to acquit Clinton, Steven, Quincy and I met in Washington to select a site. The White House had been talking with the Kennedy Center but we felt the Opera House was too small. Bundled in parkas we looked at the South Lawn of the White House and the adjacent Ellipse where the Christmas Tree Lighting takes place, as a blustery sky heralded a coming snowstorm. We were reminded that we would face uncertain weather in December. Then we stood on the marble steps of the Lincoln Memorial, and with Abe looking over our shoulders saw before us the National Mall with its long reflecting pool leading to the Washington Monument and the United States Capitol beyond. We sensed the aura of history.

"Man," said Quincy, "we could have a hundred thousand people!" We decided on the spot. This was the place.

Liz invited Quincy to dinner that night. Q's car couldn't manage the grade to Avon Lane because of the snow, and I found him in boots and a fur hat slogging up the hill in the blowing snow. Sitting by a warm fire with a whiskey, we enjoyed gallows humor about our decision to challenge Mother Nature at year end.

Hillary decided to call the White House gathering before the show the Creators' Dinner. Invitations were sent to a hundred individuals, each of whom signified American creativity. She had no interest in challenging T.R.'s hand-shaking skills but planned a post-midnight party after the show to toast the new millennium. CBS agreed to broadcast *America's Millennium* from 10 p.m. until one in the morning, and we negotiated a contract with the National Park Service for the use of the Lincoln Memorial and the mall.

Quincy, Michael Stevens and I, brainstorming ideas for the climactic midnight moment, went to inspect the Washington Monument. The 550-foot-high obelisk was encased in a scaffolding—consisting of thirty-seven miles of aluminum tubing and fifty thousand feet of decorative blue mesh—designed by renowned architect Michael Graves to enable workmen to access the structure during a two-year renovation. We saw an opportunity for a striking "millennium light" scene.

The plan we developed was for President Clinton, seconds before midnight, to lead five children to the reflecting pool where they would light a "wick" in the water that would sizzle the quarter mile to the base of the Washington Monument, and there ignite three thousand pyrotechnic devices, rigged to the Graves scaffolding, that would climb the monument like a fiery waterfall during the ten-second countdown to midnight. Then a glorious golden display of fireworks would light the night sky.

The veteran bureaucrats at the National Park Service had a mantra: "If it's green it belongs to us." They responded sternly to the Millennium Light proposal, advising us that a long-standing regulation forbade any activity within a forty-five-foot radius of the Washington Monument. We were desperate for a display at the moment of the new millennium, but even after Grucci Fireworks provided detailed safety assurances, weeks of negotiation were unproductive.

Finally a meeting was arranged with the director of the Park Service and his lawyers. Right off one lawyer reminded us that the monument is a sacred building. Q, a freewheeling can-do man, was taken aback by the rigidity we faced. I spoke of the importance of the Millennium Light, explaining that international television would sequentially broadcast midnight manifestations by other nations as the international clock moved toward the west—New Delhi, Cairo, Moscow, Berlin, Paris, London (where a million-dollar dome had been created just for the occasion)—and that America needed a display that would knock the world's socks off.

We resolved some minor problems, but the lead lawyer insisted that failure to enforce the "forty-five-foot" regulation would set a precedent. The sun was going down so I made a proposal. "We will submit in writing tomorrow an appeal for an exception. We will draft it narrowly: The exception we seek is strictly for a millennium event, which will ensure that you won't have to consider another exception for a thousand years."

As we walked to our car Quincy flashed a mischievous smile. "Jesus, Kingfish. You went full ghetto in there."

Secretary of Interior Bruce Babbitt, a former governor of Arizona and presidential candidate, was a genial, cutting-edge environmentalist who presided over the National Park Service. I called Bruce and told him about our Millennium Light, the opposition we faced, and that Quincy and I were hanging by our fingernails. "This is a tough one," he said. "I'll see what I can do—but if anything good happens you can't mention my name." Twenty-four hours later the Park Service filed a revision in the *Federal Register* allowing for a light display within the "forty-five-foot area" of the Washington Monument *only* on the occasion of millennia. One member of Congress called it a "desecration," but we would have our midnight moment. I kept Bruce Babbitt's secret for twenty years. It's time he gets some credit.

We moved a small army with production trucks, dressing rooms and temporary offices to the Lincoln Memorial one week before New Year's Eve. JumboTron screens were erected on the mall, along with facilities for a crowd whose estimated size was growing as word of star participation leaked out. There were recurrent rumors of terrorist threats, and the Y2K scare put our computer-generated cameras, lights and recorders at risk. But December 29 was a cool and sunny day and an effervescent spirit was in the air as performers rehearsed the three-hour show. Quincy enlisted megastar Will Smith to be host, which delighted CBS.

We kept Hillary informed but President Clinton asked for a briefing two nights before the show, so Steven, Quincy, Michael and I met him in the Map Room. Michael took him item by item through the rundown of the show. He was curious and enthusiastic, with a point of view on every piece of music

Inside the *America's Millennium* production truck. Seated foreground, Steven Spielberg. Standing, producers Quincy Jones, Michael Stevens and George Stevens. December 31, 1999.

("Summertime" is the best song of the century, he insisted) and a familiarity with even the lesser-known artists. He seemed excited about his role in setting up the Millennium Light at midnight.

New Year's Eve was a long day of rehearsal with singers, dancers, bands and choruses on the stage built on the steps of the memorial. We made space for stars arriving at the last minute from their movie jobs and concert tours. A total of seven hundred people would be onstage that night. At day's end we made our way in black tie to the White House.

Tables for the Creators' Dinner were set in both the East Room and State Dining Room with white orchids and roses atop silver velvet tablecloths. Painters, writers, architects, scientists, athletes, historians and performing artists—ranging from Muhammad Ali to August Wilson, along with Rita Dove, Robert Rauschenberg, Murray Gell-Mann, Itzhak Perlman and Jack Nicholson—mingled during cocktail hour. President Clinton was seated between Sophia Loren and Elizabeth Taylor, who unsettled things by arriving looking gorgeous in red velvet an hour late.

The president made his toast in both rooms. "If you look at the glowing diversity of race and background that illuminates America's house on this evening, I cannot help but think how different America is, how different history is, because of those of you who were able to imagine, to invent, to inspire. So join me in a toast—to yourselves, to the First Lady, and to our shared future."

Liz, Quincy, Michael and I slipped out early for the five-minute drive to the Lincoln Memorial. We were comforted by a forecast of clear skies. As we left the White House grounds we were confronted with a stirring sight—this was a "build it and they will come" moment. Throngs of people—some carrying blankets and picnics—were ignoring rumors of terrorists and streaming on foot toward the Lincoln Memorial. The crowd grew to six hundred thousand people.

The president and his party arrived five minutes to the hour, and at precisely ten p.m. three marching bands and our eighty-five-piece orchestra took the downbeat for "Sing Sing Sing." Will Smith took the stage for a millennium-themed number reflecting the styles of American dance through the past century. The applause came in waves from the crowd, shoulder to shoulder on both sides of the Reflecting Pool all the way to the Washington Monument. They had come to have a good time.

The three-hour show included poets Maya Angelou and Robert Pinsky, popular musicians John Fogerty, Bono, Usher, Kenny Rogers, Tom Jones, BeBe Winans, Kris Kristofferson, Patti Austin, and Don McLean with his crowd-pleaser "American Pie." Classical artists Kathleen Battle and Jessye Norman paid tribute to Marian Anderson and were joined by Bobby McFerrin with a rousing "He's Got the Whole World in His Hands." Half a million people sang along.

The magic moment came when the president led five young children to the edge of the reflecting pool. They took the torch and ignited the fuse that sparkled toward the Washington Monument. John Williams conducted the orchestra as the mall lit up and the display of fire climbed the monument. The crowd was jumping and cheering, a few hearty ones splashing into the frigid reflecting pool.

There were magnificent manifestations around the world that night, but none eclipsed the Millennium Light on Washington's National Mall.

The men and women honored at the Creators' Dinner and the cast arrived back at the White House at one o'clock to find the dinner tables gone, a breakfast buffet in the State Dining Room, and the East Room set up for dancing. It was a scintillating party with guests riding high from the Lincoln Memorial experience. True to Hillary's promise at our first meeting there was dancing until dawn. I remember leaving with Liz and the beguiling Jessye Norman a little after five. We walked toward our car and looked back at the White House, the home of presidents since John Adams, still aglow, as America and the world looked to a new millennium.

The Millennium Light on the Washington Monument as seen across the
Lincoln Memorial Reflecting Pool at 12:01 a.m., January 1, 2000.

PART SEVEN

THE TEST OF TIME

December 1, 2012. Hollywood, California.

70

The 2000s

George W. and Laura Bush moved into the White House in January of 2001, the twenty-third year of the *Kennedy Center Honors* and the fourteenth year of *Christmas in Washington.* My job was to seek the embrace of the two shows by the first family. The response of Laura Bush's social secretary was comforting. "Oh yes, the Honors and the Christmas show are entitlements, just like Social Security."

The Bushes' ties to the entertainment world weren't as close as the Reagans or Clintons, and many in the arts world, perturbed by the way the election had been decided by a five to four vote in the Supreme Court to stop the recount of votes in Florida, weren't keen to associate with the new administration. We knew our choices of honorees for the first Bush event would be critical to keeping artists involved. When we announced the stellar group for 2001—Julie Andrews, Van Cliburn, Jack Nicholson, Quincy Jones and Luciano Pavarotti—it signaled that the Honors were beyond politics. The entertainment world showed up in force and discovered that George and Laura Bush were gracious hosts who saw the occasion as nonpartisan.

I continued to serve on the executive committee and the board of trustees of the American Film Institute. Jean Firstenberg was a committed leader and the organization developed in many positive ways. Yet my concept had always been for a robust national role for AFI. It was discouraging to see the institute consolidate its activities at the site of the conservatory in Hollywood—shutting its Washington offices, ceasing publication of *American Film,* and closing the theater at the Kennedy Center in favor of a new one in Silver Spring, Maryland.

The AFI Conservatory's program of seminars with the world's leading filmmakers was in its fourth decade, which made the collection of recorded and transcribed knowledge about filmmaking unparalleled. I decided to do a book, choosing and editing thirty-two seminars from the hundreds in the AFI library, and crafting essays on each filmmaker beginning with Harold Lloyd, who was our speaker at the conservatory's opening night in 1969. Other directors included King Vidor, Howard Hawks, Fritz Lang, Alfred Hitchcock, Frank Capra, William Wyler and my father. Writers Ray Bradbury and Ernest Lehman, cinematographers James Wong Howe and Stanley Cortez, and international masters Federico Fellini, Ingmar Bergman and Satyajit Ray broadened the scope.

Conversations with the Great Moviemakers of Hollywood's Golden Age at the American Film Institute, a handsome seven-hundred-page volume with carefully chosen photographs, was published by Alfred A. Knopf in 2006. It was soon followed by a sequel, *Conversations at the American Film Institute with the Great Moviemakers—The Next Generation.* Hollywood figures like Gregory Peck, Sidney Poitier, Robert Altman, Jack Lemmon and Sydney Pollock were placed in the company of younger independent artists, including Steven Spielberg, Paul Schrader, David Lynch and John Sayles. Nora Ephron, Shirley Clark and Meryl Streep began to fill the void of women that marked the Golden Age seminars.

I had been raised as an only child and was now enjoying the pleasures of a growing family. Caroline, who was living in New York and thriving in the world of documentary filmmaking, gave Liz and me our first grandchild, Anthony, and later a second, Nicholas.

Our younger son David was an unusually bright and winning child, but he struggled in school and endured constant tutoring until he met Harry Wachs, an ophthalmologist who ran a clinic helping children with learning issues. Liz and I watched Dr. Wachs test David at age thirteen and see his eyes grow red from strain. "If you work with me," Dr. Wachs told David, "we can correct this." David accepted the challenge, meeting regularly with Wachs and conscientiously doing exercises at home to address a form of dyslexia. Two years later his reading skills and perception were normal, and tutors a thing of the past.

David studied at the American University in Paris while holding a part-time job at the *International Herald Tribune.* Partial to adventure, he traveled alone across India, and joined an expedition with Russian and Hungarian boys to climb the highest mountain in Russia, hence a prized picture on my desk of David, hatless in a blue pullover, a belay rope hooked to his waist, waving an ice axe from the snow-covered summit. On graduation he was accepted in the summer program at the Williamstown Theater Festival—like a boy from a family of acrobats pursuing the family trade. David thrived in the theatrical milieu, but soon after turned up in Washington.

"Dr. Wachs changed my life," he told Liz and me. "I'm going to work for him."

David had an instinct for relating to children, and quickly became a valued associate of Dr. Wachs, even tutoring a Washington Redskins quarterback who was having perception issues tracking downfield receivers. He had found his calling. He went on to earn his doctoral degree at the Harvard University School of Education, then start his own practice helping children with learning disabilities. He founded and leads a company that develops innovative methods to support teachers and students and improve learning outcomes. Liz and I have savored the expressions of satisfaction from parents whose children David has helped over the years. I jest that David is first in the Stevens family—since my great-great-grandfather William Thompson who became president of William Jewell College in 1857—to make a living in the real world. David and his wife Lina gave us our third grandchild, Anastasia, in 1999, and a fourth, Alexander, in 2003.

Michael Stevens directed his second independent feature, *Sin,* starring Gary Oldman, Ving Rhames and Kerry Washington in 2003, and was the last to marry. His wife Ali gave birth to John Cooper Stevens the next year, and then to Lily, who was born in Hollywood in 2005 and named for Liz's mother.

In the early days of the American Film Institute while we were rescuing movie classics from the silent era, I never imagined that Paramount Pictures was so preoccupied with the bottom line in the 1950s that it would lose or destroy the negative of *A Place in the Sun* and the soundtracks for *Shane.* I prevailed on Paramount management to invest in a restoration, and worked with studio technicians using a duplicate negative and other material to craft a handsome restoration of *A Place in the Sun.* Yet the loss of the original negative means that William Mellor's Oscar-winning black-and-white photography is slightly less luminous than it was in 1951.

When we set out to restore the soundtrack of *Shane* I discovered that new digital tools can be helpful, but also problematic. I remembered in my mind's eye and ear how the film originally looked and sounded, a benefit the technicians didn't share. I had seen the opening scene countless times, where Shane arrives at the Starrett homestead and the family receives an ominous visit from the cattlemen. Listening to the new version it felt different. When the well-meaning sound technician explained that he had "de-noised" the tracks, I realized that the rippling of the stream that flowed by the homestead had been scrubbed, draining the scene of its reality. We restored the sound of the water and ended up with a superb soundtrack, but it was a lesson in the perils of using modern technology when restoring vintage films. When high definition arrived, we made a new video transfer of *Shane* that recaptured the rich textures of the original Technicolor negative.

"I watched the *Shane* Blu-ray restoration today and could not stop thinking about how happy it would have made your Dad to see his masterpiece as clear and fresh as the day it came out of the lab," said Steven Spielberg in a letter to me. "I've seen *Shane* a hundred times but today I felt like I was at the premiere in the 50s. I didn't have to hunt through grain and scratches to imagine the pristine imagery your Dad was famous for. I got to see with my own eyes what George captured with his. Great work extending for generations to come his legacy as well as your own."

My father's centenary was celebrated in 2004 with screenings across the country, capped by a showing of *Giant* at the Cannes Film Festival. Liz and I flew to France and met Elizabeth Taylor at her villa for a cheerful reunion before going together to the Olympic Theater. There were young people in the audience who had never seen *Giant* on the big screen, and it was thrilling to see a new generation so deeply engrossed in a fifty-year-old film.

Liz and I were invited to the British Embassy a few years later. At the end of dinner the ambassador rose and recited the achievements of Elizabeth Taylor, before telling us it was her birthday, and saying, "Let's raise a glass to Dame Elizabeth." Later at home I dialed the number for Elizabeth's house in Beverly Hills. A protective assistant answered. I said, simply, "It's George Stevens calling for Ms. Taylor." Minutes passed. "George!" said the voice with high-pitched surprise. "I was at the British Embassy tonight," I said, "and the ambassador made a birthday toast to Dame Elizabeth. I thought you should know." She seemed touched and was reflective in a way I had not heard before. Elizabeth and I were born five weeks apart, she in London and I in California. She said that even though we hadn't seen each other that much in recent years, she loved me. Referring to growing up inside the walls of the MGM studio, she said she wished we had been able to do the things young people did together, like go to movies and ball games. I'm glad I called that night. It was just two months later that Elizabeth died of congestive heart failure.

There was another centenary the year after my father's—my mother turned one hundred on July 31, 2005. She had visited the Pritikin Longevity Center in the 1970s and given up caffeine (but not her ration of gin before dinner), improved her diet and started walking five miles every day. She had outlived her friends, but her family—including three grandchildren and six great-grandchildren—gathered at her favorite restaurant, Kate Mantilini on Wilshire Boulevard, next door to the Academy of Motion Picture Arts and Sciences where she regularly saw movies, to help her blow out a hundred candles. Warren Beatty, an admirer, arrived with Annette Bening. After talking with my mother, Warren introduced his wife. With Laurel and Hardy timing, my mother looked at Annette, then to Warren. "You never told me," she scolded, with mock outrage.

Michael was the only member of our family who lived in Los Angeles, and he was devoted to his grandmother, taking her to doctors' appointments and movies and fixing things in her apartment. "Michael is so smart!" she would exclaim with wonder after he programmed her remote control device. It was Michael who was called by caregivers when my mother's day came, two months short of her 105th birthday. The whole family came together again for her burial near her mother and my father on the green hillside at Forest Lawn overlooking Toluca Lake.

71

Obama

On a cold and clear November morning in 2005 Liz and I climbed the steps of the Russell Senate Office Building on Capitol Hill and moved with workers and visitors through the echoing corridors to the Caucus Room—the marble-walled chamber where the Army–McCarthy and Watergate hearings took place, the room where John Kennedy announced his campaign for the presidency and where we watched Bobby declare his.

Liz had served on the board of the Robert Kennedy Memorial Foundation since its founding in 1969, and this was the day of its annual RFK Human Rights Award. In the corridor we ran into Ethel, who radiated good cheer and enthusiasm, and were soon joined by the invited speaker, a slender man in a dark suit who greeted us with an embracing smile. Barack Obama was in his first year as the junior senator from Illinois, but his good looks and winning person-ality set him apart. I met him at a fund-raiser at Vernon Jordan's house two years earlier when he was campaigning for the Senate. Standing in Vernon's small library we found common interest in Thurgood Marshall, who was a hero to the former law professor. I was struck by his courtesy and concentration, how at his first event in Washington he never glanced away to check the turnout. Vernon had asked me to come, saying, "I just need people—you don't have to contrib-ute," but I left a check on the way out. I thought this young state senator from Chicago could enliven the United States Senate.

This was the week Robert Kennedy would have turned eighty. On hand was a collection of family and friends, politicians and reporters, who lent a class re-union aura to the frequent gatherings Ethel had organized during the thirty-seven years since Bobby's death. Ted Kennedy welcomed the crowd. Seeing him at the podium with his shock of silver hair, I wondered how Bobby, forever in our memory with his lithe body and brown forelock, would have looked at eighty. Time had passed and the pain was spent from these occasions, but the subtext of unfulfilled promise remained—the inclination to imagine once more what might have been.

And that's what made Barack Obama's remarks that day so extraordinary. For the first time at one of these events Robert Kennedy was compellingly projected into the future. Obama spoke of "the unfinished legacy that calls us still." He described Bobby's trip to the Mississippi Delta with Medgar Evers in 1967, where he wept at the desperate straits of a small child with a swollen stomach: "Kennedy turns to Evers and asks, 'How can a country like this allow it?' and Evers responds, 'Maybe they just don't know.'" "Bobby Kennedy," concluded Obama, "spent his life making sure that we knew that we have it within our power to change all this, to write our own destiny. Because we are a people of hope. Because we are Americans."

I walked out of that ceremony alongside Greg Craig, who had worked with both Ted Kennedy and Bill Clinton on justice and foreign policy matters. We looked at one another with the shared sense that we had seen a man who could change our politics. I returned to my office to resume work on the upcoming *Kennedy Center Honors,* but Obama stayed on my mind.

I sat down and wrote to the senator saying that I'd been doing some math during his speech. "John Kennedy was forty-three when he ran for president. Bobby was forty-three. You will be forty-seven in 2008—hurtling toward senior citizenship." I added that the country was ready for change now, not in 2012 or 2016, and that I had watched Robert Kennedy weigh the same question in 1967. I said that in my view he was needed just as much now as Bobby was then.

A week later Jenny Yeager called from the senator's office, saying that he appreciated my thoughts but he was not running for president. "Nevertheless," I told Jenny, "Liz and I would like him to meet some of our friends."

Tim Russert of *Meet the Press* was expert at boxing politicians into "Sherman-like statements," squeezing them to say, on the record, that they wouldn't be running for higher office. In January 2006 Russert reminded Obama of their interview in 2004. "I asked, 'Will you serve your full six-year term as United States senator from Illinois?' Your answer was, 'Absolutely.'"

"So," Russert said, eager to pin him down. "You will not run for president or vice president in 2008?" Obama then made the Sherman-like statement. "I will not."

A few days later Liz and I showed up at a small fund-raiser at a downtown law office for Obama's 2010 Senate campaign. Eric Holder, who had served as deputy attorney general in the Clinton administration, and I were talking when Obama came over. "It's my mother's birthday, I called her this morning," Eric said. "She saw you say on *Meet the Press* that you weren't going to run for president. She was disappointed."

"Give me your phone," Obama said. "I'd like to wish your mother a happy birthday. I'll tell her I can always change my mind."

I saw in that moment a different kind of politician. He wasn't going to worry about Russert's games.

In June of 2006 Liz and I had a gathering at our house to introduce Obama to Washington friends, cohosted by my friend Jim Johnson, who had been Walter Mondale's campaign manager and was a continuing presence in Democratic politics. The event raised funds for Barack's 2010 Senate race four years hence, even though our hopes were loftier. Obama stood on the short stairway above our crowded living room and made a strong first impression on the guests. A group of twenty went on to Johnson's house for dinner where Obama fielded questions from leading Democrats, including Bill Daley (whose brother Richard was mayor of Chicago), Richard Holbrooke, Tom Nides, Tom Donilon and Greg Craig, some of whom had not yet met him but all of whom would one day work for him. The talk afterward among these experienced handicappers, most of whom supported Hillary, centered on whether Obama had the experience to be president. Except for Johnson and Craig the verdict was "no."

Greg and I began having lunches at the Hay Adams with John Reilly, a veteran of the Robert Kennedy Justice Department and a key adviser to Mondale's 1984 campaign, and reporter Tom Oliphant, from the *Boston Globe*. We were true believers and enjoyed scheming about how to move Obama, as Oliphant put it, beyond denial and into consideration. Others were telling him that he lacked experience and that his time would come in 2012 or 2016.

During the fall Obama became the most sought-after Democrat for appearances at fund-raisers in support of Senate and House candidates, but there was only mild speculation about him running. On October 22 he made a return appearance on *Meet the Press* to talk about his new book, *The Audacity of Hope,* that had hit the best-seller lists. This time Russert replayed Barack's statement from nine months before, then asked whether it was fair to say he was thinking of running for president. Barack said, "It's fair, yes." Reminded by Russert of his earlier statement, he responded evenly, "That was how I was thinking at that time."

On November 28, during the heat of the 2006 Kennedy Center Honors production, I took a call. "I'm thinking seriously about running," said the now familiar voice. "What do you think?" I took a deep breath. "I believe the country's ready to turn the page," I said. "I hope you do it." Obama made an exploratory trip to New Hampshire in December—still noncommittal but stirring expectations. Then on January 3, after the Christmas holiday during which he talked with Michelle and obtained her agreement, he called again. "I'm going to run for president," he said without preamble. "I hope I can count on your help."

It was exactly one year to the day before the first voting in the Iowa caucuses.

Around this time Liz and I were invited to celebrate the hanging of Vernon Jordan's picture in the National Portrait Gallery. I hadn't had contact with the Clinton world for some time and Hillary wouldn't officially enter the campaign until April, but at the reception Capricia Marshall, Hillary's aide and my good friend, came over to me. "Is it true what I've heard?" she asked, before adding, "Obama." I was surprised by her intensity. "Yes, I'm helping Barack," I replied. "You'll be back," she said sternly, before turning away. I understood then that this campaign wouldn't be all sweetness and light.

The Obama Finance Committee first met in Washington in April, chaired by Chicago businesswoman Penny Pritzker. The committee's core responsibility was raising money, but it had other functions. We were given a list of twenty-three policy advisory groups ranging from agriculture and education to housing and trade. Late in the meeting I suggested to Penny that a committee dedicated to the arts could be valuable. She welcomed the idea and asked me to chair the group. I had earlier met Broadway producer Margo Lion and crossed the room to ask her if she would be cochair, and she agreed. As we adjourned I recorded at the top of my notes a phrase from the meeting that had struck a nerve: "Put your shoulder on the wheel of history and move it."

Margo and I enlisted leading artists and educators to join the Obama Arts Policy Committee to draft arts policy positions for a future Obama government, to help with fund-raising and become surrogates at campaign events. Our conference calls, meetings and enlistment of new members would continue until election day.

I marked my seventy-fifth birthday in April and recalled our long-ago celebration of Averell Harriman's seventy-fifth—an age that back then seemed ancient. Now having reached that milestone I was involved in an exciting new political adventure. At the same time there were grim reminders of the sorrow that attends a long life. In January my beloved pal Art Buchwald died in hospice at age eighty-one, earning laughs to the end. Then in weeks to follow we lost Arthur Schlesinger, Jr., Ahmet Ertegun and Bill Styron. All were brave, witty and wise companions who enriched American life with their creativity.

Liz was impressed with Barack, but she was one of the founders in 1974 of the Women's Campaign Fund that supports progressive female candidates, and she was fully on board with Hillary. Liz and I managed our competing passions with goodwill and harmony. She agreed that I could host a fund-raiser at Avon Lane for Barack and departed on a conveniently timed trip to London.

May 24 was a blissful spring day as people began to stream into Liz's blooming garden. There was a small reception inside for cohosts in the room where noncandidate Barack had spoken just a year earlier. Three hundred enthusiastic supporters, who had contributed more than $350,000 to his campaign, gathered in the garden. When I introduced the candidate I recalled our first meeting at Vernon Jordan's house and mentioned that Vernon said, "I just need people— you don't have to contribute." When Barack took the mic his first words were, "I'm going to have to have a talk with Vernon." Liz returned from London and gracefully ignored rumors that there had been more than eighty people at her house.

There were thirteen televised debates among eight Democratic candidates in which Barack hoped to gain ground, but in the fall he was twenty-nine points behind Hillary in the Gallup Poll. There was a meeting of the Obama Finance Committee in Des Moines on Columbus Day weekend that began with a small reception on Sunday at the Des Moines Art Center. It was evident that many top supporters had grown restless. Barack had a rule of being home with his family on Sunday nights and wasn't expected to appear, but having been told he had to reenergize his core followers, he ambled in during cocktails with his lightning smile. Standing on a small stage he spoke with ease and humor, laying out the plan for his campaign with arresting confidence. Then, referring to the crucial Iowa caucuses where the first voting would take place in eight weeks, he was, let's say, audacious. "We are going to win Iowa," he promised. "And that will change everything."

At a meeting the next morning of key people from every state, Barack's soft-spoken campaign manager, David Plouffe, made a convincing presentation. He surprised us by stating that Obama's staff outnumbered Hillary's in state after state. Few of us had any idea just how strategic the campaign was.

72

Thurgood

One never knows how inspiration might arrive.

It was on March 9, 1998, during editing of *The Thin Red Line,* that Liz and I joined Sidney and Joanna Poitier for dinner at Mimosa in Los Angeles. Sidney and I were seated beside one another across from Liz and Joanna on the banquette.

"What are you up to?" I asked Sidney after the server had placed Mimosa's signature jar of olives and cornichons on the table. "It's been forty years since *Raisin in the Sun,*" he said. "I want to go back to Broadway."

My inquiry was casual and I didn't anticipate such an explicit response. I absorbed his statement and to this day I wonder at my reply. "How about I write a play about Thurgood Marshall?" I had never written a play, nor do I recall ever thinking of doing so. I remember Sidney lighting up. "I would like that," he said.

My impromptu question launched me on a new creative path—to expand our research from *Separate But Equal* to encompass Thurgood's life after the *Brown* decision—and write a play.

Liz and I kept an apartment at the Sierra Towers in Los Angeles where Sidney and Joanna lived. It was a spring afternoon a year later when he joined me in our living room. He was a striking figure as he paced the carpet in his burnt orange cashmere sweater, reading my one-man play from beginning to end. I often marveled at the determination and courage it must have required for Sidney to leave Cat Island in the Bahamas at sixteen with empty pockets, hop a freight train from Miami to New York, and become a man of such distinction. I was energized to be writing a play that might take this talented artist back to Broadway.

Justice Sandra Day O'Connor had written how when deliberations on the court reached Thurgood, he would say, "Let me tell you a story," and relay a life experience that affected the other justices. His humor and gift for storytelling fueled my writing. On each of my trips to Los Angeles Sidney would read a new draft of the play in my living room. One day he told me that he and Joanna were moving to a house on Angelo Drive in Beverly Hills. "There's a room in that house," he smiled, "where I am going to memorize your play."

Several months later Sidney invited me for lunch at his new home. "George," he said, just after we sat down, "I am seventy-five years old. I cannot learn your play." I was stunned, but my first feeling was for this proud man who was confronting the reality of diminishing powers. We parted understanding one another and I was left to absorb the disappointment.

It was Sidney's belief in me that inspired the play, so I put it aside and concentrated on other projects. Time passed and in the fall of 2004 Liz and I went to the opening of a revival of *On Golden Pond* at the Kennedy Center starring James Earl Jones. At the supper afterward I mentioned to his wife Ceci that I had written a play about Thurgood Marshall. "Send it to him," she said with an air of authority.

I wrote a letter the next day and dispatched the script. It was a Thursday night when the phone rang. Liz called out, "It's for you."

"Who is it?"

"It's either the Verizon man or James Earl."

I listened as the grandest voice in the land intoned, "You have written a kick-ass play and I want to do it!" I settled in the easy chair. "It's an exhilarating ride," he continued. "I like that he's liberal, admits his faults—he drinks and likes women and stands for all the right things. How much of this is you and how much is Thurgood?"

"I'd say 95 percent is Thurgood."

"I see a lot of you in it—and that's good."

James Earl urged me to meet Leonard Foglia, who had directed him in *On Golden Pond.* I was considering directing the play myself, but after breakfast with Leonard I realized how skilled he was and have never regretted choosing him. I spoke to Bill Haber, a founding partner at CAA now producing plays in New York, who loved the play and became our producer. I was a rookie in the Broadway jungle and discovered Bill to be a man of his word and a superb shepherd for our play. For years I had been fending off unwanted interventions on screenplays for television and movies. Now I was to enjoy the governing principle of theater—the playwright has the final word.

Bill arranged a three-week preview engagement in April 2006 at the Westport Playhouse in Connecticut which, if successful, would lead us to Broadway. During rehearsals in New York I watched James Earl's theatrical imagination give life to the written word. *Thurgood* had a splendid opening at Westport. In ninety minutes without an intermission James Earl captured Thurgood's humor, found pathos in the dramatic passages, was commanding in the Supreme Court argument in the *Brown* case, and offered an enthralling portrait of the older Thurgood as a justice on the Court. Paul Newman and Joanne Woodward lived in Westport and were supporters of the theater, and Paul's certainty on opening night about the play's importance meant more to me than he knew. Thurgood's widow Cissy and his sons Thurgood, Jr., and John came from Washington. Cissy thrilled James Earl backstage by saying mischievously, "You were better than he was."

My pal John Guare came to Westport and passed on wisdom from the great Moss Hart—the audience is yours for the first sixteen minutes, at which point they decide whether or not they will go on your journey. John provided one precious suggestion. "Thurgood comes onstage telling his story," he said. "We must know who he's talking to and why he is telling us all this." His suggestion was that Thurgood had come back to his alma mater, the Howard University School of Law, to speak to the students. Above the proscenium we placed a sign indicating this. The audience became, in the actor's mind, the students.

Broadway prospects seemed bright, but early in the run we had to address James Earl's occasional inability to remember a line. He had no problems with *On Golden Pond,* nor would he with other plays in years to come, but in a one-man play the actor is alone with no partners to fill in if there is a lapse. We concealed a teleprompter in the set as a safety net for James Earl, but once the Westport run was complete he decided not to make our planned trip to Broadway. We had a compelling play but had run aground with America's two most beloved African American actors.

It was then that Michael Stevens called from Los Angeles. "Laurence Fishburne is doing August Wilson's *Fences* at the Pasadena Playhouse. I think we ought to go see it." Laurence, in his midforties, was impressive onstage, but not certain to be the draw on Broadway that Sidney or James Earl would be. We went backstage, complimented him on his performance, and were about to leave when Michael said, "Dad, are you going to tell Mr. Fishburne about your play?" I was uncertain about mentioning it, but spurred by the impatience of youth I described the play and told of the run at Westport. "Well," Fishburne said, "should it ever be age appropriate for me, I would be interested."

I called Bill Haber in New York the next morning. "The play is strong," he said. "We can make it work with Fishburne." We would discover—the old story of how the worst thing that can happen turns out to be the best—that Laurence's youth became a strength of the play. He could come onstage acting Marshall as an older man, then dispense with suit jacket and cane, remove his black-framed glasses, and become the vital young lawyer of the *Brown* case.

The playwright on the afternoon of opening night at
the Booth Theater, April 2008.

Haber bestowed a gift by securing the ideal Broadway setting for *Thurgood,*
the historic Booth Theater on Forty-Fifth Street and Shubert Alley, home to
great plays since 1921. It provided a serendipitous connection to the Stevens
family—my great-grandmother Georgia Woodthorpe having been the youngest
Ophelia to Edwin Booth's Hamlet.

I began to enjoy time as a man of the theater. First the intense five-week rehearsal period alone in a room with Laurence and Leonard, savoring intense
hours of sharpening the text, with Leonard devising a monochrome evocation of
the Stars and Stripes to fill the back wall and serve as a screen for documentary
images of the era. I discovered the easiest subway route from the Upper East Side
to Times Square and the four-minute walk to Shubert Alley, then, each night in
the dark at the back of the house, gauged audience response—sharing their silence and laughing along with Thurgood's humor, leading up to Justice Marshall
addressing the last question in his farewell press conference at the Supreme Court.
"Our country?" he asks. "My schoolmate Langston Hughes said it pretty well."

America never was America to me.
And yet, I swear this oath—
America will be.

Broadway virtuoso and good friend Mike Nichols had *Country Girl* running
next door at the Jacobs Theater and sent an encouraging note during previews.
"I saw *Thurgood* last night and was very moved. What a perfect moment for your
superb play. With, by the way, the best last line on Broadway."

Laurence Fishburne as Thurgood Marshall, April 2008.

The large turnout of African Americans on Broadway was impressive, especially couples bringing their children so they might learn about the life experience of their parents and grandparents in segregated America.

Opening night, April 30, 2008, ten years after my dinner with Sidney, was brightened by my children and friends from our different worlds—Cicely Tyson, Paul Newman and Joanne Woodward, Whoopi Goldberg, Joan Didion, Ethel Kennedy and filmmaker daughter Rory, Vernon Jordan and Justice Stephen Breyer. During an exuberant curtain call, Thurgood's widow Cissy joined Laurence, Leonard and me onstage.

After its sold-out run on Broadway *Thurgood* transferred to the Geffen Theater in Los Angeles, then to the Kennedy Center's Eisenhower Theatre. There I relished seeing predominately African American audiences arrive each night, a rarity at the nation's cultural center. We filmed *Thurgood* at the Kennedy Center for HBO, and Michael Stevens received a Directors Guild of America nomination for his model translation of a stage play to the screen—and to a life beyond Broadway.

The icing on the cake came just before the curtain went up that first night at the Booth. My assistant Dottie McCarthy said I should check the message line at our office. I did as instructed.

"George. I know *Thurgood* is opening tonight on Broadway," said a friendly voice. "Congratulations. You know I would be there if I wasn't running for president."

73

Yes, We Can!

The year 2008 began with a political earthquake. On January 3 Barack Obama secured the upset victory he had promised in Des Moines on Columbus Day, gaining 38 percent of the vote to John Edwards' 30 percent and Hillary Clinton's 29. He went on to New Hampshire as the front-runner, but it was Hillary's turn to surprise, and she ended any dreams of Obama running the table. Barack and Michelle joined his subdued followers at a Nashua cafe for what was expected to be a victory party. He spoke without a microphone, showing in defeat wisdom beyond his years, reminding his supporters, "You don't get anointed by winning one caucus. This loss is what we needed. We know now that we have to buckle down and run a fifty-state race."

Hillary and Barack had both been seeking the support of the Kennedys, especially Ted and Caroline. Barack would call me on occasion for "Kennedy advice." During a long dinner conversation the previous August in Maine, Teddy said he would eventually support the person he thought could inspire the country and best advance the issues he cared about. Caroline seemed to be keen on Barack but felt conflicted by her ties with the Clintons.

Hillary held a twenty-four-point lead among Black democrats in South Carolina, but after Barack proved he could win in Iowa, polls flipped to give him a twenty-eight-point lead among Black voters and he won South Carolina's Saturday primary handily. On Sunday morning, spurred by her children's enthusiasm, Caroline endorsed Obama in a *New York Times* opinion piece. The next day Barack joined Teddy and Caroline onstage at a rally at American University. Teddy boomed to a rapturous crowd, "I feel change in the air!" He called for a new generation of leadership, firmly placing Kennedy family history behind Obama. On Super Tuesday Obama won fourteen states to Hillary's ten. He was now the man to beat.

Michael Kaiser had been president of the Kennedy Center since 2002, and we prided ourselves on our good working relationship. He went so far as to introduce me to the Kennedy Center trustees as the person, next to founder Roger Stevens, who had made the greatest contribution to the center's success. He called one morning to say he had spoken with Les Moonves, the head of CBS, and that they wanted 2009 to be my last year producing the *Honors.* This came as a shock because my contract had been routinely extended every three years since 1978, and the *Honors,* in addition to being one of the most prestigious shows on television, was the Kennedy Center's largest source of fund-raising. I told Kaiser that beyond my personal desire to produce the show I was concerned that the CBS objective was to make it more "popular," with less of the "artistic heft" that he and the Kennedy Center valued. "I can't go against CBS," was his response.

A few weeks later Ted Kennedy called to talk about *Thurgood,* which he'd seen in New York, before asking, "Is something going on with the Honors?" The next day we had lunch at Johnny's Half Shell on Capitol Hill and he got right to the point. "It's outrageous that CBS dictate to the Kennedy Center who should produce the show," he said. "The Honors is like the Nobel Prize. They might decide that the Honors should be awarded to young people to boost ratings." As we parted Teddy put it in personal terms. "What Jack would care about is integrity and quality."

In June Obama secured enough delegates to guarantee him the Democratic nomination. Hillary withdrew three days later and work began on unifying the party. Liz and I were cohosts of a dinner to bring Clinton and Obama forces together, hosted by Ethel Kennedy at Hickory Hill. Dinner was served under a tent on the tennis court, but for me the fondest memory was watching Barack before dinner intently examining Kennedy family memorabilia on the walls of Ethel's house, including treasured documents of the founding fathers alongside notes from Jack to the Kennedy children. Now he, who had spoken so ardently about Robert Kennedy at the Human Rights Awards in 2005, was in Bobby's house as the nominee of the Democratic Party.

There was heartbreaking news during the summer. Ted Kennedy was diagnosed with a brain tumor. Doctors gave a bleak prognosis but Ted, whose life in the Senate centered on improving health care for Americans, was unwilling to accept it. He assembled medical experts to assess his options and decided to undergo surgery at Duke University. During his subsequent regime of chemotherapy and radiation he set for himself the secret goal of being strong enough to travel in August to the Democratic Convention in Denver and speak to the delegates who would nominate Obama.

I'd had my own less urgent medical news in May when after a routine colonoscopy, doctors recommended I have a colon resection to remove a nonmalignant polyp. They agreed my operation could wait until September after the convention.

Ted Kennedy was to kick off the convention on Monday night. We learned later that he arrived in Denver Sunday night in excruciating pain on a chartered plane with his doctor. It proved to be a kidney stone attack. Hospitalized, he resisted pain medication lest he become drowsy and unable to deliver his speech. He was taken to the convention hall by ambulance, then by golf cart to the staging area. Teddy walked onstage smiling to thunderous applause and cheers. "It is wonderful to be here. Nothing—nothing! was going to keep me away from this special gathering tonight," he declared. "And this November the torch will be passed again to a new generation of Americans. The work begins anew, the hope rises again, and the dream lives on."

Once again Liz and I watched a Kennedy enthrall a Democratic convention— this time it was a heartfelt passing of a political legacy to a man who personified the promise we had been searching for since 1968.

Barack spoke on Thursday night to a triumphant crowd of eighty-four thousand people in Denver's Mile High Stadium. "Change happens because the American people demand it," he declared, "because they rise up and insist on new ideas and new leadership, a new politics for a new time. America—this is one of those moments."

I used Barack's personal email sparingly but wrote to him the next morning from the plane to Washington.

> Dear Barack. When Liz and I left the stadium last night we gathered six American flags that will go to our grandchildren so they can remember this day in our history. As we taxied to take off this morning on Delta, the pilot announced that we would have a delay for a VIP plane. Then he said, "Oh, it's the Obama plane." The passengers applauded and cheered—American travelers cheering an inconvenience—what a sublime end to a thrilling week.

74

We Are One

My task on the first Monday of September was to go to Sibley Memorial Hospital for the long-scheduled colon operation. Surgery went well and I was resting on Wednesday when Vernon Jordan walked in unannounced to cheer me up. Ten minutes after he left the surgeon came in. "We had a surprise," he said, apologetically. "The lab reports show that what we thought was benign is stage three cancer." Soon an oncologist came to see me and by then Liz was with me. He mapped out a plan for treatment and we were left to make sense of the news. Liz's beauty and charm masked her enterprise and resolve. When I came home from the hospital the next day she had arranged for me to see Dr. Leonard Saltz, head of gastrointestinal oncology at Memorial Sloan Kettering in New York.

Naturally I was concerned about coping with campaign activities and the upcoming *Kennedy Center Honors* and *Christmas in Washington.* I tried not to dwell on possible outcomes but knew that word of serious illness is not helpful in my profession, so we told no one other than family and trusted friends Tom Brokaw and Vernon Jordan. Liz and I went to New York to meet Dr. Saltz. Intelligent and personable, he mapped out six months of bimonthly chemotherapy treatments and arranged for half of them to be administered in Washington.

My first treatment at Sloan Kettering was on September 30, where I familiarized myself with the routine of sitting for two hours with two chemicals flowing into my veins through a port installed in my chest. That afternoon I had a meeting with Broadway director and choreographer Rob Ashford about the *Kennedy Center Honors.* I wasn't razor sharp but we had a productive session. It seemed that this "new normal" was going to work for me.

Soon Liz and I were in Chicago's Grant Park with our son Michael and a quarter of a million others on an unseasonably warm election night watching on JumboTrons as CNN declared Obama the winner over John McCain. Strangers were hugging one another, even the old-timers were jumping up and down waving tiny American flags. One image on the giant screens crystallized the moment—a close-up of two-time presidential aspirant Jesse Jackson with tears running down his cheeks. America had elected her first Black president. In my picture-maker's mind I was visualizing one specific television image. Americans who had for centuries faced injustice because of the color of their skin would soon see pictures of Marine One landing on the South Lawn of the White House and the handsome Obama family stepping out and walking across the lawn to their new residence.

Washington was energized as the Obama transition team worked to fill cabinet posts and a thousand jobs for his administration. I had my heart set on producing Obama's Inaugural Gala and felt I had the inside track, but others were throwing their hats in the ring, so Michael Stevens and I spent a weekend framing ideas that would blend sparkling performance with connections to history that reflected Obama's values in a way that other producers might not.

In December we entered the hectic period of the *Kennedy Center Honors* and *Christmas in Washington*—the last year for the Bushes—and during editing of the *Honors* it was confirmed that I had been chosen to produce the Inaugural Gala. Michael and I met with Jim Margolis, one of the inaugural committee chairs, who had been in charge of the Obama campaign television advertising. We outlined our thinking, and based on our experience with *America's Millennium* proposed doing it outdoors at the Lincoln Memorial. Michael and I as executive producer-writers were joined by my colleague from the early *Honors*, Don Mischer, as coproducer and director.

The date was set for Sunday, January 18, from two to four in the afternoon. We were just twenty-five days away, a period that included Christmas and New Year's, which meant our first opportunity to survey the Lincoln Memorial with our full production team was on December 30. By then it was clear that we would encounter well-meaning intrusion on the creative process from the inaugural committee. Our timetable required rapid decision making, so that night Michael, Don Mischer and I sent a memo to Hawaii to the president-elect and Michelle. They were our clients after all.

> We intend to root this event in history—interspersed and brought to
> life with entertainment that speaks to those themes that you, Barack,
> have developed over the past two years. We will seek performances
> that speak to America—that will be "anthemic" in reaching out to
> the hundreds of thousands in attendance.

The Memorial to Abraham Lincoln is our stage. His statue will be a presence looking out over the proceedings.

We hope these ideas are in line with your expectations.

The memo came back on January 2 with a note in Barack's handwriting at the top saying he liked what we proposed. We had our mandate.

The inaugural committee insisted that the initial approach to performers come from their "director of entertainment," because the contacts would be valuable to her later in the White House. We provided a few of our top names—Bono, Tom Hanks, Denzel Washington and Beyoncé. Two days later she told Michael that Bono was unavailable, and that Tom Hanks and Denzel Washington had previous commitments. This opened the door. Michael immediately sent an email to Bono in Ireland explaining that on January 18—which would be Martin Luther King Day—we wanted Bono to sing his tribute to Dr. King, "Pride (In the Name of Love)," on the steps of the Lincoln Memorial where King gave his "I Have a Dream" speech. Michael slept through a phone call in the middle of the night and found a message at six in the morning. "Bono here. Get out of bed, Michael. You have a show to put on. I have a planet to save. No time for sleeping, man." By sunset Bono and U2 were locked in.

My letter to Hanks began: "Fellow Citizens, We Cannot escape History. That is what he said, That is What Abraham Lincoln Said." Tom recognized the opening text to Aaron Copland's "Lincoln Portrait" and agreed to narrate the piece with orchestra—with Abe looking over his shoulder.

Denzel's representative said he had a family conflict but to send along what we had in mind. That evening he received the words that would be spoken to open the show.

> We gather here today—Americans standing among the monuments that symbolize our history. We stand on the steps of the memorial to the Great Emancipator, Abraham Lincoln; to the east we look to the monument of the Father of our Country, George Washington; and to the south the memorial that honors the author of our Declaration of Independence, Thomas Jefferson. On this day, we are inspired by the man we have elected to be the 44th president of the United States of America.

Denzel said he would bring his family to Washington.

HBO agreed to broadcast the show. We met with its trailblazing chairman, Richard Plepler in New York, who was thrilled by the early star bookings. We were energized by his enthusiasm and his plan to broadcast the Sunday afternoon show live on HBO and repeat it that evening. I stopped at Dr. Saltz's office for treatment number eight on the way back to Washington. When I told him about our new project that would involve outdoor rehearsals at night in eighteen-degree weather, he leafed through my lab reports. "You're taking two debilitating drugs. I believe the first one has done its work. I'll stop it for the next six weeks," he announced. "I don't want to compromise what we're doing here," I protested. "I don't compromise," he said with authority. "It's science."

In the midst of all this I had a call from Michael Kaiser informing me the Kennedy Center was now prepared to sign a three-year extension to my Kennedy Center contract. Senator Kennedy's concerns had likely been a factor. And Kaiser speculated that Moonves realized a change of producers in the first year of Obama was not propitious. I had a cordial breakfast with Moonves two weeks later at the Regency in New York where he referred to the Honors as "your baby." I decided not to spend too much time figuring out the duality of his thinking.

We created a village behind the Lincoln Memorial—offices, satellite trucks, space heaters, dressing rooms, makeup tents, commissary, music room—to accommodate a corps of five hundred performers and technicians in parkas, mufflers and ski hats. It was sunny and seventeen degrees on Saturday afternoon, twenty-four hours to show time. Mary J. Blige, dressed it seemed for the ski slopes, was first onstage to rehearse "Lean on Me." Like other artists to come she climbed to the seated statue of Lincoln for a close look.

Mary could hear Springsteen warming up in the music tent. He was followed by John Legend, James Taylor and Jennifer Nettles performing "Shower the People" as a trio. Michael convinced artists expecting to perform solo to appear onstage with others. It was a way of giving the day as much star power as possible, including a trio of Usher, Shakira and Stevie Wonder. We worked into the night with Bono and U2, Garth Brooks and Beyoncé, as the onstage thermometer showed five degrees.

Arthur Lewis was our stage manager on *Christmas in Washington* and assistant stage manager for the Honors. A natural leader and African American, he was the best person to run the *We Are One* stage, and we arranged his release from another job to join us. He did a stellar job handling complex logistical challenges for the live show. We were notified at 1:45 p.m. Sunday that the Obamas and Vice President-elect Joe Biden and his wife Jill had arrived. Michael, Arthur and I went to greet them in the security trailer behind the memorial. Arthur briefed the president-elect on the run of the show and his movements with precision, setting the tone for what was to follow.

I recall no more inspiring experience than walking with the Obamas and Bidens to the point of their entrance behind Lincoln's statue at the top of the memorial and seeing them take in the sweep of the sunlit mall—an assembly that had grown to 750,000 people, some perched in trees—extending three-quarters of a mile to the Washington Monument. On the spacious stage were flags of the fifty-eight states and territories, the United States Herald Trumpets and a combined military services orchestra. Joe and Jill Biden descended the marble steps to cheers. Then the Obamas walked down hand in hand, smiling to the roar of the shivering crowd, and took their places in the special box onstage beside Malia, Sasha and the Bidens.

The three-cushion shot of Denzel Washington's dignity and eloquence, followed by Springsteen with a swaying chorus in red gowns singing "The Rising," his anthem about a September 11 firefighter who finds resurrection in his sacrifice, and the majesty of Hanks reciting Lincoln to Copland's orchestral score, got things off to a commanding start. Film sequences shown on the large screens of Marian Anderson singing at the Lincoln Memorial in 1939 after being denied at Constitution Hall, and of Martin Luther King—and presidents Teddy Roosevelt, FDR, Eisenhower, Kennedy and Reagan—connected the audience to American history.

The multitude listened to spoken passages with what one report called reverential quiet—Martin Luther King III, Forest Whitaker, Ashley Judd, Marisa Tomei, Laura Linney, Tiger Woods, Steve Carell and Jamie Foxx reading the words of Jefferson, Robert Kennedy, Thurgood Marshall, Rosa Parks. The last was a spot-on impression by Jamie Foxx of Obama's "Change Has Come" Grant Park speech that drew laughter down the length of the mall. The president-elect was grinning.

Samuel Jackson's introduction of U2 was simple: "A band from Ireland was moved by Dr. King's message and his sacrifice, and wrote a song to remember and honor him." The appearance of Bono and U2 was a surprise, so when they were seen on the screens, the reaction was wild. After "Pride (In the Name of Love)," Bono thanked the president-elect for using a U2 song during his campaign before performing a mesmerizing "Oh, you look so beautiful tonight in the City of Blinding Lights."

With President-elect Barack Obama and Michelle Obama at the Lincoln Memorial
following the *We Are One* inaugural concert, January 19, 2009.

Obama took the stage and spoke to his largest crowd ever. "Behind me,
watching over the union he saved, sits the man who in so many ways made this
day possible," he said. "And yet, as I stand here today, what gives me the greatest
hope of all is not the stone and the marble that surrounds us, but what fills the
spaces in between. It is you—Americans of every race and region and station
who came here because you believe in what this country can be and because you
want to help us get there."

Springsteen returned with the once-blacklisted and now much-loved eighty-
nine-year-old folk legend Pete Seeger, and together they led a singalong of
Woody Guthrie's "This Land Is Your Land," followed by Beyoncé's entrance
to sing a hymnlike arrangement of "America the Beautiful." The show was
called "We Are One," which became an idea fully rendered as the entire cast
joined the thousands standing on the mall and the new First Family in the last
verse.

Barack Obama was not as prolific a note writer as the Kennedys—making
the one that arrived a day later a "keeper."

George —

THE WHITE HOUSE

The Lincoln Memorial event was simply extraordinary! What you, your son and your team accomplished in such a short span of time was remarkable, and Michelle and I will be forever grateful.

Love to the family —

Michelle Obama would say about living in the White House, "I wake up every morning in a house that was built by slaves. And I watch my daughters, two beautiful, intelligent black young women, playing with their dogs on the White House lawn."

How I wish Robert Kennedy could have heard those words.

75

The President's Committee

It was a new day in Washington. The city and the country were exhilarated and filled with hope as the new president took the reins.

David Jacobson, an affable Chicagoan who had taken a senior post in the presidential personnel office, called one morning. Would I be interested in serving as chair of the President's Committee on the Arts and Humanities? While it would be a manageable part-time responsibility, the truth is I had never been a big fan of the committee that was started by Reagan in 1982. He hoped to demonstrate that arts funding could be handled by the private sector, and appointees to the committee were mainly campaign donors, a practice continued through the years. I told David I thought the President's Committee could play an important role and be effective if the president would appoint leading artists to the panel. David promised that could be done, so revisiting our campaign alliance, Margo Lion and I agreed to be cochairs.

There were many donors to the Obama campaign seeking positions on the committee, so I had to bargain with the White House to secure places for artists. We finally agreed on a stellar group. Yo-Yo Ma was at the top of our list but he was reluctant because of his demanding concert tours. I wrote to Yo-Yo days before the death of Ted Kennedy and described the committee's potential and how significant his participation could be. "I join you and so many others in mourning Senator Kennedy's passing. How different the Kennedy Center Honors will be without him!" began Yo-Yo's encouraging response. "I am grateful for the opportunity to carry some of the Senator's work forward through President Obama's Committee on the Arts and Humanities—his election creates an extraordinary opening to bring together the political and cultural engines of America. I welcome the chance to roll up my sleeves and join you in this effort."

With Vice President Joe Biden at swearing in of the President's
Committee at the White House in June 2009.

Vice President Joe Biden swore in new members at the White House in June
of 2009. During the campaign the Obama Arts Policy Committee had proposed an
"artist corps" and the candidate endorsed the idea. The President's Committee's
first act was to initiate a study, *Reinvesting in Arts Education,* which concluded that
the arts should be an essential ingredient in a well-rounded education, and that the
children most in need of the arts are most often the ones least exposed. This led to
Turnaround Arts, an initiative to deploy artists to help children in schools on the
Department of Education's list of the lowest performing schools in the country.

Yo-Yo Ma led the way along with the other committee members—visual artist Chuck Close, dancer-choreographer Damian Woetzel and Forest Whitaker—
each of whom "adopted" one of the lowest performing schools. They spent time
with students and teachers, providing instruction and inspiration. Damian accepted the most challenging assignment—a school on a remote Cheyenne Indian reservation in Montana plagued by poverty, drugs and a startlingly high suicide rate.
He enlisted musicians from the dynamic Silkroad Ensemble, who are in residency
there to this day, to engage the children in music. Yo-Yo adopted Orchard

President Obama discusses arts policy with his President's Committee on the Arts and the
Humanities in the Roosevelt Room, May 11, 2011. Stevens on Obama's right, Margo Lion to his
left, Alfre Woodard at end of the table, Kerry Washington, far right, Jill Udall to her left.

Gardens School in Boston, leading a dramatic turnaround from the lowest performing school in Massachusetts to the most improved, a result that school leadership fully attributed to the arts. Chuck Close adopted Roosevelt School in
Bridgeport, Connecticut, not only spending time at the school but bringing students for workshops at his studios in New York City and Long Island.

We discovered that students who were withdrawn and struggling were liberated by their participation in the arts, increasing their confidence and acceler-
ating progress. Turnaround Arts provided arts supplies, musical instruments
and intensive professional development for teachers. "We really did turn these
places around," Chuck Close later observed to the *New York Times*. "My school
in Bridgeport had 60 percent truancy and it just eliminated it."

The First Lady was honorary chairman of the President's Committee. Michelle Obama, in the traditional role, made it anything but honorary. Her vitality, commitment, humor and intelligence were breathtaking. She understood the
importance of early education and the role the arts could play in building confidence in struggling children, and hosted an annual "talent show" where students
from Turnaround Arts schools were invited to perform on the East Room stage.

Sarah Jessica Parker, Alfre Woodard and Kerry Washington, who had adopted low-performing schools, prepared their students for the first show. It was

heartening to see children with so few opportunities display their talent so joyfully on the White House stage. Sitting tall in the front row, Michelle seemed to nourish their confidence with her glow of appreciation, and when presenting awards onstage she embraced and spoke with each child. Her commitment to early education in the arts energized the program.

In 2016, approaching the end of Obama's second term, we found a permanent home for Turnaround Arts at the Kennedy Center, where it was expanded to more than eighty schools in fourteen states.

We had an exciting last act leading the first American cultural delegation to Cuba. Our close-knit band ranged from playwright John Guare to Alfre Woodard and Lourdes Lopez of the Miami Ballet, along with musicians Smokey Robinson, Usher, and Dave Matthews. The last three led a rousing late-night concert with Cuba's finest.

Fifty-seven years of enforced separation was soon transformed into something more like Guare's *Six Degrees of Separation.* Cuban filmmakers knew our films, playwrights quoted from American plays, and dancers were steeped in our traditions that complemented their own. We discovered virtuoso Cuban music, dance and painting. An ensemble of Havana's outstanding female string musicians invited violinist Joshua Bell from our delegation to join them in a sublime performance of Vivaldi's *Four Seasons.*

Presidents Obama and Raul Castro had agreed the previous month to normalize relations, expressing hope that Congress would end the longstanding US trade embargo of Cuba. Artists are optimists, and as we lifted off from Jose Marti International, we felt ever more enthusiastic about using the arts to revive our country's relationship with the Cuban people.

76

Labors of Love

In 2010 my attention was drawn to three men, each of whom I admired, each one very different from the other.

The 2009 Kennedy Center Honors, which honored Merle Haggard, Bill T. Jones, Jerry Herman, Oprah Winfrey and Paul McCartney, took place on Sunday, December 5. I was editing the show when an email arrived. "This was the most memorable Honors since the night we said goodbye to Henry Fonda," wrote Richard Holbrooke. "Kati and I are honored to have been there, and with great seats! You and Michael have done it again (and again and again and again)! Hope to see you again (and again and again!) Soon."

Three days later Richard took ill during a meeting with Secretary Hillary Clinton at the State Department and was rushed to the hospital. He had been under great stress as Obama's envoy, making twenty-hour flights to Afghanistan. His friends kept watch while he underwent two surgeries to repair a torn aorta. He died the following Monday. There would be no "again and again and again."

Dick was ambitious, determined, persuasive, great fun, and at times infuriating. His wife Kati asked me to produce a memorial service at the Kennedy Center, and it occurred to me that in a serious town like Washington I might be seen as something of a court jester, the one looked to when a show was needed. But I knew one thing about Holbrooke—nothing would be "over the top" in his eyes. Presidents Clinton and Obama agreed to speak, as did Dick's boss, Hillary. There was the chairman of the Joint Chiefs, Admiral Mike Mullen, and Kofi Annan from the United Nations. And Kati, her daughter and Dick's two sons. His list of personal friends was finally pared to five of the most articulate and voluble people in the country. There was no way to impose a time limit on ex-presidents or Hillary, but we managed to enforce a five-hundred-word rule on the others.

Presidential advance meetings for the Kennedy Center Honors usually numbered ten people. When I showed up for the Holbrooke meeting there were fifty-four people overflowing a conference room. Staff and security reps for two presidents, the secretary of state, and other VIPs. I took a moment to picture Holbrooke's heavenly delight at this assemblage on his behalf.

Fifteen hundred people came to the Opera House, including the presidents of Pakistan and Georgia, three secretaries of state (the post Dick aspired to), and ambassadors from many nations. An unsentimental observer noted that the Washington contingent included those who ardently loved Dick Holbrooke along with those who hated him. All that was missing was Dick being there with Kati in his "great seats" beaming at the remembrances. "He was like Odysseus," opined his longtime colleague Les Gelb, "a leader of men and women, prone to troubles, wily, never paralyzed by self-doubt, forever in search of legendary feats." He would have been moved by soprano Renée Fleming's "Ave Maria" and gratified that Americans at home were watching on CSPAN. And he would have relished President Clinton's summing-up that spoke to his life work.

"I loved the guy because he could *do*—doing and diplomacy saved lives," Clinton declared. "There are a lot of people walking around on the face of the earth because of the way he lived his life, and I could never understand people who didn't appreciate him. Most of the people who didn't were not nearly as good at *doing*."

The next week Barbara Bush greeted Michael and me at the door of her house in Houston with two shih tzus underfoot. President George Herbert Walker Bush, aided by a high-tech scooter chair, led us to the dining room. He had, at ninety-two, decided to hold one last public event to support the Points of Light Foundation, his organization that fosters volunteerism.

"This is going to be my last hurrah," the president said with a smile. "It's important to my family that it be a classy occasion. It would give us a lot of confidence if you fellas would take this on." Michael and I promised to do it—flattered that a Republican hero would put two Democrats in charge of his swan song.

Coordinating the involvement of every living president was part of our task. Jimmy and Rosalynn Carter, Bill Clinton, and George and Laura Bush came to the Kennedy Center in tribute to Bush 41, and Barack Obama, traveling in Latin America, sent a reminder on video that "there are few greater acts of patriotism than serving your fellow Americans." We called the show *All Together Now,* and NBC agreed to broadcast it. Michael enlisted top entertainers who admired

George H. W. Bush and supported his belief in volunteerism. Reba McEntire was host and Brad Paisley, Carrie Underwood, Sam Moore, Darius Rucker, Sheryl Crow and Kid Rock performed, along with the generous and captivating Garth Brooks, who touched everyone with "America the Beautiful."

Bill Clinton thanked the younger President Bush for doing him one of the great favors of his life when he asked him on two occasions to work with his father—first in South Asia after the tsunami and then in the Gulf Coast after Hurricane Katrina.

> We took seven trips together. It was an amazing experience. This
> man who I'd always liked and respected but who I ran against in
> a sometimes painful campaign—I really came to love. I realized
> how much energy we waste on fights over things that don't matter
> [*applause*]. It got so ridiculous, this "odd couple" relationship, that
> Barbara began to refer to me as her errant son, the Black Sheep of the
> family [*laughter*]. Now, George can do no wrong in my eyes, though
> every five years he makes me look like a wimp by insisting on
> continuing to jump out of airplanes [*laughter*].

I sensed the pleasure of George and Barbara Bush sharing with their children and grandchildren this occasion that rose above politics. Looking back at the mutual respect displayed by two Republican and two Democratic presidents makes me long for the civility of that celebratory night.

In June 2010 I gave the annual Herblock Lecture at the Library of Congress, which was an opportunity to speak about the political cartoonist Herb Block, who I considered the most creative resident of Washington during my many years in the city. His cartoons appeared under the name Herblock on the editorial page of the *Washington Post* for forty-five years, sometimes six days a week. A brilliant graphic artist whose work was underpinned with political insight, a sense of justice and great wit, he received four Pulitzer Prizes and the Presidential Medal of Freedom.

Herb was a mild-mannered Georgetown neighbor who looked more like your friendly pharmacist than a man able to boil down global complexities into stinging visual satire. He was a friend whose life intrigued me, and he regularly encouraged Michael during high school, inscribing his books "to a fellow writer"—so Michael and I decided to make a documentary. We interviewed fifty journalists, pundits and satirists including Ben Bradlee, Bob Woodward,

Backstage with the Bushes after the show. Ali Stevens, George Stevens, Jr., Barbara Bush,
George H. W. Bush, Liz Stevens, Michael Stevens.

Carl Bernstein, Gwen Ifill, Tom Brokaw, Jules Feiffer and Jon Stewart. They
spoke to the way Herblock took on big oil, corporate polluters, the gun lobby,
racists and demagogues in cartoons that, despite being drawn decades ago, speak
to twenty-first-century concerns.

Herb kept generations of politicians on their toes, showing Nixon with five
o'clock shadow popping out of a manhole, and Clinton, in a cartoon called
"Balance," on a tightrope with a wan smile balancing the budget on one side and
Monica Lewinsky on the other.

Herb was compensated with Class A *Washington Post* stock in his early days
at the paper, which meant that this man who never owned a car died with an
estate in the neighborhood of $90 million. He left the money to start the Herb
Block Foundation, managed by his coworkers, to fight prejudice and discrimi-
nation, and to support editorial cartoonists. "The free press was established,"
Herb said, "to serve as a reminder to public servants that they are, well, public
servants."

There was a time when I wondered if I was where I was because of my father,
so it was rewarding to see my son step out of the shadow and demonstrate his
gifts as a director and writer and to speak for our film. "It was a wrestling match,"

"Here I Am, Copper"

From the pen of Herblock during Watergate, July 27, 1973.

he told *Written By,* the Writers Guild of America magazine. "It had to be written, there was no way we could just walk into the editing room as you might
with other documentaries and hope to figure it out." He structured a story of a
decent man with timeless ideals who took on the mightiest of public figures with
his pen, and HBO presented *Herblock: The Black & the White* to the nation.

77

Surprise

One night in September of 2012 I picked up the ringing phone in the kitchen around midnight.

"George. This is Hawk Koch, president of the Motion Picture Academy, calling from Los Angeles."

"Hello, Hawk. Good to hear from you."

"I'm calling to let you know that the Board of Governors meeting just ended, and you were chosen to receive an Honorary Academy Award for your lifetime contribution to motion pictures."

It had never occurred to me that I would be singled out by the Academy because of my prominent identification with AFI. Koch mentioned that the awards dinner would be on the first of December in Los Angeles. Only after he hung up did I realize that was the Saturday of Kennedy Center Honors weekend, the day each year that we often likened to choreographing a hurricane. Liz had gone to bed so I called Michael in L.A. He seemed thrilled with the news and congratulated me. I mentioned my concern about the date. Michael, as was his nature, said, "Oh, Dad, we'll work something out." The next morning the significance of the Academy recognition hit home. I was on cloud nine.

We were facing an especially challenging Kennedy Center show that included an elaborate tribute to Led Zeppelin. We figured out that I could remain onstage in Washington until 3 p.m. on Saturday, then leave Michael in charge and expand my carbon footprint by taking a private plane offered by a Canadian friend to Los Angeles to accept the award. Liz managed the preparations for the Saturday dinner for the honorees at the State Department, then flew out Friday afternoon, as did Caroline from New York and David from New Hampshire. Our dear friends Tom and Meredith Brokaw came from New York and met us at our table where we were joined by Annette Bening and Warren Beatty, Quincy Jones, and Irena and Mike Medavoy.

With presenter Annette Bening and Warren Beatty at the Oscars ceremony.

Annette was a member of the board of governors and unbeknownst to me had been my advocate during the selection process in which seventeen Academy branches advance candidates for three openings. Annette confided how moved she was by the way Michael had quietly provided her with a binder of research and arranged letters from Steven Spielberg and other admirers.

That evening, surrounded by family and dear friends, I received more than my share of adulation (reminding me of Adlai Stevenson's phrase, "Flattery is fine if you don't inhale"). Annette did the spoken tribute, referring to me as "producer, playwright, activist, politician, archivist, champion, gate-keeper, benevolent despot, artist, author and mentor." She introduced the short biographical film produced by Davis Guggenheim, son of my late colleague Charles, that lived up to the Guggenheim standard. When the lights came up Sidney Poitier stood onstage.

George and I have worked together on films and fought the causes that we both believe in. When he commits to something he will get

Sidney and George. December 1, 2012.

it done. You may not know that George is also an extremely gifted director. I had the unique privilege of being directed by both George in *Separate But Equal* and by his father in *The Greatest Story Ever Told*. On behalf of the Academy I am proud to present this Honorary Oscar to George Stevens, Jr.

To be handed an Academy Award by Sidney—with his stature and humanity—was the crowning touch. I recall, as I began to speak, Steven Spielberg, Tom Hanks, Daniel Day-Lewis and Tony Kushner being seated directly in my line of sight. I told the story of my first trip to the Oscars at age twelve, standing in for my father at war, when he lost to *Casablanca,* and me saying, "We wuz robbed," to the amusement of my mother and the leading ladies seated around us. I closed with these words:

I thank Dad for opening the door to a creative life that has been so rich and gave me so many wonderful friends in our profession—and for "the test of time." I know there are filmmakers among us who will swim into the currents to make films filled with passion and glory and pity and sacrifice, that reach the depths of our humanity. So tonight I say, here's to the great films of the future.

And I should add—tonight "we wasn't robbed."

Tom and Meredith Brokaw joined Liz and me (and Oscar) for the overnight flight to Washington. I was on the bustling Opera House stage in the morning— only slightly distressed by the news that things had proceeded expeditiously without me. We were about to have what might be our best ever Kennedy Center Honors.

78

The Honors Tradition

My years with the Kennedy Center Honors expanded my appreciation of the performing arts and my regard for those who choose to devote their lives to what may be the most precious of human endeavors. The words of the man for whom the Kennedy Center is named remains our North Star: "I am certain that after the dust of centuries has passed over our cities, we, too, will be remembered not for victories or defeats in battle or in politics, but for our contribution to the human spirit."

It had been my job for nearly four decades to tell the stories of 190 of our most accomplished contributors to the human spirit. We began the five-minute biographical films with childhood images—the idea was to reveal the starting point of each artist and trace their journeys. In year one I assured Leonard Bernstein that our intention was to create a show that was true to arts at the highest level and would also be popular on television. "Like Beethoven," Lenny replied. "Accessible without being ordinary."

Wisdom and insight like Lenny's were common among the honorees, as was pursuit of perfection. Our tribute to the brilliant and prickly Jerome Robbins was a performance of *Fancy Free,* his timeless ballet of three sailors on leave in New York City, one of whom was danced by Mikhail Baryshnikov. Jerry arrived at rehearsal suspicious that the "TV people" would degrade his piece. Sleeves rolled up, he sternly examined every detail, checking lighting, sound and camera angles. "You see," he said as he walked out satisfied, "I'm a worker. Instead of being a plumber, I'm a choreographer." Isaac Stern always raised our spirits. He arrived at a Sunday rehearsal to prepare a violin solo in tribute to conductor Eugene Ormandy and noticed Yves Montand, a stranger to him, who had just arrived from Paris, rehearsing his tribute to Gene Kelly. As

Onstage with Bruce Springsteen, 1997 Kennedy Center Honors.

Montand passed him leaving the stage Isaac lifted his violin and played "La Marseillaise."

Rock music made its first appearance at the Honors in 1997 when Bob Dylan was honored. "He's disturbed the peace and discomforted the powerful," said President Clinton during his tribute at the White House. The bard of the counterculture was seated in the honorees box between Lauren Bacall and Jessye Norman. When Gregory Peck, an admirer of Dylan's, took the stage to pay tribute, the light on the phone at my table in the back of the theater started blinking. "Dylan just walked out of the Box," whispered the director. Dashing upstairs, I wondered if this was an antiestablishment protest. I entered the anteroom of the Presidential Box and saw the toilet with the door slightly ajar. A moment later Bob Dylan stepped out adjusting his black string tie and reentered the box to hear the last half of Peck's tribute. During the ovation after the film biography Dylan was kissed first by Bacall, then by Jessye Norman. Bruce Springsteen took the stage in a solo spotlight. "The song I'm going to sing was written when people's yearning for a more open and just society exploded," he said. "Bob Dylan had the courage to stand in that fire and he caught the sound of that explosion." Springsteen singing "The Times They Are a-Changin'" was a step in the evolution of the Honors.

Bob Dylan whistles his approval for fellow honoree Lauren Bacall.
Edward Villella at left. December 7, 1997.

Come senators, congressmen
Please heed the call
Don't stand in the doorway
Don't block up the hall
For he that gets hurt
Will be he who has stalled
The battle outside ragin'
Will soon shake your windows
And rattle your walls
For the times they are a-changin'

In succeeding years Chuck Berry, James Brown, Elton John, Pete Townshend,
Roger Daltrey and Brian Wilson were recognized, and Springsteen himself in

2009, alongside Mel Brooks, Dave Brubeck, Grace Bumbry and Robert DeNiro.

Jon Stewart came to the stage to honor Springsteen with the wit and intelligence that the audience cherished. "I am not a music critic, nor a historian," he began. "But I *am* from New Jersey. [*Applause*] So I can tell you what I believe, and what I believe is this. Bob Dylan and James Brown had a baby. [*Laughter and applause*] Yesss! And they *abandoned* this child. As you can imagine at that time, interracial same sex relationships being what they were—they abandoned this child on the side of the road in New Jersey. That child is Bruce Springsteen!"

Bruce was teary with laughter before Jon went on to say, "And the beautiful thing is that Bruce Springsteen always empties the tank—for his family, for his art, for his audience and for his country." Earlier soprano Angela Gheorghiu sang "Vissi d'Arte" in tribute to Grace Bumbry, and there was a Broadway tribute to Mel Brooks. Only at the Kennedy Center Honors would you hear "Born in the USA," "Vissi d'Arte" and "Springtime for Hitler" on the same night.

With his silver hair, gravity and sly humor, Walter Cronkite was a matchless host for twenty-two years. He had often mentioned retiring, then during rehearsal on Friday afternoon before the 2003 show his office called to say that Walter had torn his Achilles tendon and couldn't appear. I went to my office and started scanning lists for a name to replace the irreplaceable—and saw Caroline Kennedy's name. I put a call in to Ted Kennedy. "Walter Cronkite is ailing," I said. "I think Caroline might do a beautiful job as host." A man of instinct and quick decisions, Ted said, "Would you like me to call her?" Thirty minutes later he called back. "She has a big birthday party in New York on Saturday night. She's going to think about it. I'll call you at home in the morning." Teddy's word was gold. The phone rang at 8 a.m. "Caroline will do it." We rewrote the Cronkite script for her, incorporating one of her father's quotations on the arts. A snowstorm struck on Sunday, planes were canceled, and Caroline's train was stopped midafternoon on the tracks outside Philadelphia. She arrived by car, walking onto the Opera House stage at six wearing a parka, ski cap and jeans. This was her first such appearance but she was uncommonly assured during rehearsal. Two hours later when the announcement was made, "Ladies and gentlemen, Caroline Kennedy," the surprised audience applauded with enthusiasm as she, elegantly gowned, made a center stage entrance, with her uncle smiling brightly in the third row. Caroline became our host for a decade. It was a good fit. Her name was on the building.

That same year Michael Stevens joined the team, bringing a more exacting appreciation of contemporary music than that of his father. He produced the

With Caroline Kennedy on the Opera House stage.

James Brown tribute, bringing Rob Mathes to the *Honors,* a brilliant young composer, arranger and instrumentalist who anchored a large rock band of top musicians at the keyboard, wrote arrangements for Sting and Springsteen, as well as for Renée Fleming and Yo-Yo Ma and the Silkroad Ensemble. Michael was promoted to producer in 2007 and we functioned as partners, the younger pressing the older to be more daring while exhibiting storytelling skills that elevated all aspects of the show.

In Walter Cronkite's first year as host I handed him an introduction which included the phrase "the Honors tradition." The veteran newsman studied the page, then looked up. "Four years does not make a tradition." On our tenth anniversary when the same phrase appeared in his script, Walter gave a smiling thumbs-up. The program created to recognize excellence was itself being recognized, receiving the Peabody Award in 1986 for Meritorious Service to Broadcasting and five Emmys for Outstanding Variety, Music or Comedy Special in the eighties and nineties. Then, starting in 2004, the show was nominated for ten straight years, with my son and I accepting Emmys for outstanding special for a record-setting five consecutive seasons.

In 2010 David Rubenstein, cofounder of the Carlyle Group, became chairman of the Kennedy Center. He was generous to the center with his time and money, and we worked well together. The Honors thrived, David telling me at one point that the show was generating $20 million a year for the center. When it came to honoree selection, David, not an avid consumer of the performing arts, would search the internet for information. In 2012 I had proposed the Cuban-born ballerina Alicia Alonso, who starred with the American Ballet Theater and taught and inspired a generation of dancers. David listened attentively to my advocacy but finally sent a lengthy email saying that while his research showed that Alonso was a great ballerina, he was concerned about her connection to Fidel Castro. The Russian-born Natalia Makarova, also a great star with the ABT, replaced Alonso. Michael Stevens and I had proposed Led Zeppelin, which meant David had to overcome his concern that they might not be the Kennedy Center's type of honorees. Our lengthy email exchanges were taxing but always cordial, and the board of trustees approved Buddy Guy, Dustin Hoffman, David Letterman, Natalia Makarova and Led Zeppelin.

"ARE THE KENNEDY CENTER HONORS BIASED?" blared a *Washington Post* headline two days after the honorees were announced. The report stated that Hispanic arts advocate Felix Sanchez was shopping for ballet slippers with his teenage daughter when his cell phone rang. Kennedy Center president Michael Kaiser was on the line. Sanchez had placed three calls to Kaiser, who was now calling back. The *Post* reported that the conversation began bluntly, with Sanchez asking, "How can you continue to exclude Latinos from the Kennedy Center Honors?" And it ended badly—with Kaiser telling Sanchez to "fuck yourself."

Of course, my first thought was, "If only we had honored Alicia Alonso."

Kaiser's insult and the *Post*'s twenty-six-hundred-word article teed up the first major controversy in the thirty-five-year history of the Honors, and Rubenstein formed an eleven-person committee to examine the selection process which heretofore had few critics.

Happily, six weeks later the show was a triumph with a landmark tribute to Led Zeppelin. Vocalist Robert Plant, guitarist Jimmy Page and keyboardist John Paul Jones were in the Honor box, absent their deceased drummer, John Bonham. Ann Wilson from the band Heart was introduced with her guitarist sister Nancy—backed by a band of premier rock-and-roll musicians—to sing "Stairway

George receives his fifteenth Emmy and Michael his seventh for the 2012
Kennedy Center Honors.

to Heaven." Ann sang it as if her life depended on it. The sound was majestic and
in the rousing final section, Jason Bonham was revealed on drums, wearing his
father's famous black bowler hat, joined by a chorus of eighty—all wearing bowl-
ers. Plant, Page and Jones watched with knowing smiles and tears. Yo-Yo Ma was
shown on television, eyes closed, savoring every note. David Rubenstein wrote
saying it may have been the best show ever, and then once more to praise the high
ratings on CBS. We were awarded another Emmy, and the rendition of *Stairway
to Heaven* picked up fifty million views on YouTube.

My contract with the Kennedy Center was up for renewal and David encouraged Michael and me to schedule individual meetings to hear the views of
his new trustees committee, including its chairman, David Bohnett, a Los Angeles technology entrepreneur. Bohnett took us to lunch at the Beverly Hills
Hotel and we had a cheerful discussion of the Honors. He surprised me by
saying that I should receive the Kennedy Center Honors. David Rubenstein had
suggested this in previous years, but I explained that it was a conflict to be avoided while I was producing the show. Only later did I connect the dots—my
tendency toward paranoia having always been on the lower end of the scale.

In April David asked to meet, proposing that he come to my Kennedy Center office on Good Friday with Bohnett. "Your son would be welcome," he added. It proved to be a disturbing and somewhat bizarre meeting. The two businessmen in dark suits came into my office, its walls adorned with colorful show business photos and prizes, and greeted Michael and me wearing blazers. Bohnett sat somewhat uneasily, I thought, and David remained standing. His first words were, "You are going to receive the Kennedy Center Honors this year." He then seemed to apologize, saying that this was his most difficult meeting since the time he fired George H. W. Bush and James A. Baker from his Carlyle enterprise. I was beginning to get the picture and found little solace in being linked to a former president and a secretary of state. David then announced that he wanted to find new producers. I remember the words: "I want to look around and see what's out there."

Again, insufficient paranoia had let me down. David's riches, after all, had come from hostile takeovers of corporations—ousting existing management, cutting costs and reaping windfalls. On reflection, my response was less tempered than I would have liked. "I think you'll have to look around for a long time to find producers who will give you five consecutive Emmys." Before we adjourned I told David that it made no sense for me to be honored on a show I was producing. We agreed on a rain check.

I figured that David believed his business acumen could make the show more remunerative, but was less aware that ceding creative control of an arts-related program to a network bent on higher ratings would lead to lower ratings. I didn't argue with a New York playwright friend who later said, "That's an eccentric way to reward success."

Michael and I had six months to produce our last Honors and were determined to make it one of the best. We had a slate of gifted friends as honorees— Tom Hanks, Al Green, Patricia McBride, Lily Tomlin and Sting. All the while I was meeting with Rubenstein, falling short in reaching agreement on a reasonable royalty, considering that my Honors concept would continue for years to generate revenue for CBS and the Kennedy Center, so no announcement was made.

Each year before the Honors Gala the president pays tribute to the honorees at a White House ceremony at which the Kennedy Center is also acknowledged. After President Obama thanked Rubenstein and the center's new president Deborah Rutter, I was about to discover what it feels like to fly too close to the sun.

Not knowing our fate, President Obama said, "I want to thank George and Michael Stevens, who produce this event every year. [*Applause.*] Lately, they've won an Emmy for it just about every year, as well. So we are very proud to have them here. In fact, Michelle and I call this the 'Stevens Season.'"

We had a great turnout of stars for the 2014 Honors, ranging from the new comedienne from *Saturday Night Live,* Kate McKinnon, who joined Reba McEntire and Jane Fonda in tribute to Lily Tomlin, Whoopi Goldberg and Earth Wind and Fire for Al Green, and Lady Gaga and Springsteen who saluted Sting. After Rubenstein did the customary introduction of Michael and me at intermission, I took the occasion to announce my own departure, lest the artists and my production colleagues leave town in the dark. I was looking at faces in the audience who were so much a part of *Honors* history—Jessye Norman, Yo-Yo Ma, Steven Spielberg, Christine Baranski, Tom Hanks, Kelli O'Hara, Jacques D'Amboise, Herbie Hancock, Meryl Streep, Aretha Franklin, Itzhak Perlman and Bruce Springsteen. Acknowledging their generosity, I reminded the audience that the stars appear in service to the arts and the Kennedy Center, and never accepted payment for performing. I complimented David Rubenstein on his dedication to the center and wished him well in his efforts to polish the center's crown jewel, expressing my hope that the *Honors* would thrive far into the future. The show was watched by 9.2 million people on CBS—a two-million increase over the previous year.

David found his new producers and in a press release the new president Deborah Rutter explained that she wanted a fresh approach. "This will be quite an evolution," she said, "but I can't predict what it will look like." Soon the biographical films that portrayed each honoree's creative journey had disappeared, and justifying Ted Kennedy's misgivings, CBS was successful in getting younger honorees.

I always knew that nothing is forever—the time would come for my tenure to end at the organization that had been part of my life since the early planning with Jacqueline Kennedy in the 1960s. It's too bad it ended the way it did, but the passage of time now allows me to look back on the somewhat indecorous circumstances of my departure with what Wordsworth called "emotion recollected in tranquility."

I will forever be thankful to Roger Stevens and the Kennedy Center for enabling me to enjoy nearly four decades in the company of brilliant honorees and the world's finest performers, supported by a production team of steadfast creative compatriots. Of the latter, I loved the expression, "Each December, we come out of the hills with our machetes."

Let me call the Kennedy Center Honors the opportunity of a lifetime.

79

Courage

This is the chapter I did not wish to write.

The email I sent to friends on the morning of October 16, 2015, began like this.

> It was November two years ago that Michael Stevens was told he had stage four stomach cancer. A few days later he sat down with his beloved Ali, took out a yellow pad, and said, "We are going into production." The two of them have been so remarkable in the time since. Michael has been wise, courageous, uncomplaining and generous. Ali has been calm, brave and cheerful, and she mastered so many medical complexities in supporting Michael during his two years of arduous treatment.
>
> Michael's summer course of chemotherapy had a side effect on his lungs, and all of his strength and resolve could not overcome it. We lost Michael at 11 p.m. last night at the UCLA Medical Center.

It had come suddenly, his lungs ceasing to function despite the strenuous efforts of the expert UCLA medical team. Liz and Ali and I had left the hospital after being there all day, then were instructed to return. David had flown in from New Hampshire to see his brother. When we sensed the gravity of the situation, he drove to Studio City to pick up eleven-year-old John Cooper and Lily, ten. David spoke of this at the memorial service for Michael a week later.

> When I came to your house in the middle of the night, to take you to the hospital to say goodbye to your dad, I honestly did not know if you would be up to it. If it was me, at your age, I would have been

hiding under my bed. I pulled up to your house to find you two in the driveway, waiting for me, with your jackets on, ready to go.

John, I know when we walked into the hospital every bone in your body was telling you to turn back. If you had turned back, no one would have ever blamed you. Courage is feeling overwhelming fear but doing what needs to be done. That night your mom needed you, your sister needed you, your grandparents needed you, I needed you, and most importantly your dad needed you.

At the most challenging moment of your life, you stepped up— you were there for us.

Lily, somehow that night you managed to say everything a father could ever wish to hear from his daughter. You made it so much easier, for all of us. What your dad heard before he took his last breath was you telling him not to worry, that you were going to be ok, that John was going to be ok and that your mom was going to be ok. When he was gone, you turned and gave every nurse and doctor in the room a hug and you said, "Thank you for taking care of my daddy."

Some people go through life wondering what they have inside. John and Lily, you do not need to wonder. Your father's spirit, his confidence, his courage, his care for his friends and family and his belief in doing what is right—that spirit flows through you and will always be with you.

Ali and Liz and I were exploring a nice Episcopal church in the valley when it struck us—Michael was nowhere more at peace than walking by himself in the late afternoon on the green hills of the Bel Air golf course. We set chairs in a glen behind the eighteenth green on an idyllic Saturday afternoon. We were in the healing embrace of family and friends. An American flag that had flown over the United States Capitol the day before was on a small table, not far from Michael's golf bag. Vernon Jordan read a letter from Barack and Michelle Obama. Tom Brokaw, who was also dealing with cancer and was in regular touch with Michael, recalled his courage. His childhood friends spoke of his steadfastness.

"If I had more time, I would tell you countless stories of Michael's limitless generosity," said Neil Phillips, quarterback, basketball captain and friend from high school. "I would talk with you about his courage, his self-deprecating humor, his loyalty, his wisdom, his 'chesty' hug. I would say how he helped set me on a path of deep fulfillment through service to others."

It had been a tumultuous two years. I had observed the little boy I taught to swim showing courage far greater than my own. He welcomed Liz and me to join him and Ali with the doctors. I watched him pose questions, weigh complex explanations, and soberly decide among lifesaving options. There was chemotherapy, and a new immune therapy program at NIH in Washington, then a ten-hour operation in Philadelphia. All the while Michael was producing, directing and writing, while shepherding his family. His temperament filled him with purpose.

When he left us we became a family coming to terms with unimaginable loss. Liz and I received a flood of heartfelt and consoling letters from our friends. I recalled how distressed I had been years before on learning of the death of the son of Tommy Lasorda, who had been so generous to my boys. I had written to Tommy expressing my sympathy. I added a borrowed idea that I thought might provide perspective: "If God said at the beginning—you can only have him for thirty-three years, you would have said, 'Give me the thirty-three years.'" I now recognized the hubris of my well-intentioned letter.

Michael wanted John and Lily to enjoy the summer of 2015 with their friends at the family house in Dark Harbor, Maine, so he switched his chemotherapy from UCLA Medical Center in Los Angeles to Massachusetts General Hospital in Boston. Every other Friday he and Ali took a small plane from our little island to Boston. He would come back from the treatments and after a day or two of recovery he was again filled with purpose, doing his business on the computer, enjoying time with the children and devoting attention to others. He came to my bedroom one morning with eight pairs of Bonobos pants on his arm, a new favorite of his. I dutifully tried on each one, consulted with him on size and colors. Three days later my closet was filled with the new preferred trousers.

Michael had been, at the beginning of the summer, determined that we would play together in the annual Four Ball at the National Golf Links, only conceding that it was a bridge too far at the last minute. Michael had been a repeat champion on the modest links course at the Tarratine Club on Islesboro that includes a few dozen players each year. The usual suspects showed up on an August morning and at the last minute we saw Michael drive up in his 1958 red Oldsmobile convertible and get out with his clubs. He refused to use a cart and walked the eighteen holes. A twenty-year-old in his group mentions it to me each summer when I see him—as an unforgettable lesson in resolve.

John Cooper, Lily and Michael Stevens in Dark Harbor, Maine. 2015.

It was the fiftieth anniversary of Liz's and my wedding that summer and Michael, Caroline and David planned a surprise. They imported the Brokaws and the Jordans to Dark Harbor, bedecked our house with a joyous photo display, and put on a feast of clams and lobster for our grandchildren and friends. For Michael, everything was a "production," so he organized heartfelt and humorous toasts. It seemed on that July night that our family had never been closer.

Michael Murrow Stevens had a legacy that he embraced and honored. He elected to enter a profession where family achievement ran high, and had to rise above both the "son of" and "the grandson of" tag. He was a good and courageous man, and a beautiful storyteller who had so much more to offer. The heaviest sorrow is that John and Lily are deprived of their father's gentle influence, his example and his love. Michael worked from his office above the garage, and when they were little he was there each night to bathe the two and towel them off, on occasion offering one or the other grandparent observation rights. Then, as now, John and Lily call us Lizzie and Georgie. We cherish them and adore seeing their father's light in them as they grow into handsome and loving teenagers.

Not a day goes by that I do not think of Michael Stevens.

80

Getavasia

The passing years brought to mind what Jimmy Cagney called his "getavasia" (*get-avay—juh*), that graceful little step he did while leaving the stage.

My life was enriched by my father preserving the evidence of his life in Bekins Storage and by my mother's boxed treasure trove of family history. Were it not for the care my parents took with memories I would have less understanding of my own place in the world, so I too became a keeper of things. My professional papers, photos and films are now at the Academy of Motion Picture Arts and Sciences, along with those of my son Michael, and those of my actor grandparents and great-grandmother, and my mother, in what is now called the Stevens Family Collection that began with the donation of my father's papers in 1980. My television work is at the Library of Congress, a cache of 5,407 items encompassing thirty-seven *Kennedy Center Honors,* thirty-two *Christmas in Washington* shows, *America's Millennium,* and *We Are One,* the Obama inaugural concert.

The Library of Congress invited me to its vast underground storage and preservation facility in Culpeper, Virginia, in appreciation of my donation, as well as the American Film Institute's seminal collaboration with the library. As we entered the frigid 37-degree vaults, the director of the archive pointed down a cavernous extended corridor lined with film cans on steel shelves. With an air of ceremony, he said, "You're looking at some of the forty thousand films in your AFI Collection. It's the bedrock of the library's program."

Then he gestured to a small table. Resting beside an open film can was the original 35mm nitrate negative roll that my twenty-three-year-old father had threaded into a camera in 1928 to photograph Stan Laurel and Oliver Hardy in *Two Tars.* Beside it was the recently restored negative of *Laughing Gas,* a 1914 comedy starring my grandmother Alice Howell, and beside it a 35mm print of my own *George Stevens: A Filmmaker's Journey.* It was stirring to see family creativity stretching back a century on fragile celluloid, and reassuring to see the rigor and dedication of these archivists charged with safeguarding American culture.

On a rainy night in November of 2018 I drove from my house in Georgetown to the AFI Theater in Silver Spring, Maryland, where four recently discovered silent films starring Alice Howell were being shown in a series of silent comedies that included Buster Keaton and Harold Lloyd. What made this extraordinary was that I had never seen my grandmother on a movie screen. She was retired when I knew her, and most of the hundred films she starred in were lost, leaving me to see only a few on grainy video.

Of course those films had not been completely silent, and as I took my seat I noticed the lighted keyboard of the organ to the left of the screen. Historian Steve Massa introduced the films, explaining that film rescue efforts of the 1950s and 1960s concentrated on the great male comics—Chaplin, Keaton and Lloyd—with virtually no attention to movies that starred women. But now there was a two-disk DVD of Howell films. "Alice Howell's physical movements were as clean and precise as Keaton and Chaplin," he said, "and she could match tumbles and falls with Al St. John and Billie Ritchie."

As the lights went down notes from the organ introduced my grandmother in shimmering black-and-white images on the giant screen. I laughed with others as Alice endured, and rose above bedlam and confusion in a series of movies made between 1915 and 1925. The titles suggested their mirthful intent: *Father Was a Loafer, A Convict's Happy Bride* and *Her Lucky Day.* I loved the gags but was intrigued by the way Alice managed to create moments of pathos amidst the slapstick and the pratfalls. When she climbed out a second-story window onto a ladder, and her pursuer pushed the ladder away from the wall with Alice suspended and struggling to balance herself, I was surprised by the intense anxiety I felt for her physical safety. This, of course, is why we go to the movies. It's called willing suspension of disbelief.

In *Distilled Love* I didn't expect to see the evil bootlegger—who takes Alice from a farm to the big city and puts her to work doing eccentric dancing—played by Oliver Hardy, sporting a black mustache. Alice and Hardy became friends on this 1920 film, seven years before he and Stan Laurel achieved stardom. Were it not for their friendship, "Babe," as he was known, would never have made the fateful introduction at his house in the Hollywood hills of his young cameraman, George Stevens, to Alice's daughter, Yvonne.

The experience of seeing Alice on the screen brought to mind a night more than half a century earlier, when my mother called telling me her mother was

Alice Howell, center, in *Untamed Ladies* (1918). Russ Powell, Rosa Gore, Howell, Phil Dunham, Lee Morris, Hughie Mack.

very ill, asking that I join her. I remember my selfish disappointment canceling dinner plans with a glamorous young actress and driving to my grandmother's small house on Occidental Boulevard, on land she purchased not long after coming to Hollywood in 1913. Alice had been struggling with cancer and she didn't make it through the night. I watched my mother gently try to ease her pain. It was my first experience with death. The memory of that sorrowful night, combined with watching my grandmother shine on the big screen at the AFI Silver, leads me to believe that Alice Howell would have disputed the English tragedian Edmund Kean's famous deathbed quote, "Dying is easy, comedy is hard."

Time passing also brings milestones. In 2015 the National Endowment for the Arts invited me to be the speaker at the black-tie dinner celebrating its fiftieth anniversary, on the date that Lyndon Johnson signed legislation creating the Endowment. I was able to describe—feeling just a bit like the oldest surviving Confederate soldier—that day in the White House Rose Garden in 1965 where

Johnson declared, "We will create an American Film Institute." The AFI was now NEA's longest surviving creation.

Two years later AFI's fiftieth anniversary was celebrated in the Great Hall of the Library of Congress with a festive dinner hosted by the librarian Carla Hayden. But for me the highlight of our anniversary year was taking the stage with Sidney Poitier, AFI's founding vice-chairman and my friend for sixty years, at the Life Achievement Award dinner in Los Angeles. Sidney, still standing tall at ninety, received a passionate ovation from colleagues and admirers. He was no longer speaking in public so I did the honors, thanking AFI supporters for their commitment to an organization still thriving after half a century. Joanna Poitier explained that crowded dinners were difficult for Sidney and they wouldn't be staying, so Liz and I excused ourselves and the four of us had our own black-tie dinner at Il Piccolino. Our hearts were full with satisfaction that the institution we believed in so long ago was alive and strong at fifty. Together we remembered our collaborations and happy times. A meal never to be forgotten.

And, of course, always in mind is my father. No, I never became the best film director in my family, but I had a father who looked beyond his own self-interest to urge me to take seriously Edward R. Murrow's offer of a job in Washington. That generosity led to a life—my own filmmaker's journey—with dimensions I could not have envisioned and fulfillments I could never have imagined.

I will soon be ninety years old. I always discouraged Liz from staging parties on my "big" birthdays, feeling they would only serve as public markers of my advancing age in a profession that values youth. Years ago, having no appreciation of how timely it would become, I made a note of an observation by Bertrand Russell in his essay *The Pros and Cons of Being Ninety*. "A long habit of work with some purpose that one believes is important is a hard habit to break."

So I go to the office and ponder stories that might become films, though an awareness that each new film is a commitment of years makes me a little less keen to toss my cap over the wall. However, now that the storytelling juices that have been devoted to this book are freed up, who knows what lies ahead.

Let it be said that I have lived a life of great good fortune with a woman who, in the parlance of our family, stands the test of time with uncommon grace and beauty. Dining alone with Liz is my enduring prize.

Acknowledgments

My mother and father preserved evidence of their lives and that of their fore-bears. Their sense of history led me to save my own professional papers, letters and photographs, providing a foundation for this book.

And this endeavor was in other ways a family affair.

David Stevens volunteered his time and entrepreneurial talent. His imagination and good judgment guided me in making important choices and decisions.

Caroline Stevens came to the rescue to supervise and bring coherence to the hundred and thirty photographs and images in the book, doing so with the love and sensitivity she has always demonstrated.

Michael Stevens was in my heart throughout this journey, and at those low moments when I hesitated, his voice came from on high. "Come on, Dad. Just do it."

And to those without whom this book would not have been possible.

Dottie McCarthy has been my personal assistant for thirty-four years, as well as associate producer of the *Kennedy Center Honors* and other projects. She patiently shepherded countless drafts of this manuscript while providing thoughtful and frank insights.

Paul Cronin, writer, editor, filmmaker, was the first to read early chapters and his enthusiasm encouraged me to press on. A man of generous spirit and good judgment, his detailed notes and continuing critiques made this a better book.

Tim Willocks, British novelist, historian, screenwriter, medical doctor, colleague and friend, lit the spark for this book and provided invaluable advice in its execution.

Patrick McGilligan read the manuscript twice and provided detailed editorial suggestions on each occasion, then paved the way for it to be published at the University Press of Kentucky.

A moviemaker can screen a work in progress and gain the advice of trusted viewers in a single afternoon, whereas careful reading of a manuscript is time consuming. I am fortunate to have talented friends who made that commitment and offered forthright and informed advice—Todd Purdom, Shelley Wanger, Glenn Frankel, Joe McBride, Cathie Pelletier, Don Baer, Jim Hoagland, Neil Sinyard, Harrison Engle, Heather Reisman and Gerry Schwartz.

I turned over a completed manuscript to my agent Lynn Nesbit four weeks into a pandemic. Undaunted, Lynn represented the book with her patented determination, supported by Michael Steger and Mina Hamedi at Janklow & Nesbit. Vicky Wilson, the editor of my two previous books, was the first to read the completed manuscript and her ardent belief in the book was a first confirmation of its promise. While it was not published under her banner, she volunteered precious advice.

Ashley Runyon, the director of the University Press of Kentucky, has been enthusiastic in her support of this book, always with uncommon courtesy and steadfastness. My heartfelt thanks to Ashley and her colleagues Laura Hohman, Brooke Raby, Victoria Robinson, Ila McEntire, Jewell Boyd, Jackie Wilson and Meredith Daugherty, who have been dedicated to achieving an outstanding result. Also to copyeditor Janet Yoe for her exacting attention to detail.

Chip Kidd's design of the cover is an act of taste and imagination for which I shall be ever grateful. As are the marketing skills of Dave Kass and David MacKay.

Derry Noyes generously applied her design skills and good taste in advising me on the appearance of the book and creating the Stevens Family Tree.

The Margaret Herrick Library at the Academy of Motion Picture Arts and Sciences has taken expert care of the Stevens Family Collection, making it widely available to writers and scholars. My thanks to Linda Mehr, who headed the library for thirty-six years, and her able successor Matt Severson—and to Val Almendarez, Howard Prouty, Rachel Rosenfeld, Bob Cushman and Rachel Bernstein who have all been helpful to me. Also, a deep bow to Mike Pogorzelski and Lynne Kriste, guardians of the Academy's film collection, and to programmer Randy Haberkamp.

There are institutions and individuals who helped with research and photographs: Robert Vaughan and Emily Wittenberg at the American Film Institute Library; Mike Mashon, Larry Smith and Bill Rush at the Library of Congress; Sofia Becerra-Licha and Hannah Middlebrook at the John F. Kennedy Center for the Performing Arts; and Maryrose Grossman at the John F. Kennedy Library. Margaret Ogden worked her magic in refining the photographs for publication.

There are scores of colleagues and friends whose support through the years has lifted me up and made possible the events and productions that are recounted in this book. There are so many, and only a few are named in the text, but here's to each one of you—and to the joys and travails we experienced together while creating performances and telling stories to the audiences we respect.

And to the next generation—to Liz's and my grandchildren, Alexander, Anthony, Anastasia, John Cooper, Lily and Nicholas—who inspire me and are now seeking their own places in the sun.

Left to right: Nicholas Koka, John Cooper Stevens, David Stevens, Caroline Stevens, George Stevens, Jr., Anthony Koka and Alexander Stevens. March 2019.

Illustrations

Chapters

Index

Screen Classics

Screen Classics is a series of critical biographies, film histories, and analytical studies focusing on neglected filmmakers and important screen artists and subjects, from the era of silent cinema through the golden age of Hollywood to the international generation of today. Books in the Screen Classics series are intended for scholars and general readers alike. The contributing authors are established figures in their respective fields. This series also serves the purpose of advancing scholarship on film personalities and themes with ties to Kentucky.

Series Editor
Patrick McGilligan

Books in the Series
Olivia de Havilland: Lady Triumphant
Victoria Amador

Mae Murray: The Girl with the Bee-Stung Lips
Michael G. Ankerich

Harry Dean Stanton: Hollywood's Zen Rebel
Joseph B. Atkins

Hedy Lamarr: The Most Beautiful Woman in Film
Ruth Barton

Rex Ingram: Visionary Director of the Silent Screen
Ruth Barton

Conversations with Classic Film Stars: Interviews from Hollywood's Golden Era
James Bawden and Ron Miller

Conversations with Legendary Television Stars: Interviews from the First Fifty Years
James Bawden and Ron Miller

You Ain't Heard Nothin' Yet: Interviews with Stars from Hollywood's Golden Era
James Bawden and Ron Miller

Charles Boyer: The French Lover
John Baxter